ticking time bombs

TICKING TIME BOMBS

EDITED BY ROBERT KUTTNER

THE NEW PRESS — NEW YORK

LIBRARY OF CONGRESS CATALOG CARD NUMBER 96-071802

ISBN 1-56584-346-0

PUBLISHED IN THE UNITED STATES BY THE NEW PRESS, NEW YORK
DISTRIBUTED BY W. W. NORTON & COMPANY, INC., NEW YORK

Established in 1990 as a major alternative to the large, commercial publishing houses, The New Press is a full-scale nonprofit American book publisher outside of the university presses. The Press is operated editorially in the public interest, rather than for private gain; it is committed to publishing in innovative ways works of educational, cultural, and community value that, despite their intellectual merits, might not normally be commercially viable. The New Press's editorial offices are located at the City University of New York.

BOOK DESIGN BY HALL SMYTH AND GORDON WHITESIDE OF BAD
PRODUCTION MANAGEMENT BY KIM WAYMER
PRINTED IN THE UNITED STATES OF AMERICA

9 8 7 6 5 4 3 2 1

Contents

Introduction

Robert Kuttner

On the eve of a defining election, the American republic is losing the confidence of its citizens. Deep sources of unease include escalating worry about our economic future, doubts about the competence of government to solve collective problems, an erosion of civic connection, and distrust of democracy itself. Paralysis feeds on itself. The more these interrelated problems are deferred, the more intractable they become. Frustration lends legitimacy to fringe political figures, and leads mainstream politicians to embrace ill-considered remedy. These are the hallmarks of our political era, and the ticking time bombs of our title.

In the 1996 election, as in those of the recent past, political unease is up for grabs. Part one of this book describes the tentative political realignment that occurred in the 1994 election, and the failure of Republicans to cement it. Compared to the conservative triumphalism in November 1994, the Republican disarray in mid-1996 seems nothing short of remarkable. But in retrospect, the 1994 mid-term Republican victory was far short of a mandate for sweeping change.

A relatively small number of voters deserted the Democrats in 1994. Virtually all of the net swing can be accounted for by white, male, working class voters justifiably anxious about their economic condition. Clinton had spoken for these voters in 1992, but had not delivered much by 1994. The sense of mass political counter-revolution was created mainly by the shift to Republican control of Congress. But the vaunted "Contract with America" turned out to be a melange of special-interest legislation (regulatory rollbacks, product liability "reform," tax loopholes) and insider conservative ideological favorites (constitutional revision, de-funding social programs, punative welfare reform, "devolution" of federal responsibilities to the states) with little mass appeal. Few voters had read the Contract with America or based their votes on it. When Clinton got over his 1994 shell-shock and began vetoing major elements of the Contract, there was no mass voter outrage—not surprisingly since there was no real mandate to begin with. Indeed, the main outrage was aimed at Congressional Republicans for casually shutting down the government when Clinton resisted bowing to their entire program.

Moreover, little in the Republican program addressed the concerns of the swing voters who deserted the Democrats in 1994, mainly over pocketbook frustrations. Even the most politically appealing aspect of the Contract, a proposed $500 per child tax-credit, was neutralized by other Republican attempts to reduce existing benefits to middle and working class families, such as the earned income tax credit, college tuition aid, and Medicare. By making substantial budget accommodations, seizing the political center, and then surprising critics within his own party by resisting much of the remaining Republican program, Clinton played a relatively weak hand deftly and exploited latent weaknesses in the once united Republican coalition.

However, it remains to be seen whether Democrats will regain the voter affections, or whether the economic anxiety and political distrust will find a home in the fringes. This issue is addressed in our chapters by Teixeira, Rogers, Greenberg, Brinkley, and Faux.

Seemingly, our political system is unable or unwilling to come to grips with the great economic issues of our times. Why are these popular concerns largely ignored by the political debate? Part of the problem is what Professor Walter Dean Burnham, has termed a "politics of excluded alternatives." A set of policies that might command majority support is not offered by mainstream politicians, because elites reject such policies, and because masses of ordinary voters see little appealing in the political system and stay home.

The essence of political democracy—the franchise—has eroded, as voting and face-to-face politics give way to a campaign-finance plutocracy. As Marshall Ganz's chapter suggests, there is a direct connection between the domination of politics by special-interest money, paid attack ads, strategies driven by polling and focus groups —and the desertion of citizens. The cumulative message of the negative advertising is that *all* the candidates are scoundrels. The dominance of politics by money leads candidates to spend most of their time cultivating donors rather than citizens. Fundraising and paid advertising drive out old-fashioned retail politics. People conclude that politics is something that excludes them. As bipartisan moneyed elites come to dominate politics, genuine civic participation—both voting and deliberation—dwindles.

This process is not merely a civic blight. It disproportionately disadvantages liberal and progressive candidates, and in multiple ways. Invariably, the biggest sources of money are business groups. This dynamic whipsaws progressive candidates and elected officials. Business groups pay conservative candidates to be true to their own beliefs, while they pay progressive candidates to be less progressive. If fundraising is seen as a threshhold test of electoral viability, left-of-center candidates will raise little business money. They can be financially competitive and compromised—or pure but broke. Pocketbook populism is the theme that rallies non-rich voters and bridges over the social and racial schisms in the New Deal coalition, but a centrist politics deemed acceptable to business elites disarms the progressive coalition at its base. Gay rights is less threatening to blue collar voters if the party sponsoring it also brings full employment. Affirmative action is less threatening to white voters if wages are rising across the board. But entire issues—ones that might rally ordinary people—are excluded from political discussion. This defers remedy and intensifies social frictions. Instead of a functioning democracy, our polity becomes a large oligarchy.

As ordinary people give up on politics, they also give up on government. In the 1930s and 1960s, government was able to address the economic and social needs of the day. The voters reciprocated by accepting their share of the cost. Tax-and-spend was seen as a good bargain. Today, as government neglects felt needs like health reform, paying taxes is seen as a bad deal, validating the rightwing view of the world. Part 3 of this book is about the influence of special interest money on politics, and the logic of its reform.

In the 1990s, there are immense economic and social challenges that government has deferred. The Clinton administration was not able to muster the strategic vision, the political will, or the votes to achieve more than token reform of health care, job training, campaign finance. The society continues dividing into one of haves and have nots. Educational opportunities for the children of the poor continue to lag further and further behind. Instead of addressing these and other genuine concerns, the Clinton White House has embraced a fiscal politics of budget balance. Placing budget balance at the top of the agenda means that existing government programs must be cut by something like 30 percent, and there is nothing more than token money for reform of health, education, housing, welfare, job training, public infrastructure, and countless other needs.

A political psychology sets in: government is not doing anything constructive for me, so I might as well vote myself a tax cut. As government is stripped of resources, confidence in government's basic competence falls even further. As Robert Putnam suggests, it is civil society as well as politics that is unravelling. By nearly every indicator, what Putnam terms "social capital" is dwindling. People spend less time on everything from PTAs to bowling leagues. As economic pressures claim more and more available time, and as market forms of organization drive out civic forms, the social fabric becomes threadbare. Putnam blames television, and the graying of the generation that came of age in the Great Depression and World War II, when civic life had more dynamism and legitimacy. Richard Vallely blames the decline of institutions of working class representation, such as trade unions. There is plenty of blame to go around. But the relative decline of institutions of civic and political voice, at a time when market institutions are producing rampant insecurity, is another ticking time bomb.

Democracy and capitalism exist in a complex equipoise. The first principle of democracy is one person/one vote. The first principle of capitalism is one dollar/one vote. In the quarter century after World War II, there was a tolerable balance between market, state, and society. For the past two decades, that balance has tilted in the direction of the market, and the countervailing institutions of political representation and governmental presence have weakened. The conservative remedies, described in Part 4 of this book, would only intensify that tilt.

The right would rescue democracy by hobbling it, with a variety of automatic formulas—term limits, tax limits, a constitutional mandate to balance the budget, and a shifting of responsibilities (but not resources) to the states. Peter Schrag offers a chilling glimpse of term-limit hell from California. Lenny Goldberg adroitly deconstructs the rightwing version of "devolution." It turns out that the conservative idea of devolving responsibilities and decisions to lower levels of government is less a principled commitment to decentralization and healthy localism than an opportunistic gambit intended to limit the public sector and starve government at all levels for resources. Conservatives happily use federal pre-emption when that is convenient, as in the "tort reform" crusade, and embrace states rights when that approach works to constrain government, as in welfare.

The right would also restrain government by further limiting its fiscal capacity. The strategy of dumping responsibilities (but not resources) on state and local governments is a tactic that dates to the Nixon administration, when many federal categorical programs were subsumed into block grants. Then, when fiscal hard times come, the block grant is gradually cut, leaving states and local governments holding the bag. Initially, this approach has appeal to governors and mayors, who like the idea of federal money with fewer strings. In the past, governors and mayors could be counted upon to resist the spending cuts. But many in the current crop of conservative governors are so ideologically hostile to government that they accept drastically reduced resources in exchange for a diminished federal presence. During the 1994-96 period, some of the most extreme limitations were deflected by presidential veto, but not replaced with a convincing, affirmative conception of government.

Perhaps the most serious of our time bombs is the division of America into a society of the contented rich, the anxious middle class, and the desperate poor. Several chapters of this book address the division of America—its economics and its politics. Here, the several time bombs fuse into one: in the failure of politics, government or the private market to address economic distress.

By now, it is no longer news that earnings are slowly declining for most Americans. Compared to the post-World War II boom, when the economy both grew more rapidly and became more equal, the change is epochal. In the years between 1947 and 1973, the median paycheck more than doubled, and the bottom 20 percent enjoyed the biggest gains. Since 1973, median earnings have fallen by about 15 percent; and the bottom fifth have fallen furthest behind; more than half of all earnings gains have gone to the top five percent. Inequality shows no sign of abating. In 1995, median earnings were flat, while chief executive compensation rose by 23 percent. Corporate "downsizing" and the attendant insecurity has spread from the blue collar factory worker to corporate middle managers and even to professionals such as doctors and engineers.

A decade ago, it was too easy to blame the stagnation of earnings on low productivity and sluggish growth. But in the 1990s, American productivity and competitiveness have rebounded—and inequality has only deepened. The problem is not overall economic performance, but how society divides the spoils.

Beyond sagging incomes, most Americans face unimagined economic insecurity. The presumption of career-long employment has collapsed, owing to deregulation, technology, corporate mergers and downsizings, and cheap foreign labor. With job loss comes loss of health insurance and pensions—more insecurity. Even advanced skills are no guarantee against displacement, as computer programmers, teachers, medical professionals, and engineers have lately discovered. There is little doubt that the escalating sense of economic vulnerability underlies much of the nation's sour political mood.

What is startling, however, is that this most basic issue is virtually off the political radar screen. Instead of a real debate about how to reclaim rising living standards and greater economic security for ordinary Americans, politics offers mainly surrogate issues: bitter conflicts over immigration, affirmative action, abortion, school prayer, gun control, gay rights. Even the economic debates—on tax-cutting, deregulation, and budget balance—fail to engage issues of living standards or the division of the economic pie. As both parties fail to convincingly address what really troubles much of the electorate, the voters, not surprisingly, become ever more alienated from politics itself.

For the Republicans, the problem is government. Shrink the public sector, cut taxes and red-tape, and the unleashed power of entrepreneurship will restore high growth rates and living standards. Newt Gingrich marries the information economy to the invisible hand of the free market and sees rising living standards for all. Concervatives either duck the income-distribution question issue —a fierce op-ed offensive has tried to deny its existence—or re-define it as a problem of personal values rather than economic institutions. Supposedly, if we can reclaim traditional virtues of self-discipline and deferred gratification, all Americans can move upwards.

The trouble with this story is that for more than a decade, entrepreneurship and competitiveness have indeed been on the rise—but the gaps in social classes have only widened. And it is precisely the virtuous, hard working people of the lower-middle classes, even those who get educated and stay married, who have faced dramatic declines in living standards. Despite lip service to the upwardly-striving working poor, the GOP Congressional majority is cutting education aid, funds for job training, and wage supplements intended to "make work pay" such as the Earned Income Tax Credit.

Another key element of the Republican program, deregulation of industry, adds to the downward pressure on wages. The more the private market is liberated from norms of fairness, government regulation and other counterweights such as unions and the shelter of national borders, the greater freedom business has to underpay its workforce.

Indeed, the great paradox of today's workplace is that new competitive pressure simultaneously requires business to place ever greater demands on its employees—while also treating them as an expendable cost-center. With deregulation, relatively high unemployment and relentless competition, industry can insist that employees give their utmost, yet still deny them pay increases, benefits, or employment security. This doubtlessly creates great anxiety, among professionals and hourly wage-workers alike. But people are evidently swallowing their economic fears, or displacing them onto other issues, rather than expressing them politically.

For ordinary voters worried about their economic horizons, the Democrats' economic story is only marginally more convincing than the GOP's. As a candidate, Bill Clinton skillfully identified with the electorate's economic worries. His 1992 campaign manifesto, "Putting People First," emphasized that ordinary people were working harder but falling further behind, anxious about their health insurance, their job security and the prospects of their children. He proposed an economic stimulus program of investing in human capital and in public infrastructure, as well as universal health coverage.

This strategy and rhetoric had the twin virtues of blending a more conservative, "New Democrat" notion—the importance of an old-fashioned work ethic—with a liberal appeal that working people were not getting their just rewards; and that market forces, undisciplined by government, would not assure them. This message was directed squarely at the Reagan Democrats who had deserted the party, mainly over cultural and social issues, because it was no longer delivering for them economically.

But even the original Clinton program, with its modest new funds for public works, technology, education and training, would have changed the trajectory of inequality only marginally. As early as the spring of 1993, faced with a recalcitrant Congress, Clinton abandoned his program of public and social investments aimed at economic stimulus. The chastened and centrist Clinton, who emerged after the Republican sweep of November 1994, dropped these themes almost entirely. Budget cuts embraced by Clinton himself reduced his own education and training initiatives to tokens. All that remained of "Putting People First" was fairly unconvincing rhetoric —that mocked the voters' actual condition.

Heading into an election, flickers of the old Clinton re-emerged. The administration embraced a higher minimum wage, first reluctantly and then enthusiastically when polls showed it had the support of 84 percent of the electorate. Some on the more liberal wing of the administration, most notably Labor Secretary Robert Reich, attacked corporate greed and pressed for a more assertive White House posture on behalf of workaday voters. But for the most part Clinton himself assumed a stance of "steady as she goes," relishing the Republican disarray, taking credit for the 8.5 million jobs created during his administration, the relatively low inflation and unemployment, and avoiding the broader issues of stagnant living standards and rising economic insecurity.

As the chapters in this book suggest, society is not without remedies. But these remedies would require much stronger medicine than the Clinton administration seems willing to embrace. A revival of the economic fortunes of ordinary citizens would require a commitment to full employment, stronger trade unions, global labor standards, a significantly higher minimum wage, subsidy of education and training, increased public investment, and a new social compact between industry and labor.

Every one of these approaches, however, flies in the face of key articles of faith deeply held by today's elites: that government should de-regulate and let market forces rip; that "free trade" is the highest form of free market and an unambiguous good; that federal spending should be cut and that no new public money is available; and that true full employment would be inflationary and bad for financial markets.

These basic views are shared by both the Republican majority in Congress and by President Clinton and most of his closest advisors.

Interestingly enough, economic insecurity is being taken seriously mainly on the Democratic and third-party left and the Republican right. Pat Buchanan raised the issue, but his remedy is unconvincing because it mainly scapegoats foreigners and ducks the sources of economic insecurity that are homegrown. The House Democratic leader Richard Gephardt and the Senator leader Tom Daschle talk seriously of "stakeholder capitalism" and new measures to make corporations accountable, but their message is blunted by the cautious centrism and fiscal conservatism of their president.

Indeed, the closer one gets to the political dead center in this country, say Paul Tsongas and the "Concord Coalition" or Colin Powell or Leon Panetta, the louder is the political silence on the issue of living standards. In the center, there is a misplaced conviction that balancing the budget will restore growth, and growth will restore living standards. But that ignores the fact that growth rates are already at the threshold that the Federal Reserve considers inflationary, and that even during cyclical peaks of high growth in recent years, median earnings have continued to decline. The Clinton administration's own economists, bowing to the President's refusal to take on the Federal Reserve or the corporate elite, project economic growth at a paltry 2.2 percent a year as far as the eye can see.

To deal seriously with these issues would require mainstream politicians to challenge prevailing certitudes, to the point of sounding almost radical. They would have to challenge the virtue of deregulation, of globalization; they might even have to criticize the Federal Reserve.

The proper boundary between market, state, and civil society is an enduring political question. Today's version is that debate is surprisingly one-sided, especially given how market forces are assaulting most voters.

Americans have an ambivalent view of equality. We celebrate political equality and equality before the law. We expect hard work to be rewarded, and protest when the lion's share of winnings go to an elite few. Yet we also resist explicit mechanisms of redistribution, which strike us as handouts for the undeserving poor rather than a necessary safeguard for the broad middle class. In a market economy, whatever distribution of income and wealth the market awards enjoys a presumptive legitimacy.

So, ironically, though the struggling middle class rejects the market economy's re-allocation of material prizes from the middle class to the rich, it remains skeptical of available remedies for fear that they will tax the middle class to subsidize the poor. That skepticism reflects the great success of the Republicans in impeaching government as an engine of coalition, community, or redress.

In this strange economy, a rising tide does not lift all boats, and unspoken anxiety afflicts all classes except the most affluent. Stranger still, this pocketbook anxiety is mostly absent from political debate. It portends a politics that is both more nasty and more feckless.

Democrats and liberals once reaped the loyalties of the broad middle and working classes because they stood for a practical mixed economy that produced steady growth, broadly distributed. Today, too many Democrats embrace a slightly milder version of an essentially Republican free-market philosophy—which engenders scant enthusiasm among the Democrats' historic constituencies. One can blame this shift on the Democrats' growing reliance on financial elites, or on the centrism of the current chief executive, or the more difficult economic context of globalization, or on the general disaffection with government—or on all these factors.

Thus the major sources of unease are outside the bounds of political debate, except at its edges. And this is extremely dangerous. History is replete with terrible examples of what occurs when economic distress and political and civic decay are left unremedied, and when popular frustration is voiced mainly by the extremes. The authors of this book address different faces of the problem, but our themes are interconnected. It takes activist government and robust politics to redeem the abstract promise of political democracy and to allow a capitalist economy to co-exist with a decent society. Conversely, an untrammeled market and a debilitated polity lead to a downward spiral of economic despair and political decay. It is our hope that this collection will convey the urgency of disarming these several ticking bombs, with a new affirmative conception of politics, government, civil society and economic citizenship.

What Was the "Republican Surge"?

Who Deserted the Democrats in 1994?

Ruy A. Teixeira and Joel Rogers

American elections have long best been understood as referenda on the economy, but last November the economy didn't seem to matter to voters. By most traditional measures 1992 through 1994 were years of strong economic performance, yet the incumbent Democrats took a historic beating. For exultant Republican pollsters, this was evidence of a genuine ideological victory. For social scientists who touted models of voter behavior geared to economic aggregates such as growth in gross domestic product, it was another professional embarassment. For Democratic strategists, or anyone interested in something better than Contract politics, it should be a wake-up call for a more careful analysis. Either the economy really does not matter, in which case Democrats need to find new ideological appeals to an increasingly conservative voting public. Or it matters in ways that traditional analyses do not detect, in which case Democrats need a new electoral strategy based on new economic appeals.

Which is it?

THE IMPORTANCE OF THE ECONOMY

Wisdom here begins with an analysis of which voters deserted the Democrats in 1994, by categories of voters. Compared to 1992, Democratic support declined 10 percentage points among high school dropouts, 11 points among high school graduates, and 12 points among those with some college. Support held perfectly steady among those with college degrees. The same basic desertion pattern applies if the basis of comparison is the 1990 mid-term election. The decline in Democratic support again comes mostly from among the noncollege educated: down 9 points for high school graduates and 11 points for those with some college. The chief difference is that the

1990-1994 comparison shows very little change among high school dropouts. Merging the results, Democratic support appears to be curvilinear. Democrats are doing better at either end of the education distribution while collapsing in the middle.

Unfortunately for the Democrats, the middle is where most of the voters are. Exit polls, heavily used by strategists, understate the Democrats' problem. These polls showed the Democrats maintaining their support among college graduates, which appeared to be the largest single education group in the electorate (43 percent of voters according to the VNS exit poll). But exit polls overcount better-educated voters. Evidently, college-educated voters are more articulate and more willing to cooperate with exit polls, which accounts for their overrepresentation. The more reliable voting data available from the Census Bureau indicate that college-educated voters were only 29 percent of the electorate in 1994. This is actually a smaller share of the active electorate than voters with just a high school diploma (31 percent), and far smaller than the overall noncollege-educated share (71 percent).

Among whites, where the decline in Democratic support between 1992 and 1994 was concentrated (black Democratic support actually went up slightly), the shift away from the Democrats among noncollege-educated voters was even more pronounced, especially among men. Between 1992 and 1994, Democratic support declined 20 points (to 37 percent) among white men with a high school education and 15 points (to 31 percent) among white men with some college.

Contrary to the hopes invested in the "gender gap," noncollege-educated white women also deserted in droves. For both white women with a high school diploma and those with some college, Democratic support dropped 10 points. Thus, to ascribe the falloff in Democratic support to "angry white guys," as many commentators did, is to miss the point. Large numbers of noncollege-educated white men and women alike abandoned the party.

What is true of the electorate as a whole is also true of the 1992 Perot voters, a key swing group. Adjusted to reflect voting patterns in the Census data, their ranks are even more dominated by noncollege-educated voters. And they moved massively against the Democrats, down 17 points from 1992 to just 32 percent support. If repeated in 1996, this astonishingly low level of support will doom Clinton's re-election bid. Indeed, recent polls show 1992 Perot voters breaking two to one against Clinton in trial heats for 1996.

And what does this all have to do with the economy? Approximately everything. It is precisely noncollege educated Americans, in particular noncollege-educated men, who have suffered the largest wage declines over the last two decades. Furthermore, this miserable experience of wage (and income) decline continued apace in the first two years of the Clinton administration, providing little relief to voters who have seen their living standards erode over time. (See Lawrence Mishel, "Rising Tides, Sinking Wages," page 81.) Finally, analysis of wage data cross-linked to the VNS data indicates that the Perot voters who voted Republican in 1994 were the ones under the most economic stress, with estimated post-1979 wage losses more than double those of Perot voters who voted Democratic.

In short, the economy matters as much or more than ever, even if how it matters is missed by traditional election forecasting models that stress overall growth. These models mistakenly presume a "rising-tide-lifts-all-boats" economy that no longer exists. In today's

WHITE FLIGHT AT THE POLLS

In 1994, whites with less education and larger wage losses were most likely to desert the Democratic Party.

	% change in Democratic support, 1992-94	% change in real hourly wage, 1979-1993
WHITE MEN		
high school dropout	-11	-26
high school graduate	-20	-17
some college	-15	-11
college graduate	-6	+2
WHITE WOMEN		
high school dropout	-5	-12
high school graduate	-10	-2
some college	-10	+7
college graduate	+2	+14

Source: Authors' analysis of Voter News Service and Voter Research and Surveys exit poll data, and Current Population Survey data.

economy, some boats get swamped by the same tide that elevates a few. Therefore, we need to look below the surface to see what is really going on.

HOW THE ECONOMY AFFECTS SOCIAL ISSUES

To be sure, wage data are only crude measures of how the economy affects individual voters, and narrowly material concerns hardly exhaust voter motivation. Along with their income, voters are naturally concerned about the stability of economic arrangements, the amount of time they get with their families, the quality of schooling that their kids are getting, the safety of their streets, the stability of their neighborhoods, even the robustness of those civic values on which any society depends.

Indeed, a broad definition of "living standards" would encompass all these factors, since they all influence the material quality of everyday life. All of these factors, noneconomic and economic, can and do independently motivate voter choice, with the noneconomic sometimes outweighing the economic. Still, social life is materially conditioned, and the basic material of social standing is income. Job security would be less of a worry with higher economic growth and full employment. Relentless abuse and stress at the workplace would not be tolerated if they were not thought necessary to maintaining income. Public goods would be more abundant if the taxes to pay for them were available, and taxes would be better tolerated if incomes were rising. Families and community life would get more time if less time needed to be spent working.

Thus, however enlarged a conception of "living standards" one favors, family-supporting wages and income are central. And a central fact of life for the vast bulk of noncollege-educated voters is that, increasingly, American politics does not assure it. Do that long enough, and you have an angry electorate. Do it again, and they will throw you out, almost whoever "you" happen to be.

Our quarrel is not with those who wish an expanded understanding of living standards and thus a Democratic focus on both economic and noneconomic issues. Indeed, we believe that such a synthetic approach is suggested by the 1994 election results and would be a big improvement over both the narrowly economic focus of traditional liberals and the basically noneconomic focus of orthodox New Democrats. Our real quarrel is with those who argue that 1994 marked a newly ideological turn in American politics, from which the decline in living standards can presumably be divorced. This is a widespread view in the mass media, which take 1994 as a general right turn. It's true that the percentage of self-identified conservatives increased from 30 to 37 percent between 1992 and 1994. Republican pollster Fred Steeper points to the unusually high Republican House vote among self-identified conservatives (81 percent) in 1994—a 9-point increase over 1992—as evidence of this broad conservative shift. But we are unimpressed, for two reasons.

First, this ideological shift was dwarfed by shifts reflecting voters' perceptions of the economy. Steeper's 9-point anti-Democratic shift among conservatives (37 percent of the electorate) pales compared to the 25-point shift against the Democrats among those who thought the economy was not so good or poor (about 60 percent of the electorate) and the 36-point Democratic shift among those who thought their family financial situation was getting worse (about a quarter of the electorate).

Second, 1992 and 1994 exit poll data do not show a large change in the effect of conservative ideology on the House vote. More substantial shifts take place on economic variables like family financial situation, long-term wage decline, and especially assessment of the national economy. And the most important shift of all takes place in the relationship of partisanship to the House vote, particularly among independents. Controlling for their general anti-Democratic swing, there appears to be no significant difference in the relationship between conservatism and the House vote in 1992 and 1994. What might appear to be an ideologically driven shift was really a pragmatic shift based on economic and other concerns.

If long-term (and uninterrupted) declining living standards are indeed the basic story of 1994, making progress beyond it requires clarity on two questions: Why do such declines seem to disadvantage the Democrats uniquely? And what might the Democrats (or any other progressive political formation out there) do about that fact?

Who takes the political blame for long-term changes in economy and society depends on which story the average person believes about these changes. Here, long-term changes like steadily declining living standards differ from short-term changes in the business cycle (booms and recessions), which simply benefit (or hurt) the party on whose watch the growth (or decline) takes place. The Democrats

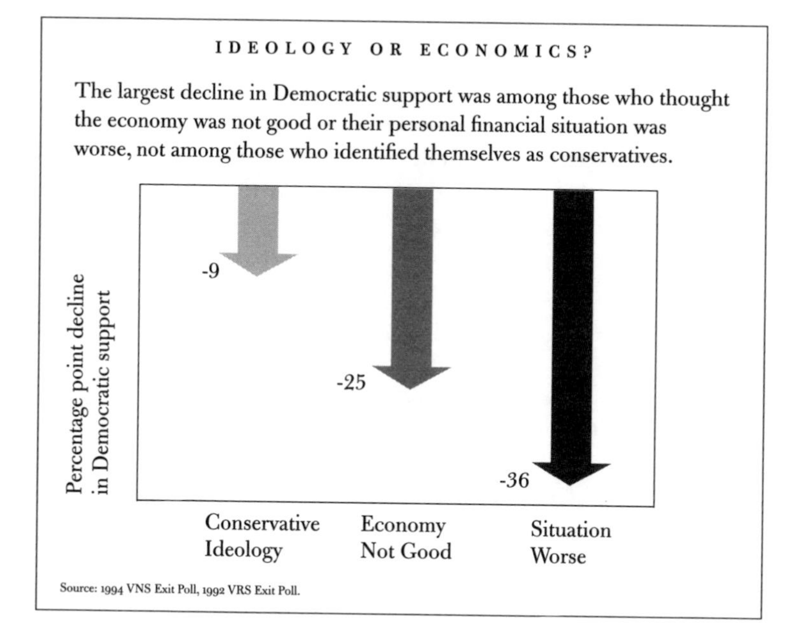

keep getting hurt by declining living standards because the story the public believes about these long-term changes casts them as the villain. The dominant story among the general public is that the long-term decline in living standards has to do with wasteful government spending (especially on the poor, minorities, and immigrants), high taxes, inefficient and obtrusive public administration, selfish behavior by interest groups, and excessive social tolerance and loss of values. Since all of this is readily identifiable with the Democrats, as the party of activist government, poor people, minorities, liberal interest groups, and social tolerance, Democrats get the blame. Because the thrust of current Democratic strategy, especially its "New Democrat" variant, implicitly accepts this dominant story, the Democrats start every election with two strikes against them. Under extraordinary circumstances they can win. Under ordinary circumstances they tend to lose.

The only way out of this box is by offering a convincing alternative in which the government and the poor don't take most of the blame for declining living standards and in which dismantling the government isn't the main policy recommendation. Certainly this alternative includes policies to reverse wage erosion, increase job security, and rebuild communities. But perhaps most important is an alternative story that shifts the blame to other targets.

The obvious candidates for such targeting are irresponsible corporate power—the source of declining living standards and feeble government response—and its political allies. An alternative story would begin by declaring that these forces have chosen a path for the country that does not inexorably accompany economic progress (globalization, the "new economy," and so on), but does inexorably drive down living standards by eroding the material basis for family and community life. It is therefore possible and necessary to choose another path—a task from which dominant corporations and politicians have disqualified themselves by their behavior.

That such alternative paths are available is obvious from the experience of virtually all other rich nations, which have survived in the new economy with vastly better income distribution and growth patterns than our own. But this alternative account does not come easily of late to Democrats. Perhaps this is because of the fight with business interests (including Wall Street, the bond traders, and Alan Greenspan) that would be necessary to advance this alternative story and agenda. Perhaps, in our private-money system of campaign finance, it reflects the Democrats' reliance on wealthy donors. Perhaps it has to do with the current weakness of organizations that represent groups that have been losing out (for example, unions or other institutions of workplace representation).

Whatever the reasons for its current timidity, unless the Democratic Party embraces an alternative story and shows a broader willingness to contest business interests and encourage mobilization along class lines, Democrats will continue to be on the defensive and Republicans will continue to have the high ground. President Dole, anyone?

After the Republican Surge

Stanley B. Greenberg

Most Democrats have a hard time being optimistic these days, and it's easy to understand why. The 1994 midterm election produced a swing to the Republicans and a new nationalization of politics that undercut Democrats who had survived in Republican districts and states. A review of polling data suggests that a conservative surge was in evidence as early as mid-1993, as ideological conservatives mobilized against the national Democratic government and its agenda. Three groups in particular—evangelical Christians, lower-income voters, and seniors—rushed to the Republicans, shifting the electoral balance against the Democrats.

But for those able to see through the smoke of battle, there is reason for hope. The conservative surge was a reaction to the defining first year of the Clinton presidency. This is a different moment, and there is plenty of evidence of emergent disillusion with the Republican agenda, leaving Democrats positioned to reclaim many of the voters lost in 1994. Downscale and older voters, the shock troops for the Republican surge, find themselves first in the line of fire and taking heavy losses. More broadly, voters have pulled back from the Republicans on a wide range of issues—welfare, education, the environment, and Social Security. Voters who were hopeful about Republican rule are now increasingly unsure and split on whom to trust, the Republicans in Congress or the president. The challenge for Democrats and progressives now is to rise to the new political moment, find their voice, and mobilize the emergent reaction.

The election of a unified national Democratic government in 1992 set off battles that produced an enlarged, energized, politicized, and mobilized conservative bloc. This historic conservative Republican surge swept away many Democrats who stood in the way and gave Republicans control of the Congress and many state governments.

Although the results were felt in November 1994, most of the surge occurred during Clinton's first year. In the face of national Democratic governance, a reaction took hold among ideological conservatives, committed Evangelicals, and Republicans who nationalized their votes. The party balance among voters across the country hardly changed, but conservatives grew more unified and emboldened.

In elections prior to 1994, many moderate and conservative voters supported Democrats for Congress even though they sometimes backed Republican candidates for president. In 1994, Republicans succeeded to an unprecedented degree in nationalizing the election. In congressional districts with a Republican presidential majority, voters held accountable incumbent Democrats who had aligned themselves with the national Democratic politics of the Clinton era.

These Democratic office holders stood undefended. The national struggles around the Clinton agenda failed to rally the left or center, and a large bloc of noncollege-educated voters stayed home. The sense of movement of the Democratic agenda by the end of 1993 concealed the gap that was emerging between Democratic leaders and the potential Democratic popular bloc. When gridlock took hold in 1994, that gap left many potential Democratic supporters disengaged. The Democrats paid a very big price at the polls.

The turn to the conservatives in 1994 proved particularly costly to Democrats because of its socioeconomic character. The surge undercut Democratic support among lower-income, noncollege-educated voters as well as among older voters. In that first year, the national discourse shifted from material concerns that historically have rallied Democrats, such as the economy and jobs, to "values" concerns, such as crime and moral decline. Along the way, the country grappled with a range of issues—including taxes, Medicare cuts, gays in the military, NAFTA, and gun control—that together created a populist and cultural gap that helped push the Democrats away from their broad working- and middle-class base.

The conservative surge, however, was specific to a particular political moment—the battles of the early Clinton presidency and a unified Democratic government pursuing change. The limits of this surge were already evident last year. This is a new moment with a unified Republican Congress pursuing change. The battles of the day center on their governance and vision, and the developing reaction suggests a possible swing back to the Democrats.

THE ANATOMY OF THE CONSERVATIVE REACTION

During the first two years of the Clinton presidency, the number of people calling themselves "conservative" grew about 7 percentage points. Conservatism also took on increased political meaning. According to the 1994 exit polls, 80 percent of conservatives voted Republican for Congress. Even at the highest point of Ronald Reagan's popularity in 1984, only 69 percent of conservatives proved that partisan. The 1994 election brought a conservative growth and unity behind Republican candidates unequaled in our time.

THE CONSERVATIVE TIDE

Growth in the conservative bloc during the Clinton presidency

POLLING ORGANIZATION	PERCENTAGE POINT GAIN
Voter News Service exit polling	+ 7
Greenberg Research	+ 9
NBC-*Wall Street Journal*	+ 8
CBS-*New York Times*	+ 3

Between 1992 and 1994, self-identified conservatives became much more polarized in their ideological thinking. In 1992, conservatives gave "conservatives" a score of 63 degrees on a thermometer scale that ranges from 0 (unfavorable) to 100 (favorable). But a year later the temperature had risen 7 degrees to 70; feelings about liberals dropped 9 degrees in the same period. By contrast, the liberal and moderate blocs seemed sidelined, as the battles of the day failed to engage them. All the elevated political energy was on the conservative side. (These results are based on work by Samuel Popkin at the University of California, San Diego.)

Conservatives comprised 70 percent of Republican identifiers and that conservative energy likely accounts for the unique increase in the conservative-Republican turnout in 1994. A survey by Times-Mirror found that 55 percent of the likely electorate intended to vote Republican—8 points more than for the registered population. In 1992, the gap was only 2 points. A large-scale Gallup survey confirms the turnout pattern: Republicans comprised 34 percent of actual voters, but only 24 percent of the nonvoters; conversely and ominously, according to CNN-USA *Today* polls, Democrats comprised just 32 percent of the voters but fully 44 percent of the nonvoters.

While conservatives were being mobilized, energy was being diffused elsewhere on the ideological spectrum. The Democratic Leadership Council's (DLC) postelection survey found that last year's nonvoters—people who stayed home but who had voted for president in 1992—were largely noncollege graduates under 50 years of age. They were disproportionately downscale Democrats who strongly favored Democratic congressional candidates to Republicans. Unfortunately, they were not sufficiently energized to vote.

A conservative swing within two broad groups, committed evangelical Christians and lower-income voters, produced the conservative surge. A surprising defection of older voters also played a significant role. A closer look at these groups tells us a lot about the character of these political developments.

COMMITTED EVANGELICALS. These voters constitute about 10 percent of the electorate; about half of them live in the South. They were already very conservative in 1992 and provided the core of the George Bush vote. But in the Clinton period, they became even more conservative. In 1994, 63 percent identified themselves as conservative, up 11 points from early 1993, making them the most conservative group in the electorate. In the 1994 exit polls, white, born-again Protestants also increased as a proportion of the electorate. And almost 80 percent voted for the Republicans.

The conservative mobilization and emerging political unity among these committed Evangelicals have given some credence to the idea, put forth by pollster Fred Steeper, that Republican gains in 1994 are a product of the rising importance of cultural issues and comparative decline of economic concerns in the electorate. But, as we shall see below, that is hardly the whole story.

WHITE DOWNSCALE AMERICA. The other push toward conservatism came among white downscale voters. Conservative identification increased 12 points among white voters with high school educations and 13 points among white men without a college degree. These downscale voters evidently soured on the Democratic course as their incomes failed to follow the rest of the economy upward and as the debate in Washington was quickly dominated by taxes, spending, NAFTA, and guns. This downscale bloc is concerned with both economic instability and "big government," and it includes many of the Perot voters who broke Republican in 1994.

SENIORS. The downscale swing to the conservatives includes a major component of older Americans: During the first year of the Clinton presidency, seniors became 14 points more conservative. That represents a dramatic turn away from the Clinton agenda by the principal beneficiaries of the New Deal state, which I will return to in a moment.

A DEFINING POLITICAL MOMENT?

The conservative surge had a powerful impact on those races in which Democrats faced their toughest tests in 1994. Near double-digit state conservative surges help account for the strong Republican statewide performances in California, Illinois, and Missouri; for the difficult Senate races in New Jersey and Pennsylvania; and for the Republican gains in the Midwest where the conservative surge was greatest (more than 10 points). The energized conservative bloc likely accounts for surprisingly strong Republican showings in Texas (with 43 percent conservative voters), Missouri (42 percent), Illinois (40 percent), and Michigan (40 percent).

The focus of most commentary on the current upheaval is naturally on the 1994 election itself as a defining political event. But the entire conservative advance had already played out by January 1994, the first-year anniversary of the Clinton presidency. After that, little

STATE CONSERVATIVE SHIFTS

Conservative proportion of the electorate, based on exit polls

STATE	1992	1994	CONSERVATIVE GAIN
California	26	36	+10
Illinois	26	40	+14
Missouri	30	42	+12
New Jersey	26	38	+12
Pennsylvania	28	37	+9

else happened except an intensification of loyalties just prior to the election. The advance came during two defining and distinctive phases of the nascent presidency, during the early Clinton slide and during the late-year Clinton resurgence.

PHASE ONE: THE EARLY CLINTON SLIDE. After an initial burst of enthusiasm for the president and his economic program, support fell off sharply in the spring and summer of 1993. The stimulus bill had been defeated, the investment program pared down, Medicare cuts and Social Security taxes were on the table, and the Democrats were under pressure to cut spending more and raise taxes less in balancing the budget. The prominence of the gays-in-the-military controversy deflected attention from the Democrats' pocketbook issues onto a politically difficult cultural issue.

In this period, according to my own research, the conservative bloc grew about 3 points. This was also confirmed by NBC-*Wall Street Journal* polling. These early conservative gains came largely among homemakers (whose conservative identification was up 6 points), retired women (up 7 points), older women (up 6 points), and the high school educated (up 6 points).

In this defining period for President Clinton and the Democrats, conservatism was well along the way to consolidating support. The ideological polarization of conservative sentiment was fully developed by May, and conservatives were becoming decisively more Republican: A 25-point Republican advantage among self-defined conservatives in early 1993 turned to a 40-point advantage by the summer. The Republican bloc as a consequence became increasingly conservative, as the proportion of moderates in the Republican bloc dropped 6 points to 31 percent.

In contrast, the political struggles around these early Clinton initiatives did not rally the left or center or produce a countervailing mobilization. The center and left were somewhat demoralized, turning slightly away from the Democrats as the party best able to address the country's problems.

PHASE TWO: THE CLINTON RESURGENCE. President Clinton regained his popularity in the fall and early winter of his first year. The passage of the budget, the introduction of the reinventing government and health care initiatives, the victories on NAFTA, and the Brady Bill brought respect and support all across the ideological spectrum. That is why it is so intriguing that this period also brought the second surge in conservative support: up about 5 points in polls by Greenberg Research and NBC-*Wall Street Journal* and 3 points in polls by CBS-*New York Times*.

The gains came among groups that established the character of the conservative surge: up 8 points with voters over 50 and, more important, 10 points with seniors (over age 65); up 8 points with the high school educated and 7 among all those without a college degree. Over the course of the year, committed Evangelicals became 11 points more conservative.

The conservative gains, against the trend of thinking about the president, likely reflected two sweeping changes in public thinking that favored the conservatives. The first was a reaction to health care reform among particular groups that shifted sentiment sharply against government. Conservatives and senior citizens were among the first to turn against health care reform. A majority of conservatives opposed it immediately after the launch. Within a month, two-thirds thought it would limit choice, and three-quarters thought that it simply would create another big government bureaucracy. The rebellion among seniors proved fateful for health care reform and contributed mightily to the conservative surge. While a majority were initially supportive of reform (57 percent), their worries about the risks and doubts about the benefits took an immediate toll, as support dropped 10 points and below a majority in just two months.

The second was a shift in the dominant worries about the country from material concerns to a renewed preoccupation with values. The number of people identifying jobs and the economy as the most important problem dropped 14 points in this period, while concern with crime and moral decline jumped 23 points. With the economy recovering, voters gave greater attention to the moral dissolution to which conservatives seemed better prepared to speak.

PHASE THREE: CONSERVATIVE CONSOLIDATION. The proportion of conservatives in the electorate remained doggedly constant at this higher level throughout 1994. The late summer and fall brought a new intensity and consolidation within the conservative bloc. In the post-Labor Day, preelection period, intense anti-Clinton sentiment jumped 10 points among conservative voters; now a near majority (48 percent) of them could be characterized as "Clinton haters." The negative energy among conservatives centered on the president, as there was no comparable increase in intense anti-Democratic sentiment. Meanwhile, moderate and conservative Democrats lost confidence in the Democrats and the parties in this late preelection period, with more than one-quarter saying they trusted "neither" party on the issues.

This late, energized anti-Clinton conservatism was most pronounced among the committed Evangelicals (58 percent held intense anti-Clinton sentiments, up 10 points at the end) and among the non-college-educated men (35 percent, up 8 points). The consolidation of the anti-Clinton right dominated the election, particularly as liberals and moderates disengaged. The evidence of gridlock on health care and other initiatives no doubt contributed to that attitude, but we know from the other data that the lack of engagement was fully evident during the first, defining year of the Clinton presidency.

A NATIONALIZED ELECTION

The Democratic takeover of national politics and the conservative reaction produced a nationalized election in 1994. And that process, rather than any sharp shifts in party loyalties, best explains the upheaval. On the Republican side, voters set aside a range of considerations that previously had allowed them to indulge Democratic incumbents and, instead, cast their ballots with extraordinary partisan consistency at all levels. Thus, in 1994, 89 percent of the electorate cast ballots for Congress that were consistent with their previous (1992) presidential vote. In 1990, just 69 percent and in 1986, just 65 percent cast such nationalized ballots. (This analysis uses findings in Gary Jacobson, "The 1994 House Elections in Perspective," delivered to the Midwest Political Science Convention, April 1995.)

For Republicans, conservatives, white born-again Protestants, and voters in the South, balloting in 1994 for Congress looked like a rerun of their balloting for president in 1988 and 1992. That simple shift had enormous consequences on the ground, particularly in the South.

The Democratic and liberal vote had already been nationalized before 1994 and, thus, was little affected by the process of nationalization in this election. The rationale for voting Democratic for Congress—the ability to deliver for the district or protect social spending—had already pushed these voters to partisan consistency. Among Democrats, 86 percent of voters backed the Democrat both for Congress and for president in 1988 and 1992; that pattern was essentially reproduced in 1994. What was new was the consistency on the Republican side. The conservative surge made the election truly national for the first time in decades by pushing conservatives and Republicans to vote Republican.

Among downscale voters, where the conservative surge was most pronounced, the election was nationalized and then some. Among those who graduated from high school but not college, for example, Democratic support for Congress dropped a stunning 13 points, compared to 1992. That is 8 points worse than their 1988 and 1992 votes for president. College graduates and postgraduates, by contrast, simply voted their presidential preference, which changed little from 1992. Democrats also lost ground beyond nationalization among Catholics (down 8 points) and white men (down 7 points).

The effect of nationalization played out dramatically in congressional districts where the Democrats were historically weak in presidential elections. The Republicans won every open congressional seat in districts that had a Republican presidential majority in 1988 and 1992; they won only 35 percent of the open seats where there had been no Republican majority. Democratic incumbents in districts that had supported the Republican presidential candidate were three times as likely to lose as Democratic incumbents in seats with no such Republican presidential majority: 29 percent of the former lost compared to only 9 percent of the latter.

In these Republican presidential districts, particularly in the South, an energized conservative bloc rebelled against the direction of Democratic politics. The more a Democratic incumbent was associated with national Democratic politics, the greater likelihood he or she would suffer at the polls.

In heavily Democratic districts—ones that had given Democratic presidential candidates 60 percent or more of the vote—Democratic House members lost no ground because of support for the president's program. In districts that had given Democratic presidential candidates 50 percent support or more, down-the-line supporters lost about 4 points, which may have tilted some of these marginal districts. But in Republican districts where Dukakis and Clinton took less than 50 percent of the vote, the Democratic incumbents paid a very high price for aligning with national Democratic politics. Across the country, these strong supporters of the Democratic program lost 7 percentage points off their expected margin; in the

South, the loss was a stunning 12 points. Strong supporters of the Clinton agenda in heavily Republican districts in the South faced three times as much erosion as weak supporters did. In weak Democratic districts (less than 40 percent for Clinton), three-quarters of pro-Clinton Democratic incumbents (those who gave him at least 75 percent support) lost their seats.

A DEMOCRATIC SURGE?

The conservative surge in 1994, while very powerful, was also specific to the political moment. That moment has changed and so, very likely, has the dynamic of our national politics. To retake the Congress and reelect the president, progressives and Democrats will have to escape the traps of the last two years and join new battles that center on the Republican ascendancy in Congress. Democrats now have the chance to forge their own reaction and their own electoral surge.

The conservative surge embodied the nation's reaction to the largely blocked Democratic national agenda and advanced a strong conservative opposition to government. But the right, contrary to the impressions of Newt Gingrich's Contract with America, did not advance a fully formed conservative agenda—only the simple and powerful idea that government messes things up.

That was enough to energize voter cynicism. In the antipolitical mood of the last election, only 20 percent of the public trusted government to do the right thing, and only 18 percent trusted Congress—down from 24 percent in 1990 and 39 percent in 1985. The voters in 1994 were deeply skeptical about the government's capacity to advance the public interest: 80 percent said the government is run for the few and special interests, not the people; 66 percent said government is the problem, not the solution. Several national polls confirmed this mood.

The conservative assault on government proved successful only because the political battles of that period allowed conservatives to obscure their broader agenda. But even at the time of the election, voters said they preferred Clinton's economic policies to Reagan's. And while voters on Election Day said they wanted the new Congress to cut government spending, they placed an equally high priority on protecting Social Security and Medicare and on ensuring affordable health insurance for everyone. Clearly, the Republicans would have faced a tougher test had they moved from their minimalist antigovernment discourse to their broader aims in social policy and government regulation. The awakening about the Republicans over the last six months has already produced sky-high doubts about the principal Republican leader, Speaker Gingrich, whose negative ratings are now at 56 percent, and growing doubts about the Congress, whose disapproval ratings are now over 60 percent. Doubts about the Congress jumped 10 points this summer alone, suggesting the price of clarity about the broader conservative agenda.

LIMITS OF REPUBLICAN SUPPORT

A self-confident, bordering on arrogant and militant, conservative Congress is now trying to enact its nationalized program. In most areas, they are moving without having laid the groundwork with the public. The overinterpretation of the 1994 election is already apparent in the sharp public turn away from the Republicans, evident even at the end of the first 100 days of the new Congress.

The debates in Congress before the summer had already produced significant movement toward President Clinton and away from the Republicans on handling the economy (a 16-point shift), on handling the federal deficit (17 points), on taxes (15 points), on crime (11 points), on welfare (10 points), and on protecting Social Security (26 points). The belated unveiling of the conservative agenda has led to an unraveling of the goodwill and trust that first characterized this period of Republican governance. At the outset of the year, voters overwhelmingly "trusted" the Republicans in Congress more than the president to address the country's problems: in one poll by 16 points, and in another by 24. But five months later, that advantage had completely evaporated. There is obviously a long way to go, but based on the current evidence, a reaction against the conservatives seems as plausible as a continuing conservative surge.

Democrats lost because they were associated with national Democratic politics and national political institutions, particularly the Congress, that were viewed as corrupt, ineffectual, or irrelevant. Indeed, when looking back on 1994, voters said their anger was directed, above all, at "politics as usual." But Republicans are now associated with a Congress whose image is sliding in nearly all the surveys. With the special-interest lobbyists on display, cuts in school lunches, and threats to Medicare, the public seems poised to sour on the latest version of politics as usual: An extraordinary 59 percent say there is a real danger that the Republicans will go "too far" in helping the rich, cutting government that benefits the poor and average Americans. This sound and fury in Washington sounds less and less like "real change" (27 percent), and more and more like "politics as usual" (68 percent). Just six months into the new Republican Congress, voters are forming new images of a corrupt politics. That is fuel for a Democratic reaction.

The conservative-Republican nationalized vote has likely reached its zenith. With conservatives casting 80 percent of their votes for Republicans—and self-identified Republicans, 91 percent—it is not clear there are more votes to get on the right. Future gains will have to be made on the left and in the center where there is clearly resistance. While some self-described moderates shifted to the conservatives in 1994, the liberal and moderate blocs held firm in their partisan preferences, despite the surge. Liberals cast 80 percent of their votes for Democratic House candidates, and moderates cast 58 percent—both unchanged from 1992. That kept the national Republican congressional vote at around 52 percent, not nearly strong enough to create a new Republican ascendancy.

Moreover, the Republicans could be victimized by their own success in 1994 in creating a Republican orthodoxy: 70 percent of Republicans are now self-identified conservatives. That provides coherence, to be sure, but also creates pressures to push beyond the public's taste for conservative policies. The Democratic Party, by contrast, is ideologically diverse, tilting toward the moderate center, with a significant liberal presence: 60 percent of self-identified Democrats describe themselves as "moderate" or "conservative." The party is led by a president who, for all his political difficulties in the last election, is seen as a "new kind of Democrat," not a "traditional liberal Democrat" (56 to 37 percent). The president is in a position to benefit from the reaction to a reign of conservative orthodoxy.

With little opportunity for partisan gain on the right—and probably on the left as well where Democrats took 80 percent of the vote—the "moderates" emerge as a kind of battleground. They comprise about 35 percent of the electorate, while liberals continue to hold around 22 percent; conservatives now hold 39 percent. Moderates, however, are no simple "centrist" challenge: While they are indeed in the middle on equal rights and abortion, they sound more like "liberals" on the role of government and social welfare and more like "conservatives" on fiscal issues. The challenge for Democrats is how to rally the liberals and moderate center and create an energy that erodes the conservative bloc.

DOWNWARD MOBILITY AND PROGRESSIVE MOBILIZATION

The battle to enact a Democratic agenda over the last few years ended up associating the Democrats with a host of negative developments—taxes, pork barrel spending, gays in the military, gun control, foreign imports, and Medicare cuts—all of which drove downscale and older voters to withdraw politically or join the Republican surge. But the Republican takeover of Congress has turned the tables. The battle to enact a Republican agenda has already associated the Republicans with a new set of negative developments—Medicare and education cuts, tax cuts for the wealthiest and big corporations, special favors for lobbyists and corporate polluters—which could reopen the debate about which party represents working people and understands the needs of older Americans. Downscale voters and seniors joined the Republican surge, but they are already having doubts.

Could these voters, newly angered as the actual Republican program unfolds, join a Democratic reaction to Republican governance? We are hardly lacking the evidence of voter discontent and reaction. What is uncertain, however, is whether the Democrats and progressive organizations can mobilize popular opposition to this reign of conservative Republicanism. If they can give voice to the skepticism and offer something better, this volatile electorate is ready to shift loyalties once again. If they fail, we will see deepening disaffection with government and politics, and not merely a surge of conservatism.

Liberalism's Third Crisis

Alan Brinkley

This is a pivotal moment in our recent political history. The 1994 elections may or may not represent a lasting realignment of party loyalties. But even if they do not, they are clear evidence of something at least equally important. They reveal how massively government, politics, and the liberalism that has for decades largely shaped them have lost popular support, even popular legitimacy.

With their longstanding assumptions about public life under siege, many liberals are in the throes of a crisis of confidence. Whatever forms liberalism takes as a result, they will almost certainly be different from those we have known. But as extraordinary as this moment may seem, it is not unprecedented.

There are at least two examples in the twentieth century of a comparable (if perhaps less abrupt) collapse in popular confidence in a prevailing model of liberal politics and government, and of the creation of another model to replace it. Liberals searching for an answer to their present dilemmas might consider how earlier generations dealt with similar challenges.

At the beginning of the twentieth century, American liberalism remained largely wedded to its Enlightenment roots. Liberals championed personal liberty, human progress, and the pursuit of rational self-interest by individuals as the basis of a free society (values most liberals would still claim to support) and stoutly resisted giving more than minimal authority to the state. This laissez-faire liberalism is often described today as "conservatism," but it was, in fact, a challenge to an earlier, nineteenth-century conservatism (often associated with the ideas of Edmund Burke and never strong in the United States) rooted in the protection of tradition and fixed social hierarchy. Laissez-faire liberalism envisioned a fluid, changing society, in which the state would not protect existing patterns of wealth and privilege and individuals could pursue their goals freely and advance according to their own achievements.

In practice, of course, the theory of laissez-faire liberalism bore little relationship to the realities of industrial society or political life in America. Like most of their contemporaries, liberals tolerated and even actively promoted what by modern standards would seem to be oppressive official restrictions on personal behavior. Ambitious entrepreneurs decried state interference in the name of liberalism when it constrained them, but they welcomed, even demanded, government assistance when it was of use to them. Nor were most liberal capitalists genuinely committed to an open competition for wealth and power. Business champions of laissez faire often benefited, for example, from government intervention that protected them against challenges from their own workers. But the "liberal" idea—however inadequately it described social reality—became a potent justification for a rapidly expanding capitalist world and for a notion of individual freedom that gained increasing sway within that world.

By the beginning of the twentieth century, the chasm separating the character of industrial society and the liberal vision of it had become too glaring to ignore. A class of corporate titans was emerging with unprecedented wealth and power. Private institutions were attaining sizes never before imagined. The freedom of individuals to pursue their economic self-interest seemed imperiled by these new centers of authority; and many erstwhile champions of laissez faire came to believe that preserving a genuinely free society required somehow constraining the private power that now threatened to dominate it.

The result was the emergence of a new "progressive" or "reform" liberalism, with broad support from across the economic, regional, and political spectrum. It was committed to (among many other things) taming the excesses of industrialism and imposing a measure of social control on capitalism. Reformers set out to protect individuals, communities, and the government itself from excessive corporate power and (more haltingly) to provide citizens basic subsistence and dignity, usually through some form of government intervention. The New Deal emerged out of this tradition of "progressive" reform, attached the word "liberal" to it, and for several years won broad popular approval for its efforts to transform the character of government.

But the New Deal model gradually generated a powerful reaction of its own—from corporate forces that felt threatened by its policies, but most of all from ordinary people who began to fear the power of government as much as (if not more than) they had once feared the power of capitalists. Even at the height of Roosevelt's popularity, public opinion surveys (crude as they were in the 1930s) revealed a striking level of concern about public spending, the size of the government bureaucracy, and the burden of federal taxes (which for the middle class were extremely light by later standards). Popular movements emerged denouncing the "dictatorial" aspirations of the president and the "tyrannical" character of the new state bureaucracies. As the 1930s wore on and the New Deal failed to end the Great Depression, such attacks steadily grew. By the beginning of World War II, New Deal liberalism was already on the defensive.

In 1942, finally, the Democratic Party suffered an electoral defeat that contemporaries considered nearly as disastrous as observers now consider the 1994 results. Democrats lost 50 seats in the House (which, when combined with substantial setbacks in 1938, reduced to 10 a majority that six years earlier had stood at 242) and 8 seats in the Senate (reducing their majority to 21 from the 60 they had enjoyed after the 1936 election). Given the power of southern Democrats, conservatives had effective control of the House and close to a majority in the Senate.

"That the Administration has completely lost control over Congress in the November elections is becoming clearer every day," a British diplomat reported to London early in 1943. "The Republicans will of course have working control of Congress," the New Deal economist Eliot Janeway wrote after the election. "On every issue enough anti-Roosevelt Democrats will be with [the Republicans] to enable Congress to boss the Administration at the point of a gun.... The balance of [Roosevelt's] term is going to be an obstacle race."

Over the next two years, congressional conservatives systematically dismantled substantial elements of the New Deal: the Civilian Conservation Corps, the Works Progress Administration, the National Youth Administration, and virtually every other relief and public works program Roosevelt had created. They abolished the government's first and only planning agency, overturned the president's efforts to limit wartime salaries to $25,000 a year, passed legislation restricting labor's right to strike and contribute to political campaigns, and reduced funding for the Office of Price Administration and the Office of War Information, war agencies conservatives considered centers of liberal sentiment.

The administration and its liberal allies had expected strained relations with Congress. But many were astonished by the intensity and bitterness of the opposition. Congress seemed to many liberals to have launched a frenzy of indiscriminate budget-cutting in an effort, as one New England Republican gloated, to "win the war from the New Deal." Vice President Henry Wallace spoke in 1943 of "powerful groups who hope to take advantage of the President's concentration on the war effort to destroy everything he has accomplished on the domestic front over the last ten years." James F. Byrnes, a former senator who had been at best moderately supportive of the New Deal in the 1930s, confided to Felix Frankfurter early in 1943 (by which time Byrnes was working in the White House) that he had been watching the performance of Congress with dismay. As Frankfurter recorded the conversation in his diary, Byrnes "never had such a sense of intellectual bankruptcy. He said there was not one thought or idea or bit of illumination in the whole outfit, and the only thing they talked about was that they were committed to abolishing 'bureaucracy.'"

Early in 1944, the poet and Office of War Information administrator Archibald MacLeish told a gathering of politicians and journalists honoring Freda Kirchwey, editor of the *Nation*, "Liberals meet in Washington these days, if they can endure to meet at all, to discuss the tragic outlook for all liberal proposals, the collapse of all liberal leadership, and the inevitable defeat of all liberal aims. It is no longer feared, it is assumed, that the country is headed back to normalcy, that Harding is just around the corner."

The political setbacks of the 1940s, and the changing political climate they represented, contributed to another redefinition of the liberal idea of the state. By the end of World War II, most liberals had begun to coalesce around a new prescription for government in which calls for structural reforms of capitalism or controls over the behavior of corporate leaders were no longer central. Postwar liberalism attempted, instead, to accommodate itself to the existing structure of American capitalism and to find new vehicles—the manipulation of fiscal and monetary levers, as Keynes, among others, had urged—by which the federal government could fight recessions and promote economic growth. Stimulating consumption, not regulating production, was the principal economic activity of postwar liberal government. "Full employment" was its goal. A generous welfare state would compensate for the inevitable shortcomings of the "free" economy and would contribute, as well, to the steady increase in purchasing power that the new vision of full employment required.

Into this changing liberal world, a different political language gradually emerged to replace the now-repudiated interest in class and economic power that had dominated the New Deal. It was the language of individual rights—a language the war, and the anti-totalitarian sentiment the war had produced, greatly strengthened. The rights-based liberalism of the post-New Deal era eventually helped lead many white liberals into a great—if, for some, short-lived—alliance with African Americans in the battle for civil rights and racial justice. It led in turn to the mobilization and empowerment of many other groups whose causes liberals generally embraced, among them racial and ethnic minorities, women, gays and lesbians, and people with disabilities. And it led as well to a growing level of tolerance for unconventional forms of personal behavior and morality—a cultural relativism that has gradually become one of liberalism's most controversial and politically damaging characteristics.

It is this newer model of liberalism—a liberalism related to but substantially different from the New Deal—that the electorate seems now to be repudiating. Its collapse is a result of the convergence of several major changes in the social and political landscape:

- Postwar liberalism has been closely identified with enhancing the role of the federal government. It has fallen victim in part to the widespread perception—a greatly exaggerated but not entirely false perception—that government itself has become as inefficient, corrupt, and menacing as earlier generations of reformers believed the corporate world had become.

- Postwar liberalism has embraced the drives for expanded rights by individuals and groups. It has fallen victim to a growing popular fear of cultural disintegration and fragmentation, a belief that the liberal commitment to "rights" has somehow run amok at the expense of society's ability to preserve some elemental sense of community.

- Postwar liberalism thrived in part on the basis of a vigorous Cold War internationalism, which not only legitimized an activist American foreign policy but also helped legitimize government itself. When the state could be seen as the defender of democracy against communism, when the president was the "leader of the free world," government had a claim to popular loyalty that it can now make with much less authority.

- Most of all, postwar liberalism flourished on the basis of its promise that government could help sustain high levels of economic growth and security—a promise government seemed to keep (even if not through the means most liberals expected) for a generation after World War II. Liberalism flounders today because of a twenty-year shift in the structure of the American economy. This shift, and the way in which the nation has adjusted to it, has weakened the popular support for, and perhaps also the viability of, the Keynsian fiscal policies on which liberals once relied to promote economic growth. It has also weakened political support for these economic tools, such as the minimum wage, that might have some effect on the increasingly unequal distribution of jobs and incomes. It is probably not too much to say that these economic frustrations, and the political world's inability to answer them, lie at the heart of liberalism's current crisis, and at the heart of the larger disillusionment with government and politics that has created that crisis.

In the embittered and ungenerous climate of American public life today, creating a new liberal vision that is both humane and politically viable will be exceptionally difficult. Liberals have been trying to recast themselves and their ideas for a generation (an effort that has been particularly visible in recent years in the pages of this magazine), and they will no doubt continue to do so. But however difficult the task, the challenge facing liberals today is an urgent one—and not unlike the challenge that faced progressives early in the twentieth century and New Dealers in the 1940s.

Recreating the New Deal, which was a far-from-perfect answer even to the problems of its own time, is certainly not the solution to liberalism's problems today. But some elements of the New Deal—including some of those repudiated and largely forgotten after the wartime redefinition of the liberal state—suggest some ways of thinking about the future of liberalism in our own time.

Among the forgotten initiatives of the New Deal was the most ambitious effort to reorganize the federal government ever undertaken by any modern administration. Roosevelt's "executive reorganization plan," the product of an extended study by a commission of distinguished scholars and planners, recommended sweeping changes in the structure of the federal government: reorganizing and relocating agencies and departments; weakening the autonomy of the civil service and the independent regulatory commissions; enhancing the budgetary and administrative capacities of the White House; creating a powerful planning mechanism within the executive branch; and others. The changes would contribute, Roosevelt said, to the "efficient and economical conduct of governmental operations."

Powerful conservatives in Congress, warning of a presidential "dictatorship," greatly weakened these recommendations by the time they were enacted in 1939. But the results were by no means inconsequential. Partly as a result of the reforms, the federal government emerged from the war better equipped than it had been in the 1930s to manage its responsibilities effectively and to assume new ones.

The Clinton administration's underappreciated and underpromoted proposal for "reinventing government" is the first major effort since 1937 to launch a serious reappraisal of how government works and how it might be reorganized. That it has generated so little attention and support from progressives is a sign of the intellectual disarray that has helped discredit liberalism in our time. Liberals need now to make the case, in an inhospitable climate, that government is not intrinsically bad. They must show that it can and must play an ameliorative and progressive role in social and economic life. And they must demonstrate that the efforts of the right to disembowel government—through the balanced-budget amendment, the attack on unfunded mandates, the supermajorities for tax increases, and other structural changes—are dangerous to society's capacity to respond to social, economic, and international crises.

But to make that case effectively, liberals must also argue with equal force for a re-examination of the way government performs its tasks. They cannot reflexively defend existing agencies and procedures just because conservatives are attacking them or just because the agencies' ostensible purposes are desirable. They must be able to demonstrate that institutions of government are capable of performing their functions effectively and, equally important, that they are capable of continually "reinventing" themselves in response to the changing world around them. In the 1990s, as in the late 1930s, a defense of government must be tightly linked to a commitment to critical thinking about government.

Buried within the confusing maze of New Deal experiments and agencies was a cluster of efforts that attempted to protect and strengthen not just individuals, but communities. The Tennessee Valley Authority, the Resettlement Administration, the Farm Security Administration, and others all experimented with ways of promoting cooperation, community spirit, and mutual responsibility, and even created model towns, communities, and camps that were designed around explicitly communitarian models.

Anyone who has read John Steinbeck's *Grapes of Wrath* (or seen John Ford's film version of the novel) may recall the wonder and delight with which the Joad family encountered a federally run camp for migrant workers—a camp explicitly designed around a concept of community engagement and shared responsibility, in stark contrast to the grim, competitive environment surrounding it. The scene depicted reasonably accurately the real camps planned and managed by the New Deal's Farm Security Administration. Not all liberals of the 1930s were interested in such goals, certainly, but there was at least a faction within the New Dealers concerned with what today's political theorists would call "civic life" or (to use Robert Putnam's phrase) the creation of "social capital." (See Putnam, "The Strange Disappearance of Civic America," page 263.)

In the 1990s, the degradation of civic life—the erosion of patterns of interaction capable of creating social bonds among substantial numbers of people—is one of our society's most troubling phenomena. And while citizens express their concern about that degradation in many different ways, few are unaware of its costs. It robs individuals of the satisfaction of group activities and shared experiences, and it robs society of the means by which men and women of different backgrounds and perspectives can learn to understand and tolerate one another. It poses a challenge to postwar liberalism's almost exclusive preoccupation with individual rights and invites attention to the problem of creating the basis for a healthier shared life.

There is, of course, a limit to what government can do to create genuine institutions and habits of community in American life. The New Deal experiments were themselves both modest and short lived. But it has surely been one of liberalism's failures to have allowed the language of community to become the almost exclusive property of the right. Political discourse at times seems to have become a stale debate between advocates of the market and advocates of the state, with all other realms of human experience floating irrelevantly in the background as "a thousand points of light."

It is, of course, possible to romanticize the institutions of "civic life." Neighborhoods, churches, schools, and voluntary associations are not only sources of healthy communal experiences. They can also be sources of bigotry and oppression, and government will always need to intervene at times to curb their excesses and injustices. But for liberal government to be credible to and valued by its citizens, it cannot seem uninterested in, or reflexively hostile to, the institutions that define the lives of many, perhaps most, Americans.

The unhappy example of some of the Community Action programs of the War on Poverty discouraged many liberals from pursuing public efforts to restore civic life. But the effort did not die entirely with the 1960s. It survived for more than twenty years in the persistent call from many liberals for a form of national service that would, they insisted, restore a sense of shared purpose to American life. President Clinton's small but promising national service program (explicitly linked in his recent State of the Union address to the idea of "civil life" and the need for the "common bonds of community") is a response to that call.

The effort to enhance community has survived in other ways as well. It has found expression recently in the controversial but at least partially successful efforts in Chicago to transfer authority over schools to local councils of parents and teachers; and even in the attempts to create councils of workers and managers within some industries. More such efforts are surely necessary for liberalism to regain respect and credibility among those who have repudiated it.

Finally, and perhaps most important, the New Dealers viewed themselves—and the world they were attempting to reshape—in terms of wealth, power, and (although liberals did not often use the word) class. The most progressive New Dealers considered taming the excesses of unbridled capitalism and empowering economically weaker groups at the expense of stronger ones their most important tasks. They carefully avoided the ethnic and cultural issues they believed had done so much damage to the Democratic Party in the 1920s, and in doing so left themselves unable to confront many problems of racial injustice. But they did manage to make the distribution of wealth and power a subject worthy of political discussion and the basis of a broad coalition that sustained the Democratic Party for more than a generation.

Unlike the New Dealers, many postwar liberals were willing and even eager to confront racial, ethnic, gender, and sexual discrimination. Their participation in the successful effort to dismantle the legal structure of segregation and the still-incomplete effort to eliminate other, less formal patterns of discrimination is one of liberalism's proudest achievements, despite the divisiveness it has created and the political costs it has imposed. But the growing commitment to rights seemed to crowd out of the liberal universe the language of class and power that was so crucial to the political success of the New Deal. Who today talks about the extraordinary and growing maldistribution of wealth in America? Why is it so difficult for liberals to articulate a critique of corporate power in an age of falling living standards and growing insecurity among workers? How has it happened that among all the powerful institutions in modern society, government has become the principal, often even the only, target of opprobrium among Americans angry and frustrated about their lack of control over their lives?

Before liberals surrender to the calls for disabling the federal government and devolving authority to states and localities, they would do well to direct attention to the increasingly centralized institutions of private power that will survive that process. It was to counter the power of such institutions that "big government" emerged in the first place. To whom would they answer in a world of weak or nonexistent national authority?

Franklin Roosevelt spoke openly in his 1936 campaign about "economic royalists," "business and financial monopoly," "reckless banking," and "government by organized money." "I should like to have it said of my first administration," he said, "that in it the forces of selfishness and of lust for power met their match. I should like to have it said of my second administration that in it these forces met their master." That is the lost language of contemporary American liberalism. We need it back.

How to Rebuild the Democratic Party

Jeff Faux

When liberal Democrats dragged themselves off the electoral battlefield after last fall's election, for the first time in 40 years they had nowhere to hide. Throughout these years, even after their defeats by Nixon and Reagan, the House of Representatives was a protected citadel to which Democrats could retreat—shielded by political warlords like Sam Rayburn and John McCormack, Tip O'Neill and Jim Wright, Dan Rostenkowski and John Dingell. With the House in Democratic hands, the core New Deal and Great Society programs survived. Labor, minority, elderly, environmental and women's organizations were safe to lick their wounds and plot revenge.

But this protection came with a price. The liberal coalition was increasingly tied to a Washington legislative agenda and became preoccupied with the lobbying and financing of the Democratic congressional majority. An unhealthy mutual dependence developed. Despite their grumbling about the chores of fund-raising, many Democrats in Congress and leaders of constituency groups had an easier life. Why spend your time driving around the congressional district to maintain a permanent organization of amateurs when fund-raising receptions in Washington could buy a professionally packaged political campaign? Why go through the effort of answering conservative critics when voters would reelect you on the basis of your seniority on an important committee? Why burden yourself with mobilizing the membership when you could get access to the Hill by writing a check?

As the Democratic Party's capacity to organize in the precincts atrophied, the party's financial foundation shifted away from labor, construction companies, and others who did business with government, to Wall Street investors and Hollywood celebrities. The eclectic political tastes of these new supporters tended toward that combination of conservative economics and social sentimentality known as "limousine liberalism." Meanwhile, the Southern conservative wing of the party reinvented itself as "New Democrats" and consciously sought to build a base on a business constituency happy to support Democrats who would attack labor and denounce welfare.

Dependent on the Democratic establishment in Washington, liberals failed to grasp the growing outrage of a financially squeezed middle class at the arrogance of those in political power. Liberal concerns such as campaign finance reforms, lobbying restrictions, and unjustified perks of the powerful went ignored because of the discomfort they caused Democrats on Capitol Hill. Major constituencies were inhibited from mobilizing for their interests for fear of damaging their relations with the congressional leadership or Bill Clinton. As a result, liberal institutions have had the worst of both political worlds: They were demonized by their enemies and increasingly seen as ineffectual by their own rank and file.

Meanwhile, the Republican right created the awesome, ideologically driven, local and national organizing network that finally captured the Democratic citadel of the House of Representatives. In the process, they rolled up the Democrats' southern flank to the point where a Republican majority in the South may be the closest thing to a sure bet in American politics. The House is now controlled by smart, seasoned reactionary politicians bent on liquidating liberalism as an organized force. The Senate is in the hands of conservative Republicans who would rather not get their hands too bloody but will gladly hold down the victim.

And the White House is no refuge. The administration has already capitulated to the right on a number of strategic fronts. Military spending will rise, the shrunken domestic budget will be squeezed dry, and consumer, labor, and environmental protections will be sacrificed. High-level administration officials speak openly of how Newt Gingrich's demolition of the House Democrats gives them a strong ally in their effort to downsize government and cut domestic spending.

BACK TO BASES

The president may change his strategy of accommodating the right, or he may not. He may decide to fight back, or he may not. At some point, he will have to stand up to the right if only as a demonstration of personal character. But one thing is clear: The administration has little interest in rebuilding an integrated grassroots political network to take on the conservative political ideology that now dominates American politics. Unlike the Nixon, Reagan, and even Bush administrations, which consciously nurtured the cadre and institutions of the partisan conservative movement, Clinton—like Jimmy Carter, his predecessor New Democrat—has loaded his administration with people who, in Robert Kuttner's phrase, are "ideologically incompetent."

In presidential politics, liberal Democrats have no credible alternative to Bill Clinton. But in the more fundamental struggle for the nation's political soul, they are on their own. Exposed and unsheltered, the core constituencies of the party must regroup, reorganize, and pursue a disciplined, independent path that uses the next election to revitalize themselves as a political force. The issue is not only their own political relevance but the relevance of the Democratic Party itself. The liberal-labor constellation of forces is the only sector of the party that has a capacity to field a grassroots challenge to the right.

The election verified that the right wing of the Democratic Party has little mass base. It is primarily a collection of conservative politicians and business lobbyists held together by a centrism calculated to appeal to the establishment press. Members of the Mainstream Forum, the major New Democrat organization in the House, lost seats at almost twice the rate of the rest of the party. The New Democrat excuse is that their members held seats in the conservative South and were therefore more vulnerable. But that is exactly their rationale: By moving to the right, they were supposed to take conservative votes from Republicans in those areas. The losing Senate bids of leading New Democrats Jim Cooper of Tennessee and Dave McCurdy of Oklahoma were particularly telling. The results validated the point attributed to Harry Truman that when faced with a choice between pseudo Republicans and Republicans the voters will choose the real thing.

The administration's effort to reinvent the Democrats as a probusiness, fiscally conservative party was a particular disaster. The business community got most of what it wanted from the administration. Yet a *Business Week* poll last fall found that 87 percent of top CEOs opposed Clinton, with only 9 percent supporting him. His successful effort to reduce the deficit also went unappreciated; a plurality of voters believed that the deficit rose under Clinton, suggesting again that the deficit is symbolic of economic anxiety rather than an informed demand for fiscal probity. (Of those who said the deficit was the most important issue, 58 percent voted Republican!)

A liberal strategy to rebuild the Democratic party must begin with an understanding that the decline in real wages and living standards is at the heart of the anger and frustration being felt by the middle class. This is particularly true of white working-age men with less than a college degree, among whom the greatest Democratic fall-off has occurred. As political scientist Ruy Teixeira reports, long-term wage declines were largest where the Democrats lost in November. To a large extent, Americans still voted their pocketbooks in the last election. Despite the solid overall economic growth of the past two years, 57 percent of the voters thought the economy was "poor or not-so-good." More than 60 percent of those people voted Republican. This does not mean that social issues—crime, gun control, gays in the military, the perennial welfare problem, family decline—were unimportant. In the absence of a strong economic appeal by the Democrats to their base, these issues defined the campaign. Indeed, they defined Clinton's "liberalism." But it is a trap for Democrats to believe that traditional American conservatism on social issues reflects a desire to buy a conservative economic package as well.

Historically, Democrats have always been out of sync with the white working class on social issues, most notably on race. Nonetheless, white workers voted Democratic for decades because they saw Roosevelt, Truman, Kennedy, and Johnson as taking their side on the central question of economic security and jobs. When Democrats sound like Republicans on economic issues, they lose because they are not as credible as social conservatives.

CLINTON'S HALF-RIGHT RESPONSE

In its rhetoric, the administration has correctly diagnosed the current condition of the middle class. The president caught the right mood in the 1992 campaign when he said that "Americans were working harder for less." Recent poll data show they still think they are. And Labor Secretary Bob Reich speaks eloquently of middle-class anxiety. It is unreasonable to expect that Clinton could have turned around 20 years of stagnant and falling wages in his first two years. But we could have expected a clear message about a credible strategy, and the Clinton prescription did not match its diagnosis.

The administration has actually had three answers to the question of declining living standards among the working classes. The first is distributional and includes the Earned Income Tax Credit (EITC), universal health coverage, and a higher minimum wage. The increase in the EITC adopted in Clinton's first year is a real benefit, but it is targeted at a small part of the population, requires filling out forms, and, unfortunately for the administration, does not actually reach its beneficiaries until this year. Health care reform in its most ambitious form would have done a great deal to alleviate middle-class economic anxiety, but the political moment was missed. The administration's call for a higher minimum wage in 1995 is a welcome move along the same lines. To his credit, Clinton has drawn a line in the dirt on this issue, and put himself on the worker's side.

The second and more troubling answer is free trade. The administration has now completely adopted the laissez-faire notion that eliminating trade barriers is the path to prosperity. Indeed, Clinton's decibel level on the subject has exceeded that of the Republicans. Even establishment economists for whom free trade is an article of faith say that the numbers and claims made by the administration for NAFTA and GATT have been widely exaggerated. In the wake of the collapse of the Mexican peso, it is now clear that the U.S. trade surplus with Mexico, upon which NAFTA job claims were based, was the creation of a deliberately overvalued peso and will now disappear. Although some might still argue that NAFTA is good for America in the long run, a year after it went into effect the administration's arguments on jobs, the trade balance, political stability in Mexico, and immigration were in shreds.

Politically, the NAFTA effort alienated many working-class voters and failed to compensate by winning over centrists and conservatives to the administration. The politics of Clinton's devotion to free trade defies common sense. "You have to imagine the Alice in Wonderland quality of this," said a senior administration official to the *New York Times* two weeks before the GATT vote. "Here we are trying to figure out how to get business leaders to put pressure on Republicans to vote for something Reagan championed and Bush almost implemented." Regardless of one's views on NAFTA or GATT, they are clearly not issues that define differences between Clinton and the Republicans or give anyone a reason to vote for Democrats.

The administration's third answer to the problem of declining living standards is training and education. The unintended message the president sent to those facing $6 an hour in a $12 an hour world was that they are the problem: they lack the skills to compete in the new flexible, brutally competitive world. No one in the administration seems to have thought through the impact of repeatedly lecturing working Americans—already working longer and harder just to stay in place—that they will have to change jobs and careers many times in this new deregulated global economy. The prospect of a life spent on a constant treadmill of retraining in a world that continually threatens you with obsolescence might seem exhilarating for the highly educated and confident policy intellectuals in Washington, but it is frightening for most people.

Moreover, the administration has not actually been able to deliver much help to workers who face this prospect. Public support will be negligible for the lifetime of education and skill upgrading the administration says workers need. Democrats abandoned Clinton's original proposal for universal on-the-job training and gave low priority even to the modest Reemployment Act, which died in the last Congress. An adequate level of investment in skills would be expensive, and the administration has given up the fight for more money. When asked about this recently, a high-level administration official shrugged his shoulders and said that working people facing job stress will just have to take responsibility to "invest in themselves."

THE REPUBLICAN DIVERSION

The Republicans did not blame the people for their anxiety. They spent two years changing the subject, diverting the economic question into a social one. The reason for your anxiety, they told the anxious middle class, is the deterioration in moral values as a result of liberal excesses—tolerance of crime in the streets, generous welfare, gun control, subsidies to immigrants. Above all, the problem is big government. Through their well-built organizing base, the talk radio network, and the constant stream of books and seminars to influence the press, they blanketed American politics with conservative propaganda. They hammered at the media for being too liberal, pushing the PBS and C-SPAN networks to more conservative programming. They trained people in the art of argument.

In effect, the right created a filter between Democrats in Washington and the electorate to screen out positive messages. A case in point was the defeat by the conservative movement of the bill to restrict lobbying in the last weeks of the Democratic Congress. Given the popular disgust with Washington, the lobbying reform bill represented a perfect opportunity to expose Republican hypocrisy—using the graphic visual images of members of Congress getting free meals and golf vacations. Yet, the right-wing network generated massive protests on patently false objections, charging that citizens writing letters would have to register as lobbyists. With many Democratic members secretly relieved, the conservative network killed the bill in a few days.

This display of political prowess clearly intimidated the White House. Since the election it has generally let Newt Gingrich set the terms and boundaries of debate. It has conceded to Gingrich the principle that government must be smaller. Federal power should be shipped to the states (where business has more leverage over government), regulation should be weakened, and the military budget should expand. In response to the incredibly destructive balanced budget amendment, the administration announced that it was not in favor, but would not fight against it.

The White House has also trapped itself into collaborating on welfare reform on the assertion that Democrats have plenty of "common ground" with Republicans. The president cannot win on this issue. Effective reforms will require more spending, particularly for training, child care, and health coverage, to enable those on welfare to qualify for jobs and make work pay. But given a climate in which prominent Democrats talk openly about cutting Medicare and Social Security, there is unlikely to be more money for welfare recipients. In the end the president can only quibble with the right over how much to take away from the poor. He will not get credit for a punitive bill, just as he did not get credit for the crime bill.

The result will be to make him look weak and without conviction, and further alienate his base. Indeed, the administration seems deliberately to run away from its own constituency, violating a fundamental rule of politics and war: secure your base. Even after deciding to propose an increase in the minimum wage, the White House staff let it be known they were worried that they would be seen as captives of organized labor.

Newt Gingrich's Contract With America is riddled with special-interest influence, yet it's hard to imagine the Republican leadership worrying about Democrats attacking them as captives of business. The combination of Republican boldness and Democratic timidity has even allowed conservatives to claim that they are the party of new ideas. In the current environment, proposals for increasing the minimum wage, which date to the 1930s, are ridiculed in the press as "old-fashioned," while proposals for orphanages and deregulation, which date to the nineteenth century, are hailed as innovations.

As an economic proposition, the Contract with America will fail. Abolishing welfare, cutting capital gains taxes, debasing the Constitution with balanced budget amendments and the rest will not reverse shrinking real earnings and opportunities for the majority of American workers. We are in many ways returning to an era of economic insecurity that predates World War II. The prospect of having to take a job at the minimum wage, or a dollar or so above it, does not seem nearly so remote to the typical 30-year-old as it did 10 or 15 years ago. The growing numbers of college graduates in the workforce have clouded this reality. Yet real earnings for college graduates have been falling since 1987. And the Bureau of Labor Statistics estimates that one in five employed college graduates is working at a job that does not require a degree. Even with continued economic growth, the forecast is that in 10 years it will be one in four.

But because they are better educated, the working- and middle-class families that make up the Democrats' natural constituency are more demanding of their leaders and more socially tolerant than they used to be. For Democrats to remobilize them, they will have to learn to speak to them with respect and intelligence. Democrats need not so much a new message as a new conversation with the majority of Americans who work for a living. They have to stop lying to the people that some marginal, insufficiently financed piece of pilot legislation is going to make a difference in their lives. They have to be willing to name and attack their enemies. They need to commit to engaging the right everywhere political discussion goes on—in Washington, on the nightly news, in local media, in neighborhood bars and churches, at the workplace, on the Internet—with their story of how the world works.

THE DEMOCRATIC STORY

We already have a "first draft" of such a story. Various liberal thinkers and Democratic politicians—including President Clinton—have been telling parts of it for a decade. Some of it was reflected in the president's 1992 campaign and in parts of his post-election Little Rock summit. It goes something like this:

The American dream is fading. More Americans will have to work harder to prevent their living standards from falling further. People now under 35 years of age are doing worse than their parents. On our current path, the future generation will do even worse.

The root causes of working people's financial stress is that America is trying to compete in the new world economy by (1) lowering our wages, (2) generating short-term profits through downsizing and speculation rather than prosperity through long-term investment, and (3) abandoning larger numbers of potentially productive people to poverty. Democrats must, therefore, raise the central question: How do Americans compete in a world of six billion people, most of whom will work for much less than Americans will? The Democratic answer must start with a vision of a permanent high-wage, full-employment economy for the twenty-first century. The choice is either to continue along the current low road—condemned forever to work harder and harder to compete in a brutal global marketplace—or to move to a higher, more productive level of economic activity.

In this brave new global economy what does it mean to be an American? Nothing, we are all on our own, say the Republicans and "Newt" Democrats. If the Chinese can undercut your job with slave labor, that's too bad. If your employer decides to throw you out in the street after 20 years of loyal service, too bad. If you can't afford health insurance, too bad. Other than through voluntary acts of personal charity, we have no obligations to each other.

The Democratic task is to challenge this dreary social Darwinist notion by reconstructing an economic framework designed to promote prosperity for the American community. For starters, the road to a high-wage full-employment economy should include:

- a low interest-rate policy that gives Main Street priority over Wall Street.
- public investment in our people, infrastructure, and the technology of the future, paid for by eliminating unnecessary subsidies and tax breaks.

- empowerment of workers and their unions through a new labor law framework to promote greater productivity and a fair sharing of its benefits.
- enhancement of family economic security through universal health care, pension portability, and higher minimum wages.
- trading only with nations that produce under accepted labor and environmental standards.
- tax, regulatory, and industrial policies that favor those who invest in long-term job creation and penalize the short-term speculator.

The fundamental objection to a high-wage, full-employment program is that the global financial markets will not permit it. The global marketplace does put new constraints on economic policy, but no iron law of international economics requires Americans to have lower wages and huge pockets of unemployment and poverty. The idea that we must abandon control of our economic destiny to the multinational corporations and global financiers is nonsense. Ninety percent of what America makes is sold in America. If Japan can keep an unemployment rate below 3 percent for decades and create a dynamic economy, so can we. It can't be done overnight, of course. But a revived Democratic answer must be based on the conviction that it can be done.

The Democratic vision must also include a spirited defense of the existing foundation of economic security. Democrats have accepted, and in many cases promoted, alarmist propaganda that casts unwarranted doubt over the future of Social Security. The logic of these attacks is flawed and the politics is suicidal. The notion that the younger generation of voters will be grateful to those who solve the "problem" of Social Security by making them wait another five years before they can get retirement benefits suggests how far out of touch the Washington policy discussion has moved.

For Democrats to succeed, the issue of what government does and should do must be taken out of the abstract. Democrats cannot run away from this question as they did during the health care debate. When challenged by attacks on government incompetence, Democrats insisted that the president's health care plan did not mean intrusion into the health care marketplace—which of course it did. Americans support a wide variety of government activities. The story of the woman who in last year's campaign demanded of a U.S. senator that he do something to stop the government takeover of Medicare is symbolic of the absurd result of Democratic cowardice on this issue.

Americans have never had any love for government per se, but they like a lot of what government does for them. Polls show, for example, that when asked about the general quality of the public schools people are highly negative. But when asked about the specific public school in their neighborhood, they are positive. The point is not that Democrats should attempt to sell Big Government. But they must be prepared to make the case for government as an instrument for solving problems that the market will not or cannot address.

But to be credible concerning government, Democrats must give the highest priority to breaking the cycle of their own large contributors. A serious effort must be made to amend the constitution, which the courts have used to strike down past restrictions on election spending. Democrats cannot be the party of both the little people and the big money.

The Democratic conversation must be both in the air and on the ground. People do not internalize political ideas just from watching television. Nor do they absorb them just by talking with their neighbors or fellow workers or working the Internet. The conversation must develop at a number of levels. It is no accident that the same phrases can be heard within days on right-wing talk radio, Christian political TV, and in the speeches of Republican candidates—and then in bars and at church suppers. Meeting this challenge will require Democrats to build a political network that can similarly combine local organizing, ideological motivation, and national media strategies that are in motion throughout the election cycle, not just every two years.

Individual political campaigns cannot create this kind of network. Consultant-dominated, media-centered electioneering has little capacity to develop issues. Hired guns shy away from them because issues get in the way of the mechanical operations—media buys, polling, focus groups—on which they make their money.

A populist conversation about economic issues powerful enough to change the national subject must be forged in the fire of the give-and-take of political experience. Economic populism has to be argued, tested, reformulated, tested again until the right language is found to connect it to the reality of the experience of the American electorate in the 1990s. It cannot be created whole in think tanks or universities or at congressional retreats. Democrats, in effect, must relearn how to speak to America.

The Democratic Party is, and will remain, a big tent that will include a variety of opinions. What is needed is not complete consensus, but a motivated core electorate of people who not only agree with a story but will themselves become storytellers. The success of the conservative movement lies not so much in the speeches of Bill Bennett or Jack Kemp or Bill Kristol or Newt Gingrich, but in the way that millions of ordinary people are repeating their message throughout the society.

Given the lack of support in the White House for this kind of effort, the immediate political purpose to which this conversation ought to be put should be to regain the House of Representatives in 1996 by electing more liberals. This is a difficult but not impossible task. At the moment Democrats need a net gain of 15 seats. Obviously Bill Clinton's re-election would help. But the evidence of the last two elections is that Clinton has no coattails. Moreover, there are sufficient historic precedents for a party losing the presidency and gaining seats in the House: In 1960, for example, while Richard Nixon lost the presidential election to Jack Kennedy, the Republicans picked up 22 seats in the House—coming after a Democratic victory in the previous House elections.

This requires a definition of a party leadership that extends beyond the White House or the Democratic National Committee, which by and large serves as a fund-raising mechanism. Start with the new minority leadership in the Congress, which is more liberal because of the greater losses last November among conservatives. Add liberals in state and local government and the leadership of the major Democratic constituencies—labor, minority and women's groups, environmentalists, and the elderly. Add the liberal intellectual community that needs to contest the right's claim to new ideas.

The mainstream left does not have the resources and corporate influence that the right enjoys. No left-wing television networks are likely to emerge in the near future. So we must start more modestly. Major liberal institutions and networks should pool resources and concentrate on three or four dozen congressional districts with the greatest chance of electing liberals. Each district would undertake a two-year program of public education and organizing of the Democratic base. Local people would be trained in how to argue with conservatives. Each situation is different and would have to be handcrafted on-site. In most areas a local committee would be formed of interested elected officials and leaders from labor, minority and women's groups, and other activists. Activities would include publicly holding conservative office holders accountable for their votes, challenging right-wing talk show hosts, talking to local journalists, and waging letter-to-the-editor campaigns on issues that illustrate Democratic themes. Regional speakers' bureaus would be formed to hammer away at the harm done by the Republican contract to the locality.

Another function would be to monitor and influence the national media's treatment of the debate over economic issues. The right devotes time and energy to tracking the major news programs. The elimination of the Fairness Doctrine provided an enormous opportunity for well-financed conservatives to influence the electronic press, which is the source of most people's learning about politics. They have succeeded in putting more conservatives on the air and intimidating the press with charges that it is too liberal. The liberal coalition does not have the resources to match the Christian Right's media network. But it can do more to put countervailing pressure on the media to get a fair share of media time.

A related task is to identify the political possibilities of the Internet and other electronic technologies that the conservatives are using to support face-to-face encounters at meetings and rallies and church suppers.

Finally, liberals also need to show more courage and fight in combating conservatives within the Democratic party. The Democratic Leadership Council has waged a relentless ideological attack on liberals that largely goes unanswered. Indeed, it spends more time attacking Democrats than Republicans, more time criticizing Clinton than Gingrich. Yet it has privileged access to the White House and influence on the national debate through the militantly middle-of-the-road Washington press. The creation of an organizational challenge to the DLC ought to be part of the new liberal agenda.

As a separate combatant in the historic battle of political ideas, liberal Democrats are in danger, if not of extinction then of dwindling relevance. The idea that salvation will come if only they wait for Newt Gingrich to go too far, or for the president to get reelected, has been shattered by the Clinton experience. Liberals waited 12 years in the wilderness for the chance once again to have access to the White House. Two years later, their political fortress is overrun, the administration's banners are emblazoned with the slogans and policies of their enemies, and they are threatened with banishment if they don't lower their already meager expectations. Liberals now have no choice. No one is coming to their rescue. They will return to power only after they have earned it in the fire of debate over the country's future.

The Divided Economy

The Crusade That's Killing Prosperity

Lester Thurow

The great untold story of the American economy in the 1990s is the disguised high rate of unemployment and its direct impact on stagnating living standards. Properly calculated, our rate of joblessness is well into double digits. No wonder workers have no bargaining power to get their share of an increasingly productive economy.

Among economists, a debate rages on why earnings inequalities began to rise rapidly and real median wages started to fall a quarter century ago. Some blame a technological shift that cut demand for uneducated labor while boosting the demand for those with greater education and skills. Others identify global "factor price equalization"—in an open global economy overseas workers with comparable skills but lower wages are forcing the wages of Americans down.

What's left out of this lengthy, if inconclusive, debate is the role played by the slack economic environment in which these two forces have been operating. While each is real, their impacts would have been very different if they had operated in an environment of labor shortages rather than one of vast labor surplus. The U.S. economy has been celebrated for creating tens of millions of jobs during the past two decades. But properly counted, our true unemployment rate is no better than Europe's. And nothing keeps wages from rising like a large pool of idle or underemployed workers.

Today's slack labor markets were produced by the war against inflation—declared in the early 1970s and still underway 25 years later. Inflation began with the mis-financing of the Vietnam War in the late 1960s, accelerated with the OPEC oil shock and food shocks of the early 1970s, expanded across the economy in the mid-1970s because of the widespread use of cost-of-living indexes in both labor and supplier contracts, and was rekindled by the second OPEC oil shock at the end of the 1970s.

While other remedies such as wage and price controls were initially tried, none seemed to work. Eventually all of the world's major governments came to the conclusion that the only cure for inflation was to use higher interest rates and tighter fiscal policies (higher taxes or lower expenditures) to restrain prices by deliberately slowing growth to push unemployment up and to force real wages down. Excess capacity and surplus labor became the key players in the anti-inflationary game.

In the end the strategy for braking the world economy worked. The world's real economic growth rate slid from 5 percent per year in the 1960s to 3.6 percent per year in the 1970s. The double-digit inflation of the early 1980s led to another round of monetary tightening, and growth further decelerated to 2.8 percent per year in the 1980s. Actions such as Federal Reserve Chairman Alan Greenspan's seven interest rate hikes between early 1994 and early 1995 and the Bundesbank's very restrictive policies in Germany slowed the world's growth rate even further, and in the first half of the 1990s world growth has averaged just 2 percent per year. Today the Federal Reserve Board designs policies to limit American economic growth to a maximum of 2.5 percent or less. Anything more is believed to be inflationary. In its annual policy recommendations, the Organization for Economic Cooperation and Development (OECD) subscribed to the view that America's maximum noninflationary growth rate was 2.5 percent.

Like a real war that has gone on far too long, all of the original reasons for the war—the mis-financing of the Vietnam War, OPEC oil shocks, food shocks, indexed wage and supply contracts, inflationary expectations—are long gone. As the war continues year after year, the negative side effects of the war, falling real wages and rising inequalities, have become far more corrosive than the original reasons for joining the battle. The battle continues even though the war against inflation has been won. The combatants have gotten so used to "fighting on" that they cannot even recognize that they have won.

Slow growth cured inflation because it directly pushed real wages down—creating very slack labor markets. Indirectly, it created an environment where factor price equalization, a skill-intensive technological shift, and other factors could generate enormous downward pressures on real wages.

Restrictive monetary and fiscal policies have produced unemployment rates not seen since the Great Depression. Today, more than 10 percent of the European workforce is officially unemployed and in three countries (Spain, Ireland, and Finland) unemployment has been above 20 percent at some point in the first half of the 1990s. Spain and Italy have youth unemployment rates of over 60 percent. While it is very fashionable to blame Europe's high unemployment rates on "rigid labor markets," which is to say unions and welfare state protections, the real culprit is macroeconomic austerity. Most of the same protections existed before 1973, and coexisted nicely with high growth, full employment, and rising wages. Japan's official unemployment rate is near 3 percent, but Japan essentially has a system of private unemployment insurance where workers who would be fired in the United States remain on private payrolls. Even the Japanese admit that if their firms acted as American firms do, their unemployment rate would be over 10 percent.

THE REAL UNEMPLOYMENT RATE

In the fall of 1995, America's official unemployment rate was hovering around 5.7 percent. But like an iceberg that is mostly invisible below the waterline, officially unemployed workers are just a small part of the total number of workers looking for more work.

If we combine the 7.5 to 8 million officially unemployed workers, the 5 to 6 million people who are not working but who do not meet any of the tests for being active in the workforce and are therefore not considered unemployed, and the 4.5 million part-time workers who would like full-time work, there are 17 to 18.5 million Americans looking for more work. This brings the real unemployment rate to almost 14 percent.

Slow growth has also generated an enormous contingent workforce of underemployed people. There are 8.1 million American workers in temporary jobs, 2 million who work "on call," and 8.3 million self-employed "independent contractors" (many of whom are downsized professionals who have very few clients but call themselves self-employed consultants because they are too proud to admit that they are unemployed). Most of these more than 18 million people are also looking for more work and better jobs. Together these contingent workers account for another 14 percent of the workforce. In the words of Fortune magazine, "Upward pressure on wages is nil because so many of the employed are these 'contingent' workers who have no bargaining power with employers, and payroll workers realize they must swim in the same Darwinian ocean." Like the unemployed, these contingent workers generate downward wage pressures.

In addition there are 5.8 million missing males (another 4 percent of the workforce) 25 to 60 years of age. They exist in our census statistics but not in our labor statistics. They have no obvious means of economic support. They are the right age to be in the workforce, were once in the workforce, are not in school, and are not old enough to have retired. They show up in neither employment nor unemployment statistics. They have either been dropped from, or have dropped out of, the normal working economy. Some we know as the homeless; others have disappeared into the underground illegal economy.

Put these three groups together and in the aggregate about one-third of the American workforce is potentially looking for more work than they now have. Add in another 11 million immigrants (legal and illegal) who entered the United States from 1980 to 1993 to search for more work and higher wages, and one has a sea of unemployed workers, underemployed workers, and newcomers looking for work.

These millions of job-hunters lead to a more human-scale result that everyone can understand. At 5 p.m. a midsized metal-ceramic firm posts job openings for 10 entry-level jobs on its bulletin board. By 5 a.m. 2,000 people are waiting in line to apply for those 10 jobs.

WHY WAGES FALL

While the economy has been generating about 2 million jobs per year since the end of the 1990-1991 recession, these gains are just barely large enough to hold even with migration and the normal internal rate of growth of the working-age population. However rapid, job growth cannot lead to wage increase, unless it is faster than the growth rate of those looking for work.

If one believes even marginally in the power of supply and demand, surplus labor of these magnitudes has to lead to falling real wages. Wages rise roughly with productivity growth only if there are labor shortages. Since slow growth throws the bottom 60 percent of the workforce into unemployment far more than it does the top 20 percent, the earnings of the bottom 60 percent should be expected to fall sharply relative to the top 20 percent in a period of high unemployment—as they have.

These direct negative effects on wages were compounded by several indirect effects. American economists used to talk about something called "efficiency wages." One of the mysteries of the post-World War II era was wages that rose even when there were unemployed qualified American workers who would have been glad to do those jobs for less. This anomaly was explained by arguing that firms deliberately paid incumbent workers above-market wages to secure a high degree of cooperation, commitment, and effort that they could not have gotten if their workforces could have quit and easily gotten equal wages elsewhere.

But in a world where there are always millions of unemployed and underemployed workers, firms do not have to pay efficiency wages. The same degree of cooperation, commitment, and effort can be achieved by using the motivation factor called "fear"—the fear of being thrown into this enormous sea of unemployment and underemployment. In the last five years examples abound of profitable firms that simply marched in and dramatically lowered the wages of their existing workforces by 20 to 40 percent. Workers complain but they don't quit.

Similarly, two decades of surplus labor have broken the linkage between productivity gains and wage increases. The early 1990s demonstrated that no government would come running to the rescue with large fiscal and monetary packages designed to stimulate demand during recessions. Instead, recessions would be allowed to run their course and governments would simply wait for a recovery—or as happened in 1994 in the United States, adopt monetary policies to actually slow what was already by historical standards a very weak recovery.

Knowledge that governments won't shorten recessions radically changes expectations. If downturns are sharper and longer, business firms have to reduce prices if they wish to survive. As a result, in the 1990s more of America's productivity gains are showing up as falling prices and fewer are showing up as rising wages. Higher labor productivity doesn't lead to higher labor wages as it used to. Wages can fall while productivity rises—as has happened in the last 20 years.

The best example is the computer industry—an industry that pays very low wages for its production workers. Productivity is growing very rapidly, but all of that productivity gain shows up in lower prices or higher profits for chip-makers or software firms. None shows up as higher wages as used to occur in industries such as automobiles or steel. This sea of excess labor accentuates the downward pressures of a skill-intensive technology shift and global factor price equalization. Tight labor markets would offset much if not all of the impact on the bottom 60 percent of the wage distribution, but they don't exist.

A skill-intensive technological shift should raise the wages of the skilled and lower the wages of the unskilled, but in the context of vast supplies of excess labor the expected higher wages even for skilled workers don't appear. The upward wage pressures that should be seen are more than offset by the downward pressures from surplus unemployed skilled laborers. For males, real wages are now falling at all education levels, even for those with graduate degrees. For the unskilled the downward wage pressures that flow from this technological shift are magnified because of the surplus labor that already exists.

The war on inflation has also intensified the downward wage pressures coming from a number of other sources. Some capitalists certainly plotted to kill America's labor unions. President Reagan's firing of all of America's unionized air traffic controllers legitimized a deliberate strategy of de-unionization. In the private sector, consultants were hired who specialized in getting rid of unions, decertification elections were forced, and legal requirements to respect union rights were simply ignored—firms simply paid the small fines that labor law violations brought and continued to violate the law. The strategy succeeded in shrinking union membership to slightly more than 10 percent of the private workforce (15 percent of the total workforce). And even where unions still existed they lost much of their power to influence wages or negotiate working conditions. Combined with corporate compensation committees who in the past 25 years have escalated CEO salaries from 35 to 157 times that of entry-level workers, one could argue that the capitalists had declared class warfare on labor—and were winning.

While the economics literature is inconclusive as to whether unions affect average wages (equally productive companies with and without unions tended to pay the same wages in the past), there is no doubt that unions affect the distribution of wages. Wage distributions are much more equal where unions exist. High school-college wage differentials, for example, have always been smaller in the union sector than in the nonunion sector. As a result, with the demise of unions as a force in the American economy, wage differentials should be expected to rise. In addition, as company worries about unionization have waned, the gap between union and nonunion wages has doubled. Higher wages no longer need to be paid in nonunion firms to keep unions out.

The attack on unions could not have succeeded in an environment of tight labor markets. But in this sea of surplus labor, unions have little negotiating power to offer prospective members.

Deregulation has also led to some wage reductions. In regulated industries such as trucking and airlines, workers collected some of the excess profits—what economists call "rents"—that accrued from regulation. Truck driver wages and the wages of some airline employees fell dramatically with deregulation. In the case of truck drivers, wages fell three times as fast as elsewhere. The rents that had been built into their wages were transferred back to the consumer or to corporate profits. But in a world of tight labor markets more of those rents would have stayed with workers.

Since wages in the many advanced industrial countries are now above those in the U.S., most of the factor price equalization flowing from other First World countries is behind us. But ahead lies the integration of the Second World into the First World and a very different Third World. The communist countries did not run effective civilian economies but they ran excellent education systems. The Soviet Union was a high-science society with more engineers and scientists than anyone other than the United States. China is capable of quickly generating hundreds of millions of medium-skill workers. The end of communism and the success of the "little tiger" countries on the Pacific Rim countries have led the Third World to junk import substitution as a route to economic development, and to become export oriented. Where countries with only a few million workers used to be export oriented (Singapore, Hong Kong, Taiwan, and South Korea), Third World countries containing billions of people now want to be export oriented (Indonesia, India, Pakistan, Mexico). As a result, exports from low-wage Third World countries are apt to be much larger in the years ahead. Whatever one believes about how much of real wage declines and increases in wage dispersion can be blamed on globalization in the past, the forces of factor price equalization are going to grow enormously. If they continue to operate in a world of slack labor markets inside the United States, the rate of decline in real wages will accelerate.

THE REAL INFLATION RATE

Inflation itself has already ended. But as long as the policymakers are convinced that the ghost of inflation will at any minute reappear, they will operate their policies as if inflation were a real threat.

It is possible, in fact, that inflation is even lower than its low official rate. The broadest measure of inflation, the implicit price deflator for the gross domestic product, fell from 2.2 percent in 1993 to 2.1 percent in 1994, and in the third quarter of 1995 inflation was running at the rate of 0.6 percent.

Having fallen during the previous recession, the producer's price index for finished consumer goods in December 1994 was below where it had been in April 1993 and annual rates of increase decelerated from 1.2 percent in 1993 to 0.6 percent in 1994. In 1994 and 1995 labor costs rose at the slowest rate since records had been kept and the core rate of inflation (the rate of inflation leaving out volatile energy and food prices) was the lowest rate recorded since 1965.

Officially the rate of inflation in the consumer price index (CPI) fell from 3 percent in 1993 to 2.6 percent in 1994, and to 2.5 percent in 1995, but Chairman Greenspan had himself testified to Congress that the CPI exaggerated inflation by as much as 1.5 percentage points since it underestimated quality improvements in goods (in computers, for example, it has performance rising at only 7 percent per year) and since it gives no credit at all for quality improvements in services. The Boskin Commission, appointed by the Senate Finance Committee, has estimated the upward bias in the CPI at between 1 and 2.4 percentage points. If one is willing to assume that the sectors where quality improvements are hard to measure are in fact improving quality at the same pace as those sectors where quality is easy to measure, the over-measurement of inflation may be closer to 3 percentage points.

Health care is a sector whose inflationary dynamics have little to do with macroeconomic pressures. Since health care accounts for 15 percent of GDP and health care prices were rising at a 5 percent annual rate in 1994, mathematically another 0.75 percentage points of inflation can be traced to health care (more than one-third of 1994's total inflation).

Put all of these factors together and it is clear that the rate of inflation in the sectors where inflation is controllable with slower growth is certainly very low and probably actually negative. While some economists argue that the CPI does not in fact overstate inflation [see Dean Baker, "The Inflated Case Against the CPI," TAP, Winter 1996] it is bizarre that Alan Greenspan is among those who think that inflation is significantly below its officially measured rate since it undercuts his arguments for contractionary monetary policy.

Left to their own devices, those who operate central banks are never going to declare a permanent victory over inflation. The reasons are simple. If the battle against inflation is primary, central bankers will be described as, and actually be, the most important economic players in the game. Without inflation, they run rather unimportant institutions.

It is important to remember that in 1931 and 1932 as the United States was plunging into the Great Depression, economic advisers such as Secretary of the Treasury Andrew Mellon were arguing that nothing could be done without risking an outbreak of inflation —despite the fact that prices had fallen 23 percent from 1929 to 1932 and would fall another 4 percent in 1933. The fear of inflation was used as a club to stop the actions that should have been taken. Central banks are prone to see inflationary ghosts since they love to be ghostbusters. While it is true that no human has ever been hurt by a real ghost, it is equally true that ghostbusters have often created a lot of real human havoc.

Central bankers will of course tell us that when they gain "anti-inflationary credibility," rapid noninflationary growth will resume. But this is a mirage shimmering in the hot desert air. If any central bank has anti-inflationary credibility, it should be the German Bundesbank, yet Germany has one of the industrial world's lowest real growth rates. If the Bundesbank has not yet achieved anti-inflationary credibility, no central bank ever will obtain this exalted status.

As a result, if policies are to change it will require a change in political perceptions. Rising inequalities and falling real wages have to come to be seen as more important problems than the ghost of inflation when it comes to getting elected or reelected. Social welfare programs for the poor are not politically viable as long as the poor do not vote for the politicians who support the programs that benefit them. Tight labor markets are equally politically unviable unless voters reward the politicians who are willing to reverse the macroeconomic policies that have been in place for the past 25 years.

The long-run answer to falling wages is a much better-skilled bottom three-quarters of the American workforce, but without a reversal in our macroeconomic policies no set of human-capital investment policies can hope to work.

The Inequality Express

Barry Bluestone

In his 1958 book, *The Rise of the Meritocracy, 1870-2033*, British sociologist Michael Young predicted that growing inequality in Britain's income distribution would spark a great populist rebellion in the year 2034. As British society moved closer to realizing the ideal of equal opportunity, Young wrote, it would also abandon any pretense of equal outcome: Each individual's socioeconomic status would depend less on lineage, family connections, and political influence, and more on intelligence, education, experience, and effort. Outright racial and gender discrimination and iniquitous privilege would be gone; inequality based on merit would take their place. The victims of this new inequality—those who were once protected by good union wages, civil service status, or seniority—would then take to the barricades.

We haven't seen any such revolution yet, but the rest of Young's prophecy today seems uncomfortably prescient. Virtually every number cruncher who has perused contemporary income data from the United States and the United Kingdom reports three clearly defined trends, each consistent with Young's forecast. First, the distribution of earnings in both countries increasingly reflects the distribution of formal education in the workforce. Second, the gap in earnings between the well educated and the not-so-well educated is steadily increasing. And finally, the real standard of living of a large proportion of the workforce—particularly those with less than a college degree—has steadily and sharply declined.

Universal acceptance of these trends has not, however, led to any agreement about their source. Some scholars emphasize increasing demand for skills in a high-technology economy. Others claim globalization of the economy has thrown workers in high-wage countries into competition with workers in low-wage ones. Still others indict deindustrialization, the decline of unions, rising immigration, and the proliferation of winner-take-all labor markets. This lack of consensus about causes has produced a lack of consensus about remedies.

Here we will attempt to solve the mystery of rising wage inequality, and in so doing consider what might be done to stymie it. The best primer for this exercise is Agatha Christie's *Murder on the Orient Express.*

MERIT OR MARKET?

When Young penned his satire, there appeared little reason to heed his warning. In the immediate postwar period, while Europe and the United States were enjoying the heady days of rapid growth, economic expansion almost always spawned greater equality. Class warfare was giving way to an implicit and generally peaceful social contract. The big trade-off between equality and growth so elegantly detailed by the American economist Arthur Okun seemed to hold more true in theory than in practice. In the U.S., real average weekly earnings would grow by 60 percent between 1947 and 1973. Median family income literally doubled. And over the same period, personal wages and family incomes became tangibly more equal, not less. Along with growth and greater equality, poverty declined across the nation. Those at the bottom of the distribution gained more—on a percentage basis—than those at the top. The higher wages of unionized workers did not come at the expense of other workers' living standards. If anything, the rising wages of higher-paid labor were extracted from the profits that traditionally went to the wealthy.

There is little dispute that by 1973 this trend had come to an end. Inequality actually rose, especially during the 1980s. Many initially blamed a slowdown in overall economic growth. But the expansion of the economy after the 1980-82 recession suggested a new dynamic at work: Faster growth no longer reduced inequality or did much to increase the earnings of those at the bottom of the skill ladder. Wage dispersion returned to levels not seen since before the 1960s. By the late 1980s, family income inequality was higher than at the end of World War II.

Wage dispersion, of course, is not the only source of economic inequality. Another source is demographic trends, such as the simultaneous rise in the number of dual income couples and single-parent families. The tremendous increase during the 1980s in non-wage sources of income for the well-to-do—interest, dividends, rent, and capital gains—plays an important role as well. But whatever role these other causes may play, changes in the distribution of wages and salaries are clearly a primary factor in rising inequality.

Racial and gender discrimination continue to be the basis of large earnings differences. However, as the influence of more virulent prejudices has declined in the labor market, differences in education and skill have had a greater impact on wages. One manifestation of this trend is the increasing wage ratio of college-educated workers to high school dropouts. In 1963, the man annual earnings of those with four years of college or more stood at just over twice (2.11 times) the mean annual earnings of those who had not completed high school. By 1979, this ratio had increased to 2.39. This was but a harbinger of things to come. By 1987, the education-to-earnings ratio had skyrocketed to nearly three to one (2.91). The trend continues today.

In fact, the entire pattern of wage growth during the 1980s reflects a remarkable labor market "twist" tied to schooling. During this decade, the average real wage of male high school dropouts fell by over 18 percent, while male high school graduates suffered nearly a 13 percent real earnings loss. At the other end of the distribution, men who completed at least a master's degree emerged as the only real winners. Their earnings rose by more than 9 percent. Note that even men who had attended college without graduating saw a serious erosion in their earning power. And men who completed college discovered that their undergraduate degrees merely served to prevent a decline in inflation-adjusted wages. Women fared better than men in terms of overall wage growth, but the imprint of a labor market twist is clearly discernible here as well.

That three out of four U.S. workers have not completed college provides some indication of how large a proportion of the entire labor force has been adversely affected by the new meritocratic distribution. If we take some liberty with Robert Reich's definition of symbolic analysts—people such as research scientists, design engineers, and public relations executives whose work focuses on problem-solving, problem-identifying, and strategic brokering activities—and limit the use of this term to those with two or more years of schooling beyond the bachelor's degree, the successes in the new economy account for just 7 percent of the U.S. labor force. If we include with men with the equivalent of at least a master's degree plus women with at least a bachelor's, we could say the proportion of real earnings winners includes about 15 percent of the workforce. The extreme losers in this new meritocratic society—those with no more than a high school diploma—still comprise more than half of all U.S. workers.

In economic terms, the "return" of education, or how much one earns with a given level of education, has diverged sharply from its "rate of return," or how much an additional year of education is worth. What we have seen is a reduction in the return of education —a decline in earnings for high school graduates, for example— while the increment in earnings due to a little more schooling pays off a whole lot, most notably at the high end. This is why the college degree for men has become a defensive good. It provided almost no wage growth during the entire decade of the 1980s, but at least it kept college graduates from suffering the nearly 13 percent loss sustained by those with only a high school diploma. For men, completing college during the 1980s became the equivalent of donning a brand new pair of running shoes to go bear hunting with a companion. If the bear ends up attacking you, you cannot outrun it. But in order to survive you need to outrun your friend. Anyone who has visited a vocational guidance counselor lately will recognize this as the principal underlying message. The college degree still outfits women with the equivalent of a new pair of Reeboks, but any less schooling leaves women trying to run in quicksand.

THE ECONOMISTS' LINEUP

To explain the crisis, economists have offered up ten suspects:

SUSPECT ONE: TECHNOLOGY. Robert Lawrence of Harvard's John F. Kennedy School of Government and Paul Krugman, now at Stanford University, are the leading advocates of this position. They believe that the new information technologies skew the earnings distribution by placing an extraordinary premium on skilled labor while reducing the demand, and hence the wage, for those of lesser skill. This, they contend, is about all you need to explain current earnings trends.

The problem is that no one has any direct measure of the skill content of technology. Proving this hypothesis would require proving not just skill-biased technological change but also a tremendous acceleration in new technology during the 1980s. After all, at least some level of technological change occurred in earlier decades without such an adverse impact on earnings equality. What's so different about technology in the 1980s and 1990s? According to David Howell (see Howell, "The Skills Myth," page 89), and Lawrence Mishel and Jared Bernstein in an Economic Policy Institute working paper, there is little evidence that the pace of innovation—the speed at which new machines are brought to factories and new products are developed—was any faster than during the 1960s and 1970s. Most businesses are not introducing technology that requires vastly improved skill. Many are simply paying less for the same skills they have been using all along while others are hiring better educated workers at lower wage rates to do the work previously relegated to lesser-educated employees.

SUSPECT TWO: THE SERVICE-BASED ECONOMY. Other researchers, including George Borjas of the University of California at San Diego, have argued that a primary suspect is deindustrialization—the shift of jobs from goods-producing sectors to the service sector. In previous writings, I have estimated that between 1963 and 1987 the earnings ratio between college graduates and high school dropouts working in the goods-producing sector (mining, construction, and manufacturing) increased from 2.11 to 2.42—a jump of 15 percent. In the service sector, however, the education-to-earnings ratio mushroomed from 2.20 to 3.52—a 60 percent increase. All of the employment growth in the economy during the 1980s came in the services sector, where wages were polarizing between high school dropouts and college graduates four times faster than the goods-producing industries. Hence, this could explain at least part of the dramatic increase in earnings inequality.

SUSPECT THREE: DEREGULATION. Government deregulation of the airlines, trucking and telecommunications industries very likely has produced the same effect. In each of these industries, intense competition from new non-union, low-wage entrants, such as the short-lived People Express in the airline industry, forced existing firms to extract large wage concessions from their employees to keep from going bankrupt. How much this has contributed to overall earnings inequality remains an open question.

SUSPECT FOUR: DECLINING UNIONIZATION. Unions have historically negotiated wage packages that narrow earnings differentials.

They have tended to improve wages the most for workers with modest educations. As Richard Freeman of Harvard and a number of other economists have noted, the higher rate of union membership is one of the reasons for the smaller dispersion of wages found in manufacturing. That unions have made only modest inroads into the service economy may explain in part why earnings inequality in this sector outstrips inequality in the goods-producing sector.

SUSPECT FIVE: DOWNSIZING. The restructuring of corporate enterprise toward lean production and the destruction of internal job ladders as firms rely more heavily on part-time, temporary, and leased employees is still another suspect in this mystery, according to Bennett Harrison of Carnegie Mellon. The new enterprise regime creates what labor economists call "segmented" labor force of insiders and outsiders whose job security and earnings potential can differ markedly.

SUSPECT SIX: WINNER-TAKE-ALL LABOR MARKETS. The heightened competitive market, which forces firms toward lean production, may also, according to Robert Frank and Philip Cook, be creating a whole new structure of free-agency, "winner-take-all" labor markets. As Frank has explained ("Talent and the Winner-Take-All Society," *The American Prospect*, Spring 1994, No. 17), in winner-take-all markets, "a handful of top performers walk away with the lion's share of total rewards." The difference between commercial success and failure in such markets may depend on just a few "star" performers—in movies the director and leading actor or actress; in the O.J. Simpson trial the conduct of just one or two trial attorneys. Given the high stakes involved in a multimillion dollar movie project or a murder trial involving a well-to-do client, investors are willing to pay a bundle to make sure they employ the "best in the business."

Today, the fields of law, journalism, consulting, investment banking, corporate management, design, fashion, and even academia are generating payoff structures that once were common only in the entertainment and professional sports industries. Just a handful of Alan Dershowitzes, Michael Milkens, and Michael Eisners can have a sizeable impact on the dispersion of wages in each of their occupations. There is considerable evidence that inequality is not only rising across education groups but within them, very likely reflecting such winner-take-all dynamics.

SUSPECT SEVEN: TRADE. Even more fundamental to the recent restructuring of the labor market—and a likely proximate cause of deindustrialization, deunionization, lean production, and perhaps even the free-agency syndrome—is the expansion of unfettered global trade. According to trade theory, increased trade alone is sufficient—*without* any accompanying multinational capital investment or low-wage worker immigration—to induce the wages of similarly skilled workers to equalize across trading countries. Economists call this dynamic "factor price equalization." As the global economy moves toward free trade, lower transportation costs, better communications, and the same "best practice" production techniques available to all countries, factor price equalization is likely to occur.

Unfortunately, in a world like ours where there is a plentiful supply of unskilled labor juxtaposed to a continued relative scarcity of well-educated workers, this "price equalization" *within* skill categories leads to a "wage polarization" *between* skill categories. The gap between the compensation of low-skilled workers and high-skilled workers everywhere will tend to grow. According to the well-respected trade theorist Edward Leamer of the University of California at Los Angeles, freer trade will ultimately reduce the wages of less-skilled U.S. workers by about a thousand dollars a year, partly as a result of NAFTA. If factor price equalization is a chief source of wage dispersion today, just consider the implications when China and India with their immense unskilled workforces enter fully into global markets.

SUSPECT EIGHT: CAPITAL MOBILITY. Freer trade generally provides for the unrestricted movement of investment capital across borders. This inevitably accelerates the process of growing wage inequality. Modern transportation and communications technologies, combined with fewer government restrictions on foreign capital investment, have led to increased multinational capital flows between countries. To the extent that companies move to take advantage of cheaper unskilled labor, transnational investment adds to the effective supply of low-skilled workers available to American firms, thus reinforcing factor price equalization.

SUSPECT NINE: IMMIGRATION. Increased immigration potentially has the same effect, if a disproportionate share of new immigrants enters with limited skills and schooling. This is true at least for legal immigrants. The typical legal immigrant in the U.S. today has nearly a year less schooling than native citizens. Undocumented immigrants surely have even less. As such, while many immigrants to the U.S. come here with excellent education and skills, there is little doubt that the large number of Central American, Caribbean, and Southeast Asians seeking refuge in this country has had the unfortunate side effect of at least temporarily boosting the supply of low-skill workers seeking jobs.

SUSPECT TEN: TRADE DEFICITS. The trade gap has contributed to the decline in those sectors of the economy that have in the past helped to restrain earnings inequality. Moreover, trade data indicate that the import surplus itself is disproportionately composed of products made by low-skilled and modestly skilled labor. This boosts the effective supply of workers at the bottom of the education-to-earnings distribution and thus depresses their relative wages.

WHODUNNIT?

Thus, in our rogue's gallery we have ten suspects: skill-based technological change, deindustrialization, industry deregulation, the decline of unions, lean production, winner-take-all labor markets, free trade, transnational capital mobility, immigration, and a persistent trade deficit. Quantitatively parsing out the relative impact of all of these forces on wage distribution is fraught with enormous difficulty. Still, Richard Freeman and Lawrence Katz have attempted to do something like this, at least for the wage gap between men with a college degree and those with a high school diploma.

SOURCES OF INEQUALITY

Factors responsible for the increase in the male college/high school wage differential during the 1980s

Factor	Share
Technological Change	7% - 25%
Deindustrialization	25% - 33%
Deunionization	20%
Trade and Immigration	15% - 20%
Trade Deficit	15%

Source: Richard B. Freeman and Lawrence F. Katz, "Rising Wage Inequality: The United States vs. Other Advanced Countries," in Richard Freeman, ed., *Working Under Different Rules*. Russell Sage, 1994.

What do these results suggest? If the Freeman and Katz estimates are in the right ballpark, the answer to our mystery is the same denouement as Agatha Christie's in *Murder on the Orient Express*. They all did it. Every major economic trend in the U.S. contributes to growing inequality largely linked to merit. None of these trends shows the least sign of weakening.

Each trend reflects the growth of market forces and the decline of institutional constraints on competition. This was Young's essential message more than 30 years ago. Increased reliance on domestic market dynamics as the sole determinant of earnings produces inequality. Heightened competition within these markets, as a consequence of fuller integration into the global economy, exacerbates this wage dispersion. While it may be sinister, there is nothing conspiratorial about this phenomenon. It is embedded in the very nature of laissez-faire market dynamics. For this reason, meritocratic inequality is much harder to remedy than overt forms of discrimination based on race and sex.

POLICY ENDGAMES

Even economists who tout the merits of the market have come to recognize the need to soften the potentially devastating social impact of current income trends. Yet given the long-standing resistance to most forms of public intervention in the marketplace, the search for solutions has been restricted to just three types of countermeasures: education and training, immigration reform, and direct tax-and-transfer policy.

In theory, education can offset the effect of skill-biased technological change and factor price equalization. If somehow we could produce a true glut of symbolic analysts in place of high school dropouts, meritocratic inequality would begin to resolve itself. Education reduces the surplus of low-skilled workers and relieves the shortage of skilled workers. If this strategy also happens to increase the overall level of education, it has the added advantage of improving overall labor productivity and ultimately real wages.

A number of education and training programs have widespread appeal. These include expanding the Head Start program for disadvantaged preschool children, levying a corporate tax to finance on-the-job training, instituting a national apprenticeship program, and converting current grant and loan programs into income-contingent loans for college and university students. Other possibilities under consideration for education reform include setting national standards for school performance, introducing merit systems to reward successful teaching, instituting voucher systems, and increasing teacher and parent control over schools.

Legal restriction of immigration is a second possible means of reducing wage inequality. Canada has a higher rate of immigration than the United States. But immigration laws in the two countries have produced very different effects on their respective labor markets. Since the 1960s, U.S. policy has stressed family reunification. Canada, in contrast, employs a point system designed to produce a more skilled immigrant labor pool. This approach has produced legal immigrants in Canada who average 1.3 more years of education than native Canadians. If we ignore the thorny ethical issues surrounding the rights of political refugees and judgments about the worthiness of individuals seeking to immigrate—a whole other debate—one could imagine tilting immigration policy toward greater use of skill-based criteria.

Finally, if immigration control and education cannot do the job, there is the old standby of progressive tax-and-transfer policy to effect greater equality after wages are paid. Traditionally, most contemporary liberal economists have favored this method, for it entails the least interference with market forces.

On the surface, this complement of liberal policies seems germane for coping with meritocratic inequality. Not surprisingly, all three policies are at the top of the domestic agenda of the Democratic Party. Yet, given the powerful set of national and global forces at work in the economy, these policies may not be enough.

A case in point is education and training. Greater equality in schooling does not by itself produce more equal earnings. The distribution of education has become significantly more even over the past three decades. Among year-round, full-time workers, the overall variation in completed years of schooling has declined by more than 25 percent since 1963. The performance of black students and other minorities on the Scholastic Aptitude Test (SAT) is further evidence of this convergence. In 1976, the average verbal SAT score for blacks stood at the 74th percentile of whites; by 1990 the average score was up to the 80th percentile. Math SAT scores for black students improved by the same amount.

But even as education backgrounds have converged, the importance of small differences in education has increased—enough so to offset any equalizing effect education would otherwise have. Recall the distinction between the return and the rate of return of schooling. As such, no matter what other benefits might flow from increased schooling, expanded education is not, by itself, a certain cure for inequality.

Job training programs have made even less headway. While the federal government has experimented with a bevy of programs from the original Manpower Development and Training Act (MDTA) of the Great Society to the Job Training and Partnership Act (JTPA) of the 1980s, repeated evaluations suggest mixed results at best. Some programs like the Job Corps, which provide long-term training opportunities to disadvantaged youth, have been cost effective. The vast majority, however, have provided dubious returns. And even when these programs are deemed successful, the earnings advantage they give participants produces only the slightest deviation in the trend toward income inequality.

James Heckman of the University of Chicago has estimated just how small this deviation really is. Assuming a generous 10 percent rate of return on investment, he calculates that the government would need to spend a staggering $284 billion on the U.S. workforce to restore male high school dropouts to their 1979 real incomes. To restore education-based wage differentials to 1979 levels without reducing the real incomes of existing college-educated workers would take more than $2 trillion.

Future investments in human capital programs may have a somewhat better track record than past attempts, particularly if they are well targeted. But one cannot ignore the enormous increases in inequality that have already taken place. And to keep inequality from growing even more quickly, government would have to expand these programs at a frenetic pace. This is not to say that there is no role for training in solving America's labor market problems. While more training may not significantly reduce inequality, it is nevertheless useful for raising overall productivity, providing individual workers with a defense against further wage decline, and for rectifying specific skill shortages which could otherwise lead to wage-led inflation.

Immigration reform may also have a marginal impact on the earnings distribution, but any improvement will be largely limited to regions of the country where immigration flows have been disproportionately large—California, Texas, Florida, and perhaps a few states in the Northeast.

That leaves tax-and-transfer programs as the centerpiece for adjusting distributional outcomes. On paper, a suitably progressive set of tax rates combined with sufficiently generous transfer assistance could radically redistribute income after it is earned in the market. But in practice even such hard-to-win liberal measures as President Clinton's 1993 tax initiative produce relatively little redistribution. In 1977, when the federal tax system was significantly more progressive than today, the richest fifth of American families had 9.5 times the pretax total income of the poorest fifth. Federal taxes reduced the overall gap in relative shares by less than 20 percent; regressive state and local taxes wiped out this improvement. Given increased reliance on regressive payroll taxes and an aversion to any further increase in progressive income taxation, the tax system is unlikely to do much more.

The same is true of public transfer programs. Over the past 20 years, the New Deal safety net of unemployment insurance and welfare assistance has come under attack. Unemployment insurance covered more than 60 percent of the jobless during the 1961 and 1975 recessions. Despite the greater severity of the 1982 recession, only 43 percent of jobless Americans collected unemployment benefits. During the 1991 recession, coverage was down to 40 percent. While the Clinton administration implemented important reforms of the federal unemployment insurance system, the states and the federal government are unlikely to greatly expand coverage of the unemployed. As for the traditional welfare system, including Aid to Families with Dependent Children (AFDC), real benefit levels have been cut in many states and the government has imposed greater eligibility restrictions. Most of the proposed reforms of the AFDC program would change the dynamics of dependency, but do nothing to change the final distribution of income—and they could, by forcing welfare recipients off the roles after two years, makes matters worse.

Education and immigration reform, as well as redistributive tax-and-transfer policy, could contribute to reducing inequality, but they are by themselves—even under the best of political scenarios—no match for the concerted forces now driving the labor market. Indeed, relying exclusively on redistributive tax-and-transfer schemes to redress the growing inequality problem would likely require tax rates and transfer sums so large that there would be not only massive political resistance but real economic costs in terms of disincentives to investment and growth.

THE END OF INEQUALITY?

There is, however, an additional policy agenda which a progressive government could embrace. This agenda would focus attention on the market forces that generate greater inequality. First, there is direct regulation of the labor market. As the empirical evidence demonstrates, the growth in earnings inequality has materialized in part because of a serious erosion in wages at the bottom of the skill distribution and a sharp decline in unionization. Higher minimum wage standards are one way government can affect the distribution of employee compensation. While raising the mandatory wage minimum theoretically entails some trade-off in the form of job loss, some recent studies prove the positive earnings impact of modest increases in the statutory minimum far outweighs any unemployment effect. Thus, the aggregate wage bill paid to less-skilled workers increases, improving the living standards of those on the bottom rungs of the earnings ladder.

Labor law reform makes it easier for unions to organize workers and provides an indirect method of accomplishing the same objective. While there are many reasons why union membership is dwindling, the recent *Fact Finding Report* of the U.S. Commission on the Future of Worker-Management Relations found undeniable evidence that the playing field is tilted heavily toward employers. Employers can permanently replace striking employees, which reduces the ability of unions to organize and to freely negotiate collective bargaining agreements. Unions do not have free access to employees during membership drives, and the penalties for employer unfair labor practices are trivial. To remedy this, government could ban permanent striker replacements, permit union organizers access to in-plant bulletin boards and public forums, impose more costly penalties on employers who violate the rights of union organizers, expedite legal remedies, and authorize binding arbitration for first contracts.

There are also industrial and trade policies to consider. Advocates of industrial policy can cite the success of the U.S. aircraft and agriculture industries, in which government purchases and research-and-development subsidies helped to create and maintain industries that now dominate world markets. The Carter administration's

Chrysler loan guarantee, which provided an eleventh-hour reprieve from certain bankruptcy for the then-hapless automaker, turned around an old smokestack company and saved tens of thousands of well-paying jobs—not only at Chrysler but at hundreds of its suppliers. With a new lease on life, Chrysler has surged back as a world leader in automotive technology. There are, of course, many instances of failed industrial policy—the government's ill-fated Synfuels Corporation, for example—but there are an ample number of cases on the other side of the ledger. Maintaining the nation's manufacturing base would have a salutary effect on incomes.

The other policy that can bolster the goods-producing sector is implementation of fair-trade language in trade agreements. One way of doing this is to use tariffs and trade barriers designed to give *temporary* protection to key industries, promoting industrial revitalization and economic transition. Another form of managed trade would tie the offer of reduced protection to a trading partner's compliance with certain environmental and labor standards. Critics of NAFTA argued for side agreements that would have linked the pace of tariff reduction to the rate at which Mexican wages caught up with Mexico's rapidly rising productivity. To be sure, government-imposed limits on trade can have detrimental effects on prices and therefore reduce average real incomes from what they might be under a free trade regime. Nevertheless, a carefully crafted set of trade policies that condones temporary protection of selected domestic markets and sets minimum labor and environmental standards can soften the distributional impact of factor price equalization. The trick is to keep such protection from becoming permanent or prompting a trade war.

One last point: What about the use of macroeconomic stimulus to counteract inequality? As noted above, growth per se is no longer an antidote to increased wage dispersion. But it is important to realize that it is the sine que non for providing the tax revenue and the political will to address inequality through government action. Hence, overzealous attacks on government deficits that reduce aggregate demand and overly restrictive monetary policies that unnecessarily boost interest rates can poison the environment for possible egalitarian reforms.

Is there any evidence that more aggressive structural policies can help? Critics like Mickey Kaus, the *New Republic* columnist and author of

The End of Equality, think not. In declaring that "the venerable liberal crusade for income equality is doomed," Kaus argues that

> you cannot decide to keep all the nice parts of capitalism and get rid of all the nasty ones. You cannot have capitalism without 'selfishness,' or even 'greed,' because they are what make the system work. You can't have capitalism and material equality, because capitalism is constantly generating extremes of inequality as some individuals strike it rich... while others fail and fall on hard times.

This may sound sensible, but it will come as remarkable news to a large number of our foreign capitalist competitors. A comparison of earnings trends across countries suggests that different institutional frameworks, all operating within a capitalist framework, produce substantially different distributional outcomes.

Kaus confuses capitalism with laissez-faire economics. All nations now face nearly identical pressures from technological change and global competition. Yet not all are experiencing the same degree of growing income inequality. Those countries with stronger unions, national wage solidarity agreements, generous social welfare programs, and more vigorously pursued industrial and trade policies have greater wage equality than countries pursuing pure free-market strategies. Relying on an extensive review of comparative statistics, Richard Freeman and Lawrence Katz conclude that while educational and occupational skill-wage differentials were growing rapidly in the United States and the United Kingdom during the 1980s, the experience elsewhere was quite different. Wage equality increased in the Netherlands; wage differentials did not change noticeably in France, Germany, and Italy; and wage dispersion increased modestly —if at all—in Australia, Canada, Japan, and Sweden.

In all of these capitalist countries, intensified global competition and technological innovation pushed the distribution of earnings and income toward greater inequality. Structural protection against this onslaught was greater in countries that did not follow the Reagan-Thatcher road to full-scale deregulation and laissez-faire trade policies.

True, the flexibility of the U.S. market may be partly responsible for lower overall unemployment rates compared with these other countries, but the price of this flexibility seems to be much higher levels of economic polarization and social inequality. Moreover, recent research by Rebecca Blank, a labor economist at Northwestern University, suggests there is little empirical evidence that social protection programs substantially affect labor market flexibility. Expansive social protection problems, then, are not the most important factor behind the high rate of unemployment in Europe, as many others suggest. Blank goes on to show that cutting back on social protection policies does not automatically reduce unemployment or increase the speed of labor market adjustment. Instead she finds that by enhancing worker well-being, social protection policies may actually permit flexibility that would not otherwise be possible. All of which means that the U.S. can adopt policies to directly redress income inequality without raising the specter of double-digit unemployment.

So can we avoid fulfilling Michael Young's prophecy for 2034? Can a society with high- and low-skill workers have a reasonably equitable distribution of income? The answer is a qualified, "yes," but it requires that we focus on equal outcome, not just equal opportunity. There is a fundamental distinction separating progressives from neoconservatives and neoliberals, and it turns largely on this point. Progressives are willing to consider a broader and more balanced array of public policies to keep the free market from perpetrating and then perpetuating socially destructive levels of inequality.

How the Pie Is Sliced

AMERICA'S GROWING CONCENTRATION OF WEALTH

Edward N. Wolff

Conservative economic policy has one central idea: just create a bigger pie, and everyone will have a bigger slice. In fact, conservatives predict that if we cut the rich a bigger piece by lowering their tax rates, the resulting growth will enlarge everyone else's slice, too. This was the core idea of Reagan's tax cuts, and it is central to such current conservative goals as lower capital gains taxes.

Unfortunately, since the 1980s the great majority of Americans have not been getting bigger slices from a growing pie. As many people have noted, median family income has failed to grow. The picture is even more stark for gains in wealth than for gains in income. New research, based on data from federal surveys, shows that between 1983 and 1989 the top 20 percent of wealth holders received 99 percent of the total gain in marketable wealth, while the bottom 80 percent of the population got only 1 percent. America produced a lot of new wealth in the '80s—indeed, the stock market boomed—but almost none of it filtered down.

Few people realize how extraordinarily concentrated the gains in wealth have been. Between 1983 and 1989 the top 1 percent of income recipients received about a third of the total increase in real income. But the richest 1 percent received an even bigger slice—62 percent—of the new wealth that was created.

The most recent data suggest these trends have continued. My preliminary estimates indicate that between 1989 and 1992, 68 percent of the increase in total household wealth went to the richest 1 percent—an even larger share of wealth gain than between 1983 and 1989. As a result, the concentration of wealth reached a postwar high in 1992, the latest year for which data are available. If these trends continue, the super rich will pull ahead of other Americans at an even faster pace in the 1990s than they did in the '80s.

Growing inequality in the distribution of wealth has serious implications for the kind of society we live in. Today, the average American family's wealth adds up to a comparatively meager $52,200, typically tied up in a home and some small investments. While *Forbes* magazine each year keeps listing record numbers of billionaires—in 1994 *Forbes* counted 65 of them in the U.S.—homeownership has been slipping since the mid-1970s. The percentage of Americans with private pensions has also been dropping. And, with their real incomes squeezed, middle-income families have not been putting savings aside for retirement. The number of young Americans going to college has also begun to decline, another indirect sign of the same underlying phenomenon. In fact, international data now indicate that wealth is more unequally distributed in the U.S. than in other developed countries, including that old symbol of class privilege, Great Britain.

Economic worries may be at the root of much of the political anger in America today, but there is almost no public debate about the growth in wealth inequality, much less the steps needed to reverse current trends. The debate needs to start with an understanding of how and why America's pie is getting sliced so unequally.

REVERSAL OF FORTUNES

The increasing concentration of wealth in the past 15 years represents a reversal of the trend that had prevailed from the mid-1960s through the late 1970s. The share of total wealth owned by the rich depends, to a large extent, on asset values and therefore swings sharply with the stock market, but some trends stand out. During the twenty years after World War II, the richest 1 percent of Americans (the "super rich") generally held about a third of the nation's wealth. After hitting a postwar high of 37 percent in 1965, their share dropped to 22 percent as late as 1979. Since then, the share owned by the super rich has surged—almost doubling to 42 percent of the nation's wealth in 1992, according to my estimates.[1]

Two statistics—median and mean family wealth—help to tell the story of growing wealth inequality in America. A median is the middle of a distribution, the point at which there are an equal number of cases above and below. Median family wealth represents the holdings of the average family. Mean family wealth is the average in a different sense: total wealth divided by the total number of families. If a few families account for a large bulk of the nation's wealth, the mean will exceed the median. The changing ratio between the mean and median is one measure of changes in wealth inequality.

Data from the 1983, 1989, and 1992 Survey of Consumer Finances conducted by the Department of Commerce show that mean wealth has indeed been much higher than the median: $220,000 versus $52,000 in 1992. And mean wealth has grown more rapidly—by 23 percent from 1983 to 1989, and by another 12 percent in the following three years, while median wealth increased by only 8 percent between 1983 and 1989 and then barely moved up at all from 1989 to 1992. As a result, between 1983 and 1989 the ratio of mean to median wealth jumped from 3.4 to 3.8.

Data for 1992 are as yet incomplete. However, the figures available indicate that the ratio of mean to median wealth saw another steep rise between 1989 and 1992, from 3.8 to 4.2. On the basis of a regression analysis of the historical relation between this ratio and the share of wealth held by the top 1 percent of families, I estimated their share at 42 percent in 1992.

Income inequality also increased over the same period. From 1983 to 1989, the share of the top 20 percent increased from 52 to 56 percent, while that of the remaining 80 percent decreased from 48.1 to 44.5 percent. The preliminary evidence from the 1992 Survey of Consumer Finances suggests a further rise in income inequality between 1989 and 1992 (the ratio of mean to median income increased from 1.57 to 1.61), though this change is much more muted than from 1983 to 1989 (when the ratio moved upward from 1.42 to 1.57).

By the 1980s the U.S. had become the most unequal industrialized country in terms of wealth. The top 1 percent of wealth holders controlled 39 percent of total household wealth in the United States in 1989, compared to 26 percent in France in 1986, about 25 percent in Canada in 1984, 18 percent in Great Britain, and 16 percent in Sweden in 1986. This is a marked turnaround from the early part of this century when the distribution of wealth was considerably more unequal in Europe (a 59 percent share of the top 1 percent in Britain in 1923 versus a 37 percent share in the U.S. in 1922).

The concept of wealth used here is marketable wealth—assets that can be sold on the market. It does not include consumer durables such as automobiles, televisions, furniture, and household appliances;

these items are not easily resold, or their resale value typically does not reflect the value of their consumption to the household. Also excluded are pensions and the value of future Social Security benefits a family may receive.

Some critics of my work, such as the columnist Robert Samuelson of the *Washington Post,* argue that a broader definition of wealth shows less concentration. To be sure, including consumer durables, pensions, and entitlements to Social Security reduces the level of measured inequality. The value of consumer durables amounted to about 10 percent of marketable wealth in 1989; including them in the total reduces the share of the top 1 percent of wealth holders from 39 percent to 36 percent. Adding pensions and Social Security "wealth," which together totaled about two-thirds of marketable wealth, has a more pronounced effect, reducing the share of the top 1 percent from 36 percent to 22 percent. However, even though pensions and Social Security are a source of future income to families, they are not in their direct control and cannot be marketed. Social Security "wealth" depends on the commitment of future generations and Congresses to maintain benefit levels; it is not wealth in the ordinary meaning of the term.

Moreover, the inclusion of consumer durables, pensions, and Social Security does not affect trends in inequality. With these assets included, the share of the richest 1 percent reached its lowest level in 1976, at 13 percent, and nearly doubled by 1989 to 22 percent. Nor does it affect international comparisons. For example, using this broader concept of wealth, we still find that the share of the top 1 percent in the U.S. is almost double that of Britain in 1989—22 percent versus 12 percent.

WHY THE RICH GOT RICHER

Part of the explanation for growing wealth concentration lies in what has happened to the different kinds of assets that the rich and the middle class hold. Broadly speaking, wealth comes in four forms:

- homes
- liquid assets, including cash, bank deposits, money market funds, and savings in insurance and pension plans
- investment real estate and unincorporated businesses
- corporate stock, financial securities, and personal trusts.

Middle-class families have more than two-thirds of their wealth invested in their own home, which is probably responsible for the common misperception that housing is the major form of family wealth in America. Those families have another 17 percent in monetary savings of one form or another, with only a small amount in businesses, investment real estate, and stocks. The ratio of debt to assets is very high, at 59 percent.

In contrast, the super rich invest over 80 percent of their savings in investment real estate, unincorporated businesses, corporate stock, and financial securities. Housing accounts for only 7 percent of their wealth, and monetary savings another 11 percent. Their ratio of debt to assets is under 5 percent.

Viewed differently, more than 46 percent of all outstanding stock, over half of financial securities, trusts, and unincorporated businesses, and 40 percent of investment real estate belong to the super rich. The top 10 percent of families as a group account for about 90 percent of stock shares, bonds, trusts, and business equity, and 80 percent of non-home real estate. The bottom 90 percent are responsible for 70 percent of the indebtedness of American households.

Thus, for most middle-class families, wealth is closely tied to the value of their homes, their ability to save money in monetary accounts, and the debt burden they face. But the wealth of the super rich has a lot more to do with their ability to convert existing wealth—in the form of stocks, investment real estate, or securities—into even more wealth, that is, to produce "capital gains."

Sure enough, we find that when wealth inequality was on the rise, so was the relative importance of capital gains. Between 1962 and 1969, conventional savings—the difference between household income and expenditures—accounted for 38 percent of the growth of wealth, but from 1983 to 1989 conventional savings accounted for just 30 percent of increased wealth. Conversely, capital gains became a bigger factor in the '80s. The immediate causes lay in a falling savings rate and more rapid growth in the value of stocks than in the value of homes. In addition, the homeownership rate (the percentage of families owning their own home), which had risen 1 percent during the 1960s, fell during the 1980s, by 1.7 percent. The extension of homeownership would suggest a widening diffusion of assets to the middle class. Alas, the homeownership rate peaked in 1980 at 65.6 percent and has been falling ever since.

Widening income inequality was clearly a factor in the growing concentration of wealth. Income inequality did not change much during the 1960s but has risen markedly ever since the early '70s. The wealthy save proportionally more than the middle class. So when the wealthy get a larger share of total income, their share of savings will increase even more. Not surprisingly, between the 1960s and 1980s, the percentage of income saved by the upper third of families has more than doubled, from 9.3 to 22.5 percent. That increase was partly spurred by generous tax cuts during the Reagan years, which were intended precisely to bring about that result.

In contrast, the middle third of the population saved almost 5 percent of its income during the 1960s but by the 1980s saved virtually nothing. This drop in savings reflected the growing squeeze on the middle class from stagnating incomes and rising expenses; the Reagan tax cuts did not produce their predicted effects on this group. The bottom third has historically saved none of its income, and the Reagan years did not turn them into savers and investors as Jack Kemp's happy vision suggested.

According to my estimates, the chief source of growing wealth concentration during the 1980s was capital gains. The rapid increase in stock prices relative to house prices accounted for about 50 percent of the increased wealth concentration; the growing importance of capital gains relative to savings explained another 10 percent. Increased income inequality during the decade added another 18 percent, as did the increased savings propensity of the rich relative to the middle class. The declining homeownership rate accounted for the remaining 5 percent or so.

In short, wealth went to those who held wealth to begin with. For those who didn't have it, savings alone were not sufficient to amass wealth of great significance.

ARE THERE REMEDIES?

These trends raise troubling questions. Will the increasing concentration of wealth further exacerbate the tilt of political power toward the rich? might it ultimately set off an extremist political explosion? Is it compatible with renewed economic growth?

At least the surface evidence suggests that equality and growth are complementary. The high growth rates of the 1950s and 1960s occurred during a period of low inequality. The slowdown in growth that began in the 1970s was accompanied by rising inequality in both income and wealth. High levels of inequality put better training and education out of the reach of more workers and may breed resentment in the workplace.

Diffusing wealth more broadly will not be easy. Some of the causes of growing income and wealth inequality lie in changes in the global economy for which no one has any ready policy response. However, the experiences of European countries as well as our neighbor Canada, which are subject to the same market forces, suggest that shifting the tax burden toward the wealthy would spread wealth more widely. In the U.S., marginal income tax rates, particularly on the rich and very rich, fell sharply during the 1980s. Although Congress raised marginal rates on the very rich in 1993, those rates are still considerably lower than they were at the beginning of the 1980s. And they are much lower than in western European countries with more equal distributions of income and wealth.

Another strategy to consider is direct taxation of wealth. Almost a dozen European countries, including Denmark, Germany, the Netherlands, Sweden, and Switzerland, have taxes on wealth. A very modest tax on wealth (with marginal tax rates running from 0.05 to 0.3 percent, exempting the first $100,000 in assets) could raise $50 billion in revenue and have a minimal impact on the tax bills of 90 percent of American families. Even with an exemption of $250,000, such a tax would raise $48 billion.

On the other side of the ledger, the financial well-being of the poor and lower-middle class would be much improved by social transfers similar to Canada's, including child support assurance, a rising minimum wage, and extension of the earned income tax credit.

None of these measures appears politically feasible today. Instead, the current majority leader of the House is promoting a flat tax that would cut in half income tax rates for the rich and entirely eliminate taxes on capital gains. Many prominent Republicans have embraced the flat tax and argued that it should be central to the 1996 election. The rush to give the rich an even bigger piece of the pie ought to be stimulus enough to start a national conversation about where America's wealth is going.

1 See Top Heavy: The Increasing Inequality of Wealth in America and What Can Be Done about It (New York: The New Press, 1996) for technical details on the construction of this series.

Rising Tides, Sinking Wages

Lawrence Mishel

The economy seems to be in great shape. The growth rate in 1994 was a brisk 4.1 percent. Unemployment has been hovering at about 5.5 percent, well below the 6 to 6.5 percent level that many economists (wrongly) consider full employment. Job growth has been so strong that President Clinton's campaign pledge to create eight million jobs may well be fulfilled in the third year of his first term. Corporate profitability has reached postwar records. The stock market is booming. Inflation is nowhere to be found except in the imagination of central bankers and bond traders.

We are also witnessing a revival of productivity growth and a celebration of America's renewed competitiveness, as U.S. products close the quality gap with imported goods and unit labor costs continuously fall relative to those of other advanced countries. Some analysts feel that our productivity growth is so strong and the promise of computerization so great that we are on the verge of a new, golden economic age.

There's only one problem with this celebration: The living standards of the broad middle class have remained in continuous decline despite the robust aggregate performance. This recovery has demonstrated that improved competitiveness, productivity, and overall economic growth do not necessarily translate into improved incomes for most families.

DOWN THE UPSWING

In the 1980s, family incomes were stagnant. Only the continued rise in two-earner families prevented a significant erosion in middle-class incomes in the face of declining real wages for men. Meanwhile, poverty grew at the bottom end while income and wealth soared among the top 1 percent. In a decade, all of the postwar progress toward greater equality was reversed.

In the 1990s, income trends have been even worse than in the 1980s. Median family income fell in every year from 1989 to 1993, the last year for which the Census Bureau has released family income data. This was the only time in the postwar period that incomes fell four years in a row and the first time that incomes fell during the first two years of an economic recovery. By 1993, the median family's income was down $2,700, or 7 percent, from its 1989 level of roughly $40,000. It will take five to eight years of steady growth to recoup these income losses—not a likely event. The economy also set records for the breadth of income deterioration as incomes steadily fell among the bottom 80 percent of families from 1989 through 1993.

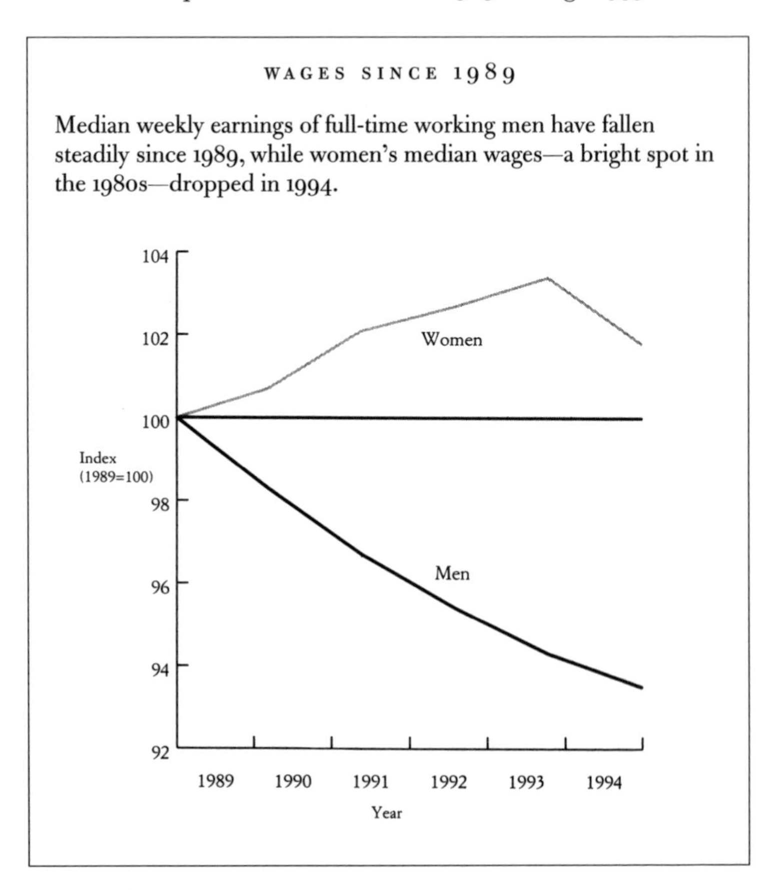

While complete data on household incomes are not yet available, it is very unlikely that these trends have improved since 1993. The real median weekly earnings of men who work have been falling since 1989, including from 1993 to 1994. Even women's median earnings, one of the few bright spots in the 1980s, dropped in 1994. The available wage data from early 1995 suggest that wages for both men and women have continued to lag behind inflation over the last 12 months.

Part of the problem is that the rate of return to capital—profits, interest, dividends—has surged to postwar records and thereby dampened wage growth. The larger part of the problem is that the continuing growth of wage disparities has demonstrated that even though average productivity and average wages may be increasing, the wages for the vast majority can still be falling. Productivity (output per hour worked) has grown 25 percent since 1973, a weak performance by historical standards, but quite enough (about 1 percent a year) to enable all workers to achieve real wage growth. In fact, average hourly compensation has roughly tracked average productivity, at least until recently. But that "average" is composed of a small part of the workforce at very high pay whose earnings are increasing while the bottom 80 percent see their pay falling. Hourly compensation

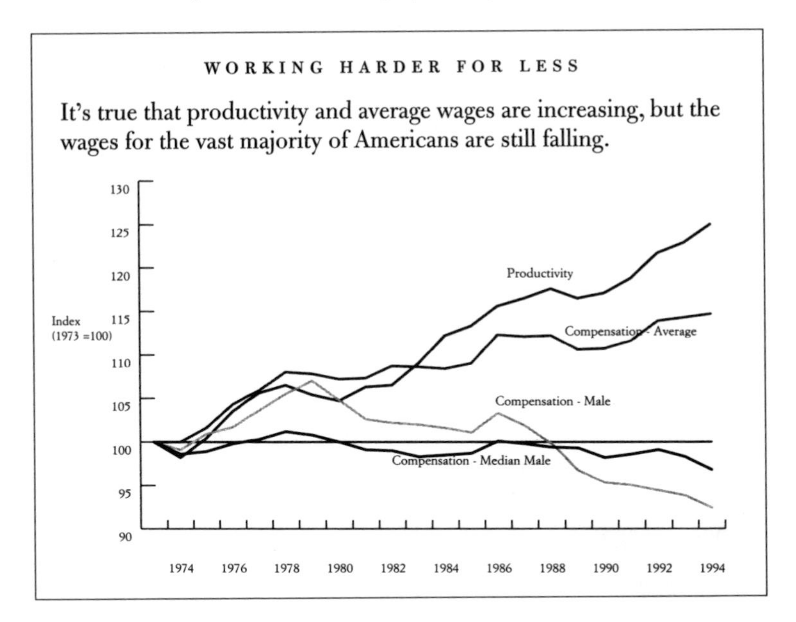

WORKING HARDER FOR LESS

It's true that productivity and average wages are increasing, but the wages for the vast majority of Americans are still falling.

of the median worker was stagnant over the 1970s and 1980s and has been declining in the 1990s. The median male has seen his hourly compensation fall 1 percent annually since 1979.

CAUSES OF WAGE INEQUALITY

Growing wage inequality is not the inevitable consequence of technological progress. Most wages have been falling despite rising productivity for one simple reason. Workers—union and nonunion, college- and noncollege-educated, white-collar and blue-collar—have lost bargaining power relative to their employers. Corporate America today has the power to respond to increased domestic and global competition by cutting labor costs. Public policies have generally accommodated or reinforced this effort, by failing to pursue full employment, fair trade, higher minimum wages, or renewal of the labor movement.

The failure of rising productivity to raise living standards is something new in the postwar American experience. As Lawrence Chimerine of the Economic Strategy Institute points out, virtually every macroeconomic model has been predicting far faster wage growth than ever materializes. At the peak of an economic recovery, one expects workers to be able to approach their bosses with propositions such as "I need a 5 percent wage increase or I'll get another job." This has not been happening in the current business cycle, even among the managerial-professional workforce whose unemployment is only 2.5 percent. The steady growth of temporary employment, which accounts for about 15 percent of job growth in this recovery, and the continued use of other forms of contingent work indicate that broad segments of the workforce have little power to shape their terms of employment. According to the Bureau of Labor Statistics (BLS), early 1995 saw the lowest compensation growth in two decades. This must be a curious phenomenon for our central bankers who have been doing their best to slow the economy lest wages accelerate and inflation take off.

In our recent book, *The State of Working America, 1994–95*, Jared Bernstein and I attribute growing wage inequality primarily to two clusters of factors, each of which can explain about one-third of the phenomena.

GLOBALIZATION AND SERVICE EMPLOYMENT. The combined effect of globalization (including the trade deficit, low-wage competition, immigration, and foreign direct-investment trends) and the continued expansion of employment in the lowest-paid portion of the service sector together explain at least a third of the wage problem. BLS attributes 25 to 30 percent of the growth of wage inequality to sectoral shifts in the pattern of employment alone. In addition, import pressure has lowered wages for many middle- and low-wage industrial workers, and undercut the wages of workers generally. Only a few ideologues in the economics profession, particularly near important congressional votes on trade policy, deny that expanding trade significantly depresses wages for noncollege-educated workers.

These factors are all influenced by policy decisions—by omission or commission. For example, the shift to service employment would be far less consequential if health care and pension benefits were not so tightly linked with one's particular job but were universally provided. A service-sector job would not be a sentence to wage reductions if America had stronger unions, or fuller employment. The wage disparities between manufacturing and services are far smaller in other industrial countries where market forces have less free rein.

AN INSTITUTIONAL COLLAPSE. The other prime culprit is the weakening of labor market standards and institutions that empower workers. The erosion of the minimum wage, a nearly 30 percent drop in value from its 1979 level, has particularly affected wage levels of working women. Deunionization and the weakening of union bargaining power has had a particularly adverse effect on noncollege-educated men. This erosion of wage-setting institutions can explain roughly another third of the recent wage deterioration among workers. Other factors that are harder to quantify have also had an impact: deregulation, privatization, and the growth of contingent work—and these also reflect the policy climate.

MYTHICAL ORIGINS

Big government is a popular scapegoat for the erosion of living standards. The Republican House Majority Leader, Dick Armey, has claimed that people are working harder and getting less because the government is taking a bigger bite out of their paycheck. In reality, it is pre-tax pay that has collapsed. According to the Congressional Budget Office, the effective federal tax rate on the middle class was stable or declining in the 1980s.

Moreover, the projections for 1995, which include all of the effect of the early Clinton budgets, show tax rates declining among the bottom four-fifths while rising among the best-off fifth. Even the conservative National Tax Foundation reports stable tax rates over the 1980s. If anything, government was stable or shrinking—as measured by shares of total employment or expenditure or by regulatory costs—since 1979 when the wage implosion originated. Unfortunately, according to a recent *Business Week* poll, the public seems to believe the big government, high taxes story. This only proves that "Big Lies Frequently Told in Many Forums" is still an effective communications strategy.

A related, and disingenuous, claim is that large fiscal deficits are the cause of income problems. At most, deficits may be a factor if they somehow eroded investment and thereby productivity growth. But, we have already seen that the productivity growth that did occur was not shared with most workers. Even more damning is that the productivity slowdown preceded the era of large structural fiscal deficits by nearly ten years. The claim that fiscal deficits have shrunk workers' paychecks is without foundation.

Among economists and editorial writers the most widely cited explanation of widespread wage deterioration and growing wage inequality is that technological change has raised the demand for skills so that the wages of more highly skilled and educated workers have been bid up and the wages of other workers have suffered because there is less demand for them. Curiously, economists also acknowledge that there is very little direct evidence for the technology story and that their belief is based on eliminating competing explanations and putting a technology label on what they cannot explain. (See Howell, "The Skills Myth," page 89)

It is implausible to rely on an explanation that describes three-fourths of the workforce—those whose wages have been declining since 1979—as "low-skilled." It is hard to imagine the "bidding up of skilled workers' wages" as an apt description of a process that has lowered the real wages of male white-collar and college-educated workers continuously since 1987. To believe the technology story, we must also believe that a technological revolution is dramatically affecting our wage and employment structures but somehow fails to raise productivity growth enough to improve living standards. And, of course, technological change in the workplace is not new. For the technology story to make sense, technology has to have had a greater impact on labor markets in the 1980s and 1990s than in earlier periods, either through a faster rate of introduction or due to new types of technologies. My recent research with Jared Bernstein has shown that no such "acceleration" has taken place.

Absent strong countervailing forces, we should expect wage inequality to grow and wages to continue to fall for large segments of the workforce. Conceivably, productivity growth could accelerate so significantly that even smaller shares of a larger pie would mean more pie for all. But this hope rests primarily on conjectures of an eventual payoff to computerization so huge that it would offset all the pressures leading to increased inequality. Put me down as a skeptic.

A second possibility is for so many new college graduates to enter the labor market that college wages fall relative to those of non-college-educated workers. This is an unlikely scenario because, even though a greater proportion of young adults are completing college, the size of the college-going-age cohort is shrinking, limiting the absolute growth of college graduates. A more plausible scenario is that wage inequality continues to grow or, *at best*, stalls.

BACK TO POLITICS

In any event, nothing in the Republican economic program will reverse or forestall continued wage erosion and the accompanying pressures on family incomes. The macroeconomic effect of balancing the budget and reducing the deficit will be to slow economic growth over the next ten years. Any long-term effect of deficit reduction on productivity is uncertain, slight, and at least a decade away. Clinton's Council of Economic Advisers estimated the payoff for their very sizable deficit package at two-and-a-half percent more consumption after twenty years, without considering the income losses from the initially slower growth. The Republican growth program of deregulation and tax reduction will, at best, increase jobs and productivity slightly but do nothing to upgrade the quality of jobs or to translate productivity growth into broad-based wage gains.

The issue of wage growth will thus be with us for a long time, and it is time the nation and politicians started focusing on it. We will not make progress unless we can sustain the necessary conditions for wage growth. That means the Federal Reserve Bank must adjust its views of the "natural" rate of unemployment and cease creating a recession at the first signs of robust growth. Public investments in skills, infrastructure, and technology are in order to maintain productivity growth. The character of growth must change as well. Public policy needs to inhibit financial speculation and corporate strategies driven by short-term profit, in favor of production strategies that rely on broadly skilled workers and widely shared rewards. Trade policy, including international labor and environmental standards, must be used to shape global capital and trade flows and inhibit the "race to the bottom."

Most of all, we need to re-empower workers and change the dynamics of wage setting. Part of the solution is a significantly higher minimum wage, which will greatly help the bottom half of the income distribution. Another part is to enable workers to choose unionization and collective bargaining, especially in the service sector where a wage push from below may be our only hope for forcing employers to become more efficient and to generate productivity growth. New forms of representation, such as works councils and occupational associations, may be needed to achieve a wider empowerment of workers. Greater economic security through training and education, along with greater health security and pension mobility are valid policy in their own right, and can also help change the dynamics of wage bargaining.

Understanding these income problems is key to understanding the current shredding of our social fabric as well as the elections of 1992 and 1994. Moreover, policies to regenerate broad-based wage growth may be the key to political success in 1996 and beyond. In fact, this theme is already central in the rhetoric of Secretary of Labor Robert Reich and House Minority Leader Richard Gephardt.

However, before we can pursue appropriate remedies, we first need broad agreement that the erosion of living standards is a problem—indeed, the problem—that can be addressed through policy. That recognition, unfortunately, is still almost totally absent from political discourse.

The Skills Myth

David R. Howell

After almost three decades of rising incomes, average real earnings have fallen relentlessly since 1973. In 1982 dollars, the weekly wage for full-time workers was $327 in 1973, $303 in 1979, $277 in 1982, and just $265 in 1990. During the same period, the income distribution became steadily more unequal. The most dramatic earnings collapse was for poorly educated men, a pattern that accelerated in the 1980s.

The single most widely accepted explanation for the earnings crisis is "skill mismatch." According to this view, there has been a fundamental shift in industry's demand for skills, leading to a collapse in opportunities and wages for low-skill workers. This shift in the demand for skills is widely attributed to technological changes. The beauty of this account is its apparent consistency with both the textbook labor market, in which relative wages reflect relative skills, and a wealth of anecdotal evidence on the skill-upgrading effects of computer-based technologies. The Clinton administration, accordingly, has placed heavy emphasis on skill mismatch in promoting its job training initiatives.

However, a review of the statistical evidence casts considerable doubt on the skill-mismatch hypothesis. There is little direct evidence that the rate of skill upgrading was substantially greater in the 1980s than in earlier decades, or that technological change was the main source of the skill upgrading that we can measure. Nor is there evidence that changes in the mix of skills can explain much of the recent growth in either earnings inequality or the share of low-wage jobs.

There is another explanation, one that does not fit neatly into a standard supply-and-demand diagram but that does offer a better fit with the facts. First, there was a marked increase in competitive pressures (globalization and deregulation) and an ideological shift in favor of markets in the late 1970s. In this climate, business strategies and government policies severely undermined traditional wage-setting institutions (collective bargaining, internal labor market norms, minimum wages) that had protected low-skilled workers from the full force of labor market competition. Second, the *effective* supply of labor competing for low-skill jobs substantially increased; and, consequently, labor lost relative bargaining power.

Several factors contributed to the crowding at the hiring gate. Employment opportunities in the *middle* of the earnings distribution, notably high-wage blue-collar jobs and moderately skilled white-collar jobs, disappeared. Fewer good job opportunities, rising numbers of displaced workers, and sharply rising numbers of low-skill immigrant workers fed the pool of workers competing for moderate and low-skill jobs paying low wages. Blue-collar labor markets also became more competitive than at any time since the early 1930s because of the decline in union memberships and the growing capacity of firms to relocate to and buy supplies from low-wage areas.

The result was a collapse in the wage paid for low-skill work. In this alternative view, the main restructuring trend among nonsupervisory male workers in the 1980s was not a massive shift away from lower skill jobs. Indeed, the share of low-skill jobs was remarkably stable from 1983 into the 1990s. Rather, the real shift was away from higher wage jobs.

In short, employers in the 1980s responded to increased competitive pressures by taking a "low-road" human resource strategy, one aimed above all at reducing current labor costs. In direct contrast to technology-induced skill mismatch story, the fundamental problem in the 1980s was that most employers did *not* follow a high-tech, high-skills path. In a great many industries, workers learned new skills to work with more advanced production technologies—but their higher productivity was not reflected in higher wages.

Note that technology plays a key role in both accounts. In the skills-mismatch story, workers were not keeping up with the rising skill requirements demanded by new computer-based technologies. In the dissenting account, technology facilitated both globalization and displacement, as well as strategies of contracting out to small, low-wage suppliers. In a context of high unemployment, hostile management and government policies, and weaker unions, these trends all eroded wages. So technology did contribute to wage collapse, but not primarily through skill restructuring.

These contrasting stories, not surprisingly, have political overtones.

If the skill mismatch explanation is correct, the market is only paying workers what they are truly "worth" and is signaling workers to upgrade their skills. More competition in the labor market, as in the market for shoes or computers, is better because competition ensures that resource allocation will be efficient. Since technological change is held to be the main cause of the restructuring, and since few would favor inhibiting the use of new technologies, declining wages become inevitable for those without, say, a good college education or at least a competent technical one.

If the alternative story is right, however, the erosion in wages is mainly the result of an asymmetry in bargaining power, reflecting low-wage strategies by employers, a failure of government to help maintain traditional labor market institutions, and increased wage competition in the external labor market. Growing shares of workers with low wages reflect neither major skill shifts not the use of new technologies. There is nothing inevitable or "natural" about the growing earnings problems of two-thirds of the workforce without college degrees.

These contrasting explanations of the wage collapse suggest dramatically different policy strategies. If the earnings problems of low-skill workers are mainly the result of a shift in the demand for skills due to increasing use of information technology, public policy must substantially upgrade the cognitive skills of large portions of the current and future workforce. On the other hand, if the real mismatch in the 1980s was between skills provided and wages paid, improvements in education and training programs per se are unlikely to have much effect on the problem of earnings or earnings-distribution. There is little doubt that American workers need better skills, but a purely human capital approach will do little to reverse the downward shifts in wage norms in the last decade.

WAGES AND SKILLS

If the wage reflects the value a worker produces for the employer, and this value reflects the worker's skills, a collapse of wages for a particular skill group reflects a drop in the demand for these skills. But much empirical research since at least the 1940s indicates that the productivity of workers provides only a partial explanation of wages and wage trends.

Relative wages reflect not only skills and education, but a variety of other factors, such as gender, race, union coverage, firm size and industry of employment. One only has to ask, for example, why most jobs dominated by women (child care workers, secretaries, teachers, librarians, etc.) pay substantially less than those dominated by men despite higher average educational attainment required in the "female jobs." Moreover, "female" jobs in small firms in competitive industries will tend to pay even less over time, even if their relative skill levels have risen. In addition to these easily measured determinants, wage setting is also affected by such hard to measure factors as changes in collective bargaining laws, changes in enforcement of government regulations affecting earnings and conditions of work, and changes in labor-management relations.

Consistent with many earlier studies, recent scholarly work by Lawrence Summers and Lawrence Katz found that similar workers in the same occupations are paid substantially different wages in different industries. My own research with Edward Wolff, using data from the *Dictionary of Occupational Titles*, found that the wage distribution was not a good proxy for the skill distribution at the occupation or industry level, whether skills are measured by cognitive skills, motor skills or interactive ("people") skills. The link was particularly weak for nonsupervisory occupations. In short, skills help determine individual wage levels, but so do a lot of other factors.

Economists agree that raising real earnings requires raising the rate of productivity growth. As the 1994 *Economic Report of the Presidents* states, "Periods of rapid productivity growth have been accompanied by increases in real wages." What the report doesn't say is that this relationship did not hold in the 1980s. As the accompanying figure demonstrates, manufacturing wages grew with productivity between 1967 and 1973, continuing a trend that began with the postwar boom. But manufacturing wages have stagnated since 1973, despite productivity growth in the 1980s that compares favorably to anything we've seen since the 1950s. Despite the introduction of productivity-enhancing technology such as optical scanners, the wages of retail sector workers have dropped even more dramatically.

SOURCES OF INEQUALITY

Additional evidence on the imperfect link between wages and skills can be found in the earnings inequality literature. Attempts to account for the unprecedented increase in male earnings inequality throughout the 1980s have naturally turned to measures of skill. If the wage distribution mirrors the skill distribution, persistent growth in earnings inequality within industries should be associated with widening skill differentials. But the data show little support for this expectation. Confirming earlier research by economist Lynn Karoly, Susan Wieler, a research associate at the Center for Education and the Economy at Columbia University, found that changes in the variation of educational attainment and work experience do a poor job of accounting for the steady increase in earnings inequality within industries observed in the 1980s. Wieler went one step further and examined the effect of changes in the mix of cognitive, interactive and motor-skill requirements on the job from the *Dictionary of Occupational Titles* on earnings inequality. Examining 33 industries between 1973 and 1990, she found no statistical effect at the industry level in either decade. Unlike the substantial widening of the *wage* distribution in the 1980s the dispersion of *skill* requirements was unchanged in the 1980s, even among technologically advanced manufacturing industries.

If demand for skills is not increasing as fast as the standard account suggests, perhaps the problem is that workers are getting dumber. However, according to a 1990 report from Educational Testing Service, 83.5 percent of white 17 year old high school students in 1971 read at "intermediate" or higher levels; this figure rose to 87.3 percent in 1980 and 89.3 percent in 1988. Even more impressive were the results for black students, who increased from just 39.7 percent in 1971 to 76 percent in 1988. Yet, real wages for young black men—even those with a college degree—declined over this period.

In the 1980s, higher skills have simply not led to higher wages. In industry after industry, average educational attainment rose while wages fell. Indeed, wages fell more rapidly for young workers, despite their higher educational attainment. Young workers (16-39) in the stone, clay, glass and primary metals industry showed a 9 percent decline in workers with a high school degree or less, but a 76 percent increase in those paid an hourly wage below that necessary to keep a family of three 50 percent above the poverty line.

The communications industry saw its low-skill share decline by 33 percent and its low-wage share increase by 33 percent. Even more dramatically, the automobile industry's low-skill employment share declined by 6 percent despite its low wage share growth of 142 percent. Goods industries with high-wage, low-skill workforces appear to have restructured in the early 1980s by radically lowering wages and gradually raising skill requirements—in short, by moving in the direction of the typical service sector workplace.

MASSIVE SKILL RESTRUCTURING?

Much of the attraction of the skills-mismatch story lies in its consistency with both the observed declines in the relative wages of low-skill workers in the 1980s and the popular vision of the effects of computer-based mechanization in the workplace. In the new "high performance" workplace, workers must possess the cognitive and diagnostic skills necessary to perform a broad range of frequently changing tasks. Computers and related technologies require higher skills and workers with obsolete or insufficient skills inevitably get paid less and ultimately lost their jobs, leaving behind a more skilled workforce. This transformation is undoubtedly underway. But was the demand for higher skills in the 1980s substantially greater than in earlier decades? And does it explain the wage collapse?

In a recent study of changing employment shares in manufacturing, Eli Berman, John Bound, and Zvi Griliches call attention to a sharp increase in the ratio of non-production to production workers and attribute this "skill" restructuring to computer-based technological change. Interestingly, the change in this ratio over time shows that virtually all of the "skill upgrading" took place in just 3 years—the recession years 1980, 1981 and 1982. Although the authors note that employers use recessions to restructure, there is no evidence of a substantial shift in skill mix (as they measure it) in the 1990-91 downturn. If the technology-induced skill mismatch hypothesis story is right, why would new workplace technologies cause a sharp skill restructuring between 1980 and 1982 but not between 1983 and 1992, when the latter period was characterized by a far higher rate of investment in computer-based equipment?

In fact, there was great stability of skill mix in manufacturing after the recessions of 1980-82. Between 1983 and 1988, the ratios of craft to semi-skilled workers, technicians to clerical workers, and professionals to managers remained virtually unchanged. And the ratio of craft workers to laborers actually *declined* steadily from about 4 to 1 in 1983 to to 3.4 (it then rose slightly to 3.5 in 1988). These figures do not suggest the kind of skill restructuring that could explain the enormous earnings decline suffered by low-skill workers or the considerable widening of the earnings gap between low- and high-skilled workers observed in the last decade.

In recent research with Maury Gittleman, an economist at the Bureau of Labor Statistics, I allocated private sector workers to 621 jobs and grouped these into six job contours and three labor market segments based on a variety of measures of job quality using a statistical technique known as cluster analysis. We found that the worst jobs, labelled the "secondary segment," included 39 percent of the workforce in 1979. This share remained almost constant in the 1980s, falling slightly to 37.9 percent in 1990. The major restructuring that we found was not at the bottom, away from secondary jobs, but away from the middle—good nonsupervisory jobs—and towards the best white collar jobs. Most these shifts took place between 1979 and 1983, well before most of the investment in computer-based technologies.

Over the long term, there has doubtless been a gradual increase in the demand for more highly skilled workers. As the renowned economist Fritz Machlup pointed out back in the early 1960s, the increase in the demand for information workers—those with relatively high cognitive skills—dates to at least the turn of the century. Indeed, as my own research with Edward Wolff indicates, the share of semi-skill and low-skill manual workers in total employment declined substantially in each decade from 1950 to 1980.

But in contrast to the skill mismatch story, the evidence does not indicate an acceleration in skill upgrading in the 1980s. Indeed, my own studies with Wolff, as well as research by Lawrence Mishel and Ruy Teixera using detailed occupational employment data matched to *Dictionary of Occupational Titles* skill measures show a *deceleration* in skill growth between the 1960s and 1980s. Using different data and methods, economists Kevin Murphy and Finis Welch, writing in the *American Economic Review*, concluded that "we do not find that the demand for skill grew particularly rapidly during the 1970s and 1980s, a period when wage inequality expanded in comparison to the three earlier decades...." Similarly, Lawrence Katz, chief economist of the U.S. Department of Labor, has noted that "estimates of within- and between-industry demand shifts indicate little or no acceleration in the 1980s" and suggests that "differences in the 1970s and 1980s depend substantially on differences in relative supply shifts."

The 1990 Report of the Commission on the Skills of the American Workforce, "America's Choice: High Skills or Low Wages!," despite its vivid title, found that only 5 percent of firms surveyed were actually concerned about a skill shortage. This is consistent with the key finding of a new study on international competitiveness by a prominent commission, assembled by the McKinsey consulting firm and headed by Professor Robert Solow of MIT, that it was not primarily skills or technology that distinguished productivity rates among nations, but rather management and labor relations policies. Based on the recent practices of employers, a more apt description might be "High Skills *and* Low Wages."

TAKING THE LOW ROAD

The more convincing explanation for the wage collapse is the intensifying product market competition and the ideological shift away from government intervention and towards laissez faire. These developments undermined traditional wage setting institutions, leading to a declining willingness to pay low- and moderate-skill workers "living-wage" paychecks. At the same time a slower growth and globalization led to an oversupply of workers competing to perform low- and moderate skill jobs.

At the end of the 1970s, firms began to fundamentally reassess their employment and wage-setting practices. Large integrated (high-wage) firms began to downsize and rely more heavily on low-wage suppliers. Advances in telecommunications and transportation facilitated the relocation of lower-skilled operations to low-wage sites, leaving behind a core of permanent, relatively skilled employees supplemented increasingly by part-time and temporary workers.

Consistent with this alternative account, George J. Borjas and Valerie A. Ramey have argued that much of the increase in earnings inequality in the 1980s can be traced to the erosion of "rents" earned by low-skilled workers in concentrated industries—an erosion they attribute to increased foreign competition in durable goods manufacturing. The show that trade competitiveness in this sector has closely mirrored trends in wage inequality since the 1970s. A 1993 study by Maria Papadakis underscores the role of durable goods industries in the worsening of the trade balance in the early 1980s. She reports that the trade balance shifted from a $3.6 billion surplus in 1982 to a $67.8 billion deficit just two years later. By 1987 the manufacturing trade deficit rose to $125 billion. She attributes about 55 percent of the increase in the trade deficit to four durable goods industries that pay relatively high wages: motor vehicles (24.5 percent, nonelectrical machinery (14.7 percent), electronic equipment (9.7 percent) and electrical machinery (5.5 percent).

Other economists, including Paul Krugman and Robert Lawrence, argue that trade shifts do not account for the bulk of the wage collapse. These studies, however, focus exclusively on various indicators of import penetration and export shares, and not on how trade patterns affect labor's bargaining power.

By the 1980s, concession bargaining had become widespread. According to labor economist Daniel Mitchell, the proportion of workers with private-sector union contracts whose wages were frozen or cut ranged from 0 to 5 from 1964 through 1980, rose to 8 percent in 1981, jumped to 44 percent in 1982 and 37 percent in 1983. While dropping to 23 percent in 1984 and 26 percent in 1985, by historical standards these rates have remained at remarkably high levels. In the eminently mainstream *Brookings Papers on Economic Activity,* Mitchell describes the increasingly confrontational approach of employers:

> [T]he longevity of the (wage) concession movement and its spread to less-than-dire situations suggest that the initial concessions have encouraged other employers to try their luck in demanding similar settlements. ... Management, cheered by what is perceived as a shift in the balance of power, has changed its bargaining goals...

Downsizing often works in tandem with wage concessions. For example, General Motors has recently agreed to sell most of its ownership in three plants employing some 2,000 employees. These workers, currently covered by a UAW contract that guarantees them the same wage as assembly line workers, will have to negotiate a separate agreement with the new company at the end of the contract, virtually guaranteeing wage concessions in the near future.

Another way to reduce labor costs is to substitute part-time and temporary workers for permanent full-time workers. The temporary help industry grew eight times faster than employment in all non-agricultural industries between 1978 and 1985 and increased from 620,500 workers in 1984 to 1,031,500 in 1989.

While the same technological advances have been occurring in Canada and Western Europe, there has not been a comparable collapse of wages. A key difference, of course, is that unions and other wage setting institutions remain much stronger in other industrial nations. Labor economists John DiNardo and Thomas Lemieux have compared wage inequality trends in Canada and the U.S. in the 1980s. Despite the similar labor markets, DiNardo and Lemieux find that "during this period, union density fell precipitously in the United States but declined very little in Canada. Similarly, the real minimum wage declined by 23 percent in the United States but by only 12 percent in Canada...We find that unions and the minimum wage accounted for 80 percent of the difference in the growth of inequality in the two countries." Another study, by Gary Loveman and David Blanchflower, concludes that unions and the minimum wage help to explain the different experiences of France (low inequality growth) and Great Britain (increasing wage inequality) during this period.

Moreover, our national social policies have undermined traditional wage-setting norms in the private sector. The U.S. continues to rely heavily on employers to provide health insurance, pensions, child care, and other fundamental benefits—benefits that appear as labor costs to employers. These costs are assumed by the public sector in most other developed countries. As the costs of benefits rise, our "privatized" benefits system encourages employers to substitute part-time and temporary low-wage jobs. This magnifies the gap between primary and secondary labor market jobs, increasing both the share of low earners and wage inequality.

The undermining of traditional wage-setting institutions has lowered wages for those with the least bargaining power in the labor market, thus increasing inequality between skilled and unskilled workers. It may have also tended to increase wage inequality among workers in the same education, age, and gender group in the same industry. While the conventional view is that technological change has increased the demand for skill, leading to an increased premium for "unobserved skills" within these groups, it may be that the de-institutionalization of the labor market has had a greater effect. Wage norms appear to have broken down *within firms* (as internal labor markets are opened up to external competition), *within industries* (as increasing competition causes differences among firms to become a more critical factor in wage outcomes), and *among communities* (as transportation and telecommunications facilitate the relocation of some, but not all, firms to lower wage areas). In short, the "law of one price" that supposedly characterizes free markets may have been undermined, not promoted, by the heightened competition in labor markets.

CROWDED LOW-WAGE JOB MARKETS

Today, more workers are crowding into a pool of "secondary" jobs that remained a fairly constant share of total jobs throughout the 1980s, tending to lower the wages of what were already the worst jobs in the labor market. One source of this crowding is displacement from high-wage blue-collar jobs. According to a recent Department of Labor study by Diane E. Herz, more than 4.3 million workers were displaced during the boom years of 1985-89. Only 72 percent had been re-employed by January 1990 and of these, about 10 percent worked part-time. Among those re-employed full-time, about 40 percent earned less in current dollars than on their previous job. Not surprisingly, those least successful in the labor market after displacement were high-wage blue-collar men.

There has also been a stream of highly educated workers forced to compete in the low-skill, secondary labor market. Despite the rising *average* premium for a college degree relative to a high school degree in the 1980s, a weak job market has forced many lower-level white-collar workers with college degrees to compete for relatively low-skilled jobs. This became particularly pronounced at the end of the decade, during the "white-collar recession" of 1990-91. The same computer-based technologies and corporate restructuring have made large numbers of middle-level managers redundant. According to the U.S. Labor Department, throughout the 1980s about 20 percent of college graduates were working at jobs that don't normally require a degree, and this is expected to increase to 30 percent at the end this decade. The share of black and Hispanic college graduates with poverty-level wages rose dramatically in this decade, from about 9 percent to just under 15 percent. One consequence of declining opportunities for moderately skilled white-collar jobs has been to increase competition, contributing a downward pressure on their wages.

Relocation of operations to low-wage, high unemployment regions has also contributed to a rising *effective* supply of labor. This shift to lower-wage labor markets, and not a search for more highly-skilled workers, is behind most recent relocation decisions. For example, according to spokespersons of Pratt and Whitney, the firm's decision to relocate as many as 9,000 high paying production jobs from a high-skill state (Connecticut) to lower-skill states (Maine and Georgia) was expressly designed to reduce labor costs.

Not long ago, it was an article of faith that new foreign workers were a net plus for the U.S. economy. They did unpleasant jobs at low wages, which native-born Americans were unwilling to perform, and had little downward effect on prevailing wages. That story is no longer accurate. At a time of extraordinarily high levels of nonrecessionary unemployment and declining real wages for low-skill workers, the flow of low-skill (legal and illegal) foreign workers into the U.S. reached record levels in the 1980s. According to Vernon M. Briggs the *counted* foreign-born population was 9.6 million (4.7 percent) in 1970 (6.2 percent) in 1980, and 19.8 million (7.9 percent) in 1990. A recent study by Borjas, Freeman and Katz found that the combination of rising imports and growing numbers of low-skill foreign workers had substantial negative effects on the relative earnings of native low-skill workers. The authors concluded that "between 30 percent and 50 percent of the… decline in the relative weekly wage of high school dropouts from 1980 to 1988 can be attributed to trade and immigration flows." Federal immigration policy, at least until 1990, helped supply an already overflowing pool of low-skill workers.

Case study evidence also suggests that, particularly in large urban centers, increased competition from recent immigrants has had negative employment impacts on native-born workers. In his study of the Los Angeles restaurant and hotel industry, Roger Waldinger concluded that "the story of black displacement in restaurants and hotels can be traced not to skill upgrading, but rather to competition with rapidly growing immigrant population." Similarly, a General Accounting Office study found that "Janitorial firms serving downtown Los Angeles have almost replaced their unionized black workforce with non-unionized immigrants." Again, it appears to have been labor costs, not skill restructuring, that explains this replacement of black with immigrant workers. A study by Katherine Newman, an urban anthropologist at Columbia University, found that despite a 25 percent decline in the value of the minimum wage in the 1980s, there was intense competition for minimum wage jobs in two fast food restaurants in Harlem. Over the first six months of 1993, over 400 people applied for 50 jobs in these establishments. Only a handful of the job winners were high school dropouts. Half had high school degrees, about one-quarter were currently enrolled students, and the remainder were mainly foreign-born adults.

In sum, much of the low-wage problem appears to be just the reverse of that proposed by the technology-induced skill mismatch hypothesis: in the face of mounting competition, employers have reduced unit labor costs and increased flexibility in the production process by following the "low road"—lower wages, little training, and fewer permanent employees. This strategy has been facilitated both by the undermining of traditional wage-setting institutions and regulations, such as unions, labor relations laws and the minimum wage, and by an increasing supply of workers forced to compete for low-wage jobs. Since the late 1970s, federal and local government policies have played a central role in both of these developments, and in so doing have contributed to the adoption of low-wage competitive strategies by many private sector employers.

Few will, or should, oppose the Labor Department's "get smart" policies for workers, but the reality is that changes in the ability of workers to provide the skills needed in technologically advanced workplaces had little to do with the startling growth in poverty-wage jobs, the drop in real earnings, and the growth of earnings inequality in the 1980s.

We do need to improve our education and training system, but making workers smarter will not, by itself, have much impact on the distribution of earnings. Training policies can only be relied upon to pay off for workers in a high-employment context. In addition to a better educated workforce, we need policies and strategies—both macroeconomic and structural—to restore labor bargaining power so that workers with rising skills in an economy with rising productivity will again command rising wages.

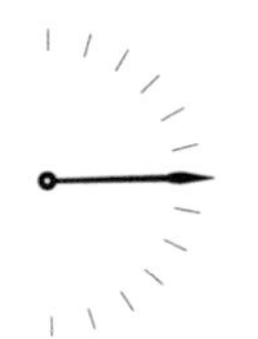

The Surrender of Economic Policy

James K. Galbraith

There is a common ground on economic policy that now stretches, with differences only of degree, from the radical right to Bill Clinton. Across the spectrum, all declare that the main job of government is to help markets work well. On the supply side, government can help, up to a point, by providing education, training, infrastructure, and scientific research—all public goods that markets undervalue. But when it comes to macroeconomic policy, government should do nothing except pursue budget balance, and leave the Federal Reserve alone.

To accept a balanced budget and the unchallenged monetary judgment of the Federal Reserve is, by definition, to remove macroeconomics from the political sphere. Thus, the remaining differ-ences between Clinton and the Congress are over details. Should we head for budget balance in seven years, eight, or ten? Should we cut (or impose) this or that environmental regulation? Do Head Start, the AmeriCorps, and technology subsidies justify their cost? And so on, in long litanies that no one believes will make a fundamental difference in American lives. Even if there were substantial gains to be made by public investments on the supply side, the conservative fiscal consensus precludes them by denying the resources.

We have now seen two Democratic presidents—Carter and Clinton—deeply damaged because they did not dispute this orthodoxy in good time and therefore could not control the levers of macro policy. Macroeconomics, not microeconomics, is the active center of power. Practical conservatives understand this. It is no accident that conservatives always seek to control the high ground of deficit and interest rate policy, nor any surprise that liberals defeat themselves from the beginning when they concede it.

Yet, the economics behind this consensus is both reactionary and deeply implausible. It springs from a never-never-land of abstract theory concocted over 25 years by the disciples of Milton Friedman and purveyed through them to the whole profession. Liberals—and anyone else concerned with economic prosperity—should now reject this way of looking at the world.

THE RIGHT-WING CONSENSUS ON EMPLOYMENT AND INFLATION

The conservative macroeconomic creed is built on three basic elements. They are, first, *monetarism*—the idea that the Federal Reserve's monetary policy controls inflation, but has little effect on output and employment except perhaps in the very short run. Second, there is *rational expectations*, which is the idea, for which Robert Lucas just won the Nobel Prize, that individual economic agents are so clever, so well informed, and so well educated in economics that they do not make systematic errors in their economic decisions, especially the all-important choices of labor supply. And third, there is *market clearing*: the idea that all transactions, including the hiring and firing of workers, occur at prices that equate the elemental forces of supply and demand.

Taken together, these assumptions conjure an efficient labor market that yields appropriate levels of employment and wages. The employment level generated by this abstraction is the core policy concept of mainstream macroeconomics, known as the natural rate of unemployment. (Some economists prefer the term nonaccelerating inflation rate of employment or NAIRU. The idea is essentially the same. The natural rate/NAIRU was introduced to supplant the older Phillips Curve idea of a static trade-off between inflation and unemployment, and to suggest that inflation would not only rise but inevitably accelerate, if unemployment falls too low.) If unemployment is above the natural rate, the theory dictates that prices and wages will fall. If unemployment is below the natural rate, the theory dictates that inflation will rise. Sustainable, noninflationary employment growth occurs only at the natural rate. [See Robert Eisner, "Our NAIRU Limit: The Governing Myth of Economic Policy," *The American Prospect*, Spring 1995.]

Among most economists these ideas are amazingly noncontroversial. The only dispute is over a narrow point of policy— whether there is any value in attempts to steer the economy toward the natural rate if it happens to be, for a time, either above or below it. To the strictest natural-raters, doing nothing is always and everywhere the right prescription, because the economy will always return to the natural rate on its own. Policy cannot help, and the very instruments of macro policy should be abandoned.

The self-described "New Keynesian," a breed found throughout the Clinton administration, believes a vestigial role for macro policy can be preserved. Unemployment may persist above the natural rate because wages take more time than other prices to adjust to changes in supply and demand, leading to failure of the labor market to "clear." That being so, there may be no harm in policy measures—a little stimulus now and then when there is a serious recession—to speed the return to the natural rate so long as a "soft landing" is carefully engineered.

Alas, the location of the natural rate is not actually observed. Worse, the damn thing will not sit still. It is not only invisible, it moves! This is no problem for the never-do-anything crowd. But it poses painful difficulties for would-be intervenors, those few voices in the administration who call, from time to time, for summer jobs, public works programs, and lower interest rates. How can one justify a dash to the goalposts, if you don't know where they are? New Keynesians obsessively estimate and re-estimate the location of the natural rate, in order to guide their policy judgments. Sadly, they have never yet been able to predict its location, which may be one reason why there has never yet been a successful "soft landing."

WHERE IS THE NATURAL RATE?

To the (questionable) extent that the Federal Reserve has any coherent macroeconomic theory, it tends to be implicitly New Keynesian on this issue. That is, the Federal Reserve Board is an inveterate intervenor, raising interest rates when unemployment is too low, and lowering them, grudgingly, to end or sometimes to avoid recessions. And so the Federal Reserve also spends a good deal of time and effort trying to pin down the phantom and elusive natural rate.

In 1994, with the natural rate estimated by numerous astrologers at about 6 percent, monetary policymakers faced an interesting problem.

Actual unemployment, now at 5.8 percent, had fallen below the estimated natural rate. So how then to interpret the rest of the data, which contrary to theory showed no evidence of accelerating inflation? Did the apparent lack of inflationary acceleration mean that the natural rate had perhaps fallen, and if so to what value? Or, had the barrier been broken and, in Robert Solow's phrase, was inflation "acceleration just around the corner"? Or again, was the whole theory rotten and fit for the garbage?

The Federal Reserve proved unwilling to change its estimate of the natural unemployment rate. So it tightened monetary policy, from February 1994 through early 1995, as the economy broached the 6 percent unemployment barrier. But then the Federal Reserve shifted course and started cutting interest rates in July 1995, even though unemployment remained below 6 percent. Why? It will be interesting to learn, when the full minutes are released, whether the Federal Reserve formally changed its estimate of the natural rate in July of 1995, and if so, on what ground and to what number. Or we may learn that the Federal Reserve doesn't really have a natural rate theory anymore, but is only holding on to the rhetoric of these ideas, for want of any alternative that ideological conservatives might accept.

The components of today's low inflation rate are not at all consistent with the natural rate theory. No part of present inflationary pressure, such as it is, stems from wages. Wage compensation, two-thirds of all costs, remains flat. The whole of today's modest inflation stems from a boom in profits and investment income, and from the effects of this boom on commodity prices and other incidentals of the inflation process. There has also been some contribution from the rising interest costs imposed since February 1994 by the Federal Reserve's own policy.

The old relationship between inflation and labor costs really has busted up since Reagan fired the air traffic controllers and he and Volcker overvalued the dollar. Prices may be rising at 2.7 percent annually, but real wages are scarcely moving. Indeed we find that all inflation accelerations after 1960, with the sole exception of that following Richard Nixon's election campaign in 1972 (when price controls were in force), were led by prices and not by wages.

THE NOMADIC AIRU

How is all of this to be reconciled with a theory of inflation acceleration based exclusively on the natural rate of unemployment in an aggregate labor market? It can't be done. If there is excess demand for labor, surely a good (new) classical economist must insist that real wages are rising. But they aren't—and haven't been in 20 years. Something must be wrong with the natural rate model. (Good economists at the Federal Reserve know this, and it bothers them, as it should.) In fact, something is more than wrong with the model. The model is junk, as we should have known long ago.

In the 1950s the unemployment rates at which inflation accelerated were low, in the 1970s, quite high. But recent data rather resemble the 1950s again, which would indicate that there is room for unemployment to come down without kicking off inflation. Depending on how you factor in the high-inflation decade of the 1970s, an honest estimate of the natural rate—even if you believe it—might be 6 percent or much lower.

The search for a natural rate really is fruitless. Rising inflation is essentially unpredictable: The shocks that cause it sometimes happen at high unemployment, sometimes not until unemployment is quite low. There is no sign in recent data of rising inflation as unemployment falls.

Indeed, the pattern of widening gyres reversed itself after the deep recession of 1982. Through the rest of the 1980s, unemployment fell without wage pressures and without sharp rises in inflation. The recession of 1989 hit while inflation was low by historic standards. And in the past four years, 1992 through 1995, there has been falling unemployment with falling unit labor costs and no rise whatever in inflation (see the horizontal ellipse). We do not know where the nomadic accelerating inflation rate of unemployment (AIRU) is today—because we don't know when the next shock might hit us. So why not go for full employment?

LIBERALS LOST ON THE SUPPLY SIDE

At the very least, New Keynesian acceptance of the New Classical theoretical structure reduces macroeconomic policy to the fringe role, that of large-scale intervention only in deep and lasting recessions. In all other circumstances, the macro authorities are warned off—as was Clinton himself during his brief Keynesian phase in early 1993.

What then can liberals do? The actual approach of the Clinton administration illustrates: Liberals can favor education, training, adjustment assistance, and other programs that upgrade skills and help workers move from one job to the next. They can support public investments in infrastructure, on the ground that these assist in the international competitiveness of the economy. They can support a combination of research and development assistance to advanced enterprises, alongside efforts to open foreign markets to American products, that help shore up the position of American companies in the world. If they are feeling brave, they can also support a higher minimum wage.

All of these are supply-side measures (except the last, which is a direct intervention in the labor market). Their purpose is to improve the long-term competitive performance of the American economy, on the thought that a more productive economy will generate higher average living standards. The further thought, that these higher averages will trickle down to low-paid production workers, is left as an assumption.

We can all agree that expenditures on education, training, research, development, and infrastructure are generally good things. But a macroeconomic commitment to full employment is the key to translating these investments into higher growth and living standards.

EDUCATION AND TRAINING. As work by Richard Rothstein in this journal and elsewhere has shown, the American system of public education is much better than its critics allege. To be sure, there are poorly educated Americans who are unqualified to fetch high wages in the job market. Yet as Katherine Newman and Chauncy Lennon have shown [see "The Job Ghetto," TAP, Summer 1995], there are far more qualified applicants in central Harlem than there are minimum wage jobs. In this macroeconomic climate, based on a false theory of the NAIRU, raising education standards will not call better jobs into being. That remains a demand-side problem. This does not mean we should give up on the task of improving inner-city schools. It only means that unless we also raise growth rates—indeed, even if we gave everyone Ph.D.s—so long as the Federal Reserve held the growth rate to 2.5 percent, it would not change the current trajectory of living standards. As a student of mine from Buenos Aires once cracked, if education alone were that powerful, Argentina would be much richer than it is.

RESEARCH AND DEVELOPMENT. A stronger case can be made for the idea that government R and D helps American companies become more technically advanced and more competitive in global markets. For four decades, our highly interventionist technology policy was a by-product of the Cold War. Now, a more explicit civilian technology policy may be needed to make up for reduced Pentagon R and D. There is surely a role in general terms for science and technology policy—ultimately many technologies lead to a better life. But they do not and cannot bring full employment, nor do they bring about a fairer and more just social order. To make science and technology policies the centerpiece of a progressive agenda, while giving up macroeconomics, is absurd.

INFRASTRUCTURE. Public works expenditure is the historical cornerstone of liberal interventionism. Public works are the fastest, most direct way to put the unemployed to work. They have direct and multiplier effects on total employment. They have the side benefit that the works themselves remain useful for many decades after they are completed. They also represent, in political memory, the triumph of liberalism in the first New Deal.

But the liberal supply-siders make an entirely different claim for public works spending. Renaming it "infrastructure," (as I too have done on many occasions) they argue that it contributes in definite ways to the productivity of the private business economy. The jobs created directly, by doing the work, are immaterial to this argument. What matters is how the finished work contributes indirectly to cost reduction and increased output in the private sector.

The evidence that such effects exist is, alas, regrettably thin. Almost all of it rests on aggregative statistical relationships, essentially on the bare fact that average measured productivity growth declined during the same years that saw cutbacks in gross public investment. Almost none rests on detailed analysis of the contribution of particular projects to business efficiency.

And this is not surprising. While America might well benefit from more public investments on public-amenity grounds, export-oriented American manufacturing enterprise is evidently not hamstrung by infrastructure problems. Roads, rail, electricity, and water service are adequate to their needs. Boeing is not short of runways from which to launch its planes, nor is Silicon Valley suffering brownouts. Phones work well in this country—we even have the Internet! Pollution costs do not necessarily fall on private business producers, but on their neighbors.

Infrastructure and associated environmental spending is undoubtedly of enormous need and value. But to whom? To the American citizen, as an element in the standard of living. Roads, water, sewer, power, and communications systems are all durable public consumption goods. It is consumers and workers, not the main business shippers, who hit the potholes on the road to work. It is people who breathe the air, drink the water, and boat on the rivers and lakes. All this has little to do with international competitiveness—which is very sad, but true. This explains why business interests are not demanding higher infrastructure spending and why these items were the first to fail in the face of Republican opposition in the Congress.

We are left with the unpleasant conclusion that the liberal mainstream has fallen into a self-deluding trap. The right has taken over the commanding heights of both fiscal and monetary policy, leaving liberals with token sums to spend on supply-side interventions. Education, training, and infrastructure are very important, but not for the reasons usually given. Business won't support funding them at levels that liberals desire, and it is wishful to argue to business that they should. We must find, instead, a language in which to defend them for the sake of the people themselves, and organize the people around them for the vital direct benefits they bring (as indeed the environmental, consumer protection, and health and safety movements have traditionally done). Otherwise they will continue to lose the budget battles.

And if we want full employment, we need something else—a full employment macroeconomics.

MACRO POLICY IN A STRUCTURALIST WORLD

Conservatives employ the myth of the market to oppose political solutions to distributive problems. But to leave things to the market is no less a political choice than any other.

Suppose the concept of an aggregate labor market and the associated metaphor of a natural rate of unemployment could be wiped away with a stroke from the professional consciousness (as it deserves to be). The policy notion that controlling the reduction of unemployment is the principal means of fighting inflation would lose its power. It would then become intellectually possible to revive the idea of giving a job to everybody who wants one. The issue becomes not how many jobs but rather who to employ and on what terms?

INVESTMENT AND CONSUMPTION. Creating jobs is a matter of finding things for people to do. Investment of all kinds creates jobs, and stabilization of private investment demand is the traditional macroeconomic issue. Low and stable interest rates are essential here—more on that later. Public investment can step in where private investment will not go, and should be designed and pursued for its direct benefits, not its imaginary indirect ones. But *consumption* is also an important and much maligned policy objective. People should have the incomes they need to be well fed, housed, and clothed—and also to enjoy life. Public services can help: day care, education, public health, culture, and the arts all deserve far more support than they are getting.

TECHNOLOGY. Technological renewal should be understood as part of a strategy of maintaining investment demand. It makes sense progressively to shut down the back end of the capital stock, for environmental, safety, energy efficiency, and competitive reasons. Properly designed regulation can help, and this will open up investment opportunities for new technologies. At the same time, a flatter wage structure and bigger safety net, including retraining but also more generous early retirement for older displaced workers, would reduce the cost of job loss and the resistance from affected workers. Again, this is an adjunct of high-growth macro policy, not a substitute for it.

INFLATION. Inflation policy would not go away. But the pursuit of relative price stability, rather than being the result of sluggish growth and tight money, would become concerned with the management of particular elements of cost, as the economy got closer to full employment. This includes wage pressures, and also materials prices, rent, and interest. Management of aggregate demand—an undoubted force on nonwage prices—could operate through channels with less effect on employment (a variable tax on excess profits, for example). Since wages are a major element in costs, inflation policy would be concerned with the institutional mechanisms of wage bargaining.

DISTRIBUTION. This exercise returns us to the real, inevitably political questions obscured by technical mumbo jumbo about natural unemployment rates: our overall structure of incomes and opportunities. What should be the distribution of incomes? How much range, between the bottom and the top? Between capital and labor? Between skilled and not? In my view, the present course of rising inequality must be reversed, and liberals should frankly support the political steps required for this purpose. Trade unions should be strengthened and the aggressive new organizing campaigns of the AFL-CIO strongly supported. Minimum wages should be raised. And liberals should strongly defend the progressive income tax, as well as support proposals for wealth taxation, as proposed by Edward Wolff. [See Wolff, "How the Pie Is Sliced: America's Growing Concentration of Wealth," page 74]

Once the basic distribution of income has been set right, further gains in real wages can only happen, on average, at the rate of productivity growth. But to keep the distribution from getting worse again, these gains should be broadly distributed, substantially social and only slightly industrial or individual. In other words, we need to return to the principle of solidarity—that the whole society advances together.

Higher minimum wages are especially important for this purpose. In their new book, *Myth and Measurement*, David Card and Alan Krueger argue that raising the minimum wage within a reasonable range would not cost jobs. In fact, higher minimum wages may increase employment by reducing job turnover. This is a doubly important work, once for its direct policy relevance and again because it flatly contradicts, and deeply undercuts, standard models of the aggregate labor market.

INTEREST RATES. Low and stable has to be the watchword. Interest rates should lose their present macroeconomic function, which has been to guarantee stagnation. They should serve instead to arbitrate the distribution of income between debtors and creditors, financial capital and entrepreneurship. As a first approximation, real rates of return on short-term money should be zero. And there is no reason why long-term rates of interest in real terms should exceed the long-term real growth rate of the economy. Indeed they should lie below this value, effecting a gradual redistribution of wealth away from the creditor and toward the debtor class and a long-term stabilization of household and company balance sheets. Speculation in asset markets should be heavily taxed.

DEFICITS. Ironically, the budget deficit hardly comes up in this discussion. During the postwar boom, we were a high-employment, low-inflation, low-interest-rate society with a progressive tax structure. Such societies do not have structural-deficit problems. A peacetime military budget would also greatly help. At any rate, the present fixation on balancing the budget is nonsense, as all serious economists should loudly declare.

The above, all taken together, would be a macroeconomic policy to fight for! The liberal microeconomic supply-siders can do some useful things—or think they can—by getting a little money into education, training, infrastructure. But the point is to raise living standards, to increase security and leisure, and to provide jobs that are worth having. And that requires us to reclaim macroeconomics as a major policy tool.

The Predators' Accomplice

HOW HIGH THEORY ABETTED SPECULATIVE EXCESS

Louis Lowenstein

> You are neither right nor wrong because the crowd disagrees with you. You are right because your data and reasoning are right.
>
> *Benjamin Graham*

In the 1980s some things went right on Wall Street but much went wrong. The fallout is still being felt today. Prudential Securities, which once boasted that "the most important thing we earn is your trust," now apologizes for having systematically duped many of the hundreds of thousands of investors who bought its limited partnership deals. Carl Icahn boasted of having bought TWA; but leaving none of his own money there, he succeeded only in leaving the flying public with 20-year-old aircraft and poor service. Banks and insurance companies bankrolled so many new buildings that we will not work off the excess until the end of the century, if then. As we close the books on the worst era in modern U.S. financial history, Prudential at least has the resources to make amends. The victims elsewhere must often grasp at straws.

This is a good time for a postmortem. It is not widely recognized, but scholars played an important role in the debacle, providing ingenious free-market theories to justify some of the worst excesses. One such concept, "efficient market theory," contributed to the damage then, and in its various mutations continues to do so today.

Even if you're not a student of financial economics, the phrase "efficient market theory" sounds right. After all, the stock market *is* crudely efficient; markets set the minute-to-minute value of stocks, the spreads between bid and asked prices are very small, and commissions are as little as two cents per share.

Efficient market theory (EMT), however, posits something more radical. The principal version, and the one on which this indictment will focus, states that we can trust the pricing of stocks. Supposedly, competition among sophisticated investors enables the stock market to price stocks "accurately"—that is, in accordance with our best expectations of companies' long-term prospects. (The trading by nonprofessionals is said to be random and of no net effect.) Supposedly, all relevant publicly available information is analyzed by investors, and new data, such as an earnings release, are quickly noted, digested, and then reflected in the share price.

In short, stock prices, while not perfect, are as perfect as can be. There are no better estimates of the fundamental value of a company and no systems for beating the market. A corollary is that while the wisest of us can do no better than to buy the market as a whole, the rest of us can do far worse.

EMT rests on several controversial assumptions, the most striking of which is the terribly convenient but circular assumption that mispriced stocks cannot long exist because if they did, "smart money" investors and arbitrageurs would already have eliminated them. This when-all-else-fails assumption, so central to the theory, is also the source of the well-worn joke about two economists walking across campus who spy what looks like a $20 bill. As the younger economist leans forward to examine it, her older colleague admonishes her. "If it really were a $20 bill, someone would already have picked it up."

Given the assumption that patience and intelligence are of no consequence, even a super-investor like Warren Buffet should not be able, certainly not with any consistency, to find loose money lying on the table. In fact, it is a waste of his time to look.

The defendant, EMT, is hereby indicted. The indictment is limited to four counts. EMT, we shall see, is guilty of:

- Providing the intellectual cover for the excesses in junk bonds and takeovers in the 1980s, ignoring the mounting evidence that important sectors of the economy and innocent bystanders were in jeopardy;
- Encouraging investors to indulge the fantasy that they can "trust prices" to balance risk and reward and thereby save themselves the enormous bother of analyzing actual businesses;
- Aiding and abetting the efforts of the Business Roundtable and similar interest groups to strip voting and other fundamental shareholder rights from stock ownership and have them treated as saleable bits of private property; and

- Justifying a theory of dividend policy that encourages wasteful corporate investment and expansion.

The result is that our financial markets have become increasingly desocialized, shuffling bits of paper and computer analytics in response to their own internalized signals, with too little regard for the real companies, workers, and products that are their reason for being. As in the usual indictment, the prosecution intends to show that the damage has been heavy and that it has been recklessly or even willfully inflicted. After the defendant has been tried, and as I expect, found guilty, we will consider the motives. They will affect the sentencing. But more of that later on.

COUNT 1: PROMOTING THE "MARKET FOR CORPORATE CONTROL"

For financial economists, the merger boom of the 1980s was the stuff of dreams. Ever since 1932, when Adolf Berle and Gardiner Means first described the separation of ownership and control in the modern, publicly held corporation, observers had wrestled with the dilemma that corporate democracy did not work, that these dispersed shareholders had very limited power, and that corporate managers were able to avoid any serious oversight or discipline. Then at the beginning of the 1980s, there blossomed a shiny new economic model, affectionately called the market for corporate control, which saw the emerging takeover boom as a natural selection device for replacing the poor performers. It is an appealing model. Given an efficient stock market, of which few economists then had any doubt, poor managerial performance would drive down a company's stock price to the point where it would pay a more talented group to bid a substantial premium for control, fire the incumbents, and run the firm themselves. Indeed, in a market as efficient as the one in the model, there could be no other systematic reason for takeovers.

Glory be, the merchants of deals on Wall Street could scarcely believe their ears. Long vilified on Main Street, they were now heralded all across the scholarly landscape—and by high government officials trained by scholars—as the avenging angels of economic survival. Academics, in turn, who had never before seen their theories played out on a trillion-dollar scale, were quite prepared to testify that all of this would improve the efficiency of American industry.

In the hot summer of their triumph, scholars and their converts—none of them baptized more thoroughly than Ronald Reagan's Council of Economic Advisors as seen in their 1985 annual report—ignored the perverse incentives and palpable imperfections that drove this market, eventually to wild excess. The story has been widely told in its several variations, but the basic system for takeovers and leveraged buyouts worked like this. Take a not-too-glamorous business, but one with decent prospects, and buy it with as much borrowed money as the banks will lend. As the market heated up, however, even these standards deteriorated. The investment by the new owners became hard to find, and under the pressure to make ever more deals the prices became absurd. Structured with no room for a disappointment of any kind these takeovers left many viable businesses—typically household names—and once-loyal workers and communities on the dole. The business casualties—the walking wounded as well as the outright failures—were staggering.

REAL CASUALTIES OF MARKET THEORY

Ames Department Store
Carter Hawley Hale
Centrust Savings and Loan
Continental Airlines
Federated Department Stores
Fruehauf
Grand Union
Harcourt Brace Jovanovich
Interco
Integrated Resources
Kindercare
Lincoln Savings and Loan
R.H. Macy
Memorex/Telex
National Gypsum
Ohio Mattress
Revco Drug
SCI Holdings
Seaman's Furniture
Southland
Southmark
Telemundo
Texas Air International
Trans World Airlines
USG (Gypsum)
Jim Walter Corporation
West Point Pepperell
Zale

How did it happen? EMT provided the justification. In an efficient market, one in which the stock market could not undervalue corporate assets in any meaningful way, efficiency and productivity enhancement justifies takeovers. While this was somewhat obscured by euphemisms, such as that the takeover market is one where managers "compete for the right to manage resources," the basic implication was that higher bidders can manage assets better and that the higher share price is the measure of the prospective improvement.

On a modest scale, hostile takeovers are not a bad idea, but even at the time the gaps or the theory was evident:

- If target company managements were not striving to do the best for *their* shareholders, how sure could one be that bidder managements were doing so for their own? (Indeed the history of the already failed conglomerate era should have raised doubts.)
- The extraordinary availability of borrowed money was soon allowing promotional buyers, with no operating experience and few resources of their own, to acquire major industrial and commercial enterprises.
- The tax gains generated by the substitution of debt for equity—the elimination of the corporate income tax—alone accounted for a substantial portion of the "value" being created in these buyouts.
- There were many bids for only well-managed targets, not just for the laggards assumed by the model.
- The premium prices being paid by bidders, averaging at times as much as 80 percent over the prevailing price in the market, should have raised concerns as to the likelihood of such consistently large efficiency gains.
- The unprecedented fees charged by bankers and kindred promoters, which soon dwarfed all others on Wall Street, suggested that efficiency gains may not have been the sole or even primary object of the game.

In the late '80s, the prices for significant takeover targets, *on average*, were over 14 times earnings before interest and income taxes. That amounted to a return of 7 percent, even while the bidders were then paying on average 10 or 11 percent for capital. Alas, EMT had blinded scholars, and others, too, to what was increasingly clear in the marketplace: the deals were not making sense—to anyone but the middlemen.

With well over $1 trillion of mergers in the 1980s, one should have expected to see a high degree of market efficiency. Instead, the damage has been long lasting. In financial terms, the loss was not just the high default rate, the failed S&Ls and other direct costs, but, as a recent study by the Federal Reserve Bank of New York has shown, the continuing need for refinancings devoted less to real investments than to restoring shattered balance sheets. In human terms, it was a story of workers and middle managers who had long ago invested their careers in the various target companies of the day, but who unlike senior management could not protect themselves.

Neoclassical economists now concede that leveraged-buyout magnates like Robert Campeau, who sought control of many of the nation's department store chains, may have bid too high—hubris produces a sort of winner's curse. But the concession is little more than an effort to control the damage to their prized theory. Campeau, like many another, could buy a major company, say, Allied Stores, investing no more of his own capital than necessary to pay the (not trivial, of course) fees of the bankers and lawyers. The actual purchase price, the only money still at risk, came from a broad cross-section of the banking and financial community here and abroad. It was the hubris of this far-flung institutional market, not just a handful of manic-depressives, that accounted for the excesses. Come to think of it, given their ability to control extraordinary amounts of institutional money with few constraints—First Boston, for example, chafing for fees, virtually threw capital at Campeau—the Campeaus of the day may have been the most rational players in the game.

Remarkably enough, there has not been a single serious effort by such defenders of EMT as Harvard financial economist Michael Jensen, Nobelist Merton Miller, or other traditional finance scholars to retrace their steps, to see how it was that excessive debt increased risk, instead of merely rearranging it as their models had forecast. At best, one observes grudging concessions that mistakes were made, but we learn from our mistakes and are not likely to repeat those *particular* ones again. ("An efficient market, sir, is one in which we succumb to different illusions at different times.")

COUNT 2: OFFERING BOOZE TO PERENNIAL DRUNKS

EMT now offers up a sacramental blessing to those who would like to believe the Wall Street dogma, "Don't argue with the tape." Ever since Benjamin Graham and David Dodd, and John Maynard Keynes wrote in the 1930s, we have known that the traders and other professionals on Wall Street by and large lack the temperament to invest money on a rational, long-term basis. Graham early on, others of us later on, preached the rewards of ignoring the stock market, except when the manic-depressive behavior occasionally offered opportunities to buy or sell on an advantageous basis.

For us preachers, past and present, it is indeed discouraging to see today's scholars dignify, with complex algebraic formulas and computer run-offs, the notion that it is foolish to challenge the conventional valuation of the day's market, that thinking is a waste. Certainly we should not pick stocks.

What, defendant asks—yes, we permit a word for the defendant—has been the damage? First, it lies in the extraordinary growth of index funds. A fund manager, persuaded that stocks are as correctly priced as can be, saves herself the bother and buys the market as a whole, or an index such as the Standard & Poor's 500, as a proxy for the market. Indexers rely heavily on the history that stocks, on average and over time, have performed much better than, say, bonds. But it is a truncated view of history, one that, at best, ignores the proven importance of buying in when market values are at historically sustainable levels. Are the levels today sustainable? Sorry, the question is out of order, one that an EMT-indexer is sworn not to ask.

Indexing confounds the essential logic of a discriminating capitalism, that we move capital and assets to higher valued uses. We all know not to put all our eggs in one basket. But EMT goes far beyond the usual dictates of prudence. Quoting Keynes, who had an enviable investment record with several insurance companies and Kings College funds:

> To suppose that safety-first consists in having a small gamble in a large number of different directions...as compared with a substantial stake in a company where one's information is adequate, strikes me as a travesty of investment policy.

True, there are many roads to heaven, though I doubt there is any substitute for studying annual reports, as Buffett does in hundreds a year. But it is odd, is it not, that not one EMT theorist has seen fit to study Buffett? Since he began managing money independently 35 years ago, first at the Buffet Partnership and now at Berkshire Hathaway, during strong markets and weak, he has produced average annual rates of return of over 27 percent. For 35 years he has been steadily mining the imperfect prices that EMT says do not exist!

The response to Buffett has been either a deafening silence or a clumsy attempt to avoid the engagement. He's a five-sigma event, it is said, someone whose performance is five standard deviations superior to the norm, so that as a statistical matter he can safely be ignored.

The idea seems to be that if we believe pitchers are now so "efficient" that no one can hit .300, we should study large numbers of average hitters rather than a star who has systematically studied the pitchers and the elements of hitting and best of all is willing to impart that knowledge. Or as *The Economist* suggested in August 1992, echoing the academic dogma, in any coin-tossing contest, no matter how many rounds, someone will survive to win, but the identity of the winner is of no consequence. Thus Buffett is explained: 35 lucky flips in a row. Or a few months later, in December, that same always-in-touch journal suggested that Buffett's success is attributable to his having used the "simple trading rule" of buying shares with relatively low ratios of market price to book value. Too bad, in its eagerness, *The Economist* had not bothered to notice that among Buffett's most profitable investments have been companies such as American Express, bought in the 1960s, and Coca-Cola in the 1980s, or that he has written frequently of the irrelevance of tangible book values.

EMT and indexing also stand accused—and this is ultimately the more important aspect of the charge—of being destructive of that basic aspect of capitalism, watching the managers in the store. For an indexer, of course, stocks are homogeneous commodities, as finance teachers say, and there is no need to name the companies in the portfolio, much less know or monitor them.

A second remarkable application of EMT goes by the euphonious acronym CAPM (pronounced CAP-M). This capital asset pricing model creates for stocks a measuring stick of risk and then calculates the trade-off between risk and expected returns. Starting from the appealing principle of no free lunch, it states that not only is risk measurable but the expected payoffs, the rewards, are mechanically commensurate. Increase your risk, as CAPM measures it, and your rewards will grow apace.

Just how pervasive CAPM has become can be seen from a recent survey of mutual funds in the *New York Times*, according to which each fund falls into one of five categories of risk. How can they know, I wondered? The answer was in the footnotes to the table. The *Times*, like almost everyone else, has accepted the standard wisdom that prospective risk can be measured. The *Times* assumed the existence of precise arithmetic yardsticks for the outcomes of such palpably uncertain matters as (investments in) the global oil business, discount retailing, pharmaceuticals—and I might add, newspapers—which are subject to political, competitive, and other factors that quite clearly are not measurable.

The *Times* had used a formula derived from CAPM that measures the historic short-term volatility of stock prices. As in all versions of CAPM, the *Times* assumed that prospective long-term business risk can be measured by looking at stock market fluctuations over the *short term*—in this case, the monthly prices.

CAPM has insinuated itself into the language and framework of finance so thoroughly that terms such as "risk-adjusted" and the "beta" of a stock are widely used, usually with little comprehension of what a mischievous model underlies them. (The beta of a stock is a measure of its price volatility relative to the market index, which is set at 1.0. A stock with a beta below 1.0, therefore, is said to be less volatile and less risky than the market as a whole.) CAPM confuses the past with the future and the long with the short term. It stubbornly refuses to acknowledge that in the typical business, there is no quantifiable risk but only immeasurable uncertainty. As Keynes explained a long time ago, these are two very different phenomena.

The beta of Capital Cities/ABC is 1.0, the same as that of the market index, but what could we possibly learn from that? The company owns a variety of media properties, including newspapers and the ABC network. Do we really believe that a computer, this remembrance of stock prices past, can tell us that a business with an emerging technology and in a changing regulatory environment will be no more or less risky over the next decade than the market as a whole? Or as Keynes succinctly put it, it is not simply that the calculation would be laborious but rather that very little rational basis may exist for numerical calculation and comparison of any kind.

But wait, EMT and CAPM still go further. They say that the beta, or some similar proxy for risk, measures not just the risk but the expected returns as well. If you want better than average results, buy a bunch of super-risky, high-beta stocks, such as the new issue of the latest trendy restaurant chain or biotech startup. An extra dollop of profits will follow the beta, as the night the day. (And a good night to you.)

Encouraging money managers to substitute betas for careful research and analysis is like offering Jack Daniels to an alcoholic. It is far too tempting. The crime is that it has succeeded so well.

One of the patron saints of CAPM, Eugene Fama, recently announced that the empirical basis for it had dried up. He had not given up the search for a computerized proxy for measuring business risk, but he was now ready to look elsewhere. What followed is truly sad. Scholar on scholar, and of course, *The Economist,* too, has said, well, CAPM may not be correct, but we will continue to use it until something better comes along. And so have money managers, for whom a bad model seems to be better than none at all. How are we to think about risk, they say, without some computer-based, arithmetic proxy? While a beta may not mean much, it has the one advantage that it is readily calculable.

COUNT 3: STEALING SHAREHOLDERS' VOTES

For roughly 60 years, the one share-one vote requirement of the New York Stock Exchange set the standard, not just for companies listed on the Big Board but for the market generally. It was an accepted part of the financial landscape that if a company invited the public to invest, the public would have, share and share alike, equal voting rights. What changed was the pressure of hostile takeovers in the 1980s, which many corporate managers sought to escape by disenfranchising the public. No raider would pay a premium price for low-voting common stock, or if he did, so what? Seeing that it would lose listings to the over-the-counter market, which had no such equal-voting requirement, the Big Board decided to abandon its long-standing rule and to allow a variety of limited-voting stocks.

Companies are now issuing these dual-class common stocks in greater numbers. The Securities and Exchange Commission tried to intervene in 1988, but the courts bucked the question back to Congress. The issue is currently on the table, requiring governmental action. What to do?

One would have expected free market economists to recoil with horror at the notion of shareholders without voting rights. Without votes, the much-loved market for corporate control would dry up. Much to my surprise, and to the utter delight of the Business Roundtable, scholars proceeded to marshal complex arguments to explain that new shareholders might indeed prefer an arrangement under which they turn over their capital with one hand and agree with the other that management will never, ever be held accountable to shareholders for the use of the money.

It seems odd, but inhabiting a world of (almost) perfect competition, or at least one in which regulation is heavily suspect, many economists believe that prices reflect essentially all potentialities, however remote. As a practical matter, the controversy turns primarily on how to deal with companies that go public for the first time—initial public offerings (IPOs). These economists are saying that if investors don't get voting rights when they buy new issues, they don't pay for them; and if they don't pay for them, they have no cause to complain. More to the point, neither do the rest of us. Voting rights are private property; there is no social interest in preserving for the future the right to recall or dismiss a wayward board of directors or CEO.

Whatever the textbook value of such a laissez-faire policy, in the context of the highly irrational, volatile IPO market, it is wholly out of place. As investors scrambled to buy shares of Boston Chicken when it went public last year, they gave it a market value of $770 million, even though its projected sales (not earnings) for the year were only $44 million. Caring only that the stock was likely to be "hot," how were they conceivably going to price something as remote in value as voting rights, assuming that they thought about them at all?

The Cambridge economist John Eatwell said facetiously: "If the world is not like the model, so much the worse for the world." I have never seen it seriously argued that the IPO market is efficient, even for the basics of price and value. Compared with the ordinary stock market, itself hardly a model of rationality, the IPO market is inferior in almost all respects. Continuity of volume is missing. Security analysts don't look at IPOs, and for that and other reasons, there is a stunning imbalance of information between buyers and sellers. (Buyers rarely see the prospectus that would tell them about their *nonvoting* rights until after they have decided to buy.) Transaction costs are very high, so high that the triple commissions alone should alert us to the probability that the other attributes of a "rational expectations" market are also likely to be absent.

Over the years, there have been few good studies of IPOs. But the data are very consistent: IPOs are a bad deal; the market does not price the product (new issues) properly. IPOs are bad in absolute terms, they are worse on a time-weighted basis, and they are worse yet when compared with the market as a whole. Being risky, CAPM theory tells us that on average IPOs should outperform the market. Not so; they are a crapshoot. According to an extensive but informal 1985 study by *Forbes* of almost 2,000 IPOs between 1975 and 1985, more than half failed to show any profit from the offering price. On average the group was down 22 percent relative to the Standard & Poor's 500 stock index, and the average annual return for the group was only about 3 percent. A more rigorous 1991 study by Jay R. Ritter, in the *Journal of Finance*, produced similar results.

The defendant EMT has rested its entire case on an abstract notion of rational behavior that implies, in Herbert Simon's words, "a complete, and unattainable, knowledge of the consequences of each choice." (Surely anyone who bought the Class A shares of Resorts International a few years ago could have foreseen that a Donald Trump might someday pay $135 per share for the fully voting, but closely held Class B shares while offering only $15 per share for the Class A.)

The deeper issue here transcends the private rights of shareholders. These Smithian economists assume that shareholders own their voting rights in the same sense that they own their automobiles. Not so. They have voting rights, not to be routinely traded away in private transactions, because of a fear of power without accountability that is reflected in almost every aspect of American life and law. A "smart" economics student might think that in the political arena, votes should be for sale. Or that charitable foundations should be allowed to accumulate wealth and power indefinitely. Or that one generation should be able to forbid their descendants from breaking up their landed or other estates. But as our Anglo-Saxon traditions long ago taught us, power that is frozen for all time will soon be abused. The fact that it was flash-frozen in a market-based IPO is irrelevant.

COUNT 4: LOOTING THE DIVIDENDS

For a company on Main Street USA, owned by, say ten shareholders, the issue of when to pay dividends, and how much, would seem fairly simple. Putting to one side the question of the investors' need for current income, the central issue would be whether the surplus, freely available earnings of the company would earn more for shareholders if left in the business or if distributed to them. If the reinvestment opportunities were not particularly attractive, shareholders would rightfully expect to see substantial payouts. And even if the performance has been good, some level of dividends would probably be in order. This normal pressure to pay dividends would also be a good check on management.

Sounds obvious, but EMT enthusiasts have managed to distort even this most basic issue of whether to keep the money in the corporation or return it to the owners. Through the reductionist lens of EMT, excessive cash will have no effect on how much is reinvested, and the normal desire of shareholders for an income on their investment is seen as an "irrational prejudice." ("Not only does it seem wrong," one particularly arrogant finance consultant/professor, Stephan A. Ross, wrote, "it is difficult to believe that sensible folk could have held such beliefs.") More important, they have reinforced the obvious preference of corporate managers to do what they are only too willing to do, namely to keep dividends as low as possible.

The problem began about 30 years ago, with a paper by Merton Miller and Franco Modigliani so celebrated that the thesis they propounded now goes simply by the acronym "MM." Their concept was that the value of the company in the market should not be affected by whether the dividend rate is high or low, or even whether dividends are paid at all. Assuming among other things that a company's investment program is known, and assuming too that the financial markets are efficient, the value of the company has been fixed, and shareholders should be indifferent to whether the current earnings are reinvested at the assumed rate of return or are paid out. (What is not paid out as dividends will show up as capital gains.) Scholars speak of the MM thesis as if it were a law of physics: EMT will guarantee the "conservation of value" regardless of how the corporate pie is capitalized or distributed.

The MM thesis is a basic tenet of modern financial theory, and literally hundreds of papers and books have been written on the subject. The underlying problem—and the error—are that economists and finance people would like to think only about the impact of dividend policies on stock prices, ignoring their impact on the business itself. M&M and their followers simply assume that, whether the payout is high or low, whether the company is broke or awash in cash, the size of the corporate jet and of management's acquisition spree will remain the same. In the "rational" world of finance, the rich and poor behave alike.

Efficient-rational market theory provided the essential building block for the MM thesis and, of course, encouraged this preoccupation with market pricing. The potential for mischief here is considerable. If dividends are irrelevant, finance scholars say, to incur the tax on dividends is a waste. Better for the company to keep all the money, they conclude. CEOs, of course, will agree, many of them being only too ready to expand the present business, buy-and-try a new one, or just feel as cozy as one can only feel with plenty of cash in the drawer. EMT and its offspring, the MM theory, legitimate these self-serving preferences.

At this point, the prosecution rested. Both sides summarized their arguments. The court tried the case without a jury, and the defendant was found guilty on all counts. A summary of the prosecution's recommendations on sentencing follows:

The prosecution asked that the defendant, EMT, be given a life sentence, with no possibility of parole. (The prosecuting attorney abhors capital punishment.) The sentence would be served by denying to all proponents of EMT access to any computer data base of historic stock prices.

The reason for requesting a life sentence was the heavy damage that had been inflicted. Most of it had been inflicted willfully or at least with a reckless disregard for the consequences. With no sign of remorse, the possibility of further harm could not be ignored. As part of a rehabilitation program, the prosecution suggested that EMT and its proponents receive a daily diet of annual reports and other primary financial material.

Conventional finance, the prosecution notes, had failed to recognize, say, the takeover bubble because of its deep disdain for accounting and financial analysis. A respected finance text, Thomas E. Copeland and J. Fred Westin's *Finance Theory and Corporate Policy*, fed to once-innocent business school students, still states as dogma that "investors gain little benefit from [corporate financial statements] because they contain no new information." (Remember, the information has been "impounded"—instantly reflected—in the stock price.) Efficient market theorists failed to heed, therefore, the fact that the ratio of corporate income available for interest charges on junk bonds, which had been a reasonable if modest two-to-one at the beginning of the 1980s, had by the mid-1980s so eroded that the income was 25 percent less than the interest charges. Trusting prices, indifferent to debt, blind to the predator's ball, the den of thieves and the barbarians at the gate, they stubbornly maintained that inflated prices and extravagant levels of debt implied not folly but social gains.

In response to a question from the court about motives, the prosecution said that EMT proponents had been driven by a search for elegance, a word that crops up again and again in the literature. "Elegance" reflects economists' desire for over-arching solutions, algebraically expressed, that will provide the key to a host of issues, and in any season, rather than the messy, context-sensitive responses that most other social sciences produce. Indeed, economists tend to reject the label "social science," although that is obviously what it is.

The pattern, the prosecution continued, is not new. Friedrich von Hayek—not Keynes, Hayek!—had something similar in mind in his Nobel lecture of 1974, when he criticized economists for straining to mimic the quantitative precision of the physical sciences. In so doing, he observed, they were ignoring the fact that theirs is a complex social study in which quantitative data would be hard to come by. He might as well have been referring to CAPM and the like when he chided economists for ignoring what is important in favor of that which happens to be accessible to measurement.

The defendant was duly sentenced. When last observed, the authorities were feeding the prisoner a diet that included the writings of Buffett, Philip Fischer, Graham, and Keynes, enriched with corporate annual reports. Color had returned to its cheeks, it had gained weight and was heard repeating as a mantra, "you are neither right nor wrong because the market agrees with you."

Dismayed by what they observed, the prisoner's relatives, CAPM, and others, visited but once. They did, however, maintain contact with one another, meeting in a ritualized setting. Computers were booted up, votive candles were lit, and the following prayer was said:

EMT

We believe in thee.

We are as one,

Thy will be done.

Is the American Economic Model the Answer?

Jeff Faux

> Not too many years ago, the conventional wisdom was that Europe and Japan did it all right, and the United States did it all wrong. And everything that could be learned, we could learn from them, and indeed, they had nothing to learn from us. Now, the new conventional wisdom is just the opposite; we're doing everything right, and Europe and Japan are doing everything wrong. Neither of those positions is correct.
>
> —*Secretary of Labor Robert Reich, Detroit Jobs Conference, March 14, 1994.*

The economic elites of most advanced nations now believe that the United States offers the best model for competing in the new global economy. As commonly formulated, the argument holds that, compared with Europe, the United States has:

CREATED MORE JOBS. Thus, according to a recent commentary in the *Washington Post*:

> The record is unmistakably clear. Since 1970 the U.S. economy has generated 41 million new jobs.... By contrast, the European Union—the new name for the European Community—has created 8 million new jobs since 1970. With a population nearly a third larger than ours, it has generated only 20 percent of the jobs. Its unemployment rate is 11 percent, up from 3 percent in 1970.

LOWERED LABOR COSTS. According to the *New York Times*, the United States is now the "low-cost provider of many sophisticated products and services from plastics to software to financial services."

RESTRUCTURED ITS FIRMS, which are now expanding world market shares. As another article in the *Times* recently put it:

> After more than a decade of painful change and dislocation, many American industries are leaner and nimbler, and others have seized the

leadership of the sophisticated technologies that are ushering in the information age.

These claims are commonly offered as proof that the "American model"—deregulation, weak unions, and a minimalist welfare state—offers an exemplary competitiveness strategy for surviving in the global economy. Not surprisingly, this was the preferred model of the policy, business, and media elites who frame the discussion. Supposedly, the sooner Europe accepts the American way, the better off it will be.

But competitiveness, American-style, is the wrong goal. The right goal is high, rising, and broadly diffused living standards. And even on its own terms, the series of claims about American economic success is not supported by the evidence.

A CLOSER LOOK AT JOB CREATION

It was during the Reagan years, of course, that deregulation took hold, business was encouraged to attack unions, and the social safety net was shredded. However, the record of job and economic growth during that period leaves one less than breathless about the American model. Calculations by Larry Mishel and Jared Bernstein of the Economic Policy Institute (EPI) shows that U.S. per capita GDP growth averaged 1.5 percent from 1979-89 (the business cycle peak-to-peak period), compared with 2.3 percent for eight other leading economies for which comparable data are available. Moreover, Mishel and Bernstein decompose the data to show the share of growth resulting from increases in productivity and changes in the ratio of employment to population. The share of U.S. growth attributable to productivity was the lowest of any of the other nations, save one. Thus not only was U.S. growth in the 1980s below average; it depended much more on an increase in the proportion of its population that chose, or was forced, to go to work.

U.S. job growth during the 1980s was high relative to other nations—although lower than that of Canada and Australia, which are in general more regulated, have higher rates of unionization, and have more generous welfare states. The growth of jobs relative to the population in the United States was respectable but hardly spectacular. And it certainly does not justify the conclusion that the American economy is uniquely structured to create jobs.

Alone among the advanced nations, real wages of production workers in the United State fell from 1979 to 1989. As Bill Clinton said during the 1992 campaign, Americans were working "harder for less." At the same time, we had the Reagan/Bush deficits, which clearly were a major engine of job growth through the decade. Thus, to achieve the growth in jobs that it did, the United States had to lower the living standards for the majority of its people and quadruple its debt. This record does not support the simple-minded notion—constantly repeated and amplified by politicians and the press—that the deregulated U.S. economy outperformed the rest of the industrial nations and should therefore be the model for the coming decade. Moreover, when the U.S. welfare state was at its most expansive during the business cycle of the 1970s, American job growth was even better compared to Europe than during the cycle of the 1980s.

After 1989, the U.S. economy turned downward. During the next three years, real wages for production workers continued to decline. Deficits in 1990, 1991, and 1992 rose to 4.0, 4.8, and 4.9 percent of gross domestic product (GDP), respectively. Inasmuch as employment was stagnant over the long recession in the United States, job growth during this period certainly does not provide much evidence to support the superiority of the American model.

This brings us to 1993—the remaining year left for making the case. The federal deficit was reduced, interest rates fell, and the government contribution to the economy shrunk. Even in 1993, however, the first two quarters were quite sluggish—GDP grew at 0.8 and 1.9 percent.

This narrows the case down to the last two quarters of 1993, in which growth accelerated smartly. This was certainly a good performance, but it was not out of line with previous recoveries. In fact, if current job growth was as robust as the average for previous recoveries, the United States would have another three to four million jobs. Thus, the celebrated case for the American model rests primarily on the evidence of two quarters of elevated growth in a recovery that otherwise has been somewhat anemic.

But if the U.S. economic record has been unimpressive, hasn't the European record—particularly in employment—been even worse? According to the conventional wisdom, Europe's currently higher unemployment rates stem largely from stronger labor unions and more generous social benefits that deter flexibility and discourage work. But there is little evidence to support this argument. First, the current disparity in unemployment between Europe and America reflects different stages of the business cycle; Europe has been in recession, while the United States has been in recovery for three years. Second, European-style labor organization and social benefits have not prevented Canada and Australia from outperforming the United States in job growth. Third, the Europeans in the 1980s achieved higher levels of productivity growth than did the United States. Although the full explanation is undoubtedly complex, the observable facts suggest that higher European unemployment rates are largely the result of the macroeconomic rigidities of the German Central Bank, whose tight money policies have held Europe's job needs hostage to its inflation phobias.

SHRINKING REAL EARNINGS

The press often treats the downward pressure on living standards as if it were a mysterious phenomenon independent of the improved "competitiveness" of U.S. business, but few serious advocates of the American model would deny that lower labor costs are now reflected in economic and social pain among people who work. Nor is there much doubt that lower levels of real wages and benefits, drastic corporate downsizing and jobs-shedding, and a dozen years of efforts to undercut labor unions have been the major causes.

The pattern is by now familiar. The decline of real wages has put the squeeze on family incomes, accelerating the entry of married women into the work force and the rise of the number of people working at more than one job. Employers have expanded temporary and contingent jobs at the expense of full-time workers, reducing the cost of fringe benefits and making it harder for unions to organize. Meanwhile, full-time workers have seen their work day stretched out. Among workers in nonunion firms, it is not uncommon for much of this "overtime" to be off the clock and therefore unpaid. In the lower and middle reaches of the white-collar world, many American workers report that the 50-hour week has become a standard.

Less familiar is the breadth of the earnings deterioration. The greatest losses are hitting the less educated, the younger, the nonwhites, and the males. (Women's real hourly wages for those at the median level or above grew during the 1980s but from a much lower base, and the "gender" gap in wages remains substantial.)

But the tide of job stress has been climbing up the educational pyramid; since 1987, real hourly earnings of male U.S. college graduates have been falling as well.

Corporate downsizing has struck both blue- and white-collar America with a vengeance. According to Professor Kim Cameron of the University of Michigan School of Business Administration, 85 percent of Fortune 500 companies have downsized over the last five years and 100 percent are planning to downsize over the next five years. Yet the evidence to date is that firing workers and forcing those who are left to work harder does not usually make the company better off. At least three surveys, each covering more than 1,000 firms, found one-half to three-quarters with lower productivity after downsizing.

BENIGN RESTRUCTURING?

Promoters of the American model sometimes argue that we should not expect the deregulation of the late 1970s and early 1980s to produce results in time to be adequately measured over the business cycle of the 1980s. So they cite the relative reduction in U.S. labor costs in manufacturing that occurred from the mid-1980s on as a proxy for improved U.S. competitiveness. Typically, this is presented in terms of U.S. dollars, since in the marketplace, competitive advantage includes the effects of currency fluctuations. But the improved performance resulting from the drop in the dollar during the last half of the 1980s is hardly a measure of returning economic strength. When the numbers are adjusted for currency movements, the U.S. advantage shrinks drastically, and, vis-a-vis our major competitiveness problem, Japan, it disappears.

Overall U.S. business productivity growth actually decelerated after 1985, averaging less than 1 percent per year through 1991. In 1992, productivity rose 3.3 percent but then turned negative in the first two quarters of 1993. Again, as with the job growth argument, this rests the productivity case for the American model on the narrow evidence of the second half of 1993.

Inasmuch as the numbers are not convincing, many enthusiasts of the American model cite anecdotal evidence: the reversal of fortune of some U.S. firms that now claim to be expanding their market shares, not simply on the basis of lower labor costs but by virtue of having "reinvented" the corporation. According to this argument,

U.S. management, relatively unfettered by union rules and social restraints, has reengineered its firms to make them more efficient and better able to cope with the accelerated pace of change and intense competition of the new global marketplace.

Much of this claim is overblown, filled with the self-congratulatory hot air that diffuses through the pages of business magazines to comfort a readership anxious to be reassured that its profits do not represent a taking from society but a giving of just rewards. The vast majority of U.S. firms that have "come back" are doing so by squeezing wages, outsourcing to Mexico and other Third World countries, and forcing longer hours on their workers. There is no need for fancy explanations to understand what is going on in most of them.

Yet there is some evidence of a more benign movement to reshape U.S. firms that can empower workers and enhance job satisfaction, notwithstanding the dangers of employee manipulation that may be involved. Indeed, the greater flexibility of American managers may have enabled them to move faster in this direction than managers in Europe. Eileen Appelbaum of EPI has surveyed so-called high-performance workplaces in a number of U.S. firms and has identified cases where genuine downward redistribution of power and authority has taken place as a result of management initiatives in both union and non-union settings.

But as she has also discovered, other aspects of the American model work against this kind of transformation. The tyranny of the financial markets' short-term outlook is a critical impediment. Rather than reward firms for the improved worker-management relations that a high-performance workplace requires, Wall Street investors put a premium on ruthless labor policies that they take as signals of management's dedication to efficiency. Indeed, some U.S. firms that had launched pioneering efforts to create empowering workplaces in partnership with unions have recently reversed themselves to accommodate investors, despite hard evidence of long-term success.

Appelbaum has also found that the transformation of the workplace requires a large up-front investment in training that most firms, obsessed with the next quarter's net earnings, are not willing to make. In America, training employed workers is seen almost exclusively as a private responsibility; little public money is available to defray the costs. During his campaign, President Clinton proposed a French-style program in which a small payroll tax would be levied on corporations and then forgiven to the extent that the firms establish a qualified training program. But the proposal has been shelved because of business opposition.

Another impediment to the transformation of the workplace is the high mobility of American workers. Firms that invest in training risk seeing those investments captured by other firms that can afford to pay higher wages precisely because they have not paid for training. A low-wage, contingent-work labor market discourages loyalty to the firm even more.

THE CLINTON VARIATION

Is the Clinton administration willing—or able—to revise the American model? Its domestic efforts are encouraging, but they are hobbled by a perceived shortage of funds and a reluctance to address the deeper issues posed by global economic deregulation.

The administration, happily, is trying to move America away from the model's worst aspects—mindless deregulation, hostility toward unions, and minimalist government. In a sense, Clinton is trying to respond to the failure of the Reagan/Bush policies with a minimum challenge to business ideology. Unlike his immediate predecessors, the president and most of his economic advisors acknowledge the basic principles of Macroeconomics 101. They came into office proposing a fiscal stimulus, led by public investment. When that effort failed in the Congress, Clinton shifted to a "second-best" monetary stimulus. The White House agreed to spending cuts and tax increases to reduce the deficit on the understanding that the Federal Reserve Board would accommodate lower long-term interest rates. The Treasury Department helped by shifting its financing of the deficit away from long-term bonds, which raised their prices and lowered their yields. The policy was successful, generating good growth in the second half of 1993 that was led by interest-sensitive industries such as housing and consumer durables. But the Federal Reserve has put us on notice that it has no intention of allowing the economy to reach full employment.

There is also good news in the Clinton administration's open acknowledgement that the government has a responsibility for reducing structural unemployment. The administration has initiated the beginnings of a civilian industrial policy, which includes more support for research and development and discussions with specific industries on ways in which the government can help get new ideas to market. It is also setting up regional industrial "extension services" for the diffusion of technology to small- and medium-sized businesses—an approach inspired by the agricultural extension services that have long helped to raise agricultural productivity in the United States. On the human capital side, Labor Secretary Reich has been given a modest budget increase to expand and reorganize the federal government's training and labor market services. Extra help will go to dislocated older workers and a welcome expansion of vocational programs aimed at young people who do not go on to college. And there are the stirrings in Reich's department of the first serious federal effort to nurture programs of worker empowerment at the job site.

The bad news is that these efforts are too small scale, in both size and conception, to deal with the problems of structural unemployment. The administration's budgetary commitment to the adjustment and public investment programs falls short of the minimum needed to support its trade expansion agenda. Instead of investing more in human and physical infrastructure, the administration and Congress have agreed to a five-year budget plan that will leave the United States even further behind; the share of the GDP devoted to domestic public investments will actually decline.

Unwilling or unable to buck the deficit hawks or to force more cuts on the military, Clinton does not have the money for the investments his strategy requires. All he has left is the "cut and spend" tactic of chipping away small sums from some programs to shift to others, along with yet another variant of the hoary proposition that bringing business methods to government will somehow convince voters that the public sector will become more efficient, and therefore more loved. Some of this reordering of priorities and reorganization of agencies makes sense (although after 12 years of Reagan and Bush there is not a great deal of fat left in the domestic budget). The savings will be small, however, and the president will need to become embroiled in battles with Congress even to obtain those limited resources. A telling example is Clinton's stripped-down welfare reform proposal, which could throw more people onto the low-wage labor market and leave millions of poor people economically worse off.

Bill Clinton's sentiments toward the working middle class and the poor are clearly warmer than were those of Bush. And it is a relief to have people in government who want to improve programs and can draw on a dozen years of experiments at the state and community level. America is replete with examples of projects that have worked and people who know how to run them. But the money is too scarce for much more than small-scale activities. At best, this is so far a pilot program presidency. How much difference will it make? The distinction between a government that doesn't care and a government that cares but cannot find the money is likely to be lost on people whose financial lives, and personal lives as well, may be in tatters.

A further piece of bad news is that while Clinton is moderately interventionist in his domestic initiatives, he does not follow the same approach to global economics. In embracing the North American Free Trade Agreement and General Agreement on Tariffs and Trade with only minimal attention to global standards, the administration tries to square the economic circle by yoking economic management at home to global laissez faire.

BEYOND PAIN ALLOCATION

Both the American model of low wages and high employment and the European model of high wages and low employment are ways of allocating pain—the pain of adjustment to the brutally competitive new global economy. In the predominant view, only free trade and deregulation can generate a prosperous equilibrium. Thus, it is said, if we take the punishment now, squeeze out "excessive" wages and benefits, liquidate debt, and reduce the burden of social welfare, our companies will become leaner and meaner, move ahead of other nations, and ultimately enlarge market share and restore prosperity. This is neo-liberal folly at its most destructive.

None of those who confidently jabber on about the long-term benefits of short-term pain can answer the critical question: how long will it take? For example, economic theory, as well as common sense, tells us that when low-wage and high-wage workers are thrown into competition in the same markets with similar capital equipment, their wages will tend to converge. But the gaps are so large that the process extends far beyond the practical time horizon of economic policy. To give one example: if Mexican real wages were to grow at 4 percent per year and U.S. wages were to stagnate, it would take almost 50 years for them to equalize and, presumably, at that point for both to begin to rise together.

Although the circumstances are quite different, the current conventional wisdom is eerily reminiscent of the economic discourse of the 1930s. Economists justified a stubborn insistence on balancing public budgets in the face of large-scale unemployment on the grounds that the world had to rely on market forces to "restructure" its way out of the Depression. The economist Alvin Hansen—later a prominent Keynesian—expressed the consensus in 1932 when he wrote: "We shall come out of it only through hard work and readjustments that are painful. There is no other alternative."

But, of course, the world did not wait for market-driven restructuring. Before the forces of supply and demand could drive incomes and prices low enough to spark a revival of investment, the political reaction to economic pain set in motion the most destructive war in history. As we all know, the unemployment problems of the 1930s were solved not by market forces but by government spending that was the exact opposite of the tight fiscal strategy advocated by the economic policy intellectuals of the time.

The internal economic debates in most of the advanced nations are today driven by the question, how do we compete in this new global economy? But the verb "to compete" lends itself to many interpretations. For example, balanced trade can be achieved with high levels of unemployment. Market share in individual industries can be maintained by constantly lowering wages. And a nation can often compensate for the unattractiveness of its goods by permitting its currency value to sink. Moreover, although international trade volumes are growing more rapidly than output, the majority of what most advanced industrial nations produce is still for their own domestic market. Among the member nations of the Organization of Economic Cooperation and Development (OECD), the share of GDP represented by imports is only 7 percent in Europe, 8 percent in Japan, and just 11 percent in the United States.

We should be asking ourselves a more pertinent question: How do we achieve full employment with rising real incomes? The difference between the two questions is critical. If the primary goal is to compete, European labor market systems, which support higher wages and a shorter work week, will be seen as an obstacle to reducing labor costs. But if the point is to raise incomes, such systems may well be necessary. The U.S. model requires more people to work longer hours to maintain family incomes. It's not clear that it makes a superior contribution to human happiness and social stability compared to a European economic model in which family incomes are maintained by fewer people working less.

Indeed, it is largely a waste of time to continue pondering the so-called "tradeoffs" between high-unemployment/high-wage strategies and low-unemployment/low-wage strategies. The more important issue is how to create an international economic environment that can support a high-wage path to accelerated job creation, which would give individuals the freedom to make tradeoffs between hours of work and leisure.

The advanced industrial nations not only have problems in common; their solutions must also, to some extent, be common. In the new competitive environment, there is a limit to the ability of any one nation—even one as large as the United States—to carry out policies to raise living standards at home unless other nations are taking similar steps. The challenge is to move from "beggar-thy-neighbor" policies, in which living standards are progressively sacrificed to the goal of competitiveness, to a cooperative effort in which competition serves to raise standards everywhere.

This challenge raises a question that is mostly off the table: How will the global economy be managed? The neoliberal answer is to leave it to the market. But that answer was rejected after it failed in the 1930s. After World War II, the industrial world could not have avoided the fate that befell it after World War I without a strong government hand to regulate national economies and a strong United States to regulate the global one.

That era is over. The vacuum left by the shrinking power of the United States has been partially filled by a global financial casino increasingly driven by competition for short-term profits. The effect has been to make it virtually impossible to create full employment in most advanced nations. Long before the limits of growth are reached, the demand for labor gets choked off by central banks that raise interest rates to discourage hypersensitive investors from transferring their hot money elsewhere.

There are many paths a market economy can take to prosperity; the search for a single model is an exercise in ideology, not economic policy. The much more pressing task is to reinvent the global economy, eliminating the conditions that prevent every nation from achieving full employment at rising wages. The priority items on this agenda include:

- an agreement to dampen global financial speculation, including the imposition of an international security transfer tax as suggested by the economist James Tobin;
- a strategy to synchronize advanced nations' macroeconomic policies;
- relief for the debt burdens that still plague too many developing nations and an end to demands by the World Bank and other financial institutions that developing nations follow destructive export-led growth strategies as conditions for aid;
- an international bill of worker and environmental rights as a requirement for any nation wanting to participate in world trade and financial markets.

As a first step, the leaders of other countries should scrutinize more carefully the idea that their economies could prosper if only they were to adopt the American model to suppress labor costs. They need to take a closer look at what is happening here. A lot of ordinary Americans could give them an earful. In a recent article on low-wage jobs, the *New York Times* interviewed a husband and wife who had two jobs apiece that earned them a total of $18,000 a year. When told by the reporter that the booming U.S. economy was now generating jobs at the rate of almost two million a year, the husband responded: "Sure, we've got four of them. So what?"

Money and Influence

Senator Dole's Greatest Harvest

Glenn R. Simpson

When Senate Majority Leader Robert Dole announced his presidential candidacy April 10, his Midwest roots figured prominently in the speech. "Our problems are not too difficult to handle," he said in Topeka, Kansas. "It's just that our leaders have grown too isolated from places like Topeka–embarrassed by the values here."

It's not clear whether Dole included himself in his reference to "our leaders," but perhaps he should have. Although Dole presents himself as an advocate of political reform, he maintains one of Washington's oldest and most extensive fundraising machines. He has torpedoed past efforts at reform, and in May he brought to the Senate floor a Republican proposal to scrap public financing for presidential elections. Dole's campaigns have admitted to intentionally violating campaign laws in the past, and today an array of loosely affiliated organizations that Dole created raises large sums of money from a few wealthy interests with a stake in the senator's legislative work. The laws governing political fundraising, passed in 1974, were supposed to prevent financiers from using their donations to obtain influence with public officials. But the laws do not effectively regulate money that goes to ostensibly independent bodies–a loophole Dole appears to have successfully exploited.

In a prepared statement, a Dole spokesperson said that "there is absolutely no connection between the Dole for President campaign and any other organizations that Senator Dole supports." But a closer look at Dole's record, pieced together from public records and interviews, shows that these organizations have advanced the senator's ambitions while maintaining close ties to his campaign and Senate offices:

- Campaign America, the independent political action committee Dole founded, has promoted Dole's candidacies for the Senate and the presidency by staging events at which Dole appears; it has also provided resources that work to advance Dole's ambitions. In effect, this has allowed Dole's supporters to finance Dole's causes well in excess of what they could legally give directly to Dole's campaigns.

- The nonprofit issues foundation Dole founded, the Better America Foundation, has helped the lay groundwork for Dole's presidential bid by providing staff and resources whose work directly or indirectly advances Dole's candidacy. The foundation has regular contact with Dole's Senate staff, originally resided in Campaign America's office. and has commissioned polling by the same firm Dole's campaign uses. And unlike Campaign America, the foundation does not have to disclose its sources of funding.

- Through Campaign America, Dole accepts hundreds of thousands of dollars worth of cut-rate air travel from corporations that benefit from his legislative activities–the same corporations that also donate generously to his foundation and benefit from his legislative work.

- As documented in the New York Times and elsewhere, Dole benefited from a preferential real estate deal arranged by one of Washington's most notorious influence seekers, Archer Daniels Midland ceo Dwayne Andreas. Dole continues to accept adm money for his foundations and pac, all the while doing adm's bidding on Capitol Hill.

- In another episode already reported by the press and investigated by a congressional committee, Dole used the power of his office to aid the business interest of one of his top fundraisers, who in turn used his business interests to increase the value of Dole's own financial holdings.

Of course, the real significance of this pattern—much of which has not been previously reported—may lie not in what it says about a particular senator or even a presidential candidate, but in what it tells about our system for regulating political fundraising. Dole's story is all too emblematic of how high-profile politicians use an array of loosely affiliated PACs and nonprofits to fill their fundraising coffers, shore up loyalty among potential allies and build long-term relationships with the nation's wealthiest interests. It is also indicative of how public and the press, increasingly desensitized to conflicts of interest, are willing to give veteran politicians a free pass for sins of the past. Oddly, Dole's campaign finance history has gotten virtually no ink in the national media this election cycle. To be sure, Dole is not the only prominent public official engaged in these practices. But Dole was a pioneer of these tactics, and he remains one of the most successful at employing them.

THE SENATOR'S NEW CLOTHES

Although virtually every candidate for office poses as a man of the people, the gap between rhetoric and reality is particularly glaring in the case of Dole, a millionaire who has lived in Washington for three decades and makes his home in the Watergate complex.

Dole can talk good-government reform with the best: "When these political action committees give money, they expect something in return other than good government." Dole said in 1983, observing that "there aren't any Poor PACs, or Food Stamp PACs, or Nutrition PACs, or Medicare PACs." But even as Dole championed the reform cause, he worked behind the scenes to smother it. In December 1985, during his first term as Senate Majority Leader, Dole headed off a popular reform proposal by promising it would get a vote in 1986. Congress did vote on the bill late that year, passing PAC reforms overwhelmingly; yet Dole himself voted against the PAC limits, and—as the Associated Press put it—"he appeared in no hurry to bring the matter to the floor." Bowing to that proposal's popularity, Dole promised the Senate would vote on it for final passage in a few days. It never did.

That November, Democrats captured control of the Senate, and vowed to enact reform. Again, Dole publicly supported the effort: "I do not believe there will be any effort to stall any such legislation," he promised. But the next fall, Dole led a marathon filibuster against the Democrats' bill, declaring it an incumbent-protection measure and promoting his own plan, which would have threatened him much less.

In the new session of Congress convened in 1989, Dole again proposed campaign finance reform, as did the Democrats. "We Republicans are determined to bring grassroots politics back to the campaign scene," Dole wrote in an op-ed for *The Washington Post*. Once again, however, partisan disagreements stalled the reform drive. This time a bipartisan reform panel was convened to make recommendations, with Dole selecting half the panel's independent experts. "I do believe there is some hope we can form a bipartisan compromise based on the [panel's] recommendations," Dole said in 1990. "If we're really concerned about cleaning up the campaign sewer money, then it's about time to spray the sewer stench with a big can of Lysol."

Yet just two months later, Dole and other Republicans offered legislation that completely ignored the recommendations of their own appointees for flexible spending limits. "We can either get serious or continue to make speeches and protect the status quo on Capitol Hill," Dole said, even as he insisted he could not abide by what the bipartisan reform panel recommended. Shortly thereafter, Dole and his colleagues opted for more speeches and the status quo.

The stalemate has continued through the 1990s. In 1994, Dole and his fellow Republicans killed the Democrat-sponsored campaign finance bill, the most ambitious attempt at reform since 1974. And this year, with Dole again the Senate Majority Leader and setting his party's agenda, he has uttered hardly a word about campaign finance reform. Instead, in May Dole joined conservatives in calling for a rollback of presidential public financing, the one initiative thought by most reformers to have had any success at all.

POCKET PICKING

The most familiar part of the Dole fundraising machine is his Senate campaign committee, Dole for Senate. According to records on file with the Federal Election Commission (FEC), since 1987 the committee has raised $3.26 million, with large chunks coming in from individuals and PACs associated with a few powerful interests: the Gallo winemaking family, the Fisher Brothers real estate firm, conglomerate American Financial, US Tobacco, and agri-giant Archer Daniels Midland. Though all of these companies have benefited directly from Dole's work in Congress—as we will see later—there's nothing illegal about this money. It was all raised in small increments that never exceeded the limits on contributions set in 1974. (Under that law, individuals can give only $2,000 to the committee per six-year election cycle, while PACs can give $10,000 per six-year cycle.)

But behind the Senate committee are a host of other fundraising operations that pump thousands of dollars more into events and projects that advance his political ambitions—even though they are ostensibly unconnected to Dole's candidacies. Chief among these is Campaign America, the political action committee created by Dole and staffed primarily by former Dole advisers. Campaign America calls itself "independent" and "multicandidate," and in theory enjoys no special relationship with the Dole campaign. "Senator Dole set up Campaign America to promote and assist state and federal Republican candidates, and Republican organizations and parties," a Dole spokesperson said. "For the record, in the last cycle Campaign America gave contributions to over 400 candidates in 47 states—even candidates who support other Presidential contenders."

Because of that status, Campaign America can accept donations like any other PAC, at levels well in excess of what Dole's campaign committee can take, just so long as it gives no more that $10,000 per election cycle to Dole himself. But that, of course, is the catch. In practice, Campaign America's treasury pays for political functions and maintains a large cadre of consultants, pollsters, and political staff, whose work continues to benefit the senator directly or indirectly. In addition, through the Campaign's travel account, Dole accepts tens of thousands of dollars worth of airfare from his corporate patrons (which his campaign then reimburses at minimal cost). Many of the providers of corporate aircraft to Dole are his biggest funders in hard cash, including ADM, American Financial and US Tobacco. A review of Dole's campaign filings shows that he has accepted at least 151 trips on corporate jets since 1987, including 29 on the Federal Express executive jet and 15 on a jet provided by the NTC Group of Wappinger Falls, N.Y.

Dole takes in still more money through Campaign America by using it as a conduit for contributions to other Republicans from his major financial backers. On December 26, 1990, for example, public records show that members of the Gallo family and Gallo executive J.E. Coleman gave Campaign America $10,000 that did not count against the PAC's limit because it was funneled directly to the campaigns of Republican Senators Steve Symms, Alfonse D'Amato, Robert Kasten, and John McCain. The beauty of this system is that Dole gets credit for giving money to his Republican colleagues (thus potentially buying their allegiance in future presidential bids) without having to bump up against the FEC's contribution limits.

Dole has even used Campaign America to finance his presidential bids, though these activities have attracted attention from the Federal Election Commission. In 1993, the FEC determined there had been involvement by Campaign America in Dole's 1988 presidential race. On at least four occasions in early 1987, the agency found, Campaign

America staged events in Iowa, site of the nation's first caucus, which benefited Dole's presidential bid despite Dole's failure to register as a presidential candidate and Campaign America's status as a PAC.

Invitations for the events were virtually identical to invitations later used by Dole's presidential committee and were printed by the same firm. "During this meeting I would like to hear your views and concerns while sharing some of my own with you regarding our shared Republican future," the invitations by Dole stated. Less subtle was a memo produced by Campaign America around the same time that stated, "Offer Iowans a friend in the White House," and a flyer that stated, "If Senator Dole is running for the White House, he's off on the right foot."

The events cost Campaign America some $33,000, and it spent other money on telemarketing in Iowa and purchases of voter lists in New Hampshire, site of the first presidential primary. Among other things, Campaign America obtained a business telephone line in New Hampshire that it later turned over to Dole's presidential campaign. All told, the FEC found, Campaign America spent about $47,000 on behalf of Dole's presidential bid, $42,000 more than the law allows. The FEC said Dole's presidential campaign "knowingly accepted" the help.

And that may not be the whole story. According to the agency's original investigative report on the case, Campaign America sponsored 19 events on Iowa in 1986-87. All were "town meetings" similar to the four the FEC said were in violation of the presidential campaign laws. The FEC dropped from its case these and several other instances of possible violations, such as purchases of voter lists and campaign materials, for unknown reasons. (Records of FEC negotiations are strictly confidential.) Even so, though, the FEC ultimately fined the Dole campaign a record $100,000 and ordered Campaign America to cough up another $12,000.

While the FEC required both to admit that they broke the law, Dole was unapologetic, issuing a statement admitting nothing and belittling the case, saying, "This bureaucratic process is the best example yet of why we don't need public financing of congressional campaigns." In fact, Bob Dole's offenses took place in the privately financed presidential primary campaign, not the publicly financed general election.

Today, Campaign America is alive and well. Among its other activities, in January Campaign America made contributions to 17 state legislators in New Hampshire, where Dole has been courting support for his presidential bid. The PAC also pays payroll taxes in Iowa, indicating it has staff stationed there.

SHAKY FOUNDATIONS

Dole's other big fundraising organs are his non-profit foundations. chief among them the Dole Foundation for People With Disabilities. The foundation, which raised about $1.25 million last year, is a bottomless pocket: Dole's supporters can give unlimited amounts at any time, and get a tax reduction to boot.

In accordance with the laws governing public charities, the foundation is ostensibly nonpartisan. To its credit, it is engaged in charitable works other than the senator's political operations. But look closely at the list of foundation contributors. The analysis of public information shows that better than 65 percent of its backers also happen to be Dole campaign contributors. American Financial Corporation is a supporter, as is the Andreas Foundation and the Archer Daniels Midland Company. The Gallo Foundation is a contributor, as is US Tobacco. In its 1990 report, the foundation singled out Gallo, ADM, AT&T, oilman William Keck, and Massachusetts Mutual Life Insurance Co. for having been "exceptionally generous in support of its programs." All five also happen to lavish Dole with campaign support.

"To suggest ... some link between the Dole Foundation for People with Disabilities and politics is simply insulting," Dole's spokesperson said. "Bob dole has lived with a disability for 50 years. And the purpose of his foundation is to help others deal with the same kind of challenge." To be sure, it is entirely possible that all of the foundation's supporters simply like the foundation's good works. However, it is also likely some of them want Dole to like them.

Unlike the disabilities foundation, the Better America Foundation engages in political activities. Campaign America's director quietly set up the foundation in 1993, and it has received attention only recently. Technically a broad-based social welfare organization, the unit originally resided in Campaign America's office and is now under the direction of a senior Dole aide, Jim Whittinghill, who left the Senate payroll to head the organization. Last year, the Better America Foundation raised $4 million, according to its tax return.

As with Campaign America, Dole's only official position at the foundation is "honorary chairman." But last October, right before the elections, the foundation ran a series of television ads supporting the balanced budget amendment. Produced by a consulting firm with longstanding ties to Dole's presidential campaigns, the ads prominently featured Dole. In addition, there is considerable crossover between the foundation staff and Dole's circle of political advisers. The architect of the foundation was Jo-Anne Coe, the longtime Dole aide who helped manage his previous presidential and Senate campaigns and was running Campaign America when she set up the foundation. Another former Campaign America official is the foundation's finance director, while a former Republican National Committee aide and ex-Dole staffer is the group's political director. The foundation also uses the same polling firm as Dole's presidential campaign, Public Opinion Strategies, and the Associated Press reported that Whittinghill confirmed the foundation "solicits Dole's ideas, shares its work with him, and meets regularly with his Senate staff."

Absent evidence that the Dole campaign is coordinating campaign activities with any of these agents, none of this is illegal. If Dole happens to benefit from this arrangement incidentally, the law permits it, even though that effectively allows Dole's donors to circumvent limits on individual donations and direct extra money to his political cause. The purpose of those limits, of course, is to prevent legislators from serving the interests of their financiers rather than their constituents—which is what Dole apparently did when he acted on behalf of a failed natural gas subsidy three years ago.

DOLING OUT LEGISLATION

In September 1992, Dole won passage of an amendment renewing a generous tax credit called "section 29," which subsidized natural gas taken from geologic formations that are difficult to access. First passed in 1980 during the energy shortage, section 29 sought to foster American energy independence by spurring production of alternative fuels. Since Kansas is a major producer of natural gas, Dole's motives seemed obvious enough.

But were they? By the mid-1980s, a glut of natural gas had severely depressed gas prices. When the amendment was up in 1992, most senators from natural gas states—including Republican Don Nickels of Oklahoma and Democrat John Breaux of Louisiana, patron saints of the petroleum industry—wanted to kill the credit to discourage over-production. The Natural Gas Supply Association, which represents 90 percent of the nation's natural gas suppliers, opposed the Dole rider, as did the American Petroleum Institute. Also against the program were the independent natural gas producers of Kansas, a consortium of smaller companies from Dole's home state.

But a handful of large companies with the resources to embark on these projects—Amoco, Arco, Coastal, and Enron, plus a few other large corporations with investments in drilling—were making a killing off the subsidy. Because the credit was so generous and the price of gas so low, the few companies producing the gas were getting a credit equal to about 92 percent of the price of commodity they were producing. In other words, for every dollar of gas they sold, the companies also received 92 cents in tax credits.

By 1992, Coastal and Enron were banking heavily on section 29's renewal. According to *World Oil*, a trade magazine, the two companies had accelerated their efforts on drilling projects eligible for the subsidy. By the fall, the magazine said, section 29 covered 78 percent of Coastal's gas drilling and 80 percent of Enron's. Officials from Enron and Amoco, which also drilled hundreds of section 29 wells in 1992, told *World Oil* they would eliminate virtually all such projects in 1993 if the tax credit expired, because they would no longer be economical.

Amoco, Arco, Coastal, and Enron are long-time backers of the Dole Foundation and Dole's campaigns. Since 1987, the companies' executives have given at least $48,000 to the Dole campaigns and more into the Dole Foundation. Coastal, in particular, has been extremely generous with its corporate jets, allowing Dole to use them four times in 1992 alone, including a trip to the Republican National Convention in Houston. Coastal CEO Oscar Wyatt held a $1,000-a-person fundraiser for Dole during convention week, where Enron executives gave at least $7,000, while Coastal officials put up at least $9,000.

Also profiting from section 29 was AT&T, which went into the gas business for the tax benefits. AT&T, it turns out, has given Dole at least $20,000 since 1987 through its PAC, while the AT&T Foundation has given Dole's foundation at least $100,000. Gerald Lowrie, AT&T's senior vice president for government affairs and the company's top lobbyist, serves on the board of the Dole Foundation and helps raise funds for the group.

Apparently, the investment caught Dole's attention. Dole brought his amendment to the floor in September 1992—only a month after the fundraiser at Wyatt's mansion. Dole contended the subsidy was vital to America's energy security, even though the nation then (as now) enjoyed an abundance of cheap fuel. Because the debate was so complicated and obscure, the press barely noticed. Nobody bothered to investigate whether "energy security" was the real explanation for Dole's motives.

Despite some substantial opposition–spearheaded by New Jersey Senator Bill Bradley—Dole prevailed on the Senate floor with support from Senators representing energy-consuming states whose citizens benefited from the low natural gas prices. The measure, however, died in the House-Senate conference committee, after conferees decided the government couldn't afford sustaining the giveaway.

ADM'S BUMPER CROP

A financier for whom Dole has delivered more tangible results is Dwayne Andreas, the CEO of agriculture giant Archer Daniels Midland.

Andreas has been a financial godfather to politicians of all ideological stripes for the last 25 years. He gave thousands of dollars to Hubert Humphrey, managed the late vice president's blind trust, and gave at least $70,000 to the children of Humphrey's top congressional aide, David Gartner. In 1974, Andreas made more than $100,000 in secret contributions to both Humphrey and Nixon, including $25,000 that went to the White House plumbers unit. The one constant in Andreas's life is that he gives money—lots of money—to whomever might be in a position to help his company, no matter what their politics. There's no mystery to this: As is widely known in Washington, ADM's success depends upon massive governmental favoritism toward its various enterprises, all of which are agriculture-based.

If few political financiers are better known than Andreas, few politicians have more conspicuously courted his favor than Dole. Since the two joined forces two decades ago, Andreas's money has found its way into virtually every pocket of Dole's money coat. In the last few years alone, ADM and Andreas family members have given

Dole's foundation at least $185,000, and at least $53,000 more to his various campaigns.

In 1982, Dole and his wife bought a luxury condominium in Bal Harbour, Florida from a company controlled by Andreas for the bargain price of $150,000. The condo allows Dole to live the lifestyle of the rich and famous: Fellow owners include millionaire attorney Robert Strauss, broadcaster David Brinkley, and lobbyist Howard Baker, himself a former GOP Senate leader. "There appears to be little doubt that the Doles received preferential treatment from Andreas," the *New York Times* concluded after investigating the transaction in 1987. The paper found that a condominium of the same size but in a less desirable location of the building sold for $40,000 more than the Doles paid, just three months prior to the Doles' purchase. The senator has always denied any impropriety.

Then there are the campaign flights Dole gets on ADM's corporate jet. In the last six years, Dole has made 23 campaign flights aboard ADM's corporate jet, according to FEC records. The flights amount to contributions by ADM to Dole that would be illegal were they to be made in the form of cash. Exploiting a loophole in campaign finance law, Campaign America reimburses ADM for most of the flights at the rate it would cost the senator to fly first-class on a commercial airliner. That's a significant discount: Charter jets cost as much as $20,000 per trip for fuel maintenance, staff, and other costs, and rarely less than $5,000. At a conservative estimation based on the number of trips at a rate of $5,000 per trip (surely a low estimate) minus those reimbursements, ADM has made $90,000 in corporate contributions to Dole in this manner.

Andreas says he's not out to buy influence. ADM, he once told *Fortune* magazine, is the "most impotent political animal in the world." Dole, for his part, has always claimed Andreas is just a kindred spirit with a lot of money. As the representative of a farm state, Dole says, he just happens to favor programs that also benefit ADM. But under scrutiny, this claim too falls apart. On the issues Dole has championed, the interests of ADM and Kansas voters have often diverged.

Consider Dole's long-standing and controversial advocacy of ethanol, a corn-based product ADM has touted as a cleaner-burning alternative to gasoline. In 1990, Dole held a trade bill hostage until the House would agree to extend a tax credit for domestic production of ethanol and to place duties on imported ethanol. In 1991, Dole added an amendment to a highway bill that made it harder for refiners to supply petroleum distributors with methanol–the chief competitor of ethanol. In 1992, Dole jawboned the Bush administration into issuing new regulations, boosting the role of ethanol in the government's clean air program. In 1993, Dole pushed a Senate resolution encouraging President Clinton to endorse the Bush regulations. (Uncharacteristically, it lost.) In fact, in virtually every session of Congress for the last decade, Dole has introduced legislation beneficial to ADM.

Though ethanol's environmental value remains unproven, Dole has always claimed the subsidies benefit his constituents, by increasing demand for Kansas-grown corn—an explanation the media and the public have apparently bought. But despite years of massive subsidization, no evidence exists that the ethanol program has raised corn prices significantly. Some economists say that even if ethanol production were to triple—and it would only grow 10 percent under the most generous government-subsidy scenario—the effect on corn prices would be minimal.

So who benefits from the subsidy? ADM, which controls two-thirds of the ethanol market. Last year, ADM produced some 900 million gallons of ethanol, reaping the lion's share of $500 million in government subsidies. Ethanol accounts for about a fourth of the company's earnings. Without the subsidy, the ethanol market would all but collapse. (Another fourth of ADM's earnings comes from high fructose corn syrup, a sweetener for which there also would be no market but for federal tariffs on imported sugar.)

Other large Dole financiers have benefited from Dole's work, too. Public records show that since 1987 Dole's biggest funders, the Gallo family, have given at least $193,000 in direct campaign contributions, not including the money donated to Dole's PAC and foundations. As the *Los Angeles Times* reported, Dole in 1992 used congressional oversight of the Treasury Department to fight off stricter labeling requirements on the imitation champagne Gallo manufactures. Dole has also opposed tax increases on alcoholic beverages, and in 1986 pushed through an amendment to the tax reform act which allowed the billionaire Gallo family and other super wealthy families to evade certain inheritance taxes on generation-skipping trusts.

Cincinnati billionaire Carl Linder, members of his family, and executives from the American Financial Corporation gave Dole about $34,000 for his 1986 Senate campaign, about $47,000 in 1987 for his presidential campaign, and at least $28,000 since then. Dole has also used the AFC corporate jet at least five times since 1989, FEC records show. Dole appears to have worked behind the scenes to preserve a dividend-received deduction that benefits AFC, and, as first reported in the *Cincinnati Enquirer,* Dole pressured the Clinton administration to protect Chiquita–an AFC subsidiary–in its trade disputes with Europe and Latin America.

THE TEFLON SENATOR?

Such relationships ought to raise at least a few eyebrows. But will they make a difference? Maybe not for Dole, who's already demonstrated a unique ability to avoid the taint of scandals to which he was connected. Putting aside the Federal Election Commission charges stemming from the 1988 presidential campaign—recall that the FEC required Dole's campaign to admit it broke the law—nobody seems to care about the relationship between Dole and David Owen, a longtime Dole fundraiser who served prison time for tax fraud and was accused (though never convicted) of illegal fundraising practices by the Kansas Public Disclosure Commission and state prosecutors.

Owen's ties to Dole go back at least to 1974, when Owen stepped down as Kansas lieutenant governor in order to rescue Dole's faltering campaign for a second Senate term. Owen was Dole's primary fundraiser for most of the 1980s, serving as a senior executive of Campaign America in 1986 and, for a time, national finance cochairman of Dole's 1988 presidential campaign. He once estimated that he had raised more than $20 million for Republicans during his fundraising career, at least half of it for Dole.

Questionable dealings characterized their relationship. One early one that attracted FEC scrutiny involved a $50,000 loan Owen had engineered while he was president of a Kansas bank—a loan to Elizabeth Dole that was promptly funneled into Dole's 1980 presidential campaign. According to FEC staff investigators, Owen had structured the deal to appear that Mrs. Dole was lending her husband's campaign the money, when in fact it came from the bank. Although it would have been legal for the bank to lend the campaign the money directly, the campaign may not have had sufficient assets to justify it, raising questions of whether Owen was giving his ally Dole a sweetheart deal. Mrs. Dole's trust fund, meanwhile, was not liquid, so the only way to get the money from the bank to Dole was for Mrs. Dole to put up her trust as collateral, take out her own loan, and then give it to the campaign.

Correspondence between Owen and campaign manager Jo-Anne Coe, on file with the FEC, confirms the nature of the relationship. "Dear Jo-Anne: Please find enclosed note for Elizabeth Dole in the amount of $50,000, per your request," Owen wrote on a piece of bank stationary. He then asked the campaign manager for "instructions as to where you would like the money sent. If you prefer, I can wire transfer to your bank in Washington..." Coe promptly instructed Owen to wire the funds directly into the campaign's bank account, as the funds "are needed at the earliest possible time."

FEC staff investigators concluded that the transaction violated federal campaign finance laws, which require campaigns to disclose the true source of all loans and contributions. Yet the FEC ultimately dropped the case after deadlocking on the staff recommendation to pursue the case against Dole. The politically divided agency frequently deadlocks along partisan lines when a powerful politician from either party is involved.

Another episode involved arrangements Owen made after he became adviser to Mrs. Dole's $1 million trust in 1983—investments he engineered that relied directly or indirectly on government contracts, all secured with the assistance of Dole's Senate staff.

One of the most profitable of these deals was the purchase of an office building in February, 1986. The trust bought the building for $1.39 million, netting Owen a $139,000 commission, and then sold the building a year later, netting the Doles a $100,000 profit. So far, so good. But the new buyer was no stranger. Instead, the Doles had sold the building to a company called EDP Enterprises, which was run by John Palmer, a former Dole aide. And at the same time EDP was buying the building, EDP has also won a $25 million minority set-aside contract (Palmer is black) from the Small Business Administration. EDP had pursued the contract unsuccessfully for at least a year; only after senior Dole aides intervened with the Small Business Administration did EDP get it. It turns out that Owen was a consultant to EDP, and that Owen owned a company that was one of EDP's major suppliers.

As word of this deal leaked into the press, Dole flatly denied any intervention with the Small Business Administration on behalf of Palmer. But the House Small Business Committee investigated and concluded that Dole personally had called SBA's top official on Palmer's behalf. The committee also investigated whether EDP was a front company for Owen, and concluded that it likely was. Despite these findings, the Senate Ethics Committee never took action against Dole.

Dole eventually cut Owen loose when reports of Owen's involvement with the trust threatened Dole's 1988 presidential bid. But Owen's state officials later prosecuted Owen on tax fraud and political fundraising charges unrelated to the Dole campaigns of the EDP episode. In 1993, a Kansas judge sentenced Owen to a year and a day in prison. Owen served six months, and was released in October in 1994.

"Exhaustive investigations into the case found no wrongdoing on the part of Dole," a Dole spokesperson said. "Questions about the Owen affair are frankly disingenuous." But it is instructive to compare what is known about the the Dole-Owen affair with Whitewater, a potential scandal that has attracted considerable attention in the national media during the last two years. Which episode is more recent? Which politician made more money? Which politician took official action to help his benefactor?

Barring new revelations about Whitewater, the answers to these questions appear to be Dole, Dole, and Dole. Dole, though, had the good fortune of having his scandal disclosed just as his presidential campaign was faltering. He has faced no investigations or independent counsels, and the national press, thus far, has given him a free pass. To date, no full accounting of Dole's transgressions has appeared in the national media, despite numerous articles on his presidential candidacy.

Such is the state of contemporary reporting. Reporters pore over the record of a new figure like Newt Gingrich but leave unexamined and unremarked the two-decade history of a politician many consider the odds-on favorite to be our next president. The voters, meanwhile, have grown increasingly desensitized to charges of political corruption altogether.

In all fairness, there is some reason for disillusionment. Dole may be noteworthy for his ambition and brazenness, but his practices are not that atypical. Gary Hart and Jack Kemp had non-profit think tanks, which like Dole's attracted money from their political contributors. Revelations about Gingrich's nonprofit foundation—which like Dole's had strong ties his campaigns—forced the Speaker to sever his ties earlier this year. House Minority Leader Richard Gephardt maintains a political action committee that engages in many of the same practices as Dole's PAC. In the modern campaign arsenal, loosely affiliated PACs and nonprofits are essential weapons for officials with national ambitions.

Such is the reality of the privately financed campaign system, a system reformers have targeted for years. Perversely, the only campaign finance proposal to come up in Dole's Senate this year was the measure to abolish public financing in presidential campaigns, which would complete the regression of our campaign finance system to pre-Watergate days. The measure failed, but Dole's sponsorship of it is a measure of how much of an opponent of reform he really is.

The Pressure Elite

INSIDE THE NARROW WORLD OF ADVOCACY GROUP POLITICS

John B. Judis

In the 1950s, in the midst of what C. Wright Mills called the "great American celebration," mainstream political scientists conceived of modern American democracy as a more or less equal contest among large-scale groups—the most important being farmers, workers, and business. (Chapters Two through Five of V.O. Key's classic *Politics, Parties and Pressure Groups* were aptly entitled "Agrarianism," "Workers," "Business," and "Other Interest Groups.") Each social group had its own organizations—from the American Farm Bureau to AFL-CIO to the Chamber of Commerce and the National Association of Manufacturers (NAM)—and each enjoyed special power within one of the major political parties. Since almost every adult American was either a farmer, worker, or businessman, or married to one, almost everyone was represented within this pluralistic system. It was not the direct democracy of Athens, but it was as close to a representative democracy as a large modern nation could come.

This pluralist vision vastly overstated the extent to which America's pressure groups represented the general public or were equal in power to each other. Noting the narrow slice of the population who were active in these organizations and the preponderance of power wielded by business over labor, the political scientist E.E. Schattschneider commented in *The Semi-Sovereign Republic*, "The flaw in the pluralist heaven is that the chorus sings with a strong upper-class accent. Probably about 90 percent of the people cannot get into the pressure system."

Nonetheless, the pluralist vision reflected at least a shadow of reality. In the 1950s, no more than a dozen very large pressure groups dominated Washington politics. The labor movement represented about a third of the non-agricultural workforce and enjoyed enormous power in Congress and the Democratic Party just as the key business and farm groups enjoyed the same kind of power within the Republican Party.

What distinguishes Washington politics today is the sheer proliferation of citizen organizations, trade associations, think tanks, and policy research groups. In its Spring 1991 directory of the most prominent Washington organizations, the *National Journal* listed 328 interest groups, 98 think tanks, 288 trade and professional associations, and 682 corporate headquarters. Many of the new citizen organizations such as the National Organization for Women (NOW), Greenpeace, and Common Cause boast memberships in the hundreds of thousands. Dwarfing even the AFL-CIO, the American Association of Retired Persons (AARP) has 28 million members, a legislative staff of 125, and 20 registered lobbyists.

But while the new organizations together claim far more members than the old—and therefore appear to be more representative of society as a whole—they have a far more tenuous connection to those whom they claim to represent directly. Many of them are what sociologist John McCarthy has called "professional movement groups." They are run entirely by their staff and by a board of directors that is often dominated by the staff. In organizations like the National Abortion Rights Action League (NARAL) and the Conservative Caucus, membership is primarily a fund-raising device to ensure continuous giving. Even in organizations that have local chapters and hold membership conventions, such as the National Audubon Society, the national staff and the board of directors control who is nominated for board positions and what information the members receive about the candidates. Moreover, in their funding, the new organizations represent almost as narrow an economic base as the old organizations of the 1950s. Many of them are supported by corporate and foundation contributions. Those that are supported by direct mail claim to represent a far broader public, but their donor profile tends to be overwhelmingly white, wealthy, and at least middle-aged. The best one can say about the bulk of these organizations is that they sing with an upper-middle-class accent. The old array of pressure groups fed false hopes of a new pluralistic democracy;

the new—perceived by Americans as occupying a world unto themselves—fuel cynicism about special interests and about politics "inside the beltway."

The new organizations also have a very different relationship to the political parties than the old organizations did. The old organizations strengthened party representation by functioning as honest brokers within party conclaves. The new organizations contribute to political fragmentation and to the decline of the political parties. This reflects the circumstances of their birth: these groups arose independently largely because the old organizations and political party structures ignored or spurned them.

THE NEW PRESSURE GROUP

Beginning in the late 1950s, new political movements emerged that did not fit into the structure of the old Washington pressure groups and political parties. They included on one side the civil rights movement, the antiwar movement, the women's movement, the environmental movement, the movements for gay rights, consumer rights, and abortion rights and on the other side the new conservative movement, the movements against racial desegregation and later against busing and affirmative action, the anti-abortion movement, and the right-wing evangelical movements. All these movements were initially outside the organized mainstream. Under the late George Meany, the AFL-CIO and the official Democratic Party were initially as hostile to the civil rights and antiwar movements as the established business groups and the Republican party were to Barry Goldwater's apocalyptic anti-communism and to Southern fundamentalism and segregationism.

Facing hostility from the Washington political establishment, these new movements created myriad organizations outside of Washington's established pressure groups. This was the origin of such groups as NOW, Friends of the Earth, SANE, Ralph Nader's Public Citizen, NARAL, the American Conservative Union, the Conservative Caucus, the Heritage Foundation, and the Moral Majority. But why did they choose to focus their activities on Washington?

The growth of these movements over the past three decades coincided with a dramatic expansion in the social and economic role of national government. Earl Warren's Supreme Court took an active role in shaping social relations—outlawing segregation and school prayer, granting the right to contraception and then abortion, expanding the rights of criminal suspects. John Kennedy used fiscal policy more consciously than any previous president to control the business cycle. Lyndon Johnson expanded the welfare state and convinced Congress to pass two major civil rights acts that outlawed racial and sexual discrimination. Richard Nixon sometimes promoted and sometimes acceded to an expansion of federal business regulation not seen since Woodrow Wilson's presidency, establishing new agencies like the Environmental Protection Agency, the Occupational Safety and Health Administration, and the Consumer Product Safety Agency, expanding old ones like the Office of the Special Trade Representative, and passing landmark regulatory legislation. Jimmy Carter created a new Department of Energy and carved a Department of Education out of the old Department of Health, Education, and Welfare, resulting, in both cases, in increased federal intervention. At the same time, Congress created its own regulatory apparatus through the expansion of its committees and staff.

This dramatic enlargement of official Washington's authority meant that many issues that had been predominately local or state concerns—from smog to abortion—became national concerns whose final resolution depended upon what the Supreme Court, Congress, and the President decided. As a result, both the old and the new movements became particularly concerned with influencing what happened in Washington.

From 1961 to 1982, the number of corporate headquarters in Washington increased tenfold, and there was a massive growth in trade associations and in lobbying firms. The number of lawyers in Washington tripled between 1973 and 1983. In addition, corporations began to fund new kinds of organizations—from think tanks such as the American Enterprise Institute (AEI) to congenial environmental organizations such as the Nature Conservancy. In the 1980s, as trade disputes with Japan intensified, money from Japanese corporations—as much as a billion dollars over the decade—fueled a further growth in think tanks and lobbies concerned with defending free trade.

At the same time, the new social and political movements that had been spawned in the 1960s and 1970s increasingly concentrated their efforts on swaying Washington. Older environmental groups such as the National Audubon Society and the National Wildlife Federation began monitoring federal legislation, while new groups such as the

Environmental Defense Fund and Greenpeace and the Citizens Clearing House for Hazardous Wastes based themselves in Washington. Common Cause and the Nader organizations were founded to fight corporate and government misconduct. The abortion rights and anti-abortion organizations focused on pressuring the Supreme Court. In the 1980s, People for the American Way and the Moral Majority joined the battle over court nominees and congressional legislation on school prayer. The National Rifle Association and Handgun Control locked horns over the new federal gun laws. The civil rights organizations devoted themselves to fighting for the renewal of the Voting Rights Acts and the Civil Rights Act of 1991.

The focus on Washington shaped the kind of organizations that emerged over these decades. Many of the new organizations located their headquarters in Washington, and some of those that had not chosen Washington initially, for example Friends of the Earth and the Cato Institute, later moved to the capital. Most of the groups eventually adopted a professionalized structure so that they were dominated by their Washington staff. This was partly a result of the groups' focus on influencing Congress and the White House and of the ebbing of grassroots political activity after the 1960s. But it also stemmed from the new kinds of funding that these groups enjoyed. The old organizations—from the AFL-CIO to NAM to the veterans' organizations or the American Medical Association—were financed primarily by membership dues. The new organizations were financed by grants from foundations, corporations, and unions, and by direct mail and neighborhood canvassing. This new form of funding laid the basis for the professional advocacy organization.

THE ROLE OF FOUNDATIONS

The major foundations such as Ford and Rockefeller, which are independent of direct corporate control and which claim to be nonpartisan in their grants, were instrumental in the formation of the new organizations. Foundation support was essential to the civil rights movement's voting drives and to the founding of such diverse organizations as the National Council of La Raza, Ralph Nader's Public Citizen, the Environmental Defense Fund, and the National Resources Defense Council. Foundations that have been more strictly identified with the left or right—from Rubin and Stewart

Mott on the left to Scaife and Bradley on the right—played important roles later in funding such groups as the Institute for Policy Studies and the Heritage Foundation.

By their nature, grants from foundations make an organization's staff less dependent upon members or constituents for organizational decisions, but as sociologist J. Craig Jenkins has argued, foundations also have encouraged professionalization. In studying foundation grants of social movements from 1953 to 1980, Jenkins found that only 17 percent of these grants went to "grass-roots" organizations involved in protests and demonstrations. The rest went to the professionalized groups. Jenkins attributes the foundations' preference to their vaunted caution:

> Grass-roots organizations often lack a clear track record and are more likely to become involved in protests or other activities that might stir criticism. They are also more informal and decentralized, lacking the fiscal and management devices that foundations expect from their recipients. Professionalized organizations are centrally managed by a single executive or professional staff. Their hierarchical structure is more intelligible to foundation boards, who typically come from business and academia, and affords greater assurance that the money will be used prudently as specified in the grant proposal.

Since the 1969 Tax Reform Act, foundations have also been limited to funding organizations that are not primarily "political"—meaning that they do not directly engage in lobbying or supporting candidates. Only nonpolitical organizations can receive tax-deductible gifts. This restriction has led the foundations to shy away from activist membership organizations. In 1968 the Ford Foundation provided the initial funding for the Southwest Unity Council for Social Action—an organization intended to become a Mexican-American NAACP. But after the tax reform act, the Ford Foundation discouraged the new organization from taking part in local protests. Prodded by the Ford Foundation, the group renamed itself the National Council of La Raza and shifted its headquarters to Washington, where it became, in Jenkins's words, "a professional organization with relatively weak ties to a constituency."

The limits on tax-deductible gifts have in turn influenced the way in which organizations have defined their mission. Before the 1970s, a considerable gulf existed between the quasi-academic think tank such as the Brookings Institution that sought to influence the long-range views of government officials but did not have a specific legislative agenda, and the lobby or activist group that pressured Congress or the White House to pass or block certain legislation. In the 1970s, however, new organizations arose that were intended to circumvent the law—to maintain eligibility for tax-deductible grants from individuals and foundations while still seeking to influence official Washington. Policy research organizations and think tanks such as the Heritage Foundation, the Free Congress Foundation, the Institute for Policy Studies, and later the Economic Policy Institute were not simply scholarly groups concerned with public policy; they had specific agendas and took positions on legislation, but they neither lobbied nor backed candidates. Some of these groups, the Heritage Foundation, for example, offered their donors memberships, but all of them, by their very nature, were professionalized organizations controlled by their staffs and by a board of directors representing their largest donors.

Some groups have tried to elude restrictions on tax-deductible gifts by creating nonprofit research or educational groups alongside lobbying organizations and political action committees. The educational group then becomes responsible for the organization's research and pays many of its salaries. Organizations that have adopted this structure include the American Civil Liberties Union, NARAL, Public Citizen, Consumer Federation of America, Eagle Forum, Conservative Caucus, and the Sierra Club. By its very nature this kind of cumbersome structure—requiring interminable bookkeeping and attention to grant-writing and fund-raising—reinforces centralized staff control of organizations.

By their grants, the large foundations have also affected the kind of issues organizations have pursued as well as the way they have pursued them. In 1962 Kennedy administration officials used the promise of foundation support to lure the Southern civil rights movement away from militant demonstrations toward voter registration. In the environmental movement, the large foundations have favored the legal strategies and policy research of the Environmental Defense Fund over the less tempered methods of Greenpeace. Foundations often prefer studies of action to action itself; and they prefer studies with uncontroversial conclusions that will not call into question their own impartiality. As Robert McIntyre, the director of Citizens for Tax Justice, puts it, "They usually don't like anything controversial. If we changed our name to Citizens for Tax Thinking, we'd get more money." Similarly, directors of organizations concerned with trade issues have also complained that the foundations were reluctant to fund proposals that were not endorsed by established free-trade economists.

But this does not mean that the large independent foundations have partisan agendas, only that they rigorously follow the path of respectable opinion. When the controversial becomes widely accepted, they fund it. Their major impact is structural rather than partisan or narrowly political. They encourage professionalization and discourage militant protest strategies. They project their own caution and timidity onto the organizations that they fund. And they contribute to the decline of politics and parties by stimulating the growth of a new realm of organizational activity—issue-oriented, but nonpartisan—that is cut off from the compromise and deliberation that are essential to building majority political parties.

The more ideologically oriented foundations have tended to have a symbiotic relationship with their recipients. The Youth Project, now called the Partnership for Democracy, was founded in 1970 to act as a middleman between foundations and liberal and left-wing social movements and groups. The project's board has been made up of representatives from many of the organizations that receive funds from it. Scaife, Bradley, Olin, and the other foundations that fund conservative organizations are advised by leading conservatives such as William Simon and Irving Kristol. (Kristol earned his nickname of "the Godfather" partly from his role in arranging funding for conservative groups and individuals.) Whom these foundations fund reflects the priorities of leading conservatives rather than the distinct concerns of the foundation executives.

Even the exceptions prove the rule. Last December, the *Washington Times* reported what appeared to be an attempt by the $200-million Scaife Foundation in Pittsburgh to influence the agenda of the Heritage Foundation, the most important conservative institution in Washington. According to the newspaper account, foundation president Richard Larry forced the organization to adopt a program concerned with cultural policy. Heritage concurred by hiring former Secretary of Education William Bennett as the head of a new cultural program, funded by Scaife. Bennett was also a member of the Scaife board of directors. It seemed like a coup for Scaife, but in fact represented Heritage's willing acquiescence in a long-standing trend in the conservative movement. Heritage already had a staff member assigned to cultural issues. By Scaife's funding of Bennett, Heritage gained a high-profile celebrity who will now help it exert influence over Scaife rather than vice versa.

CORPORATE FUNDING AND K STREET

Corporations and their private foundations contributed even more to the rise of new Washington-based organizations in the 1970s. Under attack from labor and the new consumer and environmental movements, and seeing their profit margins threatened by foreign competitors, businesses took the offensive. They vastly increased their lobbying budget in Washington. From 1971 to 1982, the number of registered business lobbyists increased from 175 to 2,445.

Corporations also flocked to set up political action committees—their ranks grew from 139 corporate PACs in 1974 to 1,204 in 1980. They revived the moribund U.S. Chamber of Commerce and funded new, powerful business organizations that were able to employ the media and grassroots lobbying techniques developed by the consumer and environmental movements. The Business Roundtable, composed of 192 large corporations, was credited with the defeat in Congress of Nader's proposal for a Consumer Protection Agency and the AFL-CIO's push for labor law reform. The American Council for Capital Formation successfully led the fight for reduction of corporate income and capital gains taxes. Business also funded think tanks that promoted deregulation of business, contributing to the rise of both the American Enterprise Institute—which before the mid-1970s was an insignificant backwater—and the Heritage Foundation.

During the 1980s, as trade battles heated up, foreign companies and foundations, particularly from Japan, poured more money into funding lobbies, public relations firms, trade associations, and think tanks in Washington. From 1986 to 1990, the Japanese contributed $1,015,000 to the Institute for International Economics, $1,812,408 to the Center for Strategic and International Studies, $1,610,684 to the Brookings Institution, and $846,000 to the American Enterprise Institute. The Heritage Foundation enjoyed substantial contributions from South Korean and Taiwanese companies and trade groups. The foreign contributions to think tanks were intended to reinforce congenial positions on trade and investment.

By the decade's end, foreign influence buying, combined with a sagging American trade balance, led to a backlash. A group of American corporations led by Chrysler, TRW, Corning Glass, USX, and Milliken began funding policy groups that favored using trade laws to protect American industries. These included the Economic Strategy Institute, founded by former Commerce Department official Clyde Prestowitz.

Corporations also funded coalitions to oppose changes in the laws of the General Agreement on Tariffs and Trade (GATT) favored by foreign countries. By the end of the 1980s, some of the fiercest lobbying battles in Washington were taking place between one business-funded lobby or policy group and another.

The influx of corporate money over the past two decades has created a burgeoning complex of law firms, public relations houses, lobbying firms, and policy research groups named after Washington's K Street, where many of them are located. This complex increasingly dominates politics in the city. National Republican politics has largely been run by the lobbying firm Black, Manafort, Stone and Kelly from which Charles Black and the late Lee Atwater came, while Democratic politics has been controlled by the powerful K Street law firms that house former Democratic officials and that have contributed Democratic national chairs Robert Strauss, Charles Manatt, and Ron Brown. The Democratic Leadership Council, chaired by Arkansas Governor Bill Clinton, an its policy group, the Progressive Policy Institute, were largely funded by former Democratic congressional aides turned K Street lobbyists. And many of these same lawyers and lobbyists now serve as trustees or members of the board of directors of the main Washington policy groups, from AEI to Brookings.

American and foreign corporations have also contributed to many organizations spawned or sustained by new social movements. These include NOW's Legal Defense and Education Fund, the Children's Defense Fund, many of the largest environmental organizations, including the Audubon Society, the National Wildlife Federation, and the Environmental Law Institute, the NAACP, the Urban League, the National Council of La Raza, and the Center for Community Change. The corporations had widely different motives for funding these organizations.

Corporate contributions to civil rights organizations largely stem from social conscience and from a commitment to social harmony and an educated work force. Many of the same corporations that contribute to conservative policy research groups also give to civil rights organizations that have denounced the kinds of policies that these research groups have favored. For instance, half of the corporations that fund the black policy group, the Joint Center for Policy Studies, also fund the Institute for Research on the Economics of Taxation, an organization founded by supply-sider and former Reagan Treasury official Norman Ture.

Some corporate gifts are intended to improve companies' images. Exxon and Weyerhauser hoped to improve their reputations among environmentalists through their contributions to the World Wildlife Fund, the Nature Conservancy, and Resources for the Future. Other corporations, faced with the prospect of change, have tried to throw their weight behind organizations that advocate the more palatable alternatives. In 1989, corporations gave $703,840 to the milquetoast Nature Conservancy and $3,175 to the Sierra Club. According to the *Corporate Philanthropy Report*, insurance companies, facing the likelihood of health insurance reform, now back research and programs that will preserve the private insurance industry's role and "head off unpalatable proposals such as shifting to a Canadian-style government health program."

The mixture of motives is epitomized by Waste Management, Inc., the $19-billion garbage collection giant and notorious polluter. Waste Management has given large contributions to almost every environmental organization to the right of Greenpeace, including the World Wildlife Fund, the National Wildlife Federation (on whose board of directors Waste Management CEO Dean Buntrock sits), the National Audubon Society, the Environmental Law Institute, Ducks Unlimited, the Sierra Club, the Natural Resources Defense Council, the Izaak Walton League, and the World Resources Institute. Waste Management intended its good works to deflect critics concerned about the $50 million in fines that the corporation has already incurred for illegal waste practices and for price fixing. The company accompanied its contributions with an aggressive advertising campaign in environmental magazines. For instance, it ran a full-page advertisement in the Wilderness Society's magazine that, under a photo of a butterfly, declared, "We profit by protecting the environment."

Waste Management also wanted to buy influence in the battle over environmental legislation and enforcement. In 1989, a year after Buntrock was named to the National Wildlife Federation's board of directors, he succeeded in getting Wildlife Federation president Jay Hair to set up a meeting between him and EPA administrator William Reilly. After the meeting, Reilly announced that he would challenge Southern states' attempts to restrict hazardous waste disposal. When the Wildlife Federation later signed a letter protesting the decision, Reilly told a reporter that he was surprised because Hair had "hosted the breakfast at which I was lobbied to do the very thing we are doing."

Finally, Waste Management has had a vested interest in passing stringent and complicated hazardous waste regulations that smaller companies would find too expensive to follow. According to an Audubon Society official, Waste Management is now underwriting that organization's attempt to strengthen the Resource Conservation and Recovery Act. Like the larger meat packing companies that pressed for food and drug regulation at the beginning of the century, Waste Management wants to use regulation to drive its competitors out of business.

Sometimes, corporate funding has seemed to induce organizations to steer clear of certain issues that might offend their donors, but usually only when a corporate representative already has considerable power within the organization itself. In the late 1970s, the NAACP refused to oppose the decontrol of natural gas prices. Most of the organization's leadership opposed decontrol, but Margaret Bush Wilson, who chaired the NAACP's board and served on the board of Monsanto, did not. Monsanto was also a big contributor to the NAACP

In 1980 the Heritage Foundation called for the abolition of the Synthetic Fuels Corporation. But Heritage began equivocating when President Reagan appointed as head of the corporation Edward Noble, who was active in Heritage and served as a trustee of the Noble Foundation, a major contributor to Heritage. In 1985, when Congress was on the verge of abolishing the agency, Heritage produced a briefing paper on "Salvaging the Synthetic Fuels Corporation." "We saw Noble's hand in it," said one Capitol Hill aide who had previously enjoyed Heritage's support in trying to abolish the agency.

Corporations have sought influence primarily by throwing their weight behind organizations and groups that espouse alternatives they either enthusiastically back or prefer in the face of something they deem to be much worse. Through their contributions, corporations have established a decided superiority over their rivals and critics in every area that is of vital concern to them.

When Congress takes up tax issues, business can call on the American Council for Capital Formation, the CATO Institute, the Heritage Foundation, selected scholars from Brookings, the American Enterprise Institute, Ture's Research Institute, NAM, and the Chamber of Commerce. Labor can call on Robert McIntyre's tiny Citizens for Tax Justice. In defining the party's economic agenda, business cannot only command the loyalty of conservative and Republican organizations, but also of Democratic groups such as the Democratic Leadership Council that have been funded by lobbyists and their corporations. By contrast, liberal and labor Democrats can look to Heather Booth's Coalition for Democratic Values, housed in the top floor of a warehouse off a side street in suburban Maryland.

Much of the environmental movement is funded through direct mail, but as the recession has dried up direct-mail contributions, those environmental organizations that can gain large-scale corporate funding have continued to prosper while the more radical groups such as Greenpeace have had to cut back drastically in their staff and activities. According to the *Chronicle of Philanthropy*, only organizations that "seek market-oriented solutions don't feel the pinch." This means that their voice is now more likely to be heard, and, in Washington, the power to get your opinion heard wins battles.

Taken together, the corporate PACs and lobbyists, corporate officials manning new Washington offices, the Chamber of Commerce and NAM, the new organizations like the Business Roundtable, and the corporate contributions to like-minded organizations such as AEI have completely tilted the balance of power in Washington. Business has gotten its way for the last fifteen years in every major legislative battle that directly threatens it, from labor law reform to tax reduction and deregulation.

LABOR'S DIMINISHING RETURNS

The AFL-CIO watched the initial explosion of social movements with a mixture of confusion and disdain. During Martin Luther King's

1963 march on Washington, AFL-CIO head George Meany closed the federation's headquarters for fear that the march would turn into a riot. During the 1972 election, Meany implicitly aligned the federation with Richard Nixon's attacks against the "acid, amnesty, and abortion" of the new left and the McGovern campaign. But the United Auto Workers, which left the AFL-CIO in 1968 and did not rejoin it until 1981, and the industrial and public employee unions within the federation backed the civil rights movement, helping to found the Leadership Conference on Civil Rights.

Over the next two decades, as corporate lobbying expanded, these same unions also funded several coalition efforts, including the Full Employment Action Council and the Progressive Alliance, intended to counter corporate influence. In the late 1970s, after Meany had been succeeded by Lane Kirkland and after labor had been repeatedly drubbed on Capitol Hill, the AFL-CIO itself began reluctantly and haltingly funding organizations that it did not directly control. But the bulk of union funding still comes from individual unions rather than the federation.

During the 1980s, unions helped bankroll feminist, environmental, consumer, foreign policy, and citizens organizations, becoming the mainstay of such efforts as the Citizen-Labor Energy Coalition, now part of Citizen Action. Unions have contributed the bulk of the funds for two policy research groups, the Citizens for Tax Justice and the Economic Policy Institute (EPI) and have joined business in backing Clyde Prestowitz's Economic Strategy Institute.

The unions' role in founding EPI bears out the plight of labor. The AFL-CIO's Industrial Union Department (IUD) had regularly been doing studies of the decline of manufacturing, but the mainstream press ignored its efforts because they were seen as colored by labor's special interest.

After lengthy and sometimes difficult discussions with the policy intellectuals that were putting EPI together, union officials decided they would be better off following the corporations' example and funding a group that was committed to the same principles and ideas but not tainted directly by their label. In 1986 labor unions provided the money to start EPI, and the IUD's star economist Larry Mishel transferred to EPI, doing virtually the same studies, but gaining some attention from the press corps. Yet EPI remained haunted by labor's role. The press refers to the organization as "labor-backed," while never describing AEI and other business-funded groups as "business-backed." To secure its independence, EPI has successfully won some support from foundations and business.

Both Citizens for Tax Justice and EPI are relatively low-budget operations compared to AEI or Heritage. And labor's overall contribution to organizations like these remains minuscule compared to the amount of money corporations spend on think tanks and policy groups—perhaps less than one half of one percent. Labor also spends relatively little on lobbying. Since 1960, the AFL-CIO has devoted about 2.5 percent of its budget to lobbying Capitol Hill. By comparison, the National Rifle Association, a particularly effective force on Capitol Hill, spends more than 15 percent of its budget on lobbying. At one point, the American Petroleum Institute employed more lobbyists in Washington than the entire labor movement.

What clout labor has comes from its political action committee contributions to candidates and from its power as a genuine national membership organization that can summon its troops to punish and reward public officials. But as labor's percentage of the non-agricultural work force has dropped to 16 percent, its ability to counter corporate power has diminished still further.

THE POWER OF DIRECT MAIL

Many of the organizations that grew out of the social movements of the last decade—including NOW, NARAL, Common Cause, and the Conservative Caucus—use direct mail to raise the bulk of their money. The advantage of direct mail is that it renders an advocacy organization independent of large donors, whether wealthy individuals, corporations, foundations, or unions. Some major issues—like Common Cause's campaign finance reform, NARAL's defense of abortion rights, and the Conservative Caucus's campaign against the Panama Canal Treaty, for example—could not have been financed otherwise. Most of the large vested interests opposed campaign reform, and most of the foundations and corporations have found abortion too controversial. There are myriad smaller single issues such as gun control or opposition to federal funding of the National Endowment for the Arts that can be financed through carefully targeted direct mail. "Direct mail allows organizations to raise money for things that you don't always read about in the newspapers and that foundations and big donors are not interested in," says Republican direct-mail specialist Ann Stone.

But direct mail also has had its disadvantages. It is extremely expensive to finance. Nader's Public Citizen required a foundation grant to begin direct mail. Greenpeace relied on a loan from its direct mailer. It cannot be used by smaller policy research groups such as EPI whose work cannot be capsulized in a gut-wrenching direct-mail letter. By encouraging political groups to define their own purposes narrowly and through single issues, reliance upon direct mail contributes to the fragmentation of American politics. And while its social universe is larger than that of corporations and very wealthy large donors, it is primarily upper-and upper-middle class and is therefore only appropriate for issues that appeal to that segment of America. While direct-mail solicitation allows groups to communicate part of what they are doing to the world outside Washington, it provides little real link between that world and Washington pressure groups.

Direct mail was first used in 1964 by fund-raiser Marvin Liebman for Barry Goldwater's presidential campaign, which could not rely on traditional business sources. In 1970 Roger Craver, a former fund-raiser for George Washington University, used it to launch John Gardner's new good-government organization, Common Cause. Gardner, a former secretary of Health, Education and Welfare, had become frustrated trying to create a consensus among the labor unions, foundations, and corporations that funded the National Urban Coalition, and wanted a way of raising money that would free him from large funders with conflicting priorities.

In the early 1970s Richard Viguerie, who had been Liebman's assistant, began using it to finance new conservative organizations, including the Conservative Caucus and the National Conservative Political Action Committee (NCPAC). In 1976 Viguerie associate Stephen Winchell branched out on his own and begin raising money for the Heritage Foundation, which depended on direct mail for much of its expenses in its early years and still raises about 40 percent of its funds that way. Meanwhile, Craver set up his own firm in 1976 and began raising money not only for candidates, but also eventually for NOW, NARAL, Planned Parenthood, Greenpeace, Handgun Control, and the whole array of liberal social-movement organizations.

Direct mailers boast that direct mail is a democratic means of raising money, but it is democratic only in comparison with fund-raising from corporations and the very wealthy. From 1970 through the mid-1980s, the direct-mail universe was very similar for both liberal and conservative organizations. It was predominately white, male, fifty-five-years-old and over, and with an income over $50,000. Craver refers to the liberal side of this constituency as the "toiling masses of Westchester and the peasants of Beverly Hills."

Conservative organizations like Heritage or Free the Eagle still rely on this older, male, well-to-do donor. Their funding base has not expanded and has probably shrunk slightly over the last two decades. But according to a survey that pollster Peter Hart did for Craver Matthews Smith & Co., the liberal social movements are now drawing almost a quarter of their fund from women donors age thirty-five to forty-five who have a mean income of $55,000. While the class base of Craver's mailing list has not changed, its age and sex have. This trend has already given liberal social-issue groups a decided advantage over their conservative counterparts.

Most organizations that raise money through the mail ask their donors to become members. A few groups such as Common Cause and NOW have tried to maintain real memberships through the mail, with local chapters and membership election of officers, but for most of the organizations, including NARAL, Planned Parenthood, Handgun Control, the Heritage Foundation, and Conservative Caucus, offering membership has served merely as a fund-raising technique that has allowed an organization to come back annually for contributions. It has sustained professionalized advocacy organizations.

Even in those organizations that have real members, the very size of the membership generated by direct mail has frayed the ties between the Washington headquarters and the organization's members. Typically, an organization such as Common Cause or NOW can be divided into four groups: the top staff and board of directors; an activist cadre of one to five percent who work in chapters and attend national conventions; the 25 percent of the membership that take the trouble to fill out membership ballots and opinion surveys; and the remaining passive members—about 70 percent—whose primary contribution is to send an annual donation.

The passive members influence the organization largely by increasing or decreasing their contribution and their numbers. In the last year, for instance, environmental organizations have suffered a sharp falling off in their direct-mail receipts not only because of the recession but also because the average donor no longer believes that the environment is threatened, while women's organizations, buoyed by anger from the Anita Hill-Clarence Thomas hearings and the looming battle over *Roe v. Wade*, have experienced an upsurge in contributions. Similarly, many New Right organizations furiously expanded their contributions during the last Carter years, but then went broke after Reagan took office and removed the specter of a reigning liberalism.

In the direct-mail membership organization, the key group is the activist cadre, who, if they combine with a faction within the Washington staff, can effect real changes in the organization. In 1982, for instance, Common Cause's activists united with staff members to change the organization's focus from good-government issues to stopping the MX missile, even though the organization's polls showed that the group's membership was less concerned about the MX than about the organization's traditional issues. In 1989 NOW's activists forced the organization—against the better judgment of many of its leaders—to consider building a feminist third party.

However limited their representation, organizations such as NOW and Common Cause do represent an advance in democracy. But the majority of organizations are less like NOW and Common Cause and more like the Conservative Caucus, NARAL, Greenpeace, or People for the American Way. However noble their cause, they pursue it largely within a closed universe. They are accountable to a larger public only through the ultimate veto power that these donors hold. And these donors, far from being representative of the country at large, embody a small slice of upper-income America.

Organizations that are dependent on direct mail also are limited by the preoccupations of their own donor base. The donors to organizations like NARAL or the Sierra Club tend to fit the profile of the Baby Boomer—liberal on social and environmental issues and on foreign policy, but fiscally conservative, often suspicious of unions, indifferent to poverty except in the most melodramatic forms. None of the major organizations that rely on direct mail emphasize the redistribution of income, the rebuilding of cities, the rights of workers to join unions, the need for national health insurance, or the kind of environmental issues that plague working-class neighborhoods.

CANVASSING THE MIDDLE CLASS

Some of those organizations that want to work on populist economic issues have discovered an alternative to direct mail and to contributions from business, labor, and foundations. In 1974 Chicago activist Marc Anderson, inspired by the example of door-to-door encyclopedia salesmen, began canvassing to raise money for Citizens for a Better Environment. Anderson introduced canvassing techniques to Ralph Nader's network of Public Interest Research Groups and to Citizen Action, a group of liberal state organizations that were emphasizing economic issues. Other national organizations, including Greenpeace, ACORN, Clean Water Action, and SANE-Freeze, now use canvassing to fund their operations.

Contributors to canvasses tend to be less well-to-do than direct-mail donors and more receptive to middle-class or even working class economic issues. Two years ago, Citizen Action did a profile of its donors and found that 58 percent have household incomes of less than $40,000.

Unlike the direct-mail donors, Citizen Action's donors identified jobs and unemployment as key issues. Yet Citizen Action's donor base was by no means working-class. One-third or more of those from thirty-five to fifty-four years old earned $50,000 and half of the donors identified themselves as either managers or professionals. Canvassing does widen the political universe in which groups operate—making it possible to raise money for economic issues—but it does not alter it dramatically.

When organizations began using canvasses for raising money, they also saw it as a way of educating citizens and gaining active members. Most canvassing groups continue to call their donors "members," and canvassers ask people not simply for donations, but to buy a membership. But over the last decade, canvassing has degenerated into a fund-raising technique for professional organizations that are run by their staff. Jo Patten, an official of a Chicago citizens group who has been active in several canvassing organizations, says, "Technically, it is membership but membership means nothing. You can have no impact on the organization. Internally, it is viewed as first and foremost a fund-raising method."

Adoption of a canvass has even led some organizations to abandon the group's grassroots tradition. In the early 1980s, the peace organization SANE adopted a canvass to raise money. When it proved highly successful, SANE's director changed the organization from a chapter-based, activist group into a professionalized, staff-driven Washington organization with paper members recruited by the canvass. By 1988, when it merged with the nuclear freeze movement, SANE had become a Washington-based fund-raising shell.

Harry Boyte, the author of *Community Is Possible* and an early proponent of canvassing as a means of building democratic organizations, is now disillusioned with its results. "Organizations that are heavily canvass-based not only pose issues in black and white, but lose any possibility for a strong membership base, because the money doesn't come from the members," Boyte observes. "The members don't have a sense of ownership or the challenge of raising money. [Saul] Alinsky is right that people don't have any strong stake in an organization unless they own it."

Yet for national organizations that deal with gas prices, health care, toxic waste, and other working-class economic issues, canvassing remains far more viable than direct mail or soliciting financial help from foundations, corporations, and unions. Direct mail does not work with people worried about their jobs; foundations and corporations appear interested only when discrimination occurs or when the poor huddle in front of Park Avenue apartments; and unions have their own diminishing membership to worry about.

Sociologist Pamela Oliver believes that the degeneration of organizations using the canvass into professional advocacy groups is the result of the decline of public political activity over the last decade rather than an outgrowth of the canvass itself. "Canvassing is a poor way of raising money," says Oliver, "but what is the alternative?"

Oliver is probably right, but the point remains: Canvassing by itself does not currently contribute to genuine mass membership organizations any more than direct mail does. And in the absence of a popular upsurge outside Washington, the existence of several national organizations that rely on canvassing has done little to mitigate the overwhelming tie of most Washington organizations to upper- and upper-middle-class wealth and concerns.

THE NEW POWER CENTERS

Political democracy has been breaking down in Washington. The breakdown began with the decline of the political parties. The parties have lost much of their power and coherence, the victims of misguided reform and the replacement of the precinct captain and street corner rally by the political consultant and television advertisement. Popular institutions that supported a civic political culture—the labor union, the neighborhood bar, and the ward organization—have withered or disappeared.

The new lobbies, research groups, and think tanks that have arisen over the last three decades have not provided an alternative link between citizens and their government. Instead, they have become centralized bureaucracies as remote from the average citizen as the government itself. Moreover, these new organizations—through their focus on single issues or through studied avoidance of partisanship—have contributed further to the decline of parties and of politics as a process of public deliberation and compromise toward common ends.

In the 1950s, pluralist theorists vastly overrated the power of the labor movement to act as a countervailing force to business, but labor in that era was a hulking Behemoth compared to what it has become. While labor's role in politics and pressure groups has steadily diminished, the power of business has vastly increased. Business and its organizations and lobbyists dominate the higher reaches of both political parties in Washington and set the agenda in the debate over the economic issues that directly concern it. About 8,500 of the 12,500 lobbyists, consultants, and lawyers listed in the current *Washington Representatives* work for American and foreign corporations.

As labor's role has diminished, business's lobbying has become narrower and more self-interested. It has had to concern itself less with challenging labor's right to speak for the entire society and more with securing its prerogatives and profit margins.

If there is another power center in Washington, it is the organs of social liberalism and environmentalism—groups like NOW, NARAL, Common Cause, Handgun Control, the Children's Defense Fund, the World Wildlife Fund, and the ACLU. Together, they employ about 2,500 Washington lawyers, lobbyists, and public relations experts on their behalf. The power of these organizations now dwarfs that of the conservative social-issue organizations, lending credence to the charge that liberals rule Washington. But these organizations represent overlapping constituencies with many of the business groups. They do not reflect a competing, but often a complementary vision of society: one that combines fiscal conservatism with a firm opposition to environmental pollution and racial and sexual inequality. The liberalism of these organizations bears little resemblance to the economic liberalism of the New Deal and the labor movement. They represent the triumph of Hollywood, Cambridge, and New York's Upper West Side.

These two forces—business/economic conservatism and well-to-do social liberalism—have ruled American politics over the last fifteen years. During this time, Washington's politicians have fought off attempts to weaken environmental and social legislation—even passing a strengthened Clean Air Act and a new Civil Rights Bill. But they have also acceded to a massive redistribution of wealth from the poor and lower-middle class to the upper-middle class and the wealthy, while acquiescing in the deregulation of corporations and banks. National Democrats have been particularly victimized by the erosion of parties and the growth of these new centers of power. Last spring, as the recession deepened, Robert Andrews, a freshman congressman from Bellmawr, New Jersey, recounted to me his utter bewilderment at how Washington works. While Andrews's constituents in his working-class Camden County district were becoming increasingly nervous about their jobs, Congress was preoccupied with the Brady gun control bill and a new version of the civil rights bill—measures, however meritorious, that were of no interest in his district. Echoing Ronald Reagan, Andrews described an "iron triangle" of interest groups that were dominating the Democratic Party and preventing it from attending to its traditional working-class and middle-class base. As a newcomer, Andrews saw clearly what many veteran Washington Democrats have accepted with resignation.

The Democrats' traditional middle class constituency "Roosevelt's forgotten men and women" have also been losers in this transformation of Washington politics. Many of them know that they are better off because unions exist; they are far more concerned about jobs, taxes, and health insurance than about abortion, gun control, or exotic wildlife. As the pressure groups in Washington have proliferated, as billions of dollars have poured into the city to fund lobbies, PACs, and so-called public interest groups, these Americans have found themselves on the outside, watching with growing dismay as their own fate is decided by men and women they never elected, funded, or supported.

How Money Votes

AN OKLAHOMA STORY

Robert Dreyfuss

A few blocks from the U.S. Capitol, in a street-level parking lot owned by the American Trucking Associations, one of those only in-America scenes unfolded last April.

With temperatures hovering near 90 degrees, men and women in expensive suits chafed uncomfortably as they waited in line. Young volunteers sporting bright yellow T-shirts were everywhere, bristling with the enthusiasm of what appeared to be their first political campaign. A crack unit of these scrub-faced ones patrolled the entrance to the lot, seizing the necks of new arrivals, quickly wrapping them in bright yellow bandannas, cowboy-style. In the heat, the added neckwear caused beads of sweat to form, giving the well-heeled attendees a faintly ridiculous air.

Though few tasseled loafers were apparent, the guests were mostly Washington lobbyists, for American Airlines and the National Rifle Association, for Dow Chemical and the Tobacco Institute, for Southwestern Bell and the American Pharmaceutical Association. Representatives of big oil producers like BP America and the American Petroleum Institute rubbed shoulders with drug manufacturers like Merck and Sandoz. Dozens, scores, perhaps more than a hundred milled around the parking lot, munching barbecue and trading gossip about doings in Congress.

In uneasy coexistence with the bleak landscape of the open air parking lot were the signs and sounds of classic American political hoopla, Oklahoma-style. To one side, a two-man band dressed in the cowboy way strummed "The Stray Cat Strut." Further on, a Choctaw tribal chief in full Indian dress stalked about, agreeably having his photo taken with any and all. And standing at the front of the line were the hosts of this celebration: Congressman Bill Brewster and his wife (and partner) Suzie, both dressed in colorful

Western attire that put them into high relief among the gray and navy suits.

One by one, the visitors filed past the Brewsters, engaging in a familiar ritual. The lobbyists gripped-and-greeted the member of Congress, murmured a few words, unwrapped the uncomfortable nylon bandanna, and headed for the beer. For two hours, the Brewsters courted their guests, who had paid $500, $1000, or more to attend the event. By day's end, more than $100,000 would flow into Brewster's campaign coffers from individual lobbyists and political action committees.

This is how the game is played.

By the end of 1994, Bill Brewster's campaigns will have raised and spent nearly $2 million since 1989, when Brewster began exploring the possibility of running for Congress. This article is the story of that $2 million—the story of how a working politician forms a practical, permanent alliance with big money and how that alliance taints the governing process.

Why Bill Brewster? He is emblematic of the system. He stands, politically and geographically, at Congress' dead center. A conservative Democrat, Brewster has little seniority in the House. But he is an influential member of the House's most important committee, Ways and Means, which gives him a head start raising money.

Brewster's is the tale of how a rising politician learns to tap national financial sources rather than local ones. It is also the story of how these powerful national financiers reward incumbents by providing them with a surfeit of money—enough to ward off any challengers who might disrupt the status quo. There are questions of legality here. A close look at Brewster's record suggests that some of his fundraising practices may have broken federal elections laws. But for the most part, Brewster's story is a vivid illustration of what the system still permits: fundraising practices that skew politics in favor of wealthy interests, thus promoting cumulative disaffection with the democratic process.

The evidence for this article was pieced together from Federal Election Commission records, data on file with the Oklahoma Council on Campaign Compliance and Ethical Standards, U.S. House of Representatives financial disclosure forms, and data compiled by the private National Library on Money and Politics. I also conducted dozens of interviews, including two with Brewster himself. Thanks to the periodic FEC reports that are required from every candidate for Congress, it is possible to trace the origin of nearly every dollar that finds its way into a campaign treasury. However, it is not so easy to find out why contributors support a candidate financially. The methods by which candidates manage to obtain those dollars are not readily apparent, either. In the following, we will try to answer some of those questions.

The parking lot at the American Trucking Associations, where Bill Brewster held court with the nation's lobbyists on April 26, is half a continent and a world away from the part of Oklahoma Bill Brewster calls home. Born in 1941 in Ardmore (population 20,000) in Carter County, the Brewsters now live on a ranch south of Marietta in Love County. Carter and Love counties, which form the southwest corner of the 22-county Third District, sit just north of the Red River that separates Oklahoma from Texas, in the middle of America's oil patch, about halfway between Oklahoma City and Dallas, Texas.

The district is one of the nation's poorest, populated by hardscrabble farmers who eke out a living growing peanuts and raising cattle, chicken, and hogs. Almost entirely rural—along with Ardmore, only the towns of Stillwater and Shawnee count more than 20,000 people—the area's farms are often punctuated by a lone oil rig slowly nodding up and down like some giant bird pecking at insects.

Dead armadillos litter the roadways, and the towns themselves show severe signs of wear and tear. The main streets in both Ardmore and Marietta are sadly barren and lifeless, marked by closed businesses and buildings whose paint is peeling off in great flakes. In county after county in the Third, as many as 20 to 25 percent of the people live in poverty, and many are on welfare.

The Third's voters are hard-working, conservative, God-fearing Democrats. The area's nickname is "Little Dixie," reflecting the migration of poor, southern whites in what was then known as Indian Territory before Oklahoma statehood in 1907. They brought with them the southerner's animosity toward anything Republican and while the rest of the South is increasingly embracing the Republican Party, Oklahoma's Little Dixie remains resolutely a "yellow dog Democratic" district. Over 80 percent of the voters are registered

Democrats. As one Oklahoma politician says, "They spray for Republicans in Little Dixie."

To be sure, these voters are not limousine liberals. By all accounts, most of the Third's constituents oppose gun control and abortion, support prayer in schools, and are wary of anything that happens in Washington. They are fiercely patriotic—as evidenced by popular bumper stickers like "Fly Our Flag, Don't Burn It!" In Paul's Valley, on the district's edge, Bob's Pig Shop sports a sign out front that says, "Rambo for D.A." Gun shops are everywhere. A billboard proclaims, "This town belongs to Jesus."

The overwhelmingly Democratic nature of the Third District has meant that its representatives in Congress enjoy a rare form of longevity. Since 1947, only three men have represented Oklahoma's Third: Carl Albert, who served from 1947 to 1977 and was Speaker of the House; Wes Watkins who served from 1977 to 1991, and who left to run for governor; and Bill Brewster, elected in 1990. Unless Brewster chooses to run for higher office, and barring a major scandal, it is widely assumed that Brewster will be a member of Congress for decades to come.

Running for Congress was unlike anything Bill Brewster had ever done before. His earlier campaigns for Oklahoma's House of Representatives in 1982, 1984, 1986 and 1988 were low-dollar affairs. State records on file in Oklahoma City show that in 1988 Brewster raised a total of $1,500 for his campaign, two-thirds of which came in the form of a $1,000 cash contribution from a fellow legislator.

That pattern changed in 1989. As required by state law, Brewster filed campaign financing disclosure forms with the Oklahoma Council on Campaign Compliance and Ethical Standards for 1989-90. But those forms, sketchy in the best of times, are sloppy and incomplete, making a thorough analysis very difficult. What the records do show is that Brewster raised far more funds than for the previous cycle, at least $26,710. There is very little to indicate how the money was spent; for much of it there is simply no account. But a major portion of it, nearly $11,000, was used not to finance his re-election to the state legislature but to launch his bid for Congress. Such transfers of funds, now illegal under FEC rules, were permitted in 1990.

Although Brewster announced his decision to run for Congress at the end of January 1990, it had been widely known that the incumbent member, Wes Watkins, a Democrat, was considering a race for governor, meaning that the Third District would be up for grabs. As early as the summer of 1989, Brewster had begun putting out feelers to explore the possibility of running for Congress should Watkins abandon the seat. Thus, every dollar Brewster raised in 1989 and 1990 could be tapped to commission polls, pay for travel, and buy advertising—which, in turn, allowed him to enhance his name recognition and assess his prospects for a run at Congress. When Brewster finally did announce his intentions to run for the Third District's seat, he officially transferred exactly $10,995.32 from his state campaign to his U.S. congressional campaign fund.

Only a few weeks earlier, however, state records show that Brewster received a $5,000 campaign contribution from an Ardmore, Oklahoma, oil man named Harold Holden. Even under the FEC rules at the time, most of that money could not legally be transferred into Brewster's new campaign. Under FEC rules, no individual is allowed to contribute more than $1,000 to any single federal candidate in a given contest (primaries and general elections are considered separate races). Because Harold Holden's $5,000 exceeded the FEC limits on individual contributions, it could not legally have been applied to a federal campaign.

Given the passage of time, poor record-keeping, and vagueness of memory, it is no longer possible to determine if Holden's $5,000 was spent on Brewster's campaign for state office or was included in the $10,995 that was transferred into his federal campaign. But either way, a substantial contribution from a single individual helped launch Brewster's first foray into national politics.

We will soon come across oil man Harold Holden again, under more worrisome circumstances.

Not for nothing had Bill Brewster spent eight years in the Oklahoma state legislature positioning himself as a pro-business, Chamber of Commerce Democrat. And seldom had anyone had as substantial and diverse ties to the business community as he had in the Third District and the state of Oklahoma.

But Brewster would not have a cakewalk into Congress. A tough race was shaping up against a worthy opponent in the Democratic primary—he would face Lieutenant Governor Robert S. Kerr III, scion of one of Oklahoma's premier families, whose father was a member of the board of directors of the Kerr-McGee oil company and whose grandfather had been a powerful U.S. Senator. As an underdog, Brewster knew that he would require several hundred thousand dollars to mount a credible campaign.

Though relatively well-to-do, Brewster also knew that he could not hope to finance his campaign with his own funds. According to a letter on file at the FEC, Brewster had assets of slightly more than $1 million and a net worth of $695,000 at the time he launched his campaign for Congress. While that amount certainly placed him amongst a tiny elite in rural Love County, most of his wealth was tied up in a home, a cattle ranch, mining investments, and IRAS. He would have to raise money, a lot of it—and fast.

Joe Elles of Marietta, Brewster's first campaign treasurer, notes that Brewster had organic ties to the local small business community. "Being a pharmacist by trade, that put him in a pretty lucrative position with the medical community. He'd been in the ranching business, served in a leadership position in the breeders' association, so that gave him an inherent inroad to the cattlemen. Him and his wife have both been involved in real estate for some time, as agents and brokers. He's had an auto dealership," says Elles. "He just had all the right ingredients."

Brewster tapped each of those small business networks in the early stages of the campaign, during February and March 1990. In the Third District, says a former Brewster staffer, "It's early to bed, early to rise, work like hell and advertise. That's how you make it." Virtually every meeting they had turned into a fundraiser, he said. "They'd give up a hundred dollars here and ten dollars there, and a tankful of gasoline here and someone would feed him there."

Although Elles says that the campaign "had quite a few barbecues, donations of hogs and calves," four out of every five dollars raised by Brewster in those two months came not from small contributors but from high-dollar donors (over $200), PACs, and the leftover funds from his state legislature campaign. Still, for the most part it was local money. Out of 77 big contributors who donated to Brewster in the first two months of his campaign, 53 came out of three small towns: Ardmore, Madill, and Marietta, and almost all of them came from Oklahoma. The majority listed themselves as "self-employed," and as their occupation listed "investments," "attorney," or "oil/gas/ranch." Many of the contributions were dated either

March 12, March 28 or March 30, indicating fundraisers were held on those dates. The $35,000 raised from these 77 contributors allowed Brewster to jumpstart his campaign with money from a small but wealthy elite in southeastern Oklahoma.

At the beginning, PAC money was difficult to come by. The nature of PACs, as every student of campaign financing knows, is that they like to back winners. As a rule, PAC money favors incumbents over challengers or long shots simply because incumbents are more likely to win and are already in a position to be helpful to the donor. But in the first few weeks of his campaign, Brewster did win the backing of a handful of PACs.

Brewster's first PAC money was a check for $4,950 from the National Rifle Association (NRA). (Just to be on the same side, the NRA also donated an identical sum to Bobby Kerr, Brewster's opponent.) The NRA would stay on as a "Brewster booster" for the next four years, and eventually Brewster would join the NRA's board of directors. Not to be outdone by her husband, Suzie Brewster is a gun enthusiast who is constantly seen in gun clubs and on shooting ranges, and who, in Washington, coaxed a passel of congressional wives to take up shooting. Today, Brewster is the co-chairman of the Sportsman's Caucus in the House, and his office wall displays a photograph of him out duck hunting with President Clinton.

Two more $5,000 checks arrived from the PACs of the National Association of Chain Drug Stores and the National Association of Pharmacists, both of whom hoped to cash in on the candidate's background as a licensed pharmacist. Along with a $2,000 contribution from the nurses' PAC, Brewster managed to raise a not-too-shabby $20,700 from PACs in the first 8 weeks of his campaign. But the best was yet to come.

Just outside Bill Brewster's old window at the Oklahoma Capitol Building, there is a striking view of an oil derrick. In fact, out just about any window of the capitol is an oil derrick, because the steel towers are scattered everywhere on the capitol plaza—a fitting symbol of the power of the oil and gas industry in the former capital of the oil patch, Oklahoma.

There is a lot of oil money in Oklahoma, and oil money is political money. During his eight years as a state legislator, Bill Brewster assiduously cultivated Oklahoma's oil men. In 1985, he took over the economic development committee in the state legislature, and he soon won the "Legislator of the Year" award from the Oil Marketing Association. He chaired the energy committee of the National Council of State Legislators and was elected chairman of the powerful South/West Energy Council.

Oil money is what pushed Bill Brewster over the top in 1990. From April to November 1990, 32 oil and gas company PACs backed Brewster's bid for Congress. Phillips PAC led the field with $7,500, and Amoco, Atlantic Richfield, Chevron, Exxon, Occidental, Shell, Sun, Texaco, Union and many others joined in. In all, including utility company PACs, Brewster raised nearly $39,000 from energy and mining PACs in 1990.

Besides oil PAC money, Brewster pulled in tens of thousands of dollars from wealthy independent oil men. It is difficult to determine exactly how much, because oil money comes not only from people who own and operate oil companies but from oil equipment people, investors, oil industry lawyers, bankers who finance oil industry operations, and friends, relatives and acquaintances of oil industry folks. Using a conservative estimate based on FEC records, the Brewster 1990 campaign gathered upwards of $40,000 from Oklahoma's oil and gas industry through individual contributions.

Patrick Raffaniello, chief of staff for Brewster, was in early 1990 executive director of the South/West Energy Council, located just outside of Dallas, and FEC records show that Pat and Kyle Raffaniello each donated $1,000 to Brewster's campaign on March 30, 1990. The council served as a nexus for state legislators from oil patch states to meet and work alongside representatives of major oil interests, and according to an Oklahoma legislator who served with Brewster, Raffaniello was a frequent visitor to Oklahoma City and "managed to steer a lot of big energy money to Brewster." A New Yorker by origin, Raffaniello caused a lot of grumbling in Oklahoma when he was appointed chief of staff by Brewster in 1993. "He got the job because he's a big-time fundraiser," said a former Oklahoman who has worked on Capitol Hill.

This is where Harold Holden enters the story again. Holden, you may remember, was the owner of Holden Energy Corporation. His $5,000 contribution to Brewster's state legislature campaign early in

1990 helped position Brewster for his congressional campaign. Holden Energy, described by the *Daily Oklahoman* as "one of the nation's largest independent energy companies," was only one of several companies owned and operated by the Holden family; others included Safe Tire Disposal Corp., Environmental Thermal Systems, and Red Fork Construction Co. According to several sources in Oklahoma, Holden has been one of Bill Brewster's key backers since at least 1989. Holden and Brewster had been friends for years, since Brewster served in the state legislature.

Last year, Holden was indicted and pled guilty to campaign financing abuses in connection with Oklahoma Governor David Walters' 1990 campaign. The FBI and then an Oklahoma City grand jury investigated a pattern of illegal campaign donations by Harold Holden, his family, employees, friends, and business associates. In October 1993, Holden pled guilty to making 16 illegal campaign donations totaling $32,000 during the 1990 race for governor. He was ordered to pay a fine of $21,280 and received a two-year suspended sentence.

According to the indictment, in order to evade the $5,000 limit on individual campaign contributions to a state candidate, Holden distributed $32,000 to employees, friends and business associates, who in turn funneled the money into the race for governor. Just to be on the safe side, half of the illegal money was channeled into Walters's coffers and half of it went to the campaign war chest of Walters's Republican opponent, Bill Price. Campaign records—backed up by subpoenaed evidence of bank transactions—show that Holden's $32,000 was paid out to at least 16 individuals, who, within a period of a couple of days, wrote personal checks to the Walters and Price campaigns.

FEC records reveal a highly interesting pattern to the Holden-Brewster connection. On the eve of the primary election, at an extremely critical moment in the race between Brewster and Kerr, at least 12 individuals made $1,000 contributions to Bill Brewster. Five of them were named in the indictment of Harold Holden in connection with the governor's race, along with three of their wives and several other Holden associates who came under investigation during the Grand Jury procedures. Most came on the same day, August 23, 1990. The individuals include Scott Holden, Harold's son, along with employees of Holden Energy, Safe Tire, Environmental

Thermal Systems, and Red Fork Construction, and attorneys and consultants who worked for Holden at the time.

The contributions stand out boldly because most of them are listed, one by one, on identical FEC reporting forms under the heading of "last-minute contributions" on August 23, just five days before the August 28 primary. On that same day, for the first time in the eight-month-long campaign, Bill and Suzie Brewster put up $35,000 in personal funds—money that Brewster apparently used to purchase a blitz of election-eve television commercials.

The TV commercials may well have pushed Brewster over the top. Kerr says polls showed him 15 points up less than a week before the vote. The final tally was 67,069 votes for Brewster and 54,471 for Kerr.

One plausible motivation for Harold Holden to funnel such extraordinary amounts of money into Brewster's campaign could be gratitude. In 1989, Bill Brewster sponsored a piece of state legislation that became law on July 1, 1989, called the Oklahoma Waste Tire Recycling Act (Oklahoma Title 68, Section 53001). This act created a state fund to pay for the recycling and disposal of millions of used auto and truck tires that were despoiling the state in dumps, valleys, and along roadways. The law established a $1 tax on the sale of new tires, 85 cents of which is paid to private tire recyclers for the collection, shredding and disposal of the tires.

Only one firm qualified for the program: Harold Holden's Safe Tire Disposal Corp., which, headed by Scott Holden, has collected more than $7 million since 1989 from the state of Oklahoma. "The law was written in such a way that it established a virtual monopoly for Holden's company," said an Oklahoma legislator.

Joe Elles, Brewster's campaign treasurer in 1990, recalls that Holden and his associates were big contributors to the Brewster campaign, but four years later does not recall much detail. "The Holdens hosted an event for Bill Brewster," he says, though Elles did not attend it. "Bill was doing everything he could to accumulate funds and they were appealing to quite a few people."

The Brewster campaign was unaware that Holden had given money illegally to the governor's race, Elles says, adding that he was careful to make sure that the campaign followed FEC rules carefully. But he adds that the campaign would not have known had Holden decided to channel funds through friends and associates. "You know, if they have a fundraiser and x number of people show up and contribute by individual checks, well, you just go from one place to another on the campaign trail. What contacts Bill and he [Holden] may have had, I can't speak to that."

But Pat Raffaniello, Brewster's chief aide, is unequivocal that there was no wrongdoing in connection with Holden. "All of the contributions that we received were legitimate and disclosed and all within the spirit and letter of the law," he says. "Nobody in the campaign has any knowledge of anybody violating any of the campaign laws."

And, concerning Harold Holden's $5,000 contribution to Bill Brewster's state legislature campaign fund, Raffaniello says, "I am confident that there was no illegal transfer of funds."

Holden did not return repeated phone calls.

In November 1990, against a little known and underfunded Republican opponent in the overwhelmingly Democratic Third, Bill Brewster stampeded to victory with 80 percent of the vote.

The second chapter of Bill Brewster's life in Congress began when the newly elected congressman and his wife began their journey to Washington, D.C. The freshman from Oklahoma reveled in the highly charged political atmosphere in the nation's capital. He loved the nonstop politicking, the network building, the aura and power that attached to the office of U.S. representative. Shaky at first in matters of protocol, he leaned on other members of the Oklahoma delegation, in particular Dave McCurdy, and he developed a very close working relationship with Sen. David Boren, vocal advocate of campaign finance reform. Bemused by the ways of Washington—he once expressed his shock at seeing Rep. Barney Frank (D.-Mass.), who is gay, dancing with another man at a congressional event—he nonetheless plunged in, building the connections and reputation that would catapult him into the Ways and Means Committee in just two years.

Unlike the vast majority of Democrats, Brewster received virtually no backing from organized labor. Most of the biggest PACs in Washington are labor PACs, and Democrats receive enormous sums from unions. However, Brewster had feuded with the AFL-CIO in Oklahoma ever since the 1980s, when he carried the banner for anti-union right-to-work legislation. Between February 1990 and December 1993, a period of 47 months, Bill Brewster received a mere $36,350 from labor PACs, just 5 percent of his total PAC receipts of

$670,465. In contrast, the average Democrat in Congress who accepted PAC money received one-third of it from labor PACs.

In the House, Brewster landed a spot on the Public Works and Transportation Committee, which is known for its pork barrel politics, often funding pet projects in members' districts. As a result, in addition to his already established backing from energy and health care interests, Brewster began to attract significant support from transportation and construction interests. Railroads, trucking companies, air transport interests, and builders gravitated to Brewster, funneling $39,500 in PAC money into his campaign warchest. The total represented more than three times the $12,200 he received from these interests in 1990.

And, now that Brewster was an incumbent, PACs reluctant to back an upstart found their way to Brewster. In every sector—energy, health care, banking, agriculture—Brewster's PAC totals rose sharply. Some businesses that had stayed away from Brewster in 1990 began lining up to support him because of his reputation as an outright supporter. Most ironic, perhaps, was the case of Kerr-McGee, a major energy company in Oklahoma with close ties to its namesake family, that of Robert S. Kerr III, Brewster's 1990 primary opponent. For six months in 1990, Brewster shied away from Kerr-McGee's Washington office, though the two eventually reconciled, with Kerr-McGee making a $1,000 PAC donation to Brewster.

The paradox of Brewster's first year in Congress is that while his fundraising totals rose dramatically, he faced no real threat in either the primary or general election of 1992. In the first six months of 1991, with the election behind him and no likely challengers in the wings, Brewster raised $108,805.

Enter Harold Holden once more. Holden's family, including Holden, his son and daughter, employees and associates once again came through handsomely; this time they kicked in a total of $20,000 in identical $1,000 contributions between June 24 and June 29, 1991.

Another Oklahoma heavyweight, oil man Mike Cantrell of Oklahoma Basic Economy, Inc. began organizing fundraisers for Brewster in Oklahoma City and Tulsa, each of which pulled in over a hundred people. Like most big givers, Cantrell denies any attempt to influence the way Brewster votes. "Money's not going to have any influence on where he stands at all," says Cantrell. "People give money to someone that has the same interests that they have."

During 1991, with the help of a growing number of PAC contributions, the campaign managed to gather more than $210,000. Brewster was following in the footsteps of his Third District predecessor, Rep. Wes Watkins. Watkins says that he attempted to keep "a defense fund, which I think a smart politician's got to do.... I think I'd carry something in the way of a couple of hundred thousand dollars, so you could get geared up fast if you had to." The money, Watkins said, served as a deterrent against a potential opponent who might be considering a race against him.

In the end, the November 1992 general election pitted Brewster against a 25-year-old teaching assistant who spent a total of $6,338. Brewster won with 75 percent of the vote.

As a sophomore, Bill Brewster shrewdly catapulted himself into the major leagues, securing a coveted seat on the Ways and Means Committee, the most powerful committee of all. Such a feat was nearly unprecedented for a second-term member, and it took help from some of Brewster's campaign financiers to make it happen.

Because of the high turnover in the House after the 1992 vote, then Chairman Dan Rostenkowski had to fill an unusually high number of seats on the committee. And because the committee's membership is traditionally balanced among regions of the country, Brewster knew that he had a shot to fill one of the slots accorded to the southwest. Brewster had shown Rostenkowski that he was a hard worker (Ways and Means is not kind to dilettantes) and it was known that the chairman wanted a conservative to offset liberals on the committee.

According to several sources, Brewster had influential, behind-the-scenes assistance from oil lobbyist J.D. Williams, one of the capital's premier power brokers and an Oklahoman who knew Rostenkowski well. In addition, sources report, Brewster had the backing of the National Rifle Association. Two powerful House committee chairs, John Dingell and Jack Brooks, both of whom are very close to the NRA, reportedly backed Brewster, urging Rostenkowski to elevate the junior Oklahoma Democrat. He did.

Joining Ways and Means opened the floodgates for campaign money. Marvelling at the newfound power of joining Ways and Means, a former Brewster staffer says, "That takes you out of the also-rans and puts you in with the big boys. It was almost as if we were freshmen again. A whole new group of people started coming into the office after he got on Ways and Means."

By the end of 1993, at least 313 individual PACs donated a total of $230,248 to Brewster's campaign, and 1993 was not even an election year. Again, in every category—agriculture, banking, finance, energy, health, transportation, and communications—contributions increased. The pace continued in 1994, making it likely that Brewster will pull in close to $1 million in PAC and individual donations for the 1993-1994 cycle, more than twice what he raised as a freshman.

The record shows that over Brewster's career, PACs have become increasingly involved in the Oklahoman's campaigns with each succeeding election cycle—and, each year, less and less of Brewster's funds came from his district and state. During the 1990 campaign, running for an open seat, Brewster managed to raise a total of $448,824, 37 percent ($173,244) of which came from PACs. During the 1991-1992 campaign, 62 percent ($266,973) of Brewster's total receipts of $423953 came from PACs. In the current 1993-1994 cycle, as of July 1, 1994, fully 71 percent ($519,336) of his campaign contributions was PAC money—out of a total of $728,191.

The rising tide of PAC contributions to Brewster between 1990 and 1994 puts him among Congress's elite for his ability to tap into the PAC community. In 1992, for example, the average winner of a House race drew just 42 percent of his or her funds from PACs.

"Committee is, down here in rural Oklahoma," he says.

Back in Oklahoma, though, Ways and Means seemed a lot less important than in Washington. Mack Stafford, Brewster's campaign treasurer, says that while the PACs are impressed with the congressman's position, Ways and Means does not have a lot of significance in the Third District. "A lot of people don't even know what the Ways and Means

To organize Brewster's Oklahoma fundraising operation, in 1993 the campaign established what it calls "the Century Club." Brewster boosters who contribute $100 or more to the campaign were invited to a lively fundraiser. First held last August in the town of Shawnee, the event included big-name country singers, barbecue, a 10-minute Brewster video, and speeches by Bill and Suzie Brewster to the assembled crowd of 500 well-wishers. The get-together probably raised $50,000 to $100,000 and another one is planned for this year.

At the Shawnee get-together, a select group of larger contributors, those donating $500 or more, were invited to join "the Medallion Club." About 100 people did so, attending a more private gathering in December at the Brewsters' home south of Marietta on a Sunday afternoon.

Stafford says that the Century and Medallion clubs allow the campaign to organize its fundraising more smoothly, consolidating a lot of statewide effort into a couple of central events, putting contributors on a computerized mailing list and sending them a quarterly newsletter. "So we don't have to go into each county and have individual fundraisers," he says. "It's an insider-type deal."

Asked why people give money to Brewster, especially since he appears to have no opponent, Stafford disclaims any quid pro quo. Instead, he describes a kind of harmony of interests. "I would say the main motivation is that people really believe in Bill Brewster," he says. "The energy people believe in him because they know he'll watch out for their best interest in energy. The agriculture people know he'll watch out for their best interests in agriculture." And so on.

I spoke to contributors in the Third District, but few were able to articulate a concrete reason for giving money. Some, like Madill, Oklahoma, lawyer Dan Little, had known the Brewsters for years and were "political friends." Others, like Jim Gunn of Stillwater, had explicit organizational reasons for backing the Brewster campaign. Last year, Gunn contributed $800, but he made it clear that his decision is shaped by larger forces. "I belong to an organization called the Association for Advanced Life Underwriting, based in Washington, D.C.," he said. "We have a program in which we commit to give, not a lot of money, but $1,000 a year, and basically we give it wherever it is determined by the organization that it be placed." Why? "We'd like to be able to have an opportunity to talk to people," he says. "They have to listen and sift, and we just want to be part of the listen-and-sift process... One sure way that people recognize you is that your name has been signed on the bottom of a check."

Nonetheless, Oklahoma-based fundraising is becoming less important to Brewster. Roy Dering, a Brewster critic who writes for the Ada Evening News, says, "He's getting big money, PAC money. That... says to me one of two things: he's not seeking money from home, or he's not getting it. He's getting support from big-money interests. And that's the kind of thing people get upset about, about losing touch with us."

The data support Dering's comments. In the three months ending June 30, 1994, for example, Bill Brewster raised more than $200,000, 80 percent of which came from PACs. From Ardmore, Madill, and Marietta—the area of Oklahoma where Brewster got his start, he raised only $2,750 during those three months, $1,000 of which came from Harold and Scott Holden.

Suzie Brewster is an accomplished fundraiser and the acknowledged strategist behind her husband Bill's finances. Until June 1, Suzie worked full-time as a professional fundraiser at Springer Associates, a Washington, D.C. consulting firm that organizes campaign financing for eight members of the House, including Bill Brewster.

During much of 1993 and 1994, Brewster paid Springer $3,000 a month to help the campaign pull in funds from Washington PACs and lobbyists. "Suzie is as good at it as anybody I've ever seen," says Maggie Springer, the firm's owner. Together, Springer and Suzie Brewster organized the April 26 "Oklahoma Round-Up," putting together a steering committee of industry givers, sending out invitations, making telephone calls, keeping track of the money, and filling out the required FEC forms.

The secret of Washington fundraising, Springer says, is to develop relationships with the key people in the PAC community. Raising money from PACs is kind of a mutual dance. For the most part, PACs budget donations to political campaigns on an annual basis, keeping in mind the $10,000 limit per cycle—but they rarely tell the members of Congress what they have budgeted for them.

"And having budgeted doesn't necessarily mean that they're going to give," Springer says. "They then sit back and wait to be asked. Nobody gives unless they're asked. So that's the first thing, to make sure that all the right people get asked."

Springer adds, "We have a rule around here that everybody is touched twice, once by mail and once by phone." Keeping track of trends and issues, sensing when particular PACs or industries are more or less interested in making donations, knowing how much money a PAC has available overall, even being aware of the degree of sensitivity to public perception about influence peddling—all these are things that political fundraisers must keep in mind.

"And," she says, "with PAC directors with whom I have a relationship, I can call them at the beginning of the cycle and say, 'How much have you budgeted for Bill Brewster and how do you want to give it?'"

As an example of the relationship that develops between a member and a PAC, consider United Parcel Service (UPS), which operates one of the largest PACS. Since 1991, UPS PAC has funneled $17,500 into Brewster's two campaigns. Arnold Wellman of UPS's government affairs unit says the company has worked with Brewster since the 1980s, when he helped sponsor tax incentives for converting the carrier's fleet of trucks to alternative fuels. During the debate over the North American Free Trade Agreement (NAFTA), which UPS strongly backed, the company lobbied hard, and successfully, to win Brewster's vote. But Wellman stresses that because Brewster has a longstanding relationship with UPS, because he has visited UPS's facility in the Third District "not once but a number of times," and because he is always accessible and "visits with our people"—all of that means more to the company than whether he votes "yes" or "no" on a particular issue. The PAC money, he says, "is a way for us to support candidates who are willing to listen to our point of view."

It is Brewster's relationship to the oil and gas industry that best exemplifies the true nature of the relationship between lawmakers and monied interests. As important as Oklahoma oil men like Harold Holden and Mike Cantrell are to Brewster, lobbyists and PACS representing members of the petroleum industry are the ones who now swing the really big money into the Brewster campaign fund. Since 1990, PACS from the oil and gas industry and related energy interests have poured more than $145,000 into Brewster's treasury.

Spokesmen for oil companies, on and off the record, state frankly that they coordinate on an almost daily basis with Bill Brewster and his staff, particularly Pat Raffaniello.

"In his brief time in Washington he's done a good job in representing the industry," says Don Duncan of Phillips. In February, Duncan joined a couple of dozen representatives of the oil and gas industry at a fundraising breakfast in Washington for Brewster. A steering committee comprised of Jean Mastres of Occidental Petroleum and Pete Frank of Kerr-McGee shepherded the major oil producers into a room where the lobbyists spent about 90 minutes with the congressman. Attendees included Chevron, Shell, Exxon, Texaco, Sun, Phillips, Kerr-McGee, Occidental, Conoco and others, including transporters and retailers. "We all know each other," says Mastres, making it easy to put together an event. A minimum donation to Brewster of $500 was the price of admission.

In a curious turn of phrase, Mastres said that they met as "concerned constituents, if you will, not just constituents of Oklahoma but constituents of the energy industry." It is almost as if Brewster were elected to represent not the people of Oklahoma's Third District, but the oil and gas industry.

The breakfast occurred at a critical moment for the oil industry. World oil prices were near historic lows, and many oil producers were clamoring for lower taxes, production incentives, and relief from government regulation. Small producers, like those in the Independent Petroleum Association of America (IPAA) were especially concerned about the collapse in prices. The big producers, along with pipeline operators, drillers, retailers, and others all had their concerns.

Bluntly, Mastres says that at times like that "you always look for someone (like Brewster) that can, quote, 'carry the water' on an issue." And carry the water he did. In a series of meetings, Brewster agreed to gather the combined concerns of the oil and gas industry into a single list of preferred reforms and tax changes. Working alongside IPAA and the major producers, he helped organize a bloc of 117 members of Congress determined to bring the oil industry's issues to the attention of the White House.

"They call it the Boren-Brewster tax package," Mastres says, adding that it includes tax cuts, tax incentives and regulatory relief. "It's sort of a wish list. This is the combined wish list for the industry." And the package, which would cost the U.S. Treasury $3 billion over 5 years, would probably not have seen the light of day had it not been for the two Oklahomans, Rep. Bill Brewster and Sen. David Boren.

Brewster had already earned a reputation as a bold defender of the oil industry in 1993, during the battle over the Clinton administration's proposal to enact an energy tax, called a BTU tax. Brewster astonished oil industry representatives by going directly to President Clinton, securing a face-to-face meeting at which he convinced the president to shift the point of collection for the BTU tax away from the producer and directly onto the bill that each consumer receives from the utilities. Not only did his action propose to save billions of dollars for the oil industry, but it made it easier for the industry to kill the tax entirely later on in the legislative process. Overnight, Brewster was a hero.

Don Duncan of Phillips cites Brewster's action as a "glowing example" of Brewster's record of support. "Here all of a sudden a freshman [on Ways and Means] goes directly to the president," he marvelled.

Duncan is quick to say that it would be wrong to consider what Brewster did as a quid pro quo for the oil industry's support. "It's not like the old days, [where] you give a guy a contribution and he's yours for life," says Duncan. "Members are more independent, and the nature of lobbying has changed drastically." Instead, he says, "The whole idea behind campaign giving is, you give to the members...who you feel best represent your interests."

But if money does not produce immediate favors, too many votes in the wrong direction by a member of Congress can lead to an abrupt halt in the flow of campaign funds. Says Duncan, "If a member...is gonna cast a vote that's really gonna hurt you, I've been known to call and say, 'I told you I'm coming to your event. I'm not.'" Duncan says that he receives eight to ten invitations a week to fundraisers, and he carefully examines the record of the member before recommending to Phillips' PAC that they contribute.

Another oil company PAC director is equally blunt. "If I see a vote or two votes that are diametrically opposed to a position that we've taken very strongly, I'll report back to the PAC that I think we should rescind their decision to give them money," he says.

It's a busy day on Capitol Hill. The House is just hours away from a vote on whether or not to ban certain types of automatic weapons, and Bill Brewster is hunting for votes to kill the ban. It's beginning to look bad for Brewster's side, however, and an aide tells him that they have just lost another handful of votes.

But Brewster keeps an appointment for an interview, and we sit down in a noisy corner of an antechamber in the Capitol.

It is immediately clear that Brewster does not think much of the various reforms that are being bandied about to deal with the public's perception that Congress is beholden to monied special interests. I ask him why he voted against a recent proposal to reform lobbying and prohibit gifts to members of Congress. "I think it's ludicrous that somebody takes the attitude that if you take a lunch or dinner with a lobbyist, that you can be bought," he says. "That you can be bought for any price."

One of the reforms, I note, would have barred members from accepting three- and four-day, all-expense-paid trips to resort hotels to attend conventions organized by lobbyists. Brewster, since coming to Washington, has taken at least 30 such trips; during 1993, for instance, he visited Palm Springs on the tab of the Tobacco Institute; Palm Beach, paid for by Philip Morris; Sarasota, Florida, for the American Medical Association; along with three other Florida trips, Los Angeles, San Antonio, and San Juan, Puerto Rico, all paid for by lobbyists.

"I do give speeches to constituents," he replies. "As to where they hold their conventions, uh, I don't guess that I have any control over where they hold them." I refrain from pointing out that little or no tobacco is grown in Oklahoma, so it is difficult to describe the Tobacco Institute or Philip Morris as "constituents" of his. (In fact, since 1990 Brewster has accepted more than $17,000 in tobacco money and, from his position on Ways and Means he has opposed plans to jack up federal taxes on cigarettes.)

Asked why he voted for campaign finance reform in 1992, when it was certain to be vetoed by President Bush, and then against an almost identical bill in 1993, when President Clinton said he would sign such a bill into law, Brewster says, "Because it had public financing in it the second time around... When you get into public finance, or welfare for politicians, I have a problem." But Brewster is wrong: the 1992 bill did include a provision for public financing, yet many of those who oppose reform in the House voted for it, knowing that it would die in the White House.

Confidently, Brewster says that he can run and win no matter what reformers do. "We can play within whatever rules they set. If they eliminate PACs, we'll go participate however they want," he says. "I can make it up. Any way they want to do it... We'll just go fundraise from those individuals in those particular industries, same way."

Brewster could begin with the health care industry. Although there are no known drug manufacturers in the Oklahoma's Third District, during 1993-94 Brewster has accepted a total of more than $15,000 in PAC money from Abbott, Ciga-Geigy, Eli Lilly, Glaxo,

Hoffman-LaRoche, Johnson & Johnson, Merck, Pfizer, Sandoz and many others. In all, Brewster has pocketed $139,000 from health care industry PACs since 1990, and hundreds of thousands more from business groups that oppose health care reform and, in particular, any plan that includes a mandate requiring employers to provide health insurance for their employees.

Brewster is implacably opposed to almost all versions of health care reform. How many people in your district don't have health insurance? I ask. He hesitates, talks to an aide, and replies that in a survey that his office sent out to Third District voters, 12 percent of those who replied said they lack insurance. (The actual figure for the state of Oklahoma is 18 percent, according to Census Bureau data, and in the Third District it is over 20 percent.) The plan that Brewster supports would leave that figure unchanged.

So it goes. Brewster has a string of votes in Congress that dovetail almost perfectly with the wishes of his contributors: he voted against the family leave bill, against the ban on striker replacement, against the Clinton administration's 1993 stimulus plan, against a cut in Star Wars funding, against a proposal to shut down NASA's space station, against extended unemployment benefits, and for NAFTA. More important, in crucial committee and subcommittee bargaining, he has aggressively promoted the agenda of the National Federation of Independent Business, the Chamber of Commerce, the oil industry and others.

Among people concerned about jobs, crime, health care, and schools, campaign finance reform has not yet become a priority. Ellen Miller, who heads the Center for Responsive Politics, says that Americans have yet to realize what it costs them when PACs and wealthy individuals are able to set the agenda for what gets debated in Congress. "People have to understand that the ability of these special interests to influence what happens in Congress affects their jobs, it affects how much money there is to fix up their towns, to provide help to people who need it," she says.

Tax breaks and subsidies for industries, she says, add $35 billion to the cost of energy, $30 billion to food costs, and billions more to the cost of nearly everything we buy, Miller says. A small campaign contribution of a few thousand dollars can result in a tax break worth tens of millions, she says. Only when people grasp the immediate pocketbook cost of the current patterns of campaign finance will they demand that the system be fixed.

When they do, they could throw their support behind one of several alternatives. One option would be public financing of campaigns modelled on the system now used for presidential elections, coupled with strict regulation of so-called soft money donations. This would eliminate the need for private money and provide the government with constitutional authority to regulate private fundraising. Almost every public interest group supports a version of this reform; even veteran fundraisers concede such rules would make a big difference. Alas, a similar proposal was advanced by the Clinton administration in 1993. Congress, thanks to resistance by lawmakers like Brewster, wanted nothing to do with it. Now, the issue has all but fallen off the radar screen.

Cynical voters seem indifferent to charges of corruption and campaign finance abuses. If Bill Brewster's backers did indeed play fast and loose with FEC rules, will his constituents care? A source at the FEC thinks not. "Oklahoma is one of those states, like Kentucky and Louisiana, where political corruption is seen more as theater or sport than as something to worry about," he says. "If you get caught, you're considered stupid, not bad." And, except in rare instances, the FEC has little power to impose stiff sanctions on campaign violators; instead, the FEC counts on the bad publicity associated with an FEC finding of wrongdoing to rile up voters. Often, that fails.

Asked about the prevailing notion of campaign finance abuses and political ethics in Oklahoma, a leading politician quotes Huey Long: "Never write to a man that you can talk to, never talk to a man that you can whisper to, and never whisper to a man that you can wink at." Whether Oklahomans wink at Bill Brewster remains to be seen.

The success of politicians who make maximum use of the current campaign finance system epitomizes a terrible paradox about American politics. Interest groups that can deliver large campaign contributions are well represented. Ordinary people feel unrepresented, and their dismay and disaffection have been growing. Yet despite public disaffection, declining voter turnout, and the scattered appearance of populist reform movements, the electorate fails to send to Congress the kind of people who might correct the system of campaign finance that is at the root of their own disenchantment.

Political Snipers

Robert Dreyfuss

Anybody doubting the political clout of the National Rifle Association should speak to the members of Congress—and the now former members—who supported President Clinton's ban on assault weapons as part of the 1994 crime bill. In the campaign cycle surrounding that close vote, the NRA spent some $70 million on political activities, including nearly $7 million through its political action committee, much of it targeting Democrats who had supported the measure. Although polls showed the majority of Americans approved of the weapons ban, the NRA campaign was by most accounts a success. Democrats say the NRA cost them no fewer than 20 seats, and President Clinton told one reporter that "the NRA is the reason the Republicans control the House." Speaker Newt Gingrich, meanwhile, has promised the group's service will be rewarded: "As long as I am Speaker of this House," he wrote in a letter to an NRA official, "no gun control legislation is going to move."

This is the story of how the NRA managed to accumulate so much influence over the democratic process. It is an unnerving ride through the loopholes in federal election law, which allow a powerful special interest to bring almost overwhelming force to bear in a single congressional district. It is the story of how the firearms lobby bludgeoned its opponents with slashing, near-anonymous attack commercials and buried them with bulk mailings on hot-button themes unrelated to guns. It is the story of how conservative financiers and the Republic Party used the NRA to do some of their dirty work, and the price the NRA is now extracting for those services.

This story leads to the question of how the NRA gets its money in the first place, and here, too, there is more than first meets the eye. Despite its image as a membership organization subsisting entirely on $35 membership dues, the NRA actually collects much of its money in large donations from upper-middle-class and even wealthy supporters. Big contributors, bequests, fundraising dinners, and backing from the gun industry have combined to provide the NRA with a substantial block of funds. The NRA uses that money for direct-mail solicitations, in effect converting large contributions into many smaller ones, which it then channels into political campaigns.

THE GOP CAUSE

Over the past several years, as the NRA's PAC income has grown dramatically—from $3.7 million in 1989-90 to $5.0 million in 1991-92 and finally $6.8 million in 1993-94—its spending has tilted increasingly into the Republican column. That tendency reached peak intensity in the 1994 election cycle, with the NRA's PAC devoting 79 percent of its direct grants to Republican campaigns, along with 87 percent of its independent expenditures aimed at influencing voters. This trend coincided with the NRA's shift toward a hard-line, no-compromise stance on gun issues—the result of an insurgency led by Neal Knox, a longtime NRA radical, and Tanya Metaksa, a former Reagan-Bush aide who is now executive director of the NRA's Institute for Legislative Action (ILA) and chairman of the PAC, which is called the Political Victory Fund.

According to Metaksa, this pattern of giving represents kindred interests, not behind-the-scenes coordinating: "We're not the National Republican Association," she says. But other sources, including former NRA officials and Republican and Democratic consultants, say that during the months leading up to the Republican sweep in November 1994, the NRA closely coordinated its election strategy with Republican Party officials. According to Tom King, a Democratic political strategist who calls the NRA a "wholly owned subsidiary of the Republican Party," the Republicans provided the NRA with polling data and lists of vulnerable Democrats in order to coordinate campaigns. Indeed, in October, on the eve of the elections, Metaksa solicited contributions explicitly to help Republicans take over. In a special mailing to NRA members entitled "It's Payback Time!" Metaksa said, "Make no mistake: a revolution is afoot. Just a handful of wins in key Senate races could turn the tide," resulting in "a Republican Senate."

In addition to strategizing with the Republicans, the NRA—ostensibly a single-issue organization—was throwing its lot in with other conservative groups, many of whom had little interest in guns but shared the NRA's desire to unseat Democrats. Together, these groups pursued lower taxes, free market economics, a smaller federal government, and a cutback in safety and health regulations. The NRA's "CrimeStrike" conference last year was cosponsored by the American Conservative Union, Americans for Tax Reform, and the Cato Institute, and today the NRA remains an active member of the American legislative Exchange Council, a public-private venture that boasts "3,000 pro-free enterprise legislators" from state capitals as members, along with most of the Fortune 500. Grover Norquist, an iconoclastic Republican ideologue and Newt Gingrich strategist who heads Americans for Tax Reform, says that the NRA played an indispensable role as a linchpin of the Republican Party alliance, which he calls "the leave-us-alone coalition." As the Republicans eyed their chances in November, says Norquist, they saw the NRA as a useful tool for undermining about 50 to 70 moderate Democrats in conservative districts.

That the NRA would work closely with the Republican Party and its supporters is no great surprise. But the fervor ran so deep that the NRA was even willing to mislead its own members on how fervently senators and congressmen supported the NRA position on guns. Going all out for a Republican sweep, the NRA fudged its traditional system of rating candidates for office. According to Joseph P. Sudbay of Handgun Control, who made a detailed study of the election for the gun-control group, the NRA gave borderline Republicans the benefit of the doubt, liberally handing out "A" ratings, while being far more hard-nosed about high ratings for Democrats. A former senior NRA official confirmed the pattern, noting "fairly glaring discrepancies" in the 1994 ratings and adding, "You can play a lot of games with that rating system."

Once the NRA made its decision to back the Republicans, the NRA's PAC followed suit, with devastating results for Democratic office seekers:

- In 52 House races where there was an open seat—that is, where no incumbent was running—the NRA either supported the Republican or remained neutral. In all, according to Federal Election Commission (FEC) data and the Coalition to Stop Gun Violence, the NRA spent $227,000 to help Republicans win 37 of those seats.

- In the nine races for open Senate seats, the NRA backed the Republican every time, spending more than $500,000. Republicans won them all.

- Where Democratic incumbents were running, the NRA abandoned many of its traditional friends on the pretext that they voted in favor of the Clinton administration's crime bill, which contained the provision that banned certain types of semiautomatic assault weapons. Such key members as Speaker of the House Tom Foley, Representative John Dingell of Michigan, and Representative Lee Hamilton of Indiana either lost all NRA support or found themselves the target of intense NRA opposition. Foley, who had long worked with the NRA to oppose gun-control legislation, was narrowly beaten by George Nethercutt, who received more than $80,000 in NRA support in the form of independent expenditures.

- Representative Jack Brooks of Texas, another longtime NRA supporter, was chairman of the House Judiciary Committee. In mid-1994, on the eve of the House-Senate conference to assemble the final version of the crime bill, Brooks thought he had worked out a compromise with the NRA over the controversial ban on assault weapons. Rather than ban the weapons, Brooks proposed limiting the number of rounds in magazines designed for the guns, thereby restricting their firepower. That deal, worked out by NRA lobbyist James Jay Baker, a relative moderate in NRA circles, was torpedoed by Metaksa and Knox. According to an insider, Metaksa at that point wanted to use the assault weapon ban to mobilize the NRA's hard-core activist base and deliberately wrecked chances of a compromise in order to go into the November election guns ablaze. Brooks, embittered, voted for the final crime bill and was abandoned by the NRA. His Republican successor is Steve Stockman, elected with strong support from pro-gun groups.

- The NRA's PAC concentrated more than $720,000 in independent expenditures in support of Republican Senate candidates in just six states: Tennessee, Oklahoma, Pennsylvania, Nevada, Nebraska, and North Dakota. The first three states elected four Republican senators, defeating two incumbent Senate Democrats, Harris Wofford and Jim Sasser. In Nevada, Nebraska, and North Dakota, the NRA's big-spending ways failed to bring down Democratic incumbents. In Nevada, the NRA gave $130,000 to the Republican challenger, even though the Democrat, incumbent Senator Richard Bryan, had voted consistently with the NRA during the 103rd Congress.

- The NRA vastly stepped up donations of so-called "soft money" to the Republican Party in the 1993-94 election cycle, largely through two checks totalling $275,000 to the Republican National Committee in October 1993. That infusion of cash was the NRA's contribution to successful Republican efforts to defeat New Jersey Governor Jim Florio and Virginia gubernatorial candidate Mary Sue Terry, both Democrats.

> The NRA also spent hundreds of thousands of dollars in independent expenditures to help beat Florio and Terry. In New Jersey, their last-minute $200,000 spending spree to fund a professional phone bank ran afoul of the state's campaign finance laws, and the NRA was fined $7,000. "They made several hundred thousand phone calls, from paid phone banks, without the opposition campaign knowing it was occurring," says Representative Robert Torricelli, who complained about the NRA's illegal spending to New Jersey authorities. "The NRA and the Republican Party... operate according to a single strategy."

STEALTH BOMBERS

Perhaps nowhere in the country was the NRA-Republican alliance more evident than in Oklahoma in 1994, where the NRA caught former Representative Dave McCurdy by surprise in a closely fought race against Republican Jim Inhofe for an open Senate seat. "It was a much bigger issue than I ever would have imagined," McCurdy says, marvelling at the campaign that the NRA waged against him. First elected to Congress in 1980 in Oklahoma's fourth district, which stretches south and west from Oklahoma City to the Texas border, McCurdy had long had NRA support. But his vote in 1993 for the Brady Bill, which called for a waiting period for buying handguns, and for the ban on assault weapons in the 1994 crime bill meant that he could no longer count on NRA backing.

"I knew I was drawing the line and could not cross it," says McCurdy, who did not even bother to ask the NRA for help in 1994. Yet the ferocity of the NRA's opposition took him by surprise. The NRA's PAC spent more than $150,000 in independent expenditures to run television and newspaper advertisements and put up billboards denouncing McCurdy in addition to the $9,900 it gave directly to Inhofe, just under the maximum $10,000 allowable under FEC regulations. The NRA also spent thousands of dollars more urging its Oklahoma members to turn out for Inhofe. It was an all-out attack that turned the tide against McCurdy.

But what was crucial about the NRA's attack on McCurdy was that rarely, if ever, in their onslaught did the NRA mention the issue of guns. Instead, in keeping with the Republic candidate's strategy, the NRA bankrolled a campaign to paint McCurdy as a "Clinton clone." An NRA-sponsored television ad began with the closeup of an AIDS ribbon on a lapel, then pulled back to show that the person sporting the ribbon was none other than Dave McCurdy, who was standing behind a podium delivering a speech supporting Bill Clinton at the 1992 Democratic National Convention. The NRA also paid for billboards throughout the state reading: "No Clinton Clones. Inhofe for U.S. Senate."

McCurdy says his aides detected a clear pattern that showed that the NRA was sharing the "buys" on Oklahoma television stations with the Republican Party and the Inhofe campaign—which would have been illegal under FEC rules that require that so-called "independent" expenditures not be coordinated with any election committees. McCurdy says that his staff tried to raise the issue with the FEC, but in the heat of the election campaign, just days before the vote, it was useless. (A spokesman for Senator Inhofe said that there was no coordination between the Inhofe campaign and the NRA on television advertising.)

"I wish they had come directly on gun issues," says McCurdy. "I think I could have won on the assault weapon ban with reasonable people." But, thanks to the work of pollster Frank Luntz, who also did the polling that helped Gingrich, Representative Dick Armey, and others assemble the Contract with America, the NRA knew that few Americans got excited about reversing the ban on assault weapons. (In fact, the NRA, for all of its vaunted, no-compromise reputation, meekly submitted when Gingrich did not include a promise to repeal the assault weapons ban in the Contract.) So, rather than give McCurdy and other Democrats around the country a chance to fight back, they simply ran ads thematically coordinated with Republican campaigns.

The NRA had learned that lesson in another Oklahoma race in 1992, against Representative Mike Synar, a liberal Democrat who had been a thorn in the NRA's side for years and had repeatedly crossed oil and gas, cattle, mining, and tobacco interests. In 1992 the NRA launched a high-profile attack on Synar, spending a reported $261,000 to defeat him. In that race, the NRA also ran ads against Synar on issues that had nothing to do with guns; one print ad read, "When Mike Synar voted for flag burning, so did you." According to Tom King, the Democratic consultant who worked on the Synar campaign, the NRA's PAC routinely coordinated its work with other business PACs who wanted to oust Synar. "They'd meet regularly, the different PACs—all the business PACs and the NRA got together and tried to beat Synar," he says. "And they met quite openly. They'd discuss strategy, what they were gonna do, how much money was needed."

But the NRA opened itself up to counterattack by making the gun issue a central part of its effort, and Synar countered by blasting the NRA as an extremist "special interest" group from Washington, out of touch with the views of most Oklahoma gun owners. Jim Brady, the namesake of the Brady Bill and a principal in Handgun Control, Inc., campaigned with Synar against the NRA. In a primary, a runoff, and the general election, Synar won each time.

The NRA vowed to continue its attack against Synar, and in 1994 it succeeded. But this time, the NRA ran a stealth campaign. Rather than adopt a high profile, the NRA quietly funded Synar's opponent in the Democratic primary, an NRA member named Virgil Cooper. "There were no full-page ads, no TV ads by the NRA," says Amy Weiss Tobe, a Synar aide. But anonymous flyers started showing up in union halls and shop floors around the district, carrying a reproduction of a nonexistent bill allegedly tied to Synar that would have banned hunting rifles. The NRA sponsored phone banks and mailings to its members in the district, but it was difficult for Synar to fight back. "It was different," says Tobe. "They were smart. It was like boxing ghosts."

"The NRA went in and went underground. And they've been more effective when they go underground than when they blatantly go in, because then they become a special interest and it can be used against them," says Tom King. In 1994, "there was nobody to fight against. It was an invisible target."

Synar lost the September 1994 primary, a stunning upset and a harbinger of the disaster that would befall the Democrats in November. It was a major victory for the coalition of Republicans, business groups, and the NRA, and it was trumpeted as such by Metaksa, who called Synar's defeat the "NRA's first scalp." But, though Metaksa told a reporter at the time that the NRA spent as much against Synar in 1994 as it did in 1992, none of that spending shows up on FEC records of campaign expenses—meaning that the NRA truly ran a stealthy, off-the-books effort that skirted FEC regulations. (Ironically, after helping Cooper to beat Synar, the NRA stayed out of Cooper's race against Republican Tom Coburn, who won. The NRA gave both Cooper and Coburn "A" ratings.)

Across the country in 1993-94, the NRA ran numerous ads that attacked Democrats on issues from taxes, the budget, health care, and education to the alliance with president Clinton. "They will write to my constituents about a business issue, a tax issue, or a spending issue, but guns are never mentioned. And often the NRA will never even identify itself," says Representative Torricelli, still burning about the 1993 Florio race. "Members of the National Rifle Association may be giving money to the organization because of a sporting purpose, but find the NRA is spending their money to attack a Democratic member on a Medicare or education issue."

"Unlike purists, they want to be effective," says Victor Kamber, a Washington public relations executive. "What they say is, 'We are using whatever the polling data show makes them vulnerable in their district. We're saying that Jim Florio is a bad guy because he raises taxes. The fact is that the voters cared about taxes, so we're going to the voters with a message about how bad this guy is.'" Thus the NRA integrated itself into the business-Republican coalition, consciously reinforcing the antitax, antigovernment message of the free marketeers that dominate the Republican right.

LAWYERS, GUNS, AND MONEY

What made the NRA such a useful tool to conservatives, of course, was its ability to raise and spend vast amounts of money. In 1994 the NRA was the nation's single biggest spender on elections. But how did it raise all the cash? Although the NRA's closemouthed tradition makes answering that question somewhat difficult, interviews with many current and former NRA officials, along with experts on the pro-gun movement, provide a fairly detailed picture—a picture that looks somewhat different from the grass roots, middle-American image NRA officials have nurtured for years.

It is true that like most direct-mail operations, the bulk of the NRA's daily operating revenue comes from small contributions, averaging about $18 per donor, and from annual dues of $35. Not surprisingly, most of this money comes from the ranks of American gun owners, who at last count were some 70 million strong. But that is not the entire story. Like the Republican and Democratic parties, which tout the fact that their average giver sends them between $10 and $25, the small average can obscure the presence of large backers. The NRA maintains an additional base of big contributors, who are clearly a few income levels above the typical working-class NRA member. This list includes the nation's 20,000 gun dealers and manufacturers and a small group of wealthy conservative financiers.

According to Brad O'Leary, the NRA sustains a block of 35,000 people who contribute at least $250 per year, and another 15,000 who give the NRA $125 per year. Those 50,000 people annually kick in more than $10 million. In addition, Metaksa said in an interview that she sees a fairly steady stream of checks up to $10,000 from NRA donors and has heard that the NRA treasury sometimes receives gifts "in the five figures."

The NRA conducts a broad fundraising campaign for several of its organizations, from the NRA itself to the ILA, the NRA Foundation, and the Political Victory Fund PAC. In a column in the *American Rifleman*, the NRA's monthly, NRA President Thomas L. Washington cited a single dinner held in Corpus Christi, Texas, where 907 people donated more than $175,000 to the NRA. And the NRA recently published a list of 214 "Friends of the NRA" fundraising events scheduled between April and October 1995.

The *American Rifleman* routinely lists the names of groups and individuals around the country who give the NRA at least $1,000 at a time; until earlier this year, the magazine listed those who donated special, onetime gifts of $250 or more but dropped that practice because of space limitations. And some NRA members have left the NRA bequests in the hundreds of thousands of dollars—their parting shot, so to speak.

Finally, there is the gun industry. It has long been assumed that the NRA receives financial support from firearms dealers and manufacturers, yet Metaksa, when asked about this, replied, "Baloney. Absolutely nothing." Yet the NRA in 1993 earned $8.6 million from advertising income, largely through ads from the gun industry in NRA magazines. And the NRA has arranged with gun dealers around the country to help the NRA solicit contributions from gun buyers. According to Tom Washington's "The President's Column" in the *American Rifleman*, just one dealer—Midway Arms of Columbia, Missouri—raised more than $678,000 for the NRA in four years. "It isn't just individual volunteers who benefit our Association," wrote Washington. "Many businesses donate their time and efforts as well."

Thanks to the Federal Election Commission, those millions raised by the NRA cannot be spent on federal campaigns. The FEC carefully regulates how a PAC, in this case the Political Victory Fund (PVF) of the NRA, raises or spends its cash.

Or does it?

The answer is: It does, but not very well. There are so many loopholes in the FEC rules that an organization like the NRA can do just about anything it wants to do for political objectives. Here's how.

A glance at the NRA's PAC records on file at the FEC, provided by the Center for Responsive Politics, shows that the overwhelming bulk of the NRA's PAC money comes into the PVF in donations of less than $200. Anything more than $200 must be reported to the FEC on an itemized basis. Yet over the six-year period ending December 31, 1994, the PVF reported itemized donations of only $278,631. During the same period, the PVF raised a total of $16,499,000.

One might conclude that large donors stay away from the PVF. But the FEC is not required to verify the accuracy of the NRA's filing. The forms that the NRA fills out simply list the itemized gifts as a line item, then present a lump-sum total for the bulk of the PVF income under the nonitemized heading. Even if the FEC suspects that there is something fishy about the lopsided nature of the PVF's income, it cannot investigate on its own without evidence of wrongdoing. The FEC takes the NRA's report on faith, just as it does with every other PAC.

More important, though, the FEC does not regulate the so-called "administrative and fundraising" costs associated with a PAC. That means that the NRA can spend unlimited sums, millions of dollars, to raise PAC funds, paying for repeated mailings to the NRA's 3.4 million members—and it does not have to report a single cent of those fundraising costs to the FEC. (That is also true for all other PACs, but it is particularly important for a large organization that can harvest small contributions, as opposed to, say, a trade association with a few dozen members whose executives kick in big bucks.)

And that is exactly what the NRA does. Using its corporate treasury, which is "soft money," that is, not regulated by the FEC, the NRA in 1994 spent at least $2 million—and probably much more—asking NRA members to contribute to the PVF. That, in turn, is what raised the PVF's $6.83 million during 1993-94. Through the science of direct mail, the NRA can estimate how much each dollar spent on soliciting donations to the PVF will bring in. So, while the FEC rules prevent a wealthy donor from giving more than $1,000 to a PAC, nothing prevents that donor from giving the NRA $5,000 in soft money, which the NRA then plows into PVF fundraising. A direct donation of $5,000 in soft money suddenly becomes $5,000, $10,000, or more in "hard money"—in other words, legally usable, reportable PAC cash.

That's not the only loophole the NRA has exploited. For example, the FEC has issued regulations saying that no association can solicit PAC money from its members unless (1) those members pay their dues and (2) those members have the right to vote for the governing body of the association. The purpose of these rules is to distinguish genuine member-controlled organizations from closely controlled direct-mail operations.

Under the NRA's bylaws, only so-called Life Members and Five Year Members, who pay larger chunks of dues at a time, have the right to vote for the NRA's 75-member board of directors—a none-too-subtle bit of class distinction. Thus, under the law, the NRA would be disallowed from soliciting the bulk of its membership, who pay only one-year dues of $35 and have no voting rights. To avoid FEC action, however, the NRA in 1994 engaged in a subterfuge so brazenly transparent that it boggles the mind. It added one position to its board to be elected at the NRA's annual meeting, to which any and all NRA members may come. Any NRA member, therefore, has the theoretical right to vote for one director, and one director only. Of course, only a minuscule portion of the NRA membership actually goes to the meeting.

This construct, laughable in its intent to subvert an FEC regulation, has not been challenged in court—yet. In the meantime, the subterfuge allows the NRA to continue to send PVF PAC mailings to its full membership and to put millions of dollars into the PVF bank account. And, by the way, the FEC conducts no audits of the NRA's membership records to determine how many members the NRA has and whether or not they are actually paying their dues.

NOT-SO-INDEPENDENT EXPENDITURES

Those who have found themselves in the NRA's sights, however, are generally more familiar with the organization's use of another legal loophole that allows the NRA to support candidates well beyond the limits on direct donations to campaigns.

Because the FEC cannot regulate free speech (thank goodness), the NRA—like any individual, corporation, or group—can spend unlimited amounts of money to promote its cause, even during an election, as long as the NRA does not engage in what is called "express advocacy." Express advocacy means that the NRA must cross a fuzzy line by explicit, campaign-style promotion of a particular candidate. If a promotion crosses that line, the thinking goes, the money spent on it ought to count as a direct political contribution, thus subject to the limits set by the FEC.

But the line is so fuzzy that the NRA can run television commercials criticizing a candidate and supporting the NRA's laissez-faire attitude toward semiautomatic weapons without falling under FEC regulations at all. In the 1992 Synar race, the NRA liberally took advantage of this loophole, running one attack advertisement with "hard" PVF money blasting Synar and then, sandwiched around another commercial, following up with a second spot that used the same spokesman, Charlton Heston, yet did not mention Synar by name. That second commercial was paid for by the NRA's corporate account, not by its PAC—thus giving the NRA a double bang for its buck.

All of these loopholes, including the biggest one of all, the use of independent expenditures, were used expertly by the NRA in 1994. To put the NRA's use of independent expenditures in perspective, consider this: In 1993-94, the NRA accounted for fully one-third of all independent expenditures by all groups during the election.

Asked about the role of independent expenditures, Metaksa is unable to suppress a sly grin before the questioner even finishes. "It's a chance for the organization to put itself into the political arena," she says. "And if the purpose is to get our point of view across, then it takes more than five or ten thousand dollars, especially in a big state." Indeed—and it doesn't hurt that nobody's figured out a way to regulate those amounts. The Clinton administration's campaign finance reform bill had a provision to offset the impact of independent expenditures, by providing public subsidies for candidates victimized by them. But that bill succumbed to the threat of a Republican filibuster a few months before the 1994 election.

SELF-INFLICTED WOUNDS

Stricter campaign finance law or tougher FEC regulation of the NRA seems an unlikely possibility as long as Republicans control

Congress. But the NRA's coziness with the Republican Party may yet cost the organization some loyalty among its many lower- and middle-class members, many of whom find the Republican stances on economics less appealing than the party's opposition to gun control.

In the past the NRA has been able to whipsaw organized labor, many of whose members opposed gun control. But the trade union rank-and-file is only beginning to appreciate that the NRA is an ally of bitterly anti-union legislators. Already, the AFL-CIO is launching a labor counteroffensive against the NRA. That movement is starting in the West, where key AFL-CIO state presidents and affiliates are studying the NRA's role in the 1994 elections. Don Judge, president of the Montana AFL-CIO, in a state where the NRA and the militia movement are powerful side-by-side forces, says that his organization is trying to educate union members that the candidates supported by the NRA are precisely the ones who, once in office, vote against labor on every issue from the minimum wage to right-to-work to safety and health provisions. "Many of us have decided, what have we got to lose in confronting this?" asks Judge. "The kind of people being promoted by the NRA, with rare exceptions, typically do not support the kinds of things that are important to working people, beyond the issue of gun ownership."

In Pennsylvania, the AFL-CIO was rocked by the Democrats' rout in 1994, and Rick Bloomingdale, president of the AFL-CIO there, is ready to confront the NRA. Bloomingdale points out that the NRA backed the victorious Republican Representative Tom Ridge in Pennsylvania's governor's race last year, even though Ridge had voted for the assault weapon ban in Congress in 1994. Says Bloomingdale, "We finally know what the NRA-PAC stands for: the National Republican Association." When the Pennsylvania AFL-CIO began running ads last year featuring a union member and the slogan, "I'm the NRA and I'm supporting Harris Wofford," the NRA's lawyers hit them with a cease and desist order because "I'm the NRA" is copyrighted by the organization. Adds Bloomingdale, "The same people who support the NRA are the people trying to bust unions."

A study by Professor Paul Clark of Pennsylvania State University shows that the NRA consistently backs candidates whose positions on economic issues are far to the right. "While [the NRA] claims not to take positions on overtly economic issues, the candidates they support clearly do," he says. "Significantly, they have had some success at convincing union members to support their organizations and their candidates."

Warren Cassidy, a former NRA executive vice president, card-carrying Republican, and backer of the Dole campaign, worries openly that the NRA's lurch to the right may involve a quid pro quo to support the Republicans on issues that have nothing to do with guns. "When does that quid pro quo begin to hurt your organization?" he asks. "With all the connections to a strong conservative movement, NRA got caught up in that tide and they might not be able to extricate themselves." He warns: "It isn't necessarily true that all those chits should fall to one party, the Republican Party... because we have always had a strong, strong blue-collar element, both rural and urban, in the NRA. And many, many, many of these people are union members."

In addition, many former NRA board members and leaders say that the NRA is driving away its longtime friends and allies by its roughshod tactics. Oklahoma Congressman Bill Brewster, who served on the NRA's board until 1995, quietly withdrew this year. High-profile resignations by George Bush, John Dingell, and other NRA supporters have hurt the organization's political clout. Dole, who voted for the Brady Bill in 1991 (but later opposed it 1993) and now keeps the NRA at arm's length while supporting most of its agenda, is warily watching the NRA's close relationship with Senator Phil Gramm, his rival for the 1996 presidential nomination in the Republican Party.

In the meantime, NRA officials have more immediate concerns. In its single-minded fervor to defeat even the most hesitant supporters of gun control, the NRA may have recklessly stretched its spending to the breaking point. The direct-mail scheme upon which the NRA has built its empire has been costly, and the organization recently traded a sizeable chunk of its inheritance for a posh new headquarters building. All of this has led many former NRA officials to say that the organization will crash in the near future. Reports of financial difficulties have attracted the scrutiny of the Internal Revenue Service.

Still, on Capitol Hill a healthy symbiosis between the Republicans and the NRA continues to thrive. While a good number of mainstream Republicans see the NRA as a loose cannon and an organization of zealots flirting with the far right, these Republicans still want the

NRA's money and grassroots army at election time, and they still worry that any misstep—even in the course of the routine give-and-take that occurs in a legislative session—could bring the NRA down on their heads.

On January 25, as Gingrich, Armey, and company moved to implement the Contract with America, the NRA convened a summit meeting in the Speaker's office. Attending were Gingrich, Armey, House Republican Conference Chairman John Boehner of Ohio, Republican Whip Tom DeLay of Texas, National Republican Conference Committee Chairman Bill Paxon of New York, and Crime Subcommittee Chairman Bill McCollum of Florida. From the NRA side, participants included Neal Knox, Tanya Metaksa, Wayne LaPierre, and, interestingly, NRA Board of Directors member Senator Larry Craig of Idaho. Following the meeting, Gingrich and the NRA announced that they had formed a "partnership" on gun issues in the House, inviting conservative Democrats like Brewster and Harold Volkmer of Missouri to join in. Shortly after that meeting, Gingrich sent Metaksa the letter promising his opposition to gun control, characterizing their meeting as "both a discussion among friends but more importantly among like-minded individuals."

Were it not for the Oklahoma City bombing, which tarred the NRA because of its association with some militia groups, Congress would likely have taken up a repeal of the assault rifle ban. The NRA worked so closely with congressional committees investigating the Waco disaster that there was no clear line between congressional and NRA staffers. And the NRA has thrown its weight around in committee action on so-called "cop killer" bullets. With the 1996 election just around the bend, it is a safe bet the Republicans will be reaching out to the NRA once again, confident that the group can accomplish its mission and willing, in exchange, to do its political bidding.

How the West Is Won

Samantha Sanchez

The term "wise use" comes from Gifford Pinchot, the first head of the U.S. Forest Service, who used it to describe the conservation movement. Pinchot chose words that implied balance, not to mention a fundamental concern for the well-being of the environment. Today Pinchot's term has been turned on its head, appropriated by a corporate-sponsored campaign to roll back environmental protection in the West, where billions of dollars ride on decisions about the use of government-regulated property.

This is the story of how the "wise use" movement—a coalition of timber, mining, oil, and grazing interests—has skewed the debate over land use. It is a tale of political contributions, well-connected lobbyists, and, most important, corporate-financed grassroots organizing that has become a model for kindred political operatives around the country. This is also the story of how environmentalists in the state of Washington fended off development activists in one key battle, providing some hope that real strength at the grass roots may still be better than "astroturf" substitutes.

REVENGE OF THE MARLBORO MAN

The public face of the development movement is the square-jawed individualism that recently graced the cover of *Time* magazine. It is a family version of the Marlboro Man—a movement that asks nothing more than to be left alone, free of meddlesome government regulation. The pitch sounds authentically American, rich with allusions to the spirit of the nation's founding. Yet if you trace the development movement's lineage, you'll find its roots not in the revolutionary ferment of the 1770s but in the corporate resentment that was simmering two centuries later.

American environmentalism had its breakthrough in the 1970s, the decade that witnessed not only the creation of the Environmental

Protection Agency but also the enactment of such measures as the Clean Air and Clean Water Acts. At the state level and through the courts, environmentalists were also able to hold corporations more accountable for the pollution they created and to stop the overdevelopment of forests and wetlands. The movement's petition drives, ballot initiatives, and other forms of door-to-door campaigning were vital to its success.

Not surprisingly, environmental laws were particularly controversial in the West, where economic growth continued to depend on the development of natural resources: timber in Idaho, Oregon, and Washington; coal, oil, and minerals in Wyoming, Utah, Nevada, and Montana; grazing land and hydroelectric power throughout the region. Many residents saw the new laws as the work of elite eastern outsiders who didn't care about local prosperity; industry lobbyists saw the laws as a threat to profits. This opposition helped blunt the environmental charge, as did the arrival of the Reagan administration.

Still, even in the early Reagan years there was substantial political support for environmentalists, so development interests set about building an intellectual foundation to support a more sweeping rollback—an effort that worked through organizations like the American Legislative Exchange Council (ALEC). At universities across the country, a few conservative intellectuals like Richard Epstein were already making the theoretical case for more expansive interpretations of the Fifth Amendment, which protects citizens from government seizure of property. Groups such as ALEC, which received significant funding from the Coors Foundation and various development interests, were instrumental in moving those ideas from the classroom to the legislatures, where the campaign for "property rights" gained steam. The staff wrote sample "takings laws"—laws that require government to compensate owners whose profit potential was diminished by regulation—and forwarded them to sympathetic officials in federal and state government. Industry-financed think tanks churned out op-eds and briefing papers to bolster the case. Once dismissed as radically conservative, the takings laws began to gain legitimacy.

Of course all the intellectual currency in the world wasn't going to do any good if the voters perceived the takings laws and similar measures as attempts to poison the air and water, so the developers took a page from the environmentalists' playbook. In a series of articles for

Logging Management magazine, strategist Ron Arnold proposed that the developers put citizens, not corporate spokesman, at the front of the parade. "Give them the money," Arnold advised resource companies at a meeting in 1988. "You stop defending yourselves, let them do it, and you get the hell out of the way. Because citizen's groups have credibility and industries don't."

Today the legacy of those efforts is the network of activist anti-environmental organizations that litter the western political landscape. Although these groups typically rely on donations from resource companies and developers, they specialize in rallies, petition drives, even T-shirt and bumper-sticker campaigns—anything that puts a workingman's face on the developers' profit motive. With innocuous, populist-sounding names, these organizations appeal directly to the economic frustration of blue-collar voters.

The appeal falls on receptive ears. Stories of environmentalist-inspired injunctions against logging and mining operations have been well publicized, making environmentalists a good scapegoat for slack times. The spotted owl ordeal left many timber workers in the Northwest frustrated with government intervention, particularly since attempts to limit the export of unmilled trees never got far. But is regulation really what's killing western jobs? More likely the real culprits are the forces that are fostering economic insecurity everywhere else in the country: globalization, technological advances, and reduced bargaining power of labor. (Weyerhaeuser, a leading timber company in Washington, gets 26 percent of its profits from exporting raw logs overseas.) Of course the corporate-financed anti-environmental groups don't dwell on questions about free trade, corporate profits, or executive salaries.

Typical of these organizations is People for the West!, which describes itself as "a grassroots campaign supporting western communities." The ongoing interest of these people is the preservation of an 1872 mining law that gives mining companies cheap access to mineral-rich public land. In 1992 about 96 percent of the organization's $1.7 million budget came from corporate donors, led by NERCO Minerals, Cyprus Minerals, Chevron, and Hecla Mining, according to Audubon Society researchers. PFW!'s corporate members include such timber and power companies as Boise Cascade, Potlatch, and Pacific Power and Light; the group also includes cattlemen and woolgrowers associations, as well as mining interests. The chairman of PFW!, Bob Quick, is the national director of state legislative affairs for Asarco, a mining company.

While these groups don't exactly advertise their corporate sponsorship, their close relationship with development companies provides crucial access to workers. Companies have been known, for instance, to stuff payroll checks with propaganda inserts from anti-environmental groups. The Oregon Lands Coalition, a timber-dominated coalition, has used its newsletter to publish flyers labeled "PAYROLL STUFFER" in bold typeface. In Montana, the Plum Creek timber company broke state election law by stuffing paycheck envelopes with a flyer urging workers to attend a rally against Representative Pat Williams, a Democrat who supports environmental causes. The offending item included some suggested slogans to put on placards: "No more Williams, wilderness or wolves," and "You'll need a job Pat."

The development activists have also reached out to other conservatives, cementing an ideological alliance that those nice-sounding names tend to obscure. Ron Arnold and his boss, Alan Gottlieb, president and founder of the Center for Defense of Free Enterprise, are products of right-wing political circles, not the timber or construction industries. Both have ties to Reverend Moon's Unification Church: Arnold was president of the Washington state chapter of Moon's American Freedom Coalition from 1989 through 1990, while Gottlieb was a director of the group. Gottlieb was also a board member of Young Americans for Freedom, national director of Youth Against McGovern, and a gun lobby leader who founded the Second Amendment Foundation and founded and chaired the Citizens Committee for the Right to Keep and Bear Arms.

MINING FOR DOLLARS

Organizing and networking have not supplanted the more traditional means of influencing politics, namely giving money to campaigns through both individual donations and political action committee contributions. According to public records (compiled in part by the organization I work for, the Western States Center), political donations from developers are on the rise, providing an invisible—but very substantial—helping hand to the more public efforts at the grass roots.

In Oregon, pro-development money accounted for 14.7 percent of the money statewide candidates accepted in 1990; in 1994 that number grew to 16.4 percent, with the winners on average receiving 21 percent of their campaign cash from developers. Perhaps that fact helps explain why in 1995 the legislature proposed scores of bills that would weaken water quality or destroy environmental enforcement programs, passing several. Only Democratic Governor John Kitzhaber, who vetoed more than 50 bills in that session, stood in the developers' way.

In Wyoming, development interests accounted for 26 percent of all campaign contributions in 1990 and 27 percent in 1992 (1994 figures are still unavailable), the highest of any state. In 1995 the state legislature passed a takings bill and voted to allow the dumping of nuclear waste inside the state. Polls showed that 70 to 80 percent of the voters opposed the latter, but four members of the conference committee that wrote the bill were beneficiaries of large industry donations. One of them, state Representative Jim Twiford, got three-quarters of his campaign money from the development-resource industry; two other representatives, Bob Peck and Eli Bebout, are founders of and major stockholders in the New Corporation, which according to the *Outdoor Council Legislative Report* is the only Wyoming company that has publicly expressed interest in the high-level radioactive-waste business.

Last year the Wyoming legislature also passed "audit privilege" legislation. Audit privilege laws, which have been introduced in 41 states, allow a company to audit its own environmental violations; in return, the state grants immunity from penalty and promises to keep information about violations confidential, even when the violations were intentional. The Wyoming bill limited polluter liability for lawsuits and took away citizens' rights to obtain information about pollution that may have harmed public health or property. How did the industry get such a plum? By writing it, of course. Greg Schaefer, a lobbyist for an ARCO subsidiary called the Thunder Basin Coal Company, took public credit for the bill when it was introduced to the legislature.

Such extensive industry involvement in the legislative process has become even more common since the Republicans swept into power. At the federal level, it is no coincidence that the anti-regulatory provisions of the legislation endorsed in the Contract with America were well suited to industry; their lobbyists had drafted much of the language. Those bills would have required federal agencies to use quantitative benefit-risk studies as the sole basis for evaluating regulations and would have provided a host of new opportunities for industry interests to influence those evaluations and take the agencies to court.

At the state level it has been the same story. The Idaho Association of Commerce and Industry, which is part of the Idaho Private Property Coalition, was the prime mover behind an audit privilege bill. It was one of several in 1995 to pass the Idaho House, where legislators received 25 percent of their campaign money from resource companies and developers. Among the more notorious new laws were measures that weakened water-quality protection and created a $1 million "constitutional defense fund" to be used by state officials in court cases asserting state control over federal natural resources. Bowing to the strength of the grazing lobby, legislators even passed a bill to grant grazing leases only to ranchers, in order to prevent environmentalists from buying up the leases first.

SHOWDOWN IN THE NORTHWEST

Given this history, it would be easy to write off the environment as just one more policy area hopelessly in the grasp of big money. But activists in the state of Washington proved otherwise over the last few years, as they took on the timber industry and other development interests in a series of high-profile political battles.

Like most other timber-rich states, Washington has been the scene of an ongoing dispute between logging companies and environmentalists. The timber companies, which have cut down trees faster than they can grow back, want the state to release more public lands for logging; if such access is not provided, they say they will need to lay off workers. Environmentalists oppose such measures, while calling on the state to slow down development with comprehensive land-use planning—a measure particularly troubling to the many timber companies that owned real estate subsidiaries.

When one environmental group, 1000 Friends of Washington, finally succeeded in putting a land-use measure on the ballot in 1990, the developers met the challenge. An alliance of corporate interests—not just timber companies but also such corporations as Boeing,

Darigold, and U.S. West—spent nearly $1.8 million on advertising and grassroots organizing to block the measure, which promised to affect both real estate and logging. Groups such as the Washington Contract Loggers Association organized rallies of angry timber workers; the American Pulpwood Association provided public speaking and lobbying training to potential activists. Meanwhile, the development interests poured more than $2.5 million into the campaign coffers of state legislature candidates; nearly 70 percent of that money went to eventual winners and much of it was directed at a group of 20 candidates particularly friendly to industry.

The industry coalition won their initiative fight, but ironically their failure to dislodge a Democratic legislature gave the environmentalists an opportunity to achieve through legislation what they could not through the ballot measure. Sure enough, the legislature adopted a growth management act while defeating four property rights bills—three dealing with wetlands and one takings measure—that had strong industry backing.

But the story does not end there. Heavy lobbying had already neutered some of the act's more ambitious provisions anyway: The *Seattle Post-Intelligencer* reported that developer pressure frightened the legislature into cutting $4.5 million from the program's funding and stripping some key provisions. Now, the industry groups concentrated on organizing at the county level, where the planning would actually take place. Organizations such as the Snohomish County Property Rights Alliance began to crop up and make their presence known at local meetings. The Snohomish group billed itself as "a grassroots group concerned about environmental regulation" while taking money from construction interests, such as the Master Builders Association of King and Snohomish Counties. Jim Klauser, the director of Seattle Master Builders, became the alliance's director.

Against this backdrop, the developers increased their investment in state races for 1992—a total of $3.2 million in contributions, up from the $2.5 million in 1990. Again, the results were mixed. Thanks in part to a strong turnout for Bill Clinton's presidential bid, the developers' candidates lost several key races and only 36 percent of industry money ended up in the pockets of winners. Industry sponsorship had actually become a liability for some candidates. One such candidate was land commissioner hopeful Ann Anderson, a conservative Republican legislator who had collected more than half a million dollars from various development interests. Eight timber companies alone gave her more money than any candidate for that office had ever collected. Anderson blanketed the state with television and radio ads accusing her opponent, Jennifer Belcher, of being an "outright environmentalist." Yet despite outspending Belcher by a nearly three-to-one margin, Anderson lost, in no small part because Belcher convinced voters that Anderson's logging ties constituted a conflict of interest.

But despite these losses, the Republicans—and the developers—won a crucial victory in the form of a new campaign finance initiative that imposed $500 limits on campaign contributions. Although purportedly designed to limit the influence of big money on campaigns, the measure disproportionately affected candidates dependent on donations from organized labor. PACs in general were hard hit by the contribution limits, but those PACs with well-heeled contributors were able to make up the difference with individual contributions. Labor PACs, with tens of thousands of $35 contributors, could not call on the rank and file to fill the gap. The new law also made it more difficult for labor to raise the money by payroll withholding.

Thus the new fundraising law helped lay the groundwork for the stunning Republican gains of 1994. Total labor contributions to campaigns fell 40 percent, while money from pro-development groups—most of them pro-Republican—increased slightly. Democrats, who once enjoyed a 16 percent funding advantage over Republicans, fell into a dead heat. With financial parity and Newt Gingrich's long coattails factored into the equation, the Washington House went from a 65-33 Democratic majority to a 60-38 Republican majority. Republican gains in the Senate brought them to within one vote of control (and because one Democratic senator was absent for health reasons during much of the 1995 session, the Senate was effectively split).

There was still Democratic Governor Michael Lowry with his veto, but the developers found a way around him. Earlier in the year a pro-development group, the Washington Property Protection Coalition, had tried unsuccessfully to put a takings measure on the November ballot. But with friendlier faces in the state House, the group had another option—the citizen's initiative. Under Washington law, citizens can petition to send a measure directly to the state government where it needs only a majority approval from the legislature—not a signature by the governor—to become law. Although the measure had only 12,000 of the required 182,000 signatures a month before the deadline, industry groups—including the Building Industry Association, the Association of Realtors, and Plum Creek Timber—raised $200,000 in three days and hired American Petition Consultants of California to run the signature-gathering effort.

The effort succeeded. The measure sailed through the Republican-dominated House, then passed the Senate with the support of several Democrats. On April 18, the toughest takings bill in the country became law in Washington.

THE GREENS STRIKE BACK

Environmentalists countered with their own ballot initiative to bring the new takings law up for reconsideration. They pulled together a broad coalition that included the League of Women Voters, the Association of Washington Cities, and the Association of Washington Churches, as well as labor unions and environmentalists. In less than three months they managed to collect 231,122 signatures.

Once again, the builders, realtors, and timber industries opened their checkbooks. Altogether, development interests spent $1.5 million, not including undocumented independent expenditures by the Republican Party, building associations, and the Farm Bureau. The Building Industry Association of Washington was the single largest contributor, spending $212,959, but the national and state realtor PACs together contributed $270,000. An assortment of timber companies, lead by Plum Creek, Simpson, Longview Fibre, and Boise Cascade came up with nearly $244,000.

The developers' appeal, as before, targeted ordinary folks with anecdotes about how environmental regulations had eliminated jobs and destroyed personal assets. A centerpiece of the campaign was a story of an elderly couple, the Powells, who, according to the industry advertisements, owned some land but could not build on it or even walk on it, all because of a wetlands law. Environmentalists, they said, were destroying their nest egg.

It would have been a sad story, except it wasn't true—and this time environmentalists were able to use that information as ammunition. Investigations by the environmentalist campaign showed that there were no building or walking restrictions over the Powells' land. As for the nest egg, it turned out the Powells had recently put their property—which they purchased years before for $13,000—on the market for $400,000. More digging produced contributor lists for the pro-takings law campaign. It demonstrated who really stood to gain from the takings law, and environmentalists hit hard on the $300 million to $900 million per year the measure would cost the taxpayers.

The muckraking helped energize the environmentalists. They organized an effective speakers bureau to engage the developers on the local level, blanketed events with volunteers and pamphlets, and raised money for advertising. Previous anti-regulatory actions had threatened to streamline and outsource government work—thus eliminating public-sector jobs. This allowed environmentalists to find common ground with the state's labor unions, thus undercutting the developers' would-be base of blue-collar workers. In the latest Washington battle, environmentalists and unions again joined forces.

On November 7, the voters of Washington voted down the takings law by a 60 percent to 40 percent vote. "The vote shows the state is not for sale," said Dee Frankforth, manager of the anti-takings campaign.

Whether this story offers hope for other progressive organizations frustrated by the hegemony of political money is, of course, a whole other question. Environmentalists represent perhaps the best organized movement in the left-liberal corner of the universe, with the possible exception of organized labor (which has surely seen better times but seems to be attempting a comeback). It might take a leap of faith to imagine activists toppling the corporate interests that have stalled national progress on such issues as education and health care. Yet it is instructive to see that an investment in grassroots organizing can pay dividends. Progressives could do worse than to take a closer look at how the Washington environmental movement took on big money and won.

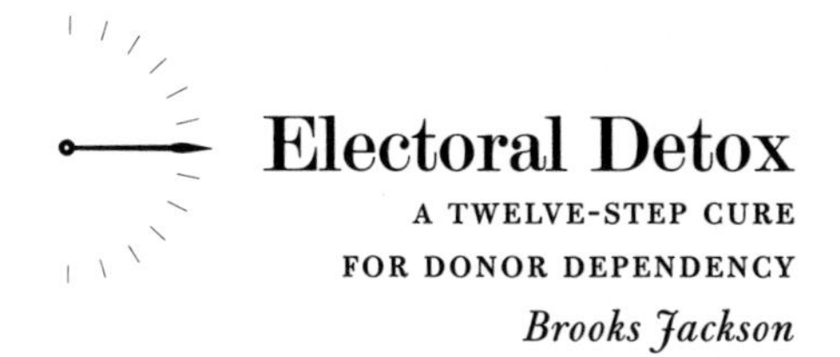

Electoral Detox

A TWELVE-STEP CURE FOR DONOR DEPENDENCY

Brooks Jackson

America's elected officials have become addicted to political money, and among the most dependent are members of the United States Congress. Everyone recognizes the more obvious symptoms: escalating campaign expenditures, growing reliance on political action committees (PACs), incessant solicitations, recurring scandals. But the underlying malady is more dangerous than most lawmakers will admit. Like addiction to alcohol or drugs, it is a disease that attacks both body and spirit.

Many lawmakers would like some changes, but not at any cost to their political party or themselves. Senate Democrats want a ceiling on expenditures that President Bush says he will veto. Bush favors the near-abolition of PACs, which House Democrats reject. The current debate is as bitter as it is shallow, like a fight between drunks over whether black coffee or a cold shower is the better path to sobriety. The odds of enacting serious change remain close to zero.

Money can destroy a democracy absolutely, but the process begins subtly. Plutarch described how it slowly corrupted the Roman republic. "The abuse of buying and selling votes crept in and money began to play an important part in determining the elections." Direct bribery of voters, the method Plutarch described, survives today only in a few backward, impoverished jurisdictions. With the rise of television and computers, money gets converted into votes in a more refined way. Yet the practical outcome is the same: candidates with money often win, and those without it almost always lose.

Most of the money for political campaigns comes from organized economic interests, whose role grows larger with each election, subtly disenfranchising ordinary voters and shifting power to economically interested donors. The nation's economy has suffered, too. While Congress listens attentively to the grievances of specific donors, it becomes less attuned to the interests of the public. One example is the way key lawmakers such as House Speaker Jim Wright and the so-called "Keating Five"—Senators Alan Cranston, Dennis DeConcini, John McCain, John Glenn, and Donald Riegle—ministered to a few renegade savings-and-loan profiteers, of whom Charles Keating is only the most notorious. Another example is the way Congress failed to see, until too late, the excessive risks to banks and insurance companies posed by junk-bond swashbucklers who recycled a few of their millions as campaign donations.

A certain amount of money has always been a necessity in American politics. But in recent years the role of money has ballooned, while the part played by individuals and political party organizations has diminished. Envelope-stuffing volunteers are less important; direct-mail consultants are more so. A county chairman of a party often counts for less than a hired "PAC director," whose job is to raise money from political action committees by systematically marketing the candidate to economic interest groups. Congressional elections have gone from being labor-intensive to being capital-intensive.

All that money is, perversely, buying a lower quality of politics. It buys poll-takers, consultants, and advertising experts who figure out what the public wants to hear and then tell it to them. Often that translates into empty symbolism, or worse, the politics of trivia, fear, and cynicism.

Congress is becoming more heavily dependent upon special-interest money with each passing election. This is especially true in the House, where members elected last year got an average of 45 percent of their funds from political action committees, up from less than 26 percent in 1976. The lion's share of PACs are sponsored by economic interest groups. The biggest are the National Association of Realtors, which gave $3 million to House and Senate candidates in the last election; the American Medical Association, which gave $2.4 million; and the Teamsters Union, which gave $2.3 million. PACs sponsored by business corporations gave $58 million; those sponsored by trade associations and professional groups gave $44 million; and those run by labor unions gave just under $35 million.

Some partisan and ideological PACs still give heavily, motivated by issues such as aid to Israel, the environment, abortion, and gun control. But the big conservative PACs that once struck fear in the hearts of liberals have faded with the passing of the Reagan era; the National

Conservative Political Action Committee itself is $3.9 million in debt and officially "inactive." PAC money is not only increasingly important but more than ever synonymous with economic lobbies.

And it is not just PACs; additional millions pour in from Washington lobbyists, executives of military contractors, real-estate developers, trial lawyers, junk-bond salesmen, and others with a direct financial interest in how Congress votes. Indeed, the special-interest donations of individuals often rival or exceed those of the PACs. Charles Keating himself did not bother with a PAC, which could legally have given only $5,000 per senator, per election. Instead, he often passed the hat among his relatives and company executives. In that way, for example, he raised $78,250 for the 1988 campaign of Senator Riegle, now chairman of the Banking Committee.

Keating's methods are widely employed. A recent study by Public Citizen of giving to congressional candidates in the 1989-1990 election cycle found that individuals in the financial industry—bankers, S&L executives, stockbrokers, commodity traders, and the like—gave $12.8 million, while the PACs in those industries gave $11.9 million. Washington-based lobbyists, lawyers, and public relations executives, who hardly bother with PACs at all, gave $19 million directly to candidates.

When it comes to buying access or influence, there is no difference between a $5,000 check from a PAC and an envelope containing checks for $500 each from ten executives of the company sponsoring the PAC. Indeed, the bundled contributions can be worse, because their economic connection is harder to trace than PAC money, and because the aggregate amount can be far greater than the legal limit for a single PAC. During the 1986 tax reform debate, for example, a group of insurance agents selling tax-sheltered policies funneled more than $250,000 into the campaign of Republican Senator Bob Packwood of Oregon, who was chairman of the Finance Committee at the time.

Lawmakers now depend for their political survival on a process that is increasingly difficult to distinguish from criminal bribery and extortion. Federal tax collectors go to jail for taking gifts from accountants, even if no explicit favors are given or promised, on the well-founded theory that any human being will tend to bend for someone who has given money and may thus give more in the future. But the Supreme Court just overturned the federal corruption conviction of a West Virginia legislator, Robert McCormick, for soliciting and accepting a $2,900 payment from a lobbyist whose legislation he was supporting. "To hold otherwise would open to prosecution conduct ...that in a very real sense is unavoidable so long as election campaigns are financed by private contributions or expenditures," Justice Byron White wrote for the majority. Unavoidable—and inherently corrosive.

Because special-interest donors are mainly seeking to sway policy, they give mainly to lawmakers who are already in office. Challengers —the instruments through whom democracy is supposed to express itself—are being systematically starved for resources.

These are the blackest days for challengers in all of American history. The re-election rate for House incumbents in the last three elections was 98 percent, 98.3 percent, and 96 percent, respectively. There has never been such a string of incumbent victories before. The signs of declining competition are evident even in the Senate, which is much less PAC-ridden than the House. Last year only one senator was defeated, while 97 percent of the incumbents running were re-elected. Incumbents have other advantages, to be sure, but their growing ability to monopolize election resources is proving decisive in more and more cases.

Ordinary people sense that something is wrong, that they are being cheated. Opinion polls show citizens are restive, cynical, overwhelmingly in favor of curbing the role of moneyed interests. After the 1990 election the National Election Studies poll showed 70 percent of the people surveyed thought "government is pretty much run by a few big interests looking out for themselves," while only 24 percent said government is "run for the benefit of all the people," and the rest were not certain. The same poll also showed only 28 percent said they "can trust the government in Washington to do what is right" most of the time.

"Increasingly, Americans have come to see their federal government as no longer responsive to their needs." Senate Majority Leader George Mitchell of Maine said during recent debate on a campaign-finance bill. "They believe Congress acts to fulfill commitments to campaign contributors, rather than to serve the interests of the people. And they believe we have created a campaign finance system that is stacked against challengers and designed especially to keep self-interested incumbents in office forever."

Like most in Congress, however, Mitchell simply denies what the public believes. "I know the reality is different," said Senator Mitchell. He and most incumbents see only a problem of perception—"the perception of the American people of our integrity and our quality."

So Congress has yet to take the first, essential step toward dealing with its own addiction. For an alcoholic, the first step to recovery is to admit he or she has a drinking problem. But so far, no incumbent lawmaker has said, "Hi, I'm Congressman Bob and I'm a money addict." Congress is still in what therapists would call the denial phase.

Listen to Senator Terry Sanford, Democrat of North Carolina: "The truth is that members of the U.S. Senate are honorable people. They do not sell their votes. They do not sell their influence. That is the reality. Unfortunately, the debate today is driven by perceptions, not reality."

Sanford, a member of the Senate Ethics Committee, told *Congressional Quarterly* recently that he thinks the Keating Five "didn't do a damn thing wrong." And when *Congressional Quarterly* reported that Sanford had used campaign contributions to pay himself back a $947,000 loan he had made to his campaign committee to get himself elected in 1986, the Senator did not see anything wrong with that, either. The money that went back into his pocket was contributed by lobbyists, PACs, bankers, and other business executives. Sanford had to be reminded that he had supported legislation to prohibit this much-criticized practice. And Sanford, incidentally, was just elevated to chairman of the Ethics Committee.

The same psychology of addiction is apparent in the House. Representative James Olin, Democrat of Virginia, recently boasted of his restraint when taking PAC funds. "The rule of thumb I have always followed, and I think it is a very good one, is to limit the PAC contributions to not more than what I get from individuals," he said. "This keeps some balance." However, a look at the record shows Olin's PAC contributions for the 1989-1990 election cycle were actually $139,875, half again as much as the $90,731 he got from individuals. When it comes to PACs, Olin is like an alcoholic who claims his drinking is under control. But why change? His ability to attract business money has helped entrench him so firmly that Republicans did not even bother to run an opponent against him last year, although the district votes heavily Republican in presidential elections.

Addiction can produce disordered thinking, and it is no different with PAC dependency. Olin, for example, says his PAC-money intake has no effect on him. "There is no way those PACs are going to influence me much because you can't please more than one or two of them at a time if you wanted to," he said. But in the next breath Olin denounced the influence of PACs sponsored by colleagues seeking to advance to leadership positions. "I think that the leadership PACs have been very, very bad in the House," he said. "People in Washington have given out jobs that have essentially bought the votes."

Congress, still in the denial phase, is doing little more than talk about cutting down. Senate Democrats pushed through a bill in May with the main purpose of putting spending limits on Senate candidates, which President Bush announced in advance he would veto. The Senate bill also would attempt to ban PACs, but House Democrats—who got 53 percent of their own re-election funds from PACs—disagree strongly. Any bill emerging from a Senate-House conference would likely have separate and different rules for Senate and House campaigns. Bush has also said he would veto any bill that would further "Balkanize" the bewildering array of federal campaign finance rules. "I don't know if anybody takes it seriously," Republican Senator Hank Brown of Colorado said in an interview. "The assumption on everybody's part is that it will be vetoed, and the veto will be sustained. So it's just an exercise in mutual bashing. It's a shame. There are a lot of things that should be changed." And Steve Stockmeyer, lobbyist for a group of business PACs, agrees. "I just don't see any change in the factors that have brought about deadlock in the past," he says. "There's a lot of symbolism and posturing and hypocrisy."

Devising real reform will take more than addressing a mere "perception problem." So long as a majority in Congress think of their money addiction as a public-relations problem, then public relations solutions are all they will accept. But such band-aids will not cure the money fever, or even fool the public very long.

A consensus is not likely to crystallize around some magical new idea or novel formula. That approach was tried last year when Senate leaders commissioned a blue-ribbon panel of three lawyers and three political scientists, evenly divided among Republican and Democratic appointees, to work up some new ideas that both parties might accept. But their plan pleased neither side and would not have changed things very much anyway. It called for high spending limits without any public subsidies for candidates, higher donation limits for individuals, and only modest limits on PACs. "I have gone back to these experts and said, 'Have you any more ideas?'" Senate Minority Leader Robert Dole of Kansas said during debate. "So far I have heard from, I think, two. They said they were out of ideas."

A bold reform plan might actually stand a better chance of passage than either the strongly partisan bills seen so far, or some weak cobbling together of whatever marginal fixes command bipartisan support. What follows—with profuse apologies to Alcoholics Anonymous and all similar twelve-step programs—are a dozen steps to end the money chase.

STEP ONE: ADMIT THE PROBLEM. The famous "Twelve Steps"of Alcoholics Anonymous begins with this declaration: "We admitted we were powerless over alcohol—that our lives had become unmanageable." Many lawmakers do complain about the amount of time they spend raising money. "When we think of the time it takes away from doing the duties we are elected to perform, we know something is wrong," said Senator David Boren, Democrat of Oklahoma. "Members of Congress are becoming part-time policymakers." But addiction to special-interest money is not just a problem of efficient time management any more than it is just an image problem. Congress has not yet admitted that money is making elections and government unmanageable.

On a partisan level, serious Democrats need to face up to what their quest for business money is doing to their credibility and their chances of regaining the White House. Accepting money from an oil or chemical company may not be a moral compromise for a Republican who sincerely believes in the primacy of commerce, but it is a real ethical problem for a Democrat claiming to stand for governmental controls on pollution. It is also a practical political problem; the watered-down Republicanism that keeps business money flowing to Democrats makes an uninspiring platform for reclaiming the White House. Is it a coincidence that Democrats now treat the idea of full national health insurance as too radical to contemplate seriously? Instead, they offer up a patchwork of health care ideas borrowed from Richard Nixon. Do the millions given by insurance companies, hospital executives, and physicians have something to do with their timidity? Consciously or subconsciously, the money has an effect.

Republicans are farther along toward recognizing the purely practical way that the special-interest money system hurts them. Bush's proposal to ban PACS shows some Republicans have already figured out that business money by its nature goes to buy influence from incumbents, not to fund a GOP revolution. Corporate PACS—*corporate* PACS—gave $17.7 million to House Democratic incumbents in the last election, and a pitiful $1.2 million to Republican challengers who ran against them. Currently, the Republican National Committee's fund-raising appeals read in part like those of Common Cause. "Congress has become a virtual prisoner to the big spending special interests," the party's chairman, Clayton Yuetter, said in a July mailing.

Once both parties concede how they are being hurt, they should find it easier to agree between them that the country is suffering as well.

STEP TWO: AGREE ON GOALS. Reform needs to accomplish two major goals simultaneously: increasing electoral competition and reducing the grip of moneyed interests on policy. Unfortunately, these policy goals often tug in opposite directions. Special-interest money could be eliminated entirely by simply outlawing all election outlays, removing the need for any donations by setting spending limits at zero. But that would eliminate election campaigns along with the money.

The most important way to increase competition is simply to get more money into the hands of challengers. Their spending does not have to equal that of incumbents; it just has to be enough to allow them to let voters know who they are and what they are trying to say. Despite what too many journalists write and most people intuitively believe, incumbents do not gain a big advantage merely by outspending a challenger.

Most political professionals now recognize as practical fact what political scientist Gary Jacobson discovered long ago—that spending is essential for challengers to become known to the public, but has little measurable benefit for incumbents, who are already well known. Indeed, Jacobson found that the more a House incumbent spends the *less* likely he or she is to win. Probably that is because the incumbents who raise and spend the most are the ones who know they are the most politically vulnerable. What is killing challengers is not so much the spending of incumbents, but their own lack of resources. The trick is to replace special-interest donations with ample supplies of money that carries no strings, such as small contributions from constituents.

A secondary goal, born of political necessity, is that any package of reforms should distribute burdens and benefits fairly equally between the major parties. Anything seen as a partisan power grab is doomed. Other secondary goals should be simplicity and ease of enforcement. They are related: complicated rules are harder to understand, easier to evade, and more prone to springing loopholes.

STEP THREE: ENACT PUBLIC FINANCING. Because they carry no strings of special-interest obligation and would provide aid to cash-starved challengers, public funds advance the fundamental goals of reform. But to a Congress in the denial phase, public funds are about as appealing as a glass of water to a drunk on a bender. In May, for example, the Senate soundly rejected an amendment that would have used public funds to pay for 90 percent of the cost of Senate general elections. It drew support from only thirty-nine Democrats, and was opposed by sixteen Democrats and all forty-two Republicans who voted. In the House, Democrats solidly opposed. Bush says he intends to veto any bill containing "taxpayer financing" of congressional campaigns.

The idea of public financing is gaining support among the public. A 1990 Greenberg-Lake poll showed, for example, that 58 percent of those polled thought it a good idea to give candidates a fixed amount of federal money and bar all private contributions. It was the highest level of support for the idea since Watergate days. Only 33 percent thought it a poor idea. But that is a more radical plan than anyone in Congress is proposing.

The Senate Democratic leadership pushed through a bill on May 23 containing a pitifully small amount of public money for Senate campaigns—perhaps $25 million, compared to the $180 million spent in all Senate campaigns last year. Yet five Democrats voted against it, four more than opposed a similar bill in the previous Congress. Democrats are so nervous about public financing that they will not speak its name. Their bill would not provide Treasury Department checks to candidates, the way the presidential system does. Instead, it would provide government vouchers that could be used for the purchase of radio and television advertising time.

Indeed, if it were not for the Supreme Court, the Democrats' bill might contain no public financing at all. What Democrats desire most strongly is a law to limit the spending of congressional candidates. But they cannot have that without giving public funds to candidates in return for accepting the limits.

That is because the Court in its 1976 *Buckley v. Valeo* decision took the dubious position that in politics, money is speech. Actually, money is more like a megaphone than speech; those with more money can speak more loudly than those with less. Spending limits do not affect the content, only the volume. Nevertheless, the Court ruled that spending limits are an unconstitutional abridgement of free speech unless candidates accept them voluntarily in return for public funds or other inducements.

Republicans, meanwhile, attack even weak public funding as just another Democratic entitlement program for the least deserving of all pressure groups: "food stamps for politicians." Last April, for example, the Senate Republicans' point man on the campaign finance issue, Mitch McConnell of Kentucky, proposed killing public funding of presidential elections to spend $50 million a year more for child nutrition. "That is a lot of school lunches," McConnell said.

But the GOP attack is both hypocritical and against the best interests of the party's own candidates. Hypocritical, because the Republican Party has never refused taxpayer subsidies for its national nominating conventions, and no GOP presidential candidate except John Connally has ever refused them either. In July the party deposited a federal check for $10,600,000 to finance its 1992 convention in Houston. Ronald Reagan accepted $89,741,125 in public funds for his three presidential campaigns, and George Bush has taken $60,149,962 for his—so far. Bush even checks off the box on his federal income tax returns every year designating $2 of the Bush family's tax money for public financing. Furthermore, public financing probably would help the GOP most because it has more of the challengers. "In terms of the impact of public financing, it probably would be a net plus for Republicans," says Senator Brown.

Republican lawmakers are even out of step with their own rank-and-file constituents. The Greenberg-Lake poll showed that among the public, Republicans like the idea of replacing private funds with public money just as much as Democrats. Furthermore, self-identified conservatives liked it as much as liberals. And that should not be surprising. A Republican President, Theodore Roosevelt, proposed the idea first.

STEP FOUR: DE-EMPHASIZE SPENDING LIMITS. Republican lawmakers are on more solid ground when they attack the concept of spending limits in congressional campaigns. For one thing, limits have simply collapsed in presidential campaigns. Walter Mondale got around them using phony "delegate committees" in 1984. And last time, Bush and Michael Dukakis both raised scores of $100,000 donations and spent tens of millions of dollars outside the limits, running the so-called "soft money" through state-regulated political party accounts. "Spending limits are like putting a rock on Jello," McConnell observes. "The Jello just oozes out to the side."

If set too low, limits would certainly hurt challengers and reduce electoral competition even further. But if set high enough to allow competition, they would do nothing to curb dependence on special-interest money. After much internal wrangling, Democrats have settled on fairly high limits. The Senate-passed bill provides a limit of about $11.1 million for a California Senate race, for example, counting various exemptions. That is not much less than the $13 million spent there by Republican Pete Wilson, who won the state's most recent Senate race in 1988. In the House, Democrats are talking about a limit of $600,000, well above the median amount spent by winning challengers in recent elections: $469,000 in 1990, $517,000 in 1988, and $435,000 in 1986.

To be sure, the idea of limits is popular with a public sickened by negative advertising and shallow, thirty-second commercials. They equate high campaign spending with low campaign quality. In a Louis Harris poll last year, 82 percent of the respondents said they favored spending limits combined with other provisions in the Democrats' bill. So Democrats have made limits the Holy Grail of campaign finance reform. "The only meaningful way to reform the Senate election finance system is to have limits on campaign spending," said Senator Mitchell. "Anything less than that avoids the real issues and simply creates the appearance of reform." But both sides should realize that limits, provided they are set high enough and indexed for inflation, are just harmless political sugar-coating, not real medicine.

STEP FIVE: LOOSEN PARTY LIMITS. "The best way to get more resources to cash-strapped challengers is to increase the limits on what the two parties can give to their candidates," said Senator Dole. "We ought to be strengthening, not weakening, the one institution that has a vested interest for removing incumbents, the two political parties, Democrat and Republican."

Dole has a point. One of the worst features of the current regulatory scheme is that it limits the amount of money that political parties can spend on behalf of their own nominees. The law limits the Democratic and Republican campaign committees, after the most recent adjustment for inflation, to about $63,000 in direct aid to each House candidate. For Senate candidates the maximum aid varies with population, from $123,000 in the fourteen smallest states to about $2.4 million in California. These sums are only a fraction of the cost of a serious campaign, so as a practical matter the election law forces candidates to rely more on moneyed interests than on their own party organizations.

Democrats oppose change, however. They rejected a plan offered by Dole to let parties give more aid to challengers by matching, dollar for dollar, whatever early contributions are raised by the candidates from within their own state. This "seed money" plan would have allowed parties an extra $150,000 each for House challengers and $250,000 each for Senate challengers. The reason is pure partisan self-interest: Republican Party organizations still raise a lot more money than the Democrats.

STEP SIX: STRENGTHEN PARTY FINANCES. Strong national parties do not have to be big Tammany Halls. Party money can be just the sort of small donations, publicly disclosed, that everybody says they want. After Watergate, Republicans learned how to raise huge amounts of this clean money through the mail. Thanks in part to Ronald Reagan's popularity, millions of gifts in the $25 to $50 range poured into GOP coffers year after year. But now their donor lists are not working as well, and Democrats are catching up. Republican Party organizations raised nearly five and one-half times more than the Democrats for their federal accounts in 1981-1982, but raised only two and one-half times more during the election cycle just ended.

Some propose filling party coffers by loosening limits on donations by wealthy individuals, or even corporations, labor unions, or PACs. But these ideas go in the wrong direction and would encourage party officials to return to the days when they acted as political money launderers, passing through special-interest contributions that would either have been illegal or politically embarrassing for candidates to accept directly.

Unfortunately, Democratic Party organizations are already becoming increasingly reliant on special-interest money. Most of their money comes from a combination of PACs, lobbyists, real estate developers, and business executives. Their small-donor efforts have never done very well, partly because direct-mail fund-raising is much more expensive than soliciting contributions from PACs, lobbyists, and the wealthy few.

The simplest way to aid the parties is through direct subsidies, as is done in some European democracies. A modest start might be made by requiring both parties to convert their convention subsidies into a trust fund to aid their challengers in House and Senate elections.

Another, possibly less controversial idea is to set up a system for the efficient collection of voluntary contributions, modeled after the enormously successful payroll check-off systems that the Teamsters and United Auto Workers unions and others won for themselves through collective bargaining. Union members who wish to support the PAC simply fill out a form requesting their employer to withhold, say $1 or $2 per week. A similar system for the parties could yield tens of millions of dollars annually, a steady stream of income without special-interest obligation. Employers would remit the voluntary donations to the Internal Revenue Service along with the money they already withhold for income taxes, Social Security, and Medicare. And only the IRS needs to know which party the employee is supporting.

The check-off idea has received little attention since I first proposed it in 1988. To succeed, it would require parties to work hard at persuading rank-and-file workers to give money. But it would be a much cheaper way than direct mail for parties to develop broad financial support.

STEP SEVEN: DE-FUND THE PACS. Currently, President Bush is calling for eliminating the ability of corporations, trade associations, and labor unions to subsidize the administration of PACs. Only the PACs that could support their own fund-raising and administrative costs from the voluntary donations of members would survive, and even those free-standing PACs would see their donation limits cut in half. The President's proposal would force a large number of PACs out of existence, because the voluntary contributions they receive do not equal the corporate or union funds spent to collect them. The President's proposal is the strongest one that stands any chance of surviving in the courts. It should be enacted.

Senate Democrats have tried to one-up Republicans with a hypocritical ploy that would preserve corporate and union PACs. Nominally, it calls for outlawing all PAC donations, but this is guaranteed to be overturned in the courts because it would criminalize even PACs that are not subsidized out of corporate or union treasury money, such as groups supporting Israel, gun control, or the environment. The courts will overturn any limit on political activity by voluntary associations as a violation of the First Amendment. Consequently, the Democratic bill has a "fallback" provision cutting down donation limits for all PACs and restricting Senate candidates from accepting more than 20 percent of their election funds from PACs. But the winners in last year's Senate elections got just 25.6 percent of their funds of PACs anyway.

House Democrats, on the other hand, collected 53 percent of their re-election funds from PACs, and they want even less change. A leading proposal would allow House members to raise up to $200,000 per election from PACs.

STEP EIGHT: CLOSE THE "SOFT MONEY" LOOPHOLE. Some really big money is back in presidential and Senate campaigns, thanks to the "soft money" loophole. It should be closed. President Bush dispensed ambassadorships—to Spain, Australia, Britain, France, Switzerland, and Barbados—to elite members of his "Team 100" club, who gave $100,000 each to finance the 1988 Republican ticket. And in last year's Senate elections, newspaper heiress Mary Bingham wrote a check for $230,000 which Democrats used to buy television commercials aiding their Kentucky candidate, Harvey Sloane.

The problem here is that many states never outlawed corporate or union money in state and local elections, as the federal government did years ago for presidential, Senate, and House elections. Also, federal limits on donations from wealthy individuals do not apply to money given ostensibly to state candidates or state party organizations for use in non-federal elections. So parties have taken to funneling big money into state coffers for such things as voter turnout campaigns and "generic" broadcast advertisements that ostensibly benefit both federal and non-federal candidates on the same ticket. Such party-building expenditures, of course, could be applauded if they were financed entirely with money raised under the federal limits and fully disclosed. That is what should be required.

STEP NINE: ENACT TAX CREDITS. There is already wide support in both parties for giving dollar-for-dollar tax credits for small donations to congressional candidates, especially donations that come from within a candidate's own state. Credits ought to be allowed for small donations to political parties, too, to further encourage them to broaden their financial bases. Donors giving, say, $100 could get the money back when they file their tax returns the following year. It is public financing, but without the bureaucracy or any government formulas for disbursing the funds. Citizens would decide directly which candidates or parties get the subsidy. Republicans do not object to this proposal as they do to sending Treasury checks to candidates. Indeed, a tax-credit measure cleared the House with bipartisan support in 1986 before being discarded in a Senate-House conference on the tax reform bill.

It should not be much of a problem to find the money for tax credits, or for direct public funding, for that matter. True, new budget rules require lawmakers to come up with new taxes or offsetting spending cuts to pay for any new spending or revenue-losing measures they propose. Senate Democrats floated the idea of eliminating business tax deductions for Washington lobbyists to raise an estimated $100 million yearly, or $200 million per election cycle. That alone might be enough; the total amount spent by all congressional candidates combined in 1989-1990 was $445 million. Some House Democrats want to tax political action committees, but that is a pale alternative to getting rid of them entirely. Imposing a slight millage on all advertising would spread the burden more broadly over an industry the public sees as profiting from campaign commercials anyway.

Congress could also reduce its own free mailings or cut the jobs of all Senate and House employees who now solicit campaign contributions. Or, how about a tax on political consultants? Negative political advertising? As amusing as it is to think of deserving targets, the soundest approach would be simply to take the money from general revenues and suspend the requirement for finding offsets.

STEP TEN: COMMANDEER CHEAP COMMERCIALS. To reduce the cost of campaigning, thereby making it easier for challengers to get their message to voters, Congress should require radio and television stations to sell commercial time to Senate and House candidates at half price. Such a plan is part of the bill already passed by the Senate, and it drew surprisingly little opposition. It is hard to find lawmakers who do not think they have been gouged by their local stations, which tend to charge premium rates in the weeks just before an election. The National Association of Broadcasters is not putting up much of a fight. It countered with a plan to provide one free commercial for every two that are purchased. Political advertising, which is highly seasonal, only accounts for an estimated 1 percent of broadcast revenues anyway.

Even at half price, television would remain out of reach for about half of all House candidates. For them, mail is the preferred advertising medium and half-price postage is the way to cut the costs. This is yet another form of public financing, but one that many Republicans find ideologically acceptable. Also, subsidizing candidates' mail would make it easier for them to prospect for small political donations.

STEP ELEVEN: IMPROVE DISCLOSURE AND ENFORCEMENT. If it were not for public disclosure, lawmakers might be even more inclined to do official favors for campaign contributors. "I just had somebody come in last week that I want to help," recalled Senator Alan Dixon, Democrat of Illinois. "I called in my people and I said, 'Has that person given me a campaign contribution?' and they said, 'Yes.' I said, 'Put everything in writing.'"

But disclosure needs improvement, especially if PACs are eliminated and moneyed lobbies react by increasing their bundling of individual donations. Public Citizen, in its survey of large contributions to last year's congressional candidates, counted $30 million from donors whose employers and occupations were not disclosed at all. Candidates should be required to list occupation and employer for *every* donor of $200 or more, or give the money back.

Also, the Federal Election Commission (FEC) should be required by law to computerize all donors to enable researchers to make sense of the millions of pages of raw data. The FEC puts all donors on computer now, but for years it omitted all donors of under $500 to save money on keypunching, thereby missing millions of dollars. And it once suspended computerization entirely during a budget pinch, saying the law did not require any such data entry.

The FEC's commitment to disclosure is so ambivalent, in fact, that it is currently seeking fines from at least two different organizations for the offense of offering commercial computer processing of donor data. The law forbids making "commercial use" of donor names, except by news organizations. This was intended mainly to prevent professional fund-raisers or name-list brokers from pirating the valuable donor lists of candidates or political parties. But the FEC, at the request of the National Republican Congressional Committee, has gone to federal court to prevent private companies from selling computerized donor information to public interest groups, academic researchers, or even news organizations, even when lists of donor names are stripped of street addresses and therefore useless as a mailing list. Congress should stop the FEC from this sort of nonsense by repealing the "commercial use" restriction, or at least narrowing it to apply only to those who actually pirate names for the specific purpose of soliciting donations or selling merchandise.

STEP TWELVE: RECOGNIZE A HIGHER POWER. Among the steps toward recovery in the Alcoholics Anonymous program is accepting that "a power greater than ourselves could restore us to sanity." For a politician, that higher power is the electorate, the American people.

One way Congress could show a change of heart would be to require that House and Senate candidates meet their election opponents in at least three of four public debates sponsored by bipartisan or nonpartisan entities. This would not only be a sign of respect toward voters; it would as a practical matter provide loads of free publicly to challengers and favor those candidates with something more to say than will fit in a thirty-second commercial. Senator Bob Graham, Democrat of Florida, proposed such a requirement, but only for presidential candidates. "The American people are smart and wise enough to be able to evaluate the quality of that exchange," he said. "It would not be limited to just what they see in a burst of highly emotional, visual images on their television screen." But many senators resisted. "It is a matter of deciding on political strategy," said Senator Boren. "There are circumstances in which you simply might not want to enter into a debate with your opponent." Senator Graham's proposal squeaked by, 44 to 43, and certainly would have failed had it applied to House and Senate candidates.

Many alcoholics seek help only after the shock of "hitting bottom," a divorce, a frightening accident while driving drunk, or being fired from a job. For Congress, the Jim Wright and Charles Keating traumas have apparently not been enough. But the pathology of addiction is such that something worse is likely to follow.

Indeed, 1992 will bring an orgy of political fund-raising because of the conjunction of a decennial reapportionment, a uniquely expensive set of Senate races, and a presidential election. The soft-money loophole will allow an escalating bidding war for wealthy donors. Unless Congress takes the pledge soon, the twentieth anniversary of the Watergate break-in could easily see the return of the $1-million fatcat, another increase in special-interest dependency, and a further erosion in public trust.

Voters in the Crosshairs

HOW TECHNOLOGY AND THE MARKET ARE DESTROYING POLITICS

Marshall Ganz

> Organize the whole state, so that every Whig can be brought to the polls ...divide the county into small districts and appoint in each a sub-committee...make a perfect list of voters and ascertain with certainty for whom they will vote...and on election day see that every Whig is brought to the polls.
>
> *Abraham Lincoln*
> *Illinois State Register*
> *February 21, 1840*

Campaigns and elections are the lifeblood of American democracy and the principal means by which citizens form and express political opinions. Any less than full and equal electoral participation puts democracy at risk. Today electoral participation is neither full nor equal, and it is getting worse. Paradoxically, new campaign technologies and practices bear significant responsibility for declining participation. While making it easier to communicate with voters and to create Lincoln's "perfect list," direct mail, databases of voters, polling, and targeted advertising also depress voter turnout and fragment the electorate. The source of this conflict lies in the combination of the technology, the new class of political consultants it has empowered, and the marketplace institutions to which the management of campaigns are increasingly relegated (like so many other public goods).

The paradox demonstrates a fundamental American dilemma: the conflict between equality and liberty and, more specifically, the conflict between a politics based on equality of voice and an economics based on inequality of resources. To the extent that voice depends on resources, an unregulated political market guarantees political inequality. The new technology has given those with more resources access to even greater voice. As a result, many elections have become for most citizens exercises in choosing between two power blocs representing similar if not identical resource-rich interests.

Not surprisingly, fewer Americans are taking part. Election scholar Walter Dean Burnham reports voter turnout in presidential elections outside the South declined from 73 percent in 1960 to 54 percent in 1988. Participation expert Sidney Verba found that turnout for local elections during a similar period declined from 47 percent to 35 percent.

Verba also found that the well-known bias that favors higher electoral turnout among wealthier voters is even greater for other forms of participation. Families with incomes below $35,000 comprise 54.6 percent of the eligible electorate but only 50.3 percent of voters. On the other hand, those earning more than $50,000 make up 24.6 percent of the electorate and 28.1 percent of voters. In campaign hours, the lower income group contributes 35.5 percent, while the upper income group contributes 50.1 percent. In campaign dollars, the lower income group gives only 16.5 percent, while the upper income group contributes 71 percent. Indeed, the top 10 percent contributes 50 percent of all the money that supports political campaigns.

Because politicians pay more attention to the people who put them in office, this pattern of participation means the interests of a major portion of the electorate, if not a majority, are consistently left out of the political calculus.

The mechanisms by which elections are conducted are a kind of electoral "means of production" for the polity. Electoral mechanics define who takes part, how they take part, what resources are needed to take part, and thus whose interests the outcome will reflect. The introduction of radical new communications technologies has dramatically altered the way in which elections are conducted. This revolution, in turn, has altered the political system itself.

HUNTERS AND GATHERERS

Since the 1830s, American political campaigns have pursued one of two basic strategies: vote "gathering" that maximizes turnout or vote "hunting" that minimizes it. During the nineteenth century, political parties "gathered" votes by using marches, rallies, patronage, and a partisan press to mobilize known supporters; in 1896 turnout outside the South reached a peak of 86 percent. Early in the twentieth century, however, an establishment fearful of populism and new immigrants used restrictive voting measures, such as voter registration, as well as a nonpartisan press and new advertising and broadcast technologies in a "hunt" for the "responsible" but undecided voter. By 1920, turnout outside the South had declined to a new low of 57 percent. With the political upheavals of the 1930s, vote gathering resumed as newly organized unions and a revitalized Democratic Party generated new political resources that were applied to renewed voter mobilization. Turnout increased, reaching 73 percent in 1940.

Modern campaigning, which began with polling and television in the 1960s, marked a return to vote hunting. Although polling developed from demographic studies by Gallup and Roper in the 1930s, it reached public acceptance only in the early 1960s when Lou Harris achieved fame as John F. Kennedy's pollster. Polling enabled politicians to learn voter opinions without attending to constituency leaders or the voters themselves. It became possible to "know" the electorate without having a relationship with it. Polling also created a role for the electoral expert whose "expertise" derived not from political or organizational experience but from mastery of the new technology.

Television transformed political campaigning along with much of American life beginning with the 1952 Eisenhower campaign. Television was also credited with Kennedy's presidential victory over Richard Nixon in 1960. Television transformed JFK's state primary victories into national events, creating a momentum Democrats could not ignore, and gave the photogenic Kennedy a critical edge over Nixon. By the 1970s, television advertising had become a key element in most major campaigns, as well as the principal factor driving up their cost. Television also introduced a second technological expert—the "media adviser" typified by long-time Democratic campaign consultants Tony Schwartz or Joe Napolitan.

Computers, which had been used to support polling, began to have a separate influence in the 1970s. Computer technology made it possible to develop direct mail fundraising campaigns on a large scale but with precise targeting. About the same time, marketing companies learned to combine census data and polling information, enabling marketers to target consumers by zip code according to their lifestyle and preferences. As voter registration lists and other electoral data became computerized at the state, county, and city level, microcomputer technology spread and there developed an industry of over 2,500 firms providing each campaign with targeted, custom-made lists. Consequently, voter contact strategies are targeted down to the level of the individual voter.

In 1984 Frank Tobe, a leading practitioner of computer targeting, described his mission:

> Campaign managers...need to be aware of the exciting, new delivery products for campaign messages afforded by today's computer technologies and decide which are most relevant and cost effective for the race they are working on...computer-prepared laser letters, pre-filled-in absentee ballots, computer-generated slate cards, tasteful and stylish response devices, urgent looking (get out the vote) messages, polished and authentic looking endorsement letters, and hundreds of other computer prepared products all improved by some level of personalization far beyond simple inclusion of the recipients' name or city into the copy.

Meanwhile, modern campaigns have become even more expensive when voter turnout has fallen to a new low. Campaign expenditures climbed from $200 million, or $2.80 a vote, in 1964 to $2.7 billion, or $29.48 a vote, in 1988, but voter turnout outside the South fell from 73 percent to 54 percent.

THE PROFESSIONALS

Each technological innovation produced a new expert—or "consultant"—who provided access to the new tool for a fee. In the absence of strong parties or public regulation of campaign activities, candidates made deals directly with consultants. No longer was running for office an organizational activity; it was now an "entrepreneurial" endeavor. The premium was on the cash to buy expertise rather than the loyalty to command organization. The campaign manager or press agent of yore, often a party operative or associate of the candidate or his supporters, was replaced by a paid professional.

The arrival of television in the early 1950s provided professional campaign consulting with its real kick-off. In *The Rise of Political Consultants*, Larry Sabato noted that by 1972, 168 out of 208 candidates for state office were reported as having hired professionals, as had 61 out of 67 U.S. Senate candidates, 38 out of 42 gubernatorial candidates, and 30 out of 37 candidates for attorney general. By 1986, after the introduction of computer targeting, consultant Frank Lutz reports that 85 percent of 138 senatorial or gubernatorial candidates hired professional pollsters, 94 percent had professional media consultants, and 4 percent had no consultants at all.

Ironically, the rise of the consultants was also spurred by the campaign finance reforms of the 1970s and the 1976 Supreme Court decision, *Buckley v. Valeo*, that declared spending limits unconstitutional. The legislative reforms attempted to regulate contributions rather than expenditures, thus trying to control supply rather than demand. The unabated demand for money, however, simply created a premium for fundraisers with expertise in the new requirements. The contribution limits also placed a premium on the ability to raise large sums of money in small amounts from many donors. Direct mail fundraising thus received a new boost, as did political action committees (PACs). The legacy of this legislation was to make campaigning still more expensive and the role of consultants still more critical.

The way in which consultants are compensated also drives up campaign costs. Consultants are usually paid a flat campaign fee plus a commission based on the cost of the services the campaign (the consultant) purchases. For example, a consultant paid a flat fee of $100,000 will also receive a commission of 15 percent to 20 percent of all the money spent on the television buy, direct mail, and even billboards. A typical television buy of $300,000 and direct mail expense of $250,000 will return the consultant an additional $120,000. Consultants also often own interests in their subcontractors (printers, mail houses, telemarketing firms, and so on), providing them with additional income. A consultant who produces a mailer for $.32 per piece will charge the client $.40 per piece. If a campaign sends, say, 27 mailings of 75,000 brochures each, the consultant nets an extra $162,000. Since top consultants handle from five to ten campaigns simultaneously, their earnings potential is impressive indeed.

The personal quality of consulting has inhibited the development of a competitive market. A winning reputation is so important that a candidate's capacity to raise money and discourage competition often depends on hiring the right consultant at the right time. Absent political parties with the resources to take advantage of the new campaign tools, and absent reforms to limit spending, consultants are able to sell their expertise for "all the market will bear."

The thrall in which many consultants hold candidates also gives these professionals greater control over the content of a campaign than candidates themselves. In a 1989 survey, 44 percent of political consultants interviewed reported that their candidates were uninvolved in setting the issue priorities in their own campaigns, and 66 percent reported candidates to be uninvolved in determining the tactics.

Consultants have thus come to play multiple roles: campaign manager, press agent, party, and even candidate. But for most political consultants, the motivation to get out the vote is private, not public, gain. For these professionals, politics is not a public domain in which each citizen is to have an equal voice. It is a business in which market principles apply and there is one criteria of success—winning. From the consultants' perspective, winning does not depend on who is right, who is the better candidate, or what is in the best interest of the community. As Stanley Foster Reed, founder of the trade journal *Campaigns and Elections*, put it in his 1980 premise issue:

> What makes the difference between winning and losing a political campaign? Is it the same thing that makes the difference between succeeding and failing in business? Yes! Management makes the difference. Management of resources: money, media, people.

Of course, candidates, parties, and constituency leaders also want to win, but this desire dovetails with the long-term interests of their political community. The consultant's calculus, on the other hand, considers only will it win and does it make money?

Although the consequences of this marketplace thinking for American democracy are serious and far-reaching, they are not the result of insidious forces or a malevolent cabal. They are the result of intelligent people making conscious and "utility maximizing" decisions under the current arrangements that govern American political campaigns.

CAMPAIGNS OLD AND NEW

The guiding principle of modern campaign management is "bang for the buck"—the allocation of each dollar to achieve maximum possible effect in the *current* election. Traditional campaigns took a more long-term, investment approach, building the party infrastructure through voter registration and precinct organization. The new campaign methods not only raise costs and empower consultants, they also require that money be spent in different ways. Today's campaign strategies have reached a new level of sophistication, where only those votes most likely to vote are wooed, messages change with demographics, issues are condensed into fleeting televised images, and campaign organizations are nearly as ephemeral.

TARGETING I: REDUCING THE UNIVERSE. Traditional campaign strategy would expand the electorate and motivate voters to participate. A voter registration drive, for example, would increase potential support in the district by targeting pockets of unregistered supporters based on the density of partisan registration. Each campaign would then target its own partisans for mobilization and a portion of the other party's adherents for persuasion. Both campaigns would target unaffiliated voters for persuasion. This logic would lead to the targeting of 60 percent of registered voters for mobilization by one of the campaigns and 40 percent of registered voters for persuasion by both campaigns. An election day get-out-the-vote program would then focus on turning out all identified supporters to vote.

This was the strategy Senator Robert Kennedy's 1968 presidential campaign used in targeting California Latinos for pre-primary voter registration, especially in East Los Angeles. The extraordinary turnout from this community was a key factor in Kennedy's primary win. Today such a registration effort would never happen, on grounds that historically lower turnout among Latinos means that precious campaign dollars should be invested in persuading more-likely voters.

For the last couple decades, campaign consultants have been perfecting ways to restrict the electorate by "reducing the universe" of voters, long before Ed Rollins caused a furor by claiming he paid New Jersey ministers not to encourage their congregation members to vote in the gubernatorial race last September. The computerization of voter registration files and emergence of "list vendors" who purchase tapes of these files and convert them into customized, campaign-specific lists make possible this new approach to targeting. Matching voter files with tapes of phone directories, ethnic surname dictionaries, county assessor records, and voter turnout reports makes it possible to generate lists of voters individually profiled by their party affiliation, age, gender, marital status, homeowner status, ethnicity, and frequency of voting. Consultant Matt Reese explains how this information is used:

> Targeting is a process of excluding people who are not "profitable" to work, so that resources are adequate to reach prime voters with enough intensity to win them. Targeting provides an ultimate "lift" to the voter contact process, allowing maximum concentration of resources to a minimum universe.

Voter registration, for example, is rarely considered because newly registered voters are less likely to turn out than established voters. Also, it requires a "ground force" of volunteers or paid registrars. In the absence of an ongoing program, there are numerous problems of management, recruitment, and quality control in creating such a team for a single campaign.

The effects of this new campaign ethos can be seen in a hypothetical district, where 55 percent of the registered voters are Democrats, 35 percent are Republicans, and 10 percent are independent or "decline to state." The first step in applying the new strategy is to buy computer tapes that describe the district by party and by voter turnout. Of all registered voters, 24 percent have no record of voting, suggesting that they are gone, and 39 percent vote only occasionally, mainly in presidential elections. These voters are ignored because they are unlikely to turn out unless stimulated. The likely voters, a bedrock 37 percent of registered voters who vote in most elections, are the prime targets of the campaign. Among these, priority is assigned to the Democratic 10 percent, Republican 5 percent, and independent 2 percent judged to be "swing" voters based on their electoral or individual histories (a Republican living with a Democrat, for example). This 17 percent is targeted for persuasion and becomes the heart of the campaign, the real determiners of the issues the campaign will address. The remaining 20 percent of the electorate who are likely voters and are likely to be loyal to their parties are contacted mainly to inform them of the candidate's identity and affiliation. They are not mobilized because they are regular voters.

As of election day, 63 percent of registered voters will not have been contacted by anyone. If, as is typical, only 60 percent of the eligible electorate were registered, 78 percent of the eligible voters in the district would never be contacted. These uncontacted voters are far more likely to be of lower socioeconomic status than those who are contacted. They never hear from a campaign and thus will likely stay at home on election day or vote the way they always have. The assumption that past voting behavior is predictive of future behavior becomes a self-fulfilling prophecy. With both campaigns in last June's Los Angeles mayoral election using this kind of reasoning, it is not so surprising that, despite the city's troubles, less than 25 percent of the Los Angeles electorate turned out to vote.

TARGETING II: THE SEGMENTED ELECTORATE. After "reducing the universe" limits the campaign to just 37 percent of the registered voters, further targeting segments it for assault by direct mail. In a recent interview, Richie Ross, consultant to California Assembly Speaker Willie Brown, described the process:

> Once a consultant goes to work for a candidate, he or she will cross-reference the district's population over and over, until the desired geodemographic groups have been isolated. These groups are always exceedingly narrow. The number of demographic groups targeted in a specific campaign ranges from 60 to 1,200 with the precise figure depending on the level of office being contested and the amount of money a candidate has to spend.... A typical congressional campaign might have around 300 groups targeted.

Information on each of these subgroups is matched with polling data, and the campaign messages are developed to deliver what Matt Reese calls "different—and compelling—truths" to those various segments.

Instead of a single campaign with a single theme that unifies a candidate's supporters, parallel campaigns emerge, each articulating themes narrow enough to appeal to the peculiar characteristics of each sub-constituency. In a recent California Assembly campaign, for example, married Catholic homeowners learned that the candidate supported family values, while single Jewish women under age 40 found the candidate had been consistently pro-choice.

Although direct mail was originally developed for small-donor fundraising, consultants adapted it to the delivery of the segmented message because it is far less expensive than television and can market politics to precisely the right voters.

Far from aggregating the interests of the electorate, the new campaign thus serves only to further disperse them.

THE 30-SECOND SPOT. As television has driven up campaign costs and given new currency to consultants, it has devalued the quality and content of political discussion. The quest for the six o'clock news sound bite and the reduction of political debate to visual-emotional images that can be conveyed in 30 seconds have been major factors in redefining American political discourse.

To the extent that voters depend on campaigns for political information, the "30 second rule" allows the medium to obstruct the message. Thus the emptiness Americans observe in their political dialogue may be mechanical as well as substantive in origin. Even worse, the 30-second bite has been a very effective tool for the negative campaigning that increasingly takes the place of issue differentiation between candidates who target the same voters.

Developments in targeting and direct mail, however, have made the economics of television advertising problematic for all but the largest campaigns and those in which district boundaries coincide with a particular media market. Television is so expensive because it is billed according to the size of the entire market a particular channel reaches. For example, if a candidate for the Los Angeles City Council in a district with 100,000 voters runs a television commercial, he or she pays for reaching all 10 million people in the Los Angeles basin.

A revival of televised political advertising may occur if it can become a visual version of direct mail. Newer wireless cable technologies and the proliferation of local and specialized carriers may both lower the cost and offer access to highly targeted audiences currently possible only through the mail.

INSTANT ORGANIZATIONS. When consultants determine a need for people-intensive tactics, they turn to "instant organization." For example, canvassing may be required to determine the identities of undecided swing voters who may then receive calls or mailings customized to their concerns. Or an election may be so close—and well funded—that occasional voters will be targeted for get-out-the-vote work. With atrophied party structures, weakened constituent organizations, and the increasingly lost art of building a campaign structure to recruit, train, and direct volunteers, consultants subcontract to purveyors of "instant organization," or IO.

Providers of IO hire a paid staff to run field operations that dissolve at the end of the campaign, leaving candidate and consultant free of costly maintenance and accountability problems. IO generally entails paid door-to-door or telephone canvassers using prepared scripts to solicit voter support and who are paid on a per head or bounty basis. The results of their contacts are then computerized and dovetailed with mailing or recontact strategies. That such efforts can be effective—for vote gathering as well as vote hunting—is demonstrated by the 1986 campaign of California Senator Alan Cranston. Six weeks before the election, after Cranston and his opponent, Ed Zschau, had spent $15 million each on television and direct mail, Cranston committed $300,000 to an IO get-out-to-vote effort. Computerized targeting identified "unlikely" voters who were supporters. The only work done by the precinct was turning them out to vote. The 160,000 unlikely voters who did turn out gave Cranston the 110,000 vote edge he needed to win.

In the absence of an institutional structure to connect with, however, almost all of these organizations have been abandoned by the candidate "the morning after" the election. Candidates' agendas shift to raising money to pay off campaign debt (and accumulate a new war chest), accommodating interest groups, and insulating themselves against opposition in the next election. This development, in turn, induces cynicism among organizers and volunteers who generally want to have a longer term role in policy as well as politics.

THE "NEW" CAMPAIGN AND AMERICAN DEMOCRACY

These developments have eroded the quality of American democracy in four important ways.

DECLINE AND BIAS IN VOTER TURNOUT. New campaign methods undermine and bias voter turnout by failing to communicate with all but the most likely voters. This denies many people the resources and motivation they need in order to participate—particularly voters at the lower end of the socioeconomic spectrum.

Resources include political information and skills; motivation includes attitudes that encourage participation, a belief in one's political efficacy, and a clear political interest. Citizens of higher socioeconomic status generally have greater access to both resources and motivation. Sidney Verba found, however, that the motivational deficit can be compensated for when "group consciousness" makes a voter's interest in participation clearer or provides a heightened sense of efficacy. The resource deficit can be offset by organizational affiliation, which allows the activist to gain political skills and information. This explains the impact that unions had on American workers in the 1930s and that many Protestant churches have on African-American constituencies today.

Diminished voter contact also inhibits the formation of political opinion. In *The Reasoning Voter,* political scientist Sam Popkin reported that voters use the information they receive from campaigns, Popkin says, because they have limited information about government and are "open to influence by campaigners who offer them...better explanations of the ways in which government activities affect them."

The voter's understanding of campaign issues is also directly related to the amount of debate to which he or she is exposed. Popkin found that "the more the candidates talked about an issue [in a campaign] and the greater their differences on it, the more accurately it was perceived." The logic of the "reduced universe" denies this information to the voters who most need it.

Finally, the "dehumanization" of voter contact techniques damages efforts to turn people out. Campaign activities that depend on popular participation for their effectiveness—such as voter registration and get-out-the-vote programs—have been widely dismissed as not cost-effective. Yet studies like those of political scientist Ray Wolfinger have verified that people are most likely to respond to other people. Wolfinger found that active precinct increased voter turnout in New Haven by as much as 10 percent.

DECLINE AND BIAS IN POLITICAL ACTIVISM. Because the new campaign devalues all forms of political activism except for giving money, the role of the political volunteer has been all but eliminated. This dampens overall levels of participation and limits it to those with the financial resources to become contributors.

The decline of the volunteer has closed off an important source for recruitment of political leadership, and many people drawn to politics today must seek entry instead as employees or interns. The reduced demand for volunteer activity has also likely contributed to a decline in membership in political organizations, according to Verba, from 8 percent of the citizenry in 1967 to 4 percent in 1987.

THE WEAKENING OF CIVIC SOCIETY. The new campaign has undercut broad-based democratic organizations through which individual citizens have traditionally participated in public life. Traditional democratic organizations, which rely heavily on volunteers, once served as important "schools for democracy"where citizens acquired resources and motivation for active political participation. These organizations—parties, unions, political clubs, and civic groups—help formulate political choices and provide organizational mechanisms to encourage voting. The atrophy of these associations and the rise of Washington-based lobbies that do little more than seek members' money through direct mail both reflect and reinforce the rising influence of money and the declining importance of citizen participation.

EROSION OF COMMON INTEREST. Segmented voter interests have undermined incentives for political leaders to articulate and act upon those interests citizens do share. Indeed, intensity of political voice seems to have become directly related to narrowness of vision, while breadth of vision is related to weakness of voice. Much of this "narrowness" can be directly traced to the new campaign and its approach to "political marketing."

The reduction of individual voters to demographic abstractions has even dampened the incentive of citizens to intelligently translate their own competing interests into coherent politics. A voter receives one piece of mail as a married Catholic, another as a 30-year-old professional, and still another as an "environmentally concerned" citizen. Each piece of propaganda asserts the overwhelming importance of its own priorities and course of action. The set of concerns that least enters the campaign are those of citizens of lower socioeconomic status. As a result, the marginal voters are rendered invisible, as their concerns go unrepresented, and silent, as their capacity to articulate those concerns remains undeveloped. Thus instead of providing an experience in "strong democratic talk" that helps to define and articulate common interests, the new campaign is a political cacophony in which one coalition of dissonant and powerful interests seeks to defeat another. This offers a grim prospect for the future of American democracy.

RESTRUCTURING VOICE

The introduction of new political technologies has crippled the American attempt to combine equal voice in politics with unequal resources in economics. Technology, however, is only a set of tools. The critical factor is the "free market" approach to the management of politics and elections. Weak parties and an ineffective method of governing elections has allowed the new tools to enhance the power of those with the resources to buy access to them.

Establishing equality of political voice for all Americans will require major institutional change: a reconstruction of the political parties and the public allocation of campaign resources.

Despite their weakened condition, political parties remain one of the few institutions with which a significant number of Americans still identify. The rule of thumb in most campaigns is that 80 percent of voters will vote for the party with which they are registered. Political parties also have the framework of a democratic structure through which participation can take place. They are uniquely positioned to have a strategic interest in gaining more adherents and thus in expanding the electorate.

Partisan "reconstruction" would begin with measures enabling them to build their own financial base from resources unavailable to candidates running for office. These resources could be used as the political capital to invest in the following partisan infrastructure:

- party-owned computerized voter files available to all endorsed candidates;
- voter registration drives targeted on the non-participating voter with the intent of expanding support for the party;
- ongoing precinct organization available to support endorsed candidates but not dependent on them for finance;
- "generic" media campaigns targeted at the non-participating electorate encouraging them to join the party, etc.

Reconstructed parties could then become vehicles for currently disempowered interests to reenter the political process and serve as a means for rebuilding a politics of inclusion and common interest.

Second, the cost of campaigns must be reduced and equalized, attacking the demand side of political resources in an equitable fashion. The mail, the radio waves, and the television airwaves belong to the public, and access to them by political campaigns—as to any limited public space—should be allocated by the public in the public interest.

In other words, bona fide candidates should receive equitable but limited access to the mail, radio, and television. This would limit the need for funds, soft and hard, thereby reducing the incentive to raise them. Public finance could be provided to campaigns agreeing to operate within this framework and denied to others. This would avoid problems created by constitutional inhibitions to limitations on campaign spending per se and yet reduce the incentive for ceaseless, seemingly limitless, fundraising. Limiting what could be purchased and the money available to purchase it could force candidates to turn back toward volunteers, parties, and other organizations able to provide the human power, which could then provide the "edge" in winning a campaign.

The paradoxical impact of the new technology is captured most clearly by the authors of *The Electronic Commonwealth:*

> Here we come to an essential irony about the impact of the computer age on our democracy. In theory, the computer is a vast force for equalizing access to information: no information is so remote or closely held as to be unobtainable by the average citizen. In practice, however, the computer tends to widen the information gap between economic classes.

The political challenge which we face is to gain control over the consequences of our own technology, finding ways to use it to bring the goal of a democracy of "equal voices" ever closer to reality. It is, however, only through a mastery of the politics of our time that we can hope to succeed.

Ticking Time Bombs

The Strange Disappearance of Civic America

Robert D. Putnam

For the last year or so, I have been wrestling with a difficult mystery. It is a classic brainteaser, with a corpus delicti, a crime scene strewn with clues, and many potential suspects. As in all good detective stories, however, some plausible miscreants turn out to have impeccable alibis, and some important clues hint at portentous developments that occurred before the curtain rose.

The mystery concerns the strange disappearance of social capital and civic engagement in America. By "social capital," I mean features of social life—networks, norms, and trust—that enable participants to act together more effectively to pursue shared objectives. (Whether or not their shared goals are praiseworthy is, of course, entirely another matter.) I use the term "civic engagement" to refer to people's connections with the life of their communities, not only with politics.

Although I am not yet sure that I have solved the mystery, I have assembled evidence that clarifies what happened. An important clue, as we shall see, involves differences among generations. Americans who came of age during the Depression and World War II have been far more deeply engaged in the life of their communities than the generations that have followed them. The passing of this "long civic generation" appears to be an important proximate cause of the decline of our civic life. This discovery does not in itself crack the case, but when combined with other data it points strongly to one suspect against whom I shall presently bring an indictment.

Evidence for the decline of social capital and civic engagement comes from a number of independent sources. Surveys of average Americans in 1965, 1975, and 1985, in which they recorded every single activity during a day—so-called "time-budget" studies—indicate that since 1965 time spent on informal socializing and visiting is down (perhaps by one-quarter) and time devoted to clubs and organizations is down even more sharply (by roughly half). Membership records of such diverse organizations as the PTA, the Elks club, the League of Women Voters, the Red Cross, labor unions, and even bowling leagues show that participation in many conventional voluntary associations has declined by roughly 25 percent to 50 percent over the last two to three decades. Surveys show sharp declines in many measures of collective political participation, including attending a rally or speech (off 36 percent between 1973 and 1993), attending a meeting on town or school affairs (off 39 percent), or working for a political party (off 56 percent).

Some of the most reliable evidence about trends comes from the General Social Survey (GSS), conducted nearly every year for more than two decades. The GSS demonstrates, at all levels of education and among both men and women, a drop of roughly one-quarter in group membership since 1974 and a drop of roughly one-third in social trust since 1972. (Trust in political authorities, indeed in many social institutions, has also declined sharply over the last three decades, but that is conceptually a distinct trend.) Slumping membership has afflicted all sorts of groups, from sports clubs and professional associations to literary discussion groups and labor unions. Only nationality groups, hobby and garden clubs, and the catch-all category of "other" seem to have resisted the ebbing tide. Gallup polls report that church attendance fell by roughly 15 percent during the 1960s and has remained at that lower level ever since, while data from the National Opinion Research Center suggest that the decline continued during the 1970s and 1980s and by now amounts to roughly 30 percent. A more complete audit of American social capital would need to account for apparent countertrends. Some observers believe, for example, that support groups and neighborhood watch groups are proliferating, and few deny that the last several decades have witnessed explosive growth in interest groups represented in Washington. The growth of such "mailing list" organizations as the American Association of Retired People and the Sierra Club, although highly significant in political (and commercial) terms, is not really a counterexample to the supposed decline in social connectedness, however, since these are not really associations in which members meet one another. Their members' ties are to common symbols and ideologies, but not to each other. Similarly, although most secondary associations are not-for-profit, most prominent nonprofits (from Harvard University to the Ford Foundation to the Metropolitan Opera) are bureaucracies, not secondary associations, so the growth of the "third sector" is not tantamount to a growth in social connectedness. With due regard to various kinds of counterevidence, I believe that the weight of available evidence confirms that Americans today are significantly less engaged with their communities than was true a generation ago.

Of course, American civil society is not moribund. Many good people across the land work hard every day to keep their communities vital. Indeed, evidence suggests that America still outranks many other countries in the degree of our community involvement and social trust. But if we examine our lives, not our aspirations, and if we compare ourselves not with other countries but with our parents, the best available evidence suggests that we are less connected with one another.

Reversing this trend depends, at least in part, on understanding the causes of the strange malady afflicting American civic life. This is the mystery I seek to unravel here: Why, beginning in the 1960s and accelerating in the 1970s and 1980s, did the fabric of American community life begin to fray? Why are more Americans bowling alone?

THE USUAL SUSPECTS

Many possible answers have been suggested for this puzzle:

- busy-ness and time pressure;
- economic hard times (or, according to alternative theories, material affluence);
- residential mobility;
- suburbanization;
- the movement of women into the paid labor force and the stresses of two-career families;
- disruption of marriage and family ties;
- changes in the structure of the American economy, such as the rise of chain stores, branch firms, and the service sector;
- the sixties (most of which actually happened in the seventies); including Vietnam, Watergate, and disillusion with public life; and the cultural revolt against authority (sex, drugs, and so on);
- growth of the welfare state;
- the civil rights revolution;
- television, the electronic revolution, and other technological changes.

The classic questions posed by a detective are means, motive, and opportunity. A solution, even a partial one, to our mystery must pass analogous tests.

Is the proposed explanatory factor correlated with trust and civic engagement? If not, that factor probably does not belong in the lineup. For example, if working women turn out to be more engaged in community life than housewives, it would be harder to attribute the downturn in community organizations to the rise of two-career families.

Is the correlation spurious? If parents, for example, were more likely than childless people to be joiners, that might be an important clue. However, if the correlation between parental status and civic engagement turned out to be entirely spurious, due to the effects of (say) age, we would have to remove the declining birth rate from our list of suspects.

Is the proposed explanatory factor changing in the relevant way? Suppose, for instance, that people who often move have shallower community roots. That could be an important part of the answer to our mystery *only if* residential mobility itself had risen during this period.

Is the proposed explanatory factor vulnerable to the claim that it might be the result *of civic disengagement, not the* cause? For example, even if newspaper readership were closely correlated with civic engagement across individuals and across time, we would need to weigh the degree to which reduced newspaper circulation is the result (not the cause) of disengagement.

Against those benchmarks, let us weigh the evidence. But first we must acknowledge a trend that only complicates our task.

EDUCATION DEEPENS THE MYSTERY

Education is by far the strongest correlate that I have discovered of civic engagement in all its forms, including social trust and membership in many different types of groups. In fact, the effects of education become greater and greater as we move up the educational ladder. The four years of education between 14 and 18 total years have *ten times more impact* on trust and membership than the first four years of formal education. This curvilinear pattern applies to both men and women, and to all races and generations.

Sorting out just why education has such a massive effect on social connectedness would require a book in itself. Education is in part a proxy for social class and economic differences, but when income, social status, and education are used together to predict trust and group membership, education continues to be the primary influence. So, well-educated people are much more likely to be joiners and trusters, partly because they are better off economically, but mostly because of the skills, resources, and inclinations that were imparted to them at home and in school.

The expansion of high schools and colleges earlier this century has had an enormous impact on the educational composition of the adult population during just the last two decades. Since 1972 the proportion of adults with fewer than 12 years of education has been cut in half, falling from 40 percent to 18 percent, while the proportion with more than 12 years has nearly doubled, rising from 28 percent to 50 percent, as the generation of Americans educated around the turn of this century (most of whom did not finish high school) died off and were replaced by the baby boomers and their successors (most of whom attended college).

So here we have two facts—education boosts civic engagement sharply, and educational levels have risen massively—that only deepen our central mystery. By itself, the rise in educational levels should have increased social capital during the last 20 years by 15-20 percent, even assuming that the effects of education were merely linear. (Taking account of the curvilinear effect in the figure, "Education and Civic Life," the rise in trusting and joining should have been even greater, as Americans moved up the accelerating curve.) By contrast, however, the actual GSS figures show a net decline since the early 1970s of roughly the same magnitude (trust by about 20-25 percent, memberships by about 15-20 percent). The relative declines in social capital are similar within each educational category—roughly 25 percent in group memberships and roughly 30 percent in social trust since the early 1970s, and probably even more since the early 1960s.

While this first investigative foray leaves us more mystified than before, we may nevertheless draw two useful conclusions. First, we need to take account of educational differences in our exploration of other factors to be sure that we do not confuse their effects with the consequences of education. And, second, the mysterious disengagement of the last quarter century seems to have afflicted all educational strata in our society, whether they have had graduate education or did not finish high school.

MOBILITY AND SUBURBANIZATION

Many studies have found that residential stability and such related phenomena as homeownership are associated with greater civic engagement. At an earlier stage in this investigation I observed that "mobility, like frequent re-potting of plants, tends to disrupt root systems, and it takes time for an uprooted individual to put down new roots." I must now report, however, that further inquiry fully exonerates residential mobility from any responsibility for our fading civic engagement.

Data from the U.S. Bureau of the Census 1995 (and earlier years) show that rates of residential mobility have been remarkably constant over the last half century. In fact, to the extent that there has been any change at all, both long-distance and short-distance mobility have declined over the last five decades. During the 1950s, 20 percent of Americans changed residence each year and 6.9 percent annually moved across county borders; during the 1990s, the comparable figures are 17 percent and 6.6 percent. Americans, in short, are today slightly more rooted residentially than a generation ago. The verdict on mobility is unequivocal: This theory is simply wrong.

But if moving itself has not eroded our social capital, what about the possibility that we have moved to places, especially suburbs, that are less congenial to social connectedness? In fact, social connectedness does differ by community type, but the differences turn out to be modest and in directions that are inconsistent with the theory.

Controlling for such characteristics as education, age, income, work status, and race, citizens of the nation's 12 largest metropolitan areas (particularly their central cities, but also their suburbs) are roughly 10 percent less trusting and report 10-20 percent fewer group memberships than residents of other cities and towns (and their suburbs). Meanwhile, residents of very small towns and rural areas are (in accord with some hoary stereotypes) slightly more trusting and civicly engaged than other Americans. Unsurprisingly, the prominence of different types of groups does vary significantly by location: Major cities have more political and nationality clubs; smaller cities more fraternal, service, hobby, veterans', and church groups; and rural areas more agricultural organizations. But overall rates of associational membership are not very different.

Moreover, this pattern cannot account for our central puzzle. In the first place, there is virtually no correlation between gains in population and losses in social capital, either across states or across localities of different sizes. Even taking into account the educational and social backgrounds of those who have moved there, the suburbs have faintly higher levels of trust and civic engagement than their respective central cities, which should have produced growth, not decay, in social capital over the last generation. The central point, however, is that the downtrends in trusting and joining are virtually identical everywhere—in cities, big and small, in suburbs, in small towns, and in the countryside.

Of course, Evanston is not Levittown is not Sun City. The evidence available does not allow us to determine whether different types of suburban living have different effects on civic connections and social trust. However, these data do rule out the thesis that suburbanization per se has caused the erosion of America's social capital. Both where we live and how long we've lived there matter for social capital, but neither explains why it is eroding everywhere.

PRESSURES OF TIME AND MONEY

Americans certainly *feel* busier now than a generation ago: The proportion of us who report feeling "always rushed" jumped by half between the mid-1960s and the mid-1990s. Probably the most obvious suspect behind our tendency to drop out of community affairs is pervasive busy-ness. And lurking nearby in the shadows are economic pressures so much discussed nowadays, from job insecurity to declining real wages.

Yet, however culpable busy-ness and economic insecurity may appear at first glance, it is hard to find incriminating evidence. In the first place, time-budget studies do not confirm the thesis that Americans are, on average, working longer than a generation ago. On the contrary, a new study by John Robinson and Geoffrey Godbey of the University of Maryland reports a five hour per week *gain* in free time for the average American between 1965 and 1985, due partly to reduced time spent on housework and partly to earlier retirement. Their claim that Americans have more leisure time now than several decades ago is, to be sure, contested by other observers, notably Juliet Schor, who in her 1991 book *The Overworked American* reports evidence that work hours are lengthening, especially for women.

But whatever the resolution of that controversy, other data call into question whether longer hours at work lead to lessened involvement in civic life or reduced social trust. Results from the GSS show that employed people belong to somewhat more groups than those outside the paid labor force. Even more striking is the fact that among workers, longer hours are linked to more civic engagement. The patterns among men and women on this score are not identical: Women who work part-time appear to be somewhat more civicly engaged and socially trusting than either those who work full-time or those who do not work outside the home at all—an intriguing anomaly, though not relevant to our basic puzzle, since female part-time workers constitute a relatively small fraction of the American population, and the fraction is growing, up from about 8 percent to about 10 percent between the early 1970s and early 1990s.

But what do workaholics do less? Robinson reports that, unsurprisingly, people who spend more time at work do feel more rushed, and these harried souls do spend less time eating, sleeping, reading books, engaging in hobbies, and just doing nothing. Compared to the rest of the population, they also spend a lot less time watching television, almost 30 percent less. However, they do not spend less time on organizational activity. In short, those who work longer forego *Nightline*, but not the Kiwanis club; *ER*, but not the Red Cross.

So hard work does not *prevent* civic engagement. Moreover, the nationwide falloff in joining and trusting is perfectly mirrored among full-time workers, among part-time workers, and among those outside the paid labor force. So if people are dropping out of community life, long hours do not seem to be the reason.

If time pressure is not the culprit, how about financial pressures? It is true that people with lower incomes and those who feel financially strapped are somewhat less engaged in community life and somewhat less trusting than those who are better off, even holding education constant. On the other hand, the downtrends in social trust and civic engagement are visible among people of all incomes, with no sign whatever that they are concentrated among those who have borne the brunt of the economic distress of the last two decades. Quite the contrary, the declines in engagement and trust are actually somewhat greater among the more affluent segments of the American public than among the poor and middle-income wage-earners. Moreover, personal financial satisfaction is wholly uncorrelated with civic engagement and social trust. In short, neither objective nor subjective economic well-being has inoculated Americans against the virus of civic disengagement; if anything, affluence has slightly exacerbated the problem. Poverty and economic inequality are dreadful, growing problems for America, but they are not the villains of *this* piece.

THE CHANGING ROLE OF WOMEN

Most of our mothers were housewives, and most of them invested heavily in social capital formation—a jargony way of referring to untold unpaid hours in church suppers, PTA meetings, neighborhood coffee klatches, and visits to friends and relatives. The movement of women out of the home and into the paid labor force is probably the most portentous social change of the last half century. However welcome and overdue the feminist revolution may be, it is hard to believe that it has had no impact on social connectedness. Could this be the primary reason for the decline of social capital over the last generation?

Some patterns in the survey evidence seem to support this claim. All things considered, women belong to somewhat fewer voluntary associations than men do. On the other hand, time-budget studies suggest that women spend more time on those groups and more time in informal social connecting than men. Although the absolute declines in joining and trusting are approximately equivalent among men and women, the relative declines are somewhat greater among women. Controlling for education, memberships among men have declined at a rate of about 10-15 percent a decade, compared to about 20-25 percent a decade for women. The time-budget data, too, strongly suggest that the decline in organizational involvement in recent years is concentrated among women. These sorts of facts, coupled with the obvious transformation in the professional role of women over this same period, led me in previous work to suppose that the emergence of two-career families might be the most important single factor in the erosion of social capital.

As we saw earlier, however, work status itself seems to have little net impact on group membership or on trust. Housewives belong to different types of groups than do working women (more PTAs, for example, and fewer professional associations), but in the aggregate working women are actually members of slightly more voluntary associations (though housewives, according to Robinson and Godbey, spend more time on them). Moreover, the overall declines in civic engagement are somewhat greater among housewives than among employed women. Comparison of time-budget data between 1965 and 1985 seems to show that employed women as a group are actually spending more time on organizations than before, while housewives are spending less. This same study suggests that the major decline in informal socializing since 1965 has also been concentrated among housewives. The central fact, of course, is that the overall trends are down for all categories of women (and for men, too, even bachelors), but the figures suggest that women who work full-time actually may have been more resistant to the slump than those who do not.

Thus, although women appear to have borne a disproportionate share of the decline in civic engagement over the last two decades, it is not easy to find any micro-level data that tie that fact directly to their entry into the labor force. Of course, women who have chosen to enter the workforce doubtless differ in many respects from women who have chosen to stay home. Perhaps one reason that community involvement appears to be rising among working women and declining among housewives is that precisely the sort of women who, in an earlier era, were most involved with their communities have been disproportionately likely to enter the workforce, thus lowering the average level of civic engagement among the remaining homemakers and raising the average among women in the workplace.

No doubt the movement of women into the workplace over the last generation has changed the *types of organizations* to which they belong. Contrary to my own earlier speculations, however, I can find little evidence to support the hypothesis that this movement has played a major role in the net reduction of social connectedness and civic engagement. On the other hand, I have no clear alternative explanation for the fact that the relative declines are greater among women, both those who work outside the home and those who don't, than among men. Since this evidence is at best circumstantial, perhaps the best interim judgment here is the famous Scots verdict: not proven.

MARRIAGE AND FAMILY

Another widely discussed social trend that more or less coincides with the downturn in civic engagement is the breakdown of the traditional family unit—mom, dad, and the kids. Since the family itself is, by some accounts, a key form of social capital, perhaps its eclipse is part of the explanation for the reduction in joining and trusting in the wider community. What does the evidence show?

First of all, evidence of the loosening of family bonds is unequivocal. In addition to the century-long increase in divorce rates (which accelerated from the mid-1960s to the mid-1970s and then leveled off), and the more recent increase in single-parent families, the incidence of one-person households has more than doubled since 1950, in part because of the rising number of widows living alone. The net effect of all these changes, as reflected in the General Social Survey, is that the proportion of all American adults currently unmarried climbed from 28 percent in 1974 to 48 percent in 1994.

Second, married men and women do rank somewhat higher on both our measures of social capital. That is, controlling for education, age, race, and so on, single people—both men and women, divorced, separated, and never married—are significantly less trusting and less engaged civicly than married people. (Multivariate analysis hints that one major reason why divorce lowers connectedness is that it lowers family income, which in turn reduces civic engagement.) Roughly speaking, married men and women are about a third more trusting and belong to about 15-25 percent more groups than comparable single men and women. (Widows and widowers are more like married people than single people in this comparison.)

In short, successful marriage, especially if the family includes children, is statistically associated with greater social trust and civic engagement. Thus, some part of the decline in both trust and membership is tied to the decline in marriage. To be sure, the direction of causality behind this correlation may be complicated, since it is conceivable that loners and paranoids are harder to live with. If so, divorce may in some degree be the consequence, not the cause, of lower social capital. Probably the most reasonable summary of these arrays of data, however, is that the decline in successful marriage is a significant, though modest part of the reason for declining trust and lower group membership. On the other hand, changes in family structure cannot be a major part of our story, since the overall declines in joining and trusting are substantial even among the happily married. My own verdict (based in part on additional evidence to be introduced later) is that the disintegration of marriage is probably an accessory to the crime, but not the major villain of the piece.

THE RISE OF THE WELFARE STATE

Circumstantial evidence, particularly the timing of the downturn in social connectedness, has suggested to some observers that an important cause—perhaps even *the* cause—is big government and the growth of the welfare state. By "crowding out" private initiative, it is argued, state intervention has subverted civil society.

Some government policies have almost certainly had the effect of destroying social capital. For example, the so-called "slum clearance" policies of the 1950s and 1960s replaced physical capital, but destroyed social capital, by disrupting existing community ties. It is also conceivable that certain social expenditures and tax policies may have created disincentives for civic-minded philanthropy. On the other hand, it is much harder to see which government policies might be responsible for the decline in bowling leagues and literary clubs. Some community institutions sponsored, organized, or subsidized by government, such as National Service, agricultural extension programs, and Head Start, may enhance trust and social capital. Which effect prevails needs to be resolved with evidence, not ideology.

One empirical approach to this issue is to examine differences in civic engagement and public policy across different political jurisdictions to see whether enlarged government leads to shriveled social capital. Among the U.S. states, however, differences in social capital appear essentially uncorrelated with various measures of welfare spending or government size. Citizens in free-spending states are no less trusting or engaged than citizens in frugal ones.

Cross-national comparison can also shed light on this question. Among nineteen member countries of the Organization of Economic Cooperation and Development (OECD) for which data on social trust and group membership are available from the 1990-1991 World Values Survey, these indicators of social capital are, if anything, positively correlated with the size of the state. This simple bivariate analysis, of course, cannot tell us whether social connectedness encourages welfare spending, whether the welfare state fosters civic engagement, or whether both are the result of some other unmeasured factor(s). Even this simple finding, however, is not easily reconciled with the notion that big government undermines social capital.

RACE AND THE CIVIL RIGHTS REVOLUTION

Some observers have noted that the decline in social connectedness began just after the successes of the civil rights revolution of the 1960s. That coincidence has suggested the possibility of a kind of sociological "white flight," as legal desegregation of civic life led whites to withdraw from community associations.

The erosion of social capital, however, has affected all races. In fact, during the 1980s the downturns in both joining and trusting were even greater among African Americans (and other racial minorities) than among the white majority. This fact is inconsistent with the thesis that "white flight" is a significant cause of civic disengagement, since black Americans have been dropping out of religious and civic organizations at least as rapidly as white Americans. Even more important, the pace of disengagement among whites has been uncorrelated with racial intolerance or support for segregation. Avowedly racist or segregationist whites have been no quicker to drop out of community organizations during this period than more tolerant whites.

This evidence is far from conclusive, of course, but it does shift the burden of proof onto those who believe that racism is a primary explanation for growing civic disengagement over the last quarter century. This evidence also suggests that reversing the civil rights gains of the last thirty years would do nothing to reverse the social capital losses.

GENERATIONAL EFFECTS

Our efforts thus far to identify the major sources of civic disengagement have been singularly unfruitful. In all our statistical analyses, however, one factor, second only to education, stands out as a predictor of all forms of civic engagement and trust. That factor is age. Older people belong to more organizations than young people, and they are less misanthropic. Older Americans also vote more often and read newspapers more frequently, two other forms of civic engagement closely correlated with joining and trusting.

Civic involvement appears to rise more or less steadily from early adulthood toward a plateau in middle age, from which it declines only late in life. This pattern seems naturally to represent the arc of life's engagements. That, at least, was how I first interpreted the data. But that would be a fundamental misreading of the most important clue in our whole whodunit.

Evidence from the General Social Survey enables us to follow individual cohorts as they age. If civic engagement deepens with age, we should be able to track this same deepening engagement as we follow, for example, the first of the baby boomers, born in 1947, as they aged from 25 in 1972 (the first year of the GSS) to 47 in 1994 (the latest year available). Startlingly, however, such an analysis, repeated for successive birth cohorts, produces virtually no evidence of such life cycle changes in civic engagement. In fact, as various generations moved through the period between 1972 and 1994, their levels of trust and membership more often fell than rose, reflecting a more or less simultaneous decline in civic engagement among young and old alike, particularly during the second half of the 1980s. But that downtrend obviously cannot explain why, throughout the period, older Americans were always more trusting and engaged. In fact, the only reliable life cycle effect visible in these data is a withdrawal from civic engagement very late in life, as we move through our eighties.

The central paradox posed by these patterns is this: Older people are consistently more engaged and trusting than younger people, yet we do not become more engaged and trusting as we age. What's going on here?

Time and age are notoriously ambiguous in their effects on social behavior. Social scientists have learned to distinguish three contrasting phenomena:

LIFE CYCLE EFFECTS represent differences attributable to stage of life. In this case individuals change as they age, but since the effects of aging are, in the aggregate, neatly balanced by the "demographic metabolism" of births and deaths, life cycle effects produce no aggregate change. Everyone's close-focus eyesight worsens as we age, but the aggregate demand for reading glasses changes little.

PERIOD EFFECTS affect all people who live through a given era, regardless of their age. Period effects can produce both individual and aggregate change, often quickly and enduringly, without any age-related differences. The sharp drop in trust in government between 1965 and 1975, for example, was almost entirely this sort of period effect, as Americans of all ages changed their minds about their leaders' trustworthiness. Similarly, as just noted, a modest portion of the decline in social capital during the 1980s appears to be a period effect.

GENERATIONAL EFFECTS affect all people born at the same time. Like life cycle effects (and unlike typical period effects), generational effects show up as disparities among age groups at a single point in time, but like period effects (and unlike life cycle effects) generational effects produce real social change, as successive generations, enduringly "imprinted" with divergent outlooks, enter and leave the population. In pure generational effects, no individual ever changes, but society does.

Returning to our conundrum, how could older people today be more engaged and trusting, if they did not become more engaged and trusting as they aged? The key to this paradox, as David Butler and Donald Stokes observed in another context, is to ask, not *how old people are*, but *when they were young*.

THE LONG CIVIC GENERATION

Beginning with those born in the last third of the nineteenth century and continuing to the generation of their great-grandchildren, born in the last third of the twentieth century, we find relatively high and unevenly rising levels of civic engagement and social trust. Then rather abruptly we encounter signs of reduced community involvement, starting with men and women born in the early 1930s. Remarkably, this downward trend in joining, trusting, voting, and newspaper reading continues almost uninterruptedly for nearly 40 years. The trajectories for the various different indicators of civic engagement are strikingly parallel: Each shows a high, sometimes rising plateau for people born and raised during the first third of the century; each shows a turning point in the cohorts around 1930; and each then shows a more or less constant decline down to the cohorts born during the 1960s.

By any standard, these intergenerational differences are extraordinary. Compare, for example, the generation born in the early 1920s with the generation of their grandchildren born in the late 1960s. Controlling for educational disparities, members of the generation born in the 1920s belong to almost twice as many civic associations as those born in the late 1960s (roughly 1.9 memberships per capita, compared to roughly 1.1 memberships per capita). The grandparents are more than twice as likely to trust other people (50-60 percent compared with 25 percent for the grandchildren). They vote at nearly double the rate of the most recent cohorts (roughly 75 percent compared with 40-45 percent), and they read newspapers almost three times as often (70-80 percent read a paper daily compared with 25-30 percent). And bear in mind that we have found no evidence that the youngest generation will come to match their grandparents' higher levels of civic engagement as they grow older.

Thus, read not as life cycle effects, but rather as generational effects, the age-related patterns in our data suggest a radically different interpretation of our basic puzzle. Deciphered with this key, the figure on page 43 depicts a long "civic" generation, born roughly between 1910 and 1940, a broad group of people substantially more engaged in community affairs and substantially more trusting than those younger than they. (Members of the 1910-1940 generation also seem more civic than their elders, at least to judge by the outlooks of relatively few men and women born in the late nineteenth century who appeared in our samples.) The culminating point of this civic generation is the cohort born in 1925-1930, who attended grade school during the Great Depression, spent World War II in high school (or on the battlefield), first voted in 1948 or 1952, set up housekeeping in the 1950s, and watched their first television when they were in their late twenties. Since national surveying began, this cohort has been exceptionally civic: voting more, joining more, reading newspapers more, trusting more. As the distinguished sociologist Charles Tilly (born in 1928) said in commenting on an early version of this essay, "We are the last suckers."

To help in interpreting the historical contexts within which these successive generations of Americans matured, the figure also indicates the decade within which each cohort came of age. Thus, we can see that each generation that reached adulthood since the 1940s has been less engaged in community affairs than its immediate predecessor.

Further confirmation of this generational interpretation comes from a comparison of the two parallel lines that chart responses to an identical question about social trust, posed first in the National Election Studies (mainly between 1964 and 1976) and then in the General Social Survey between 1972 and 1994. If the greater trust expressed by Americans born earlier in the century represented a life cycle effect, then the graph from the GSS surveys (conducted when these cohorts were, on average, 10 years older) should have been some distance above the NES line. In fact, the GSS line lies about

5-10 percent below the NES line. That downward shift almost surely represents a period effect that depressed social trust among all cohorts during the 1980s. That downward period effect, however, is substantially more modest than the large generational differences already noted.

In short, the most parsimonious interpretation of the age-related differences in civic engagement is that they represent a powerful reduction in civic engagement among Americans who came of age in the decades after World War II, as well as some modest additional disengagement that affected all cohorts during the 1980s. These patterns hint that being raised after World War II was a quite different experience from being raised before that watershed. It is as though the postwar generations were exposed to some mysterious X-ray that permanently and increasingly rendered them less likely to connect with the community. Whatever that force might have been, it—rather than anything that happened during the 1970s and 1980s—accounts for most of the civic disengagement that lies at the core of our mystery.

But if this reinterpretation of our puzzle is correct, why did it take so long for the effects of that mysterious X-ray to become manifest? If the underlying causes of civic disengagement can be traced to the 1940s and 1950s, why did the effects become conspicuous in PTA meetings and Masonic lodges, in the volunteer lists of the Red Cross and the Boy Scouts, and in polling stations and church pews and bowling alleys across the land only during the 1960s, 1970s, and 1980s?

The visible effects of this generational disengagement were delayed by two important factors. First, the postwar boom in college enrollments raised levels of civic engagement, offsetting the generational trends. As Warren E. Miller and J. Merrill Shanks observe in their as yet unpublished book, *The American Voter Reconsidered*, the postwar expansion of educational opportunities "forestalled a cataclysmic drop" in voting turnout, and it had a similar delaying effect on civic disengagement more generally.

Second, the full effects of generational developments generally appear several decades after their onset, because it takes that long for a given generation to become numerically dominant in the adult population. Only after the mid-1960s did significant numbers of the "post-civic generation" reach adulthood, supplanting older, more civic cohorts. The long civic generation born between 1910 and 1940 reached its zenith in 1960, when it comprised 62 percent of those who chose between John Kennedy and Richard Nixon. By the time that Bill Clinton was elected president in 1992, that cohort's share in the electorate had been cut precisely in half. Conversely, over the last two decades (from 1974 to 1994) boomers and X-ers (that is, Americans born after 1946) have grown as a fraction of the adult population from 24 percent to 60 percent.

In short, the very decades that have seen a national deterioration in social capital are the same decades during which the numerical dominance of a trusting and civic generation has been replaced by the dominion of "post-civic" cohorts. Moreover, although the long civic generation has enjoyed unprecedented life expectancy, allowing its members to contribute more than their share to American social capital in recent decades, they are now passing from the scene. Even the youngest members of that generation will reach retirement age within the next few years. Thus, a generational analysis leads almost inevitably to the conclusion that the national slump in trust and engagement is likely to continue, regardless of whether the more modest "period effect" depression of the 1980s continues.

OUR PRIME SUSPECT

To say that civic disengagement in contemporary America is in large measure generational merely reformulates our central puzzle. We now know that much of the cause of our lonely bowling probably dates to the 1940s and 1950s, rather than to the 1960s and 1970s. What could have been the mysterious anticivic "X-ray" that affected Americans who came of age after World War II and whose effects progressively deepened at least into the 1970s?

Our new formulation of the puzzle opens the possibility that the zeitgeist of national unity, patriotism, and shared sacrifice that culminated in 1945 might have reinforced civic-mindedness. On the other hand, it is hard to assign any consistent role to the Cold War and the Bomb, since the anticivic trend appears to have deepened steadily from the 1940s to the 1970s, in no obvious harmony with the rhythms of world affairs. Nor is it easy to construct an interpretation of the data on generational differences in which the cultural vicissitudes of the sixties could play a significant role. Neither can economic adversity or affluence easily be tied to the generational decline in civic engagement, since the slump seems to have affected in equal measure those who came of age in the placid fifties, the booming sixties, and the busted seventies.

I have discovered only one prominent suspect against whom circumstantial evidence can be mounted, and in this case, it turns out, some directly incriminating evidence has also turned up. This is not the occasion to lay out the full case for the prosecution, nor to review rebuttal evidence for the defense, but I want to present evidence that justifies indictment.

The culprit is television.

First, the timing fits. The long civic generation was the last cohort of Americans to grow up without television, for television flashed into American society like lightning in the 1950s. In 1950 barely 10 percent of American homes had television sets, but by 1959, 90 percent did, probably the fastest diffusion of a major technological innovation ever recorded. The reverberations from this lightning bolt continued for decades, as viewing hours grew by 17-20 percent during the 1960s and by an additional 7-8 percent during the 1970s. In the early years, TV watching was concentrated among the less educated sectors of the population, but during the 1970s the viewing time of the more educated sectors of the population began to converge upward. Television viewing increases with age, particularly upon retirement, but each generation since the introduction of television has begun its life cycle at a higher starting point. By 1995 viewing per TV household was more than 50 percent higher than it had been in the 1950s.

Most studies estimate that the average American now watches roughly four hours per day (excluding periods in which television is merely playing in the background). Even a more conservative estimate of three hours means that television absorbs 40 percent of the average American's free time, an increase of about one-third since 1965. Moreover, multiple sets have proliferated: By the late 1980s three-quarters of all U.S. homes had more than one set, and these numbers too are rising steadily, allowing ever more private viewing. Robinson and Godbey are surely right to conclude that "television is the 800-pound gorilla of leisure time." This massive change in the way Americans spend their days and nights occurred precisely during the years of generational civic disengagement.

Evidence of a link between the arrival of television and the erosion of social connections is, however, not merely circumstantial. The links between civic engagement and television viewing can be instructively compared with the links between civic engagement and newspaper reading. The basic contrast is straightforward: Newspaper reading is associated with high social capital, TV viewing with low social capital.

Controlling for education, income, age, race, place of residence, work status, and gender, TV viewing is strongly and negatively related to social trust and group membership, whereas the same correlations with newspaper reading are positive. Within every educational category, heavy readers are avid joiners, whereas heavy viewers are more likely to be loners. In fact, more detailed analysis suggests that heavy TV watching is one important reason *why* less educated people are less engaged in the life of their communities. Controlling for differential TV exposure significantly reduces the correlation between education and engagement.

Viewing and reading are themselves uncorrelated—some people do lots of both, some do little of either—but "pure readers" (that is, people who watch less TV than average and read more newspapers than average) belong to 76 percent more civic organizations than "pure viewers" (controlling for education, as always). Precisely the same pattern applies to other indicators of civic engagement, including social trust and voting turnout. "Pure readers," for example, are 55 percent more trusting than "pure viewers."

In other words, each hour spent viewing television is associated with less social trust and less group membership, while each hour reading a newspaper is associated with more. An increase in television viewing of the magnitude that the U.S. has experienced in the last four decades might directly account for as much as one-quarter to one-half of the total drop in social capital, even without taking into account, for example, the indirect effects of television viewing on newspaper readership or the cumulative effects of lifetime viewing hours. Newspaper circulation (per household) has dropped by more than half since its peak in 1947. To be sure, it is not clear which way the tie between newspaper reading and civic involvement works, since disengagement might itself dampen one's interest in community news. But the two trends are clearly linked.

HOW MIGHT TV DESTROY SOCIAL CAPITAL?

TIME DISPLACEMENT. Even though there are only 24 hours in everyone's day, most forms of social and media participation are positively correlated. People who listen to lots of classical music are more likely, not less likely, than others to attend Cubs games. Television is the principal exception to this generalization—the only leisure activity that seems to inhibit participation outside the home. TV watching comes at the expense of nearly every social activity outside the home, especially social gatherings and informal conversations. TV viewers are homebodies.

Most studies that report a negative correlation between television watching and community involvement are ambiguous with respect to causality, because they merely compare different individuals at a single time. However, one important quasi-experimental study of the introduction of television in three Canadian towns found the same pattern at the aggregate level across time. A major effect of television's arrival was the reduction in participation in social, recreational, and community activities among people of all ages. In short, television privatizes our leisure time.

EFFECTS ON THE OUTLOOKS OF VIEWERS. An impressive body of literature suggests that heavy watchers of TV are unusually skeptical about the benevolence of other people—overestimating crime rates, for example. This body of literature has generated much debate about the underlying causal patterns, with skeptics suggesting that misanthropy may foster couch-potato behavior rather than the reverse. While awaiting better experimental evidence, however, a reasonable interim judgment is that heavy television watching may well increase pessimism about human nature. Perhaps too, as social critics have long argued, both the medium and the message have more basic effects on our ways of interacting with the world and with one another. Television may induce passivity, as Neil Postman has claimed.

EFFECTS ON CHILDREN. TV consumes an extraordinary part of children's lives, about 40 hours per week on average. Viewing is especially high among pre-adolescents, but it remains high among younger adolescents: Time-budget studies suggest that among youngsters aged 9 to 14 television consumes as much time as all other discretionary activities combined, including playing, hobbies, clubs, outdoor activities, informal visiting, and just hanging out. The effects of television on childhood socialization have, of course, been hotly debated for more than three decades. The most reasonable conclusion from a welter of sometimes conflicting results appears to be that heavy television watching probably increases aggressiveness (although perhaps not actual violence), that it probably reduces school achievement, and that it is statistically associated with "psychosocial malfunctioning," although how much of this effect is self-selection and how much causal remains much debated. The evidence is, as I have said, not yet enough to convict, but the defense has a lot of explaining to do.

More than two decades ago, just as the first signs of disengagement were beginning to appear in American politics, the political scientist Ithiel de Sola Pool observed that the central issue would be—it was then too soon to judge, as he rightly noted—whether the development represented a temporary change in the weather or a more enduring change in the climate. It now appears that much of the change whose initial signs he spotted did in fact reflect a climatic shift.

Moreover, just as the erosion of the ozone layer was detected only many years after the proliferation of the chlorofluorocarbons that caused it, so too the erosion of America's social capital became visible only several decades after the underlying process had begun. Like Minerva's owl that flies at dusk, we come to appreciate how important the long civic generation has been to American community life just as its members are retiring. Unless America experiences a dramatic upward boost in civic engagement (a favorable "period effect") in the next few years, Americans in 2010 will join, trust, and vote even less than we do today.

In an astonishingly prescient book, *Technologies without Borders*, published in 1991 after his death, Pool concluded that the electronic revolution in communications technology was the first major technological advance in centuries that would have a profoundly decentralizing and fragmenting effect on society and culture. He hoped that the result might be "community without contiguity." As a classic liberal, he welcomed the benefits of technological change for individual freedom, and in part, I share that enthusiasm. Those of us who bemoan the decline of community in contemporary America need to be sensitive to the liberating gains achieved during the same decades. We need to avoid an uncritical nostalgia for the fifties. On the other hand, some of the same freedom-friendly technologies whose rise Pool predicted may indeed be undermining our connections with one another and with our communities. Pool defended what he called "soft technological determinism" because he recognized that social values can condition the effects of technology. This perspective invites us not merely to consider how technology is privatizing our lives—if, as it seems to me, it is—but to ask whether we like the result, and if not, what we might do about it. Those are questions we should, of course, be asking together, not alone.

POSTSCRIPT

In the "The Strange Disappearance of Civic America," Putnam sought to explain a decline in Americans' engagement with community affairs over the last several decades. Recently, we have discovered a significant error in one of the data series that supported Putnam's claim of civic disengagement. In the General Social Survey as published and distributed for the years 1989 to 1994 the entry for "number of group memberships" (MEMNUM) mistakenly excludes memberships in "service clubs" (such as Rotary clubs) and "school service groups" (such as parent-teacher associations). Correcting this error increases by approximately 15 percent the number of reported group memberships per capita during these years. As a result, the corrected aggregate number of group memberships per capita as reported in the GSS (weighted to represent American adults, but not adjusted to compensate for rising educational levels) shows only a slight decline over the period 1974–1994. The newly discovered error in the GSS time series has no effect on the various other measures of civic disengagement reported by Putnam (such as political engagement, time budgets, social trust, and membership in specific organizaitons) and, so far as we have detected, the error has no significant effect on the causal analyses reported there. In fact, in a forthcoming work we report strengthened evidence for Putnam's central conjecture that the advent of television had marked negative effect on the civic engagement of the postwar generation of Americans.

John P. Helliwell,
University of British Columbia

Robert D. Putnam,
Harvard University

What If Civic Life Didn't Die?

Michael Schudson

Robert Putnam's important and disturbing work on civic participation ("The Strange Disappearance of Civic America," see page 263) has led him to conclude that television is the culprit behind civic decline. But lest we be too disturbed, we ought to consider carefully whether the data adequately measure participation and justify his conclusions and whether his conclusions fit much else that we know about recent history. I suggest that his work has missed some key contrary evidence. If we could measure civic participation better, the decline would be less striking and the puzzle less perplexing. If we looked more carefully at the history of civic participation and the differences among generations, we would have to abandon the rhetoric of decline. And if we examined television and recent history more closely, we could not convict TV of turning off civic involvement.

Consider, first, the problem of measuring whether there has been civic decline. Putnam has been ingenious in finding multiple measures of civic engagement, from voter turnout to opinion poll levels of trust in government to time-budget studies on how people allocate their time to associational membership. But could it be that even all of these measures together mask how civic energy is deployed?

Data collected by Sidney Verba, Kay Lehman Schlozman, and Henry Brady suggest the answer is yes. In 1987, 34 percent of their national sample reported active membership in a community problem-solving organization compared to 31 percent in 1967; in 1987, 34 percent reported working with others on a local problem compared to 30 percent in 1967. Self-reports should not be taken at face value, but why does this survey indicate a slight increase in local civic engagement? Does it capture something Putnam's data miss?

Putnam's measures may, in fact, overlook several types of civic activity. First, people may have left the middling commitment of the League of Women Voters or the PTA for organized activity both much less and much more involving. As for much more: Churches seem to be constantly reinventing themselves, adding a variety of groups and activities to engage members, from singles clubs to job training to organized social welfare services to preschools. An individual who reports only one associational membership—say, a church or synagogue—may be more involved in it and more "civic" through it than someone else who reports two or three memberships.

Second, people may have left traditional civic organizations that they used for personal and utilitarian ends for commercial organizations. If people who formerly joined the YMCA to use the gym now go to the local fitness center, Putnam's measures will show a decrease in civic participation when real civic activity is unchanged.

Third, people may be more episodically involved in political and civic activity as issue-oriented politics grows. For instance, in California, motorcycle riders have become influential political activists since the 1992 passage of a law requiring bikers to wear helmets. According to the *San Diego Union,* of 800,000 licensed motorcyclists, 10,000 are now members of the American Brotherhood Aimed Toward Education (ABATE), which has been credited as decisive in several races for the state legislature. Members do not meet on a regular basis, but they do periodically mobilize in local political contests to advance their one legislative purpose. Would Putnam's data pick up on this group? What about the intense but brief house-building activity for Habitat for Humanity?

Fourth, Putnam notes but leaves to the side the vast increase in Washington-based mailing list organizations over the past 30 years. He ignores them because they do not require members to do more than send in a check. This is not Tocquevillian democracy, but these organizations may be a highly efficient use of civic energy. The citizen who joints them may get the same civic pay-off for less personal hassle. This is especially so if we conceive of politics as a set of public policies. The citizen may be able to influence government more satisfactorily with the annual membership in Sierra Club or the National Rifle Association than by attending the local club luncheons.

Of course, policy is a limited notion of government. Putnam assumes a broader view that makes personal investment part of the payoff of citizenship. Participation is its own reward. But even our greatest leaders—Jefferson, for one—complained about the demands of public life and, like Dorothy in liberating Oz, were forever trying to get back home. Getting government off our backs was a theme Patrick Henry evoked. And who is to say that getting back home is an unworthy desire?

The concept of politics has broadened enormously in 30 years. Not only is the personal political (the politics of male-female relations, the politics of smoking and not smoking), but the professional or occupational is also political. A woman physician or accountant can feel that she is doing politics—providing a role model and fighting for recognition of women's equality with men—every time she goes to work. The same is true for African American bank executives or gay and lesbian military officers.

The decline of the civic in its conventional forms, then, does not demonstrate the decline of civicmindedness. The "political" does not necessarily depend on social connectedness: Those membership dues to the NRA are political. Nor does it even depend on organized groups at all: Wearing a "Thank you for not smoking" button is political. The political may be intense and transient: Think of the thousands of people who have joined class action suits against producers of silicone breast implants or Dalkon shields or asbestos insulation.

Let us assume, for argument's sake, that there has been a decrease in civic involvement. Still, the rhetoric of decline in American life should send up a red flag. For the socially concerned intellectual, this is as much off-the-rack rhetoric as its mirror opposite, the rhetoric of progress, is for the ebullient technocrat. Any notion of "decline" has to take for granted some often arbitrary baseline. Putnam's baseline is the 1940s and 1950s when the "long civic generation"—people born between 1910 and 1940—came into their own. But this generation shared the powerful and unusual experience of four years of national military mobilization on behalf of what nearly everyone came to accept as a good cause. If Putnam had selected, say, the 1920s as a baseline, would he have given us a similar picture of decline?

Unlikely. Intellectuals of the 1920s wrung their hands about the fate of democracy, the decline of voter turnout, the "eclipse of the public," as John Dewey put it or "the phantom public" in Walter Lippmann's terms. They had plenty of evidence, particularly in the record of voter turnout, so low in 1920 and 1924 (49 percent each year) that even our contemporary nadir of 1988 (50.3 percent) does not quite match it. Putnam himself reports that people born from 1910 to 1940 appear more civic than those born before as well as those born after. There is every reason to ask why this group was so civic rather than why later groups are not.

The most obvious answer is that this group fought in or came of age during World War II. This is also a group that voted overwhelmingly for Franklin D. Roosevelt and observed his leadership in office over a long period. Presidents exercise a form of moral leadership that sets a norm or standard about what kind of a life people should lead. A critic has complained that Ronald Reagan made all Americans a little more stupid in the 1980s—and I don't think this is a frivolous jibe. Reagan taught us that even the president can make a philosophy of the principle, "My mind's made up, don't confuse me with the facts." He taught us that millions will pay deference to someone who regularly and earnestly confuses films with lived experience.

The "long civic generation" had the advantages of a "good war" and a good president. Later generations had no wars or ones about which there was less massive mobilization and much less consensus—Korea and, more divisively, Vietnam. They had presidents of dubious moral leadership—notably Nixon, whom people judged even in the glow of his latter-day "rehabilitation" as the worst moral leader of all post-World War II presidents. So if there has been civic engagement in the past decades, it may be not a decline but a return to normalcy.

If the rhetoric of decline raises one red flag, television as an explanation raises another. Some of the most widely heralded "media effects" have by now been thoroughly discredited. The yellow press had little or nothing to do with getting us into the Spanish-American War. Television news had little or nothing to do with turning Americans against the Vietnam War. Ronald Reagan's mastery of the media did not make him an unusually popular president in his first term (in fact, for his first 30 months in office he was unusually unpopular).

Indeed, the TV explanation doesn't fit Putnam's data very well. Putnam defines the long civic generation as the cohort born from 1910 to 1940, but then he also shows that the downturn in civic involvement began "rather abruptly" among people "born in the early 1930s." In other words, civic decline began with people too young to have served in World War II but too old to have seen TV growing up. If we take 1954 as a turning-point year—the first year when more than half of American households had TV sets—Americans born from 1930 to 1936 were in most cases already out of the home and the people born the next four years were already in high school by the time TV is likely to have become a significant part of their lives. Of course, TV may have influenced this group later, in the 1950s and early 1960s when they were in their twenties and thirties. But this was a time when Americans watched many fewer hours of television, averaging five hours a day rather than the current seven, and the relatively benign TV fare of that era was not likely to induce fearfulness of the outside world.

All of my speculations here and most of Putnam's assume that one person has about the same capacity for civic engagement as the next. But what if some people have decidedly more civic energy than others as a function of, say, personality? And what if these civic spark plugs have been increasingly recruited into situations where they are less civically engaged?

Putnam accords this kind of explanation some attention in asking whether women who had been most involved in civic activities were those most likely to take paying jobs, "thus lowering the average level of civic engagement among the remaining homemakers and raising the average among women in the workplace." Putnam says he "can find little evidence" to support this hypothesis, but it sounds plausible.

A similar hypothesis makes sense in other domains. Since World War II, higher education has mushroomed. Of people born from 1911 to 1920, 13.5 percent earned college or graduate degrees; of those born during the next decade, 18.8 percent; but of people born from 1931 to 1950, the figure grew to between 26 and 27 percent. A small but increasing number of these college students have been recruited away from their home communities to elite private colleges; some public universities also began after World War II to draw from a national pool of talent. Even colleges with local constituencies increasingly have recruited faculty nationally, and the faculty have shaped student ambitions toward national law, medical, and business schools and corporate traineeships. If students drawn to these programs are among the people likeliest in the past to have been civic spark plugs, we have an alternative explanation for civic decline.

Could there be a decline? Better to conceive the changes we find as a new environment of civic and political activity with altered institutional openings for engagement. Television is a part of the ecology, but in complex ways. It is a significant part of people's use of their waking hours, but it may be less a substitute for civic engagement than a new and perhaps insidious form of it. TV has been more politicized since the late 1960s than ever before. In 1968, *60 Minutes* began as the first money-making entertainment news program, spawning a dozen imitators. *All in the Family* in 1971 became the first prime-time sitcom to routinely take on controversial topics, from homosexuality to race to women's rights. *Donahue* was first syndicated in 1979, *Oprah* followed in 1984, and after then, the deluge.

If TV does nonetheless discourage civic engagement, what aspect of TV is at work? Is it the most "serious," civic-minded, and responsible part—the news? The latest blast at the news media, James Fallows's *Breaking the News,* picks up a familiar theme that the efforts of both print and broadcast journalists since the 1960s to get beneath the surface of events has led to a journalistic presumption that no politician can be trusted and that the story behind the story will be invariably sordid.

All of this talk needs to be tempered with the reminder that, amidst the many disappointments of politics between 1965 and 1995, this has been an era of unprecedented advances in women's rights, gay and lesbian liberation, African American opportunity, and financial security for the elderly. It has witnessed the first consumers' movement since the 1930s, the first environmental movement since the turn of the century, and public health movements of great range and achievement, especially in antismoking. It has also been a moment of grassroots activism on the right as well as on the left, with the pro-life movement and the broad-gauge political involvement both locally and nationally of the Christian right. Most of this activity was generated outside of political parties and state institutions. Most of this activity was built on substantial "grassroots" organizing. It is not easy to square all of this with an account of declining civic virtue.

Robert Putnam has offered us a lot to think about, with clarity and insight. Still, he has not yet established the decline in civic participation, let alone provided a satisfying explanation for it. What he has done is to reinvigorate inquiry on a topic that could scarcely be more important.

Unravelling from Above

Theda Skocpol

If only folks would turn off the TV and start attending PTA meetings, America's future could be as bright as its civically engaged past. This diagnosis is taking shape in foundation-sponsored gatherings and among highbrow columnists. Privileged men and women—who spend most of their waking hours in their offices, on jet airplanes, and in front of computer screens—are converging on the belief that civic irresponsibility is the fault of average Americans.

Today's concern with civic engagement is widely shared, deceptively suggesting a consensus. "We find ourselves at a unique moment in American history," applauds multimillionaire Arianna Huffington writing in the *Wall Street Journal*, "when thoughtful people all across the political spectrum are coming together to recognize the primacy of civil society to our national health." Americans are "returning to Tocqueville," agrees Michael Barone in a *Washington Post* commentary that concludes that 1990s "new" Democrats must develop "an acceptable variant of the Republican faith," where "government leaves to voluntary associations... functions that elsewhere and at other times have been performed by the state." But this conclusion is too hasty.

On the right, civic responsibility means drastic reductions in the role of the national government. In the words of George Will, "swollen government, which displaces other institutions, saps democracy's strength. There is...a zero-sum transaction in society: As the state waxes, other institutions wane." Accordingly, Newt Gingrich wants to "renew America" by "replacing the welfare state with an opportunity society" featuring market incentives and "volunteerism and spiritual renewal." And Arianna Huffington promotes Gingrichism through a new Washington-based advocacy group called the Center for Effective Compassion.

Many conservatives are rallying around this notion of civil society as an alternative to extra-local government. Fresh from years of successful government bashing inside the Beltway, the Heritage Foundation has rechristened its journal *Policy Review as Policy Review: The Journal of American Citizenship*. "We think of our mission as 'Applied Tocqueville,'" declare the editors. "We will focus on the institutions of civil society—families, communities, voluntary associations, churches and other religious organizations, business enterprises, public and private schools, local governments—that are solving problems more effectively than large, centralized, bureaucratic government.... We hope many liberals and centrists will join us in this endeavor."

But liberals and thoughtful centrists are rightfully reluctant to conflate business and the market with civil society, while pitting voluntarism and charity in zero-sum opposition to government. The United States has never had much of a "centralized bureaucratic" welfare state; instead the federal and state governments have often subsidized and acted in partnership with the efforts of voluntary, religious, and nonprofit agencies such as Catholic Charities and the Salvation Army. It is not at all clear that spontaneous local voluntarism would take up the slack should national social provision be destroyed. Besides, economic forces can hurt civil society as much as needlessly intrusive government. "The market acts blindly to sell and to make money," Senator Bill Bradley aptly declared in a February 1995 speech to the National Press Club. "Too often those who trash government as the enemy of freedom and a destroyer of families are strangely silent about the market's corrosive effects on those very same values in civil society."

ENTER EMPIRICAL RESEARCH

At the center of this discussion are the writings of Harvard University's Robert D. Putnam. By embellishing the idea of "social capital" borrowed from the late James Coleman, Putnam has persuaded his fellow political scientists, and even the occasional economist, to take up issues of the sort usually relegated to lowly and underfunded sociologists. With admirable gusto, he has plunged into empirical data to look for causes of the "disappearance" of civic America.

"Disappearance" is too strong a word, of course. As Putnam acknowledges, Americans remain more likely to join churches and other voluntary groups than the citizens of any other advanced industrial nation. Some researchers do not agree with Putnam that volunteering has declined in recent years. Questions can be asked about the General Social Survey (GSS) on which he chiefly relies. The GSS asks respondents about "types" of organizations to which they belong, not concrete group memberships; as groups have proliferated within certain categories, the extent of individuals' involvements may well be undercounted. What is more, newer types of involvements—such as parents congregating on Saturdays at children's sports events, or several families going together to the bowling alley (just visit one and look!)—may not be captured by the GSS questions. As many fathers and mothers have pulled back from Elks Clubs and women's clubs, they may have turned not toward "bowling alone" but toward child-centered involvements with other parents.

Despite qualms about the data, I accept Putnam's broad finding of a generational disjuncture in the associational loyalties of many American adults, starting around the mid-1960s. Once-vibrant federations of locally rooted associations (such as the PTA, the American Legion, and many fraternal groups) did not continue to attract younger adults as readily as they had in the past. Moreover, the group involvements of U.S. adults coming of age after the 1950s may not hold the same significance for U.S. civic life as the PTA, the American Legion, and other such voluntary federations.

These federations once had an enormous impact, both locally and nationally. Early in this century, the PTA (then the National Congress of Mothers) joined with other women's voluntary federations to push for historic breakthroughs in social policy, including mothers' pensions (later to become Aid to Families with Dependent Children); the establishment of the federal Children's Bureau; and the enactment of the federal Sheppard-Towner program to promote maternal and infant health (later to become part of the Social Security Act). Similarly, during the 1940s the American Legion formulated the GI Bill, modern America's greatest program of federal investment in higher education and youthful family formation. Millions of Legionnaires, arrayed in thousands of local posts and in state and national headquarters, waged a popular campaign calling upon Congress to enact this program. Without the American Legion, access to college would not have been so fully opened up to working- and middle-class Americans after World War II. Conservatives may imagine that popular voluntary associations and the welfare state are contradictory opposites, but historically they have operated in close symbiosis. Voluntary civic federations have both pressured for the creation of public social programs, and worked in partnership with government to administer and expand such programs after they were established.

Putnam has put his finger on a historic break in U.S. associational life. Yet as others delve deeper into the dynamics of civic engagement in U.S. democracy, they should critically examine the largely individualist and localist premises on which Putnam has so far based his research. To be sure, Putnam's research on the decline in social capital does not demonize the welfare state. Nevertheless, fresh inspirations need to come into play, to avoid an inaccurate picture of how and why American civil society has historically flourished and recently declined.

LOOKING BEYOND DISCONNECTED INDIVIDUALS

Ironically for a scholar who calls for attention to social interconnectedness, Putnam works with atomistic concepts and data. He writes as if civic associations spring from the purely local decisions of collections of individuals—with everyone in the socioeconomic structure potentially counting the same as everyone else. Putnam sorts individuals by gender, educational levels, job-market involvements, and "exposures" to television. He tries to derive group outcomes by testing one variable at a time against such highly aggregated individual-level data. Perhaps unintentionally, Putnam largely ignores the cross-class and organizational dynamics by which civic associations actually form and persist—or decay and come unravelled.

An association may decline not only because people with the wrong sorts of individual traits proliferate in the population, but also because opportunities and cultural models for that association (or type of organization) wither in the larger society and polity. An association may also decline because the defection of crucial types of leaders or members makes the enterprise less resourceful and relevant for others.

Consider what occurs when better-educated women shift from family and community endeavors into the paid labor force. As capable women who once devoted energies to the PTA (and similar locally rooted federations) have switched their allegiances to workplaces and national professional groups, PTAs may have become less attractive for other potential members, including housewives. PTAs may also have become less powerful in local, state, and national politics. Such trends are magnified if, at the same time, more and more privileged two-career married couples move to high-income neighborhoods or switch their children from public to private schools. Putnam argues that female entry into the paid labor force cannot explain membership decline because employed women join more groups than housewives. But he does not tell us what kinds of groups employed women have joined; nor does he explore the potential unravelling effects of the withdrawal of women leaders from locally rooted cross-class federations like the PTA.

Throughout U.S. history, well-educated and economically better-off citizens have been key founders, leaders, and sustaining members of voluntary associations. The commitment of business people and professionals, and of women married to them, has been especially important for the great cross-class and cross-regional associations—such as veterans groups, fraternal bodies, temperance associations, ethnic benefit societies, and women's federations—that played such a major role in U.S. civic life from the nineteenth through the mid-twentieth century.

Maybe what has changed recently has less to do with TV watching than with shifting elite allegiances. Members of a burgeoning upper-middle stratum of highly educated and munificently paid managers and professionals may have pulled out of locally rooted civic associations. At one time participation and leadership in the American Legion or the PTA were stepping stones for professionals, business people, and privileged homemakers. But now their counterparts do better if they work long hours and network with each other through extra-local professional or trade associations, while dealing with politics by sending checks to lobbying groups headquartered in Washington, DC. If this scenario is credible—and I suggest it is just as plausible, given the data, as Putnam's TV argument—then maybe the quest for "who done it" strikes uncomfortably closer to home for the privileged people (myself included!) who fly off to elegant meetings to ponder the civic misbehaviors of the great unwashed.

A GENERATIONAL DIVIDE

Another irony: Although Putnam directs our attention toward succeeding generations, he gives short shrift to the cultural splits between older and younger Americans that occurred in the 1960s and 1970s. Putnam does not view a "sixties and seventies period effect" as an important cause of declining civic engagement, on the grounds that everyone would have dropped out in equal numbers. But ever since the work of Karl Mannheim, historical social scientists have hypothesized that epochal watersheds have their biggest influence on the outlooks of young adults. Perhaps Americans reaching adulthood in the sixties and seventies looked anew at the world, and did not find so attractive those civic associations that their elders still held dear.

The sixties and seventies did bring divisions in outlook between Americans who came of age from World War II to the height of the Cold War versus those who reached maturity during the era of the civil rights struggle and the war in Vietnam. We know that this contentious watershed adversely affected enrollments in the American Legion and the Veterans of Foreign Wars. The sixties and seventies also brought changes in race and gender relations, which may well have rendered mostly segregated associations less attractive to younger people—again, without necessarily loosening the established group loyalties of their parents.

POLITICAL CHANGES AND ASSOCIATIONAL LIFE

But why didn't new locally rooted federations emerge to replace those that started to fade in the 1960s? To some degree they did, for example in the environmental movement. Yet new federations did not grow enough to carry on the organizational tradition of the PTA, the Elks, and the American Legion. Why not brings me to my last argument—about the Tocqueville romanticism that not only undergirds right-wing versions of the civil society debate, but also influences aspects of Putnam's research. Of course Putnam does not share Gingrich's hostility to the welfare state. Yet he often speaks of social capital as something that arises or declines in a realm apart from politics and government.

A romantic construction of Tocqueville supposes that voluntary groups spring up de novo from below, created by individuals in small geographic areas who spontaneously decide to associate to get things done "outside of" government and politics. Supposedly this is what Alex de Tocqueville saw in early national America. But local spontaneity wasn't all that was going on back then. True, once local villages and towns passed a threshold of 200 to 400 families apiece, voluntary associations tended to emerge, especially if there were locally resident business people and professionals. But research on America in the early 1800s shows that religious and political factors also stimulated the growth of voluntary groups. In a country with no official church and competing religious denominations, the Second Great Awakening spread ideas about personal initiative and moral duty to the community. In addition, the American Revolution, and the subsequent organization of competitive national and state elections under the Constitution of 1789, triggered the founding of newspapers and the formation of local and translocal voluntary associations much faster and more extensively than just nascent town formation can explain. The openness of the U.S. Congress and state legislatures to organized petition drives, the remarkable spread of public schooling, and the establishment of U.S. post offices in every little hamlet were also vital enabling factors, grounded in the very institutional core of the early U.S. state. (As a nobleman critical of the centralized bureaucratic state of contemporary post-revolutionary France, Tocqueville naturally riveted on the absence of a bureaucratic state in early America. He briefly acknowledged but did not emphasize the effects of early American government on the associations of civic society.)

In the latter part of the nineteenth century came another great wave of U.S. voluntary group formation—this time prominently featuring three-tiered federations of associations at the local, state, and national level. Again, political events and processes were critical, along with industrialization, urbanization, and immigration. The Civil War and its aftermath encouraged ties between central and local elites and groups. Between the mid-1870s and the mid-1890s the intense electoral competition of locally rooted, nation-spanning political parties encouraged the parallel formation of voluntary federations, and gave them electoral or legislative leverage if they wanted it—as groups such as the Grand Army of the Republic, the Grange, and the Women's Christian Temperance Union most decidedly did.

Twentieth-century voluntary federations were often built from the top down, deliberately structured to imitate and influence the three tiers of U.S. government, and encouraged by parts of the federal government itself. Thus the American Legion was launched from the top by World War I military officers and later nurtured by the Veterans Administration. And the American Farm Bureau Federation was encouraged by the U.S. Department of Agriculture. The PTA itself, now romanticized as a purely local voluntary group, did not originally bubble up from below. It was founded in 1897 as the National Congress of Mothers (and renamed the PTA in 1924). The original Congress of Mothers was knit together from above by elite women. It started out as the brainchild of a new mother married to a prominent lawyer in Washington, DC. She decided to launch a women's organization resembling the U.S. Congress and paralleling the levels of U.S. government, so that "mother thought" could be carried into all spheres of American life. Once the Congress of Mothers began to take shape, as prominent women wrote to their counterparts in states and localities, it immediately turned to influencing local, state, and national governments to work in partnership with it for the good of all mothers and children. From its very inception, the Congress of Mothers/PTA was actively involved in public policymaking and the construction of a distinctively American version of the welfare state.

Although U.S. history contradicts the premises of Tocqueville romanticism, this vision has insinuated itself into current scholarship about U.S. civil society. Political patterns and developments (such as levels of trust in government, and rates of electoral participation or attendance at public meetings) are treated simply as "dependent variables." The assumption is that local voluntarism is fundamental, the primary cause of all that is healthy in democratic politics and effective governance, in contrast to the dreaded "bureaucratic state." But just as Marxists are wrong to assume that the economy is the primal "substructure" while government and politics are merely "superstructure," so Tocqueville romanticists are wrong to assume that spontaneous social association is primary while government and politics are derivative. On the contrary, U.S. civic associations were encouraged by the American Revolution, the Civil War, the New Deal, and World Wars I and II; and until recently they were fostered by the institutional patterns of U.S. federalism, legislatures, competitive elections, and locally rooted political parties.

CIVIL DECLINE RECONSIDERED

From the 1960s onward the mechanics of U.S. elections changed sharply. Efforts to mobilize voters through locally rooted organizations gave way to television advertising, polling and focus groups, and orchestration by consultants paid huge sums with money raised from big donors and mass mailings. Around the same time, the number of lobbying groups exploded in Washington, DC. Both business groups and "public interest" groups proliferated. Advocacy groups have clashed politically, yet their structures have become remarkably similar.

By now, almost all are led by resident professional staffs, and funded more by outside donors or commercial side ventures than from membership dues. If today's advocacy groups connect at all to society at large, they do so through mailings of magazines, newsletters, and appeals for donations to millions of individuals. The American Association of Retired Persons (AARP), founded in 1958, now has around 35 million members fifty years of age and older. But only 5 to 10 percent of AARP members participate in local affiliates, and new members join after getting a letter in the mail, not an invitation to a local club meeting. The AARP is not like the locally rooted federations that once dominated the ranks of nationwide U.S. voluntary associations.

Just as younger adults were turning away from traditional voluntary associations, America's ways of doing electoral politics and legislative advocacy were sharply transformed. Television was certainly a major factor, as were computerized modes of data analysis and direct-mail targeting. Complementary changes happened in the media, and in ways of doing policy business in the federal bureaucracy and Congress. Interlocking transformations added up to a new set of constraints and opportunities for voluntary groups. No longer do the great local-state-national federations, rooted in face-to-face meetings in localities, have a comparative advantage in mediating between individuals and politicians, between localities and Washington, DC. Professional and business elites increasingly bypass such federations. One exception, on the right, is the Christian Coalition, which since the late 1980s has successfully melded top-down and bottom-up styles of political mobilization.

Throughout much of U.S. history, electoral democracy and congressionally centered governance nurtured and rewarded voluntary associations and locality-spanning voluntary federations. But since the 1960s, the mechanics of U.S. politics have been captured by manipulators of money and data. Among elites new kinds of connections are alive and well. Privileged Americans remain active in think tanks, advocacy groups, and trade and professional associations, jetting back and forth between manicured neighborhoods and exotic retreats. Everyone else has been left to work at two or three poorly paid jobs per family, coming home exhausted to watch TV and answer phone calls from pollsters and telemarketers.

How ironic it would be if, after pulling out of locally rooted associations, the very business and professional elites who blazed the path toward local civic disengagement were now to turn around and successfully argue that the less privileged Americans they left behind are the ones who must repair the nation's social connectedness, by pulling themselves together from below without much help from government or their privileged fellow citizens. This, I fear, is what is happening as the discussion about "returning to Tocqueville" rages across elite America.

Progressives who care about democratic values should pause before joining this new "consensus." They should not hastily conclude that the answers to most of America's problems lie in civil society understood apart from, or in opposition to, government and politics. The true history of civic associationalism in America gives the lie to notions propagated by today's government bashers and government avoiders.

Organized civil society in the United States has never flourished apart from active government and inclusive democratic politics. Civic vitality has also depended on vibrant ties across classes and localities. If we want to repair civil society, we must first and foremost revitalize political democracy. The sway of money in politics will have to be curtailed, and privileged Americans will have to join their fellow citizens in broad civic endeavors. Re-establishing local voluntary groups alone will not suffice.

Couch-Potato Democracy?

Richard M. Valelly

Robert Putnam's analysis of the decline of civic engagement suggests that Americans have become a nation of couch-potatoes, turning to television for solitary entertainment, leaving bowling leagues, PTA meetings, and the Rotary Club behind. If true, this shift to homebody-ness entails a vast cost to public spirit. A long line of democratic theory stretching from Thucydides to Tocqueville suggests that a dynamic and diverse polity requires civic engagement, else threats to liberty and prosperity emerge.

As compelling as Putnam's argument is, he has left out the organizations that draw people into political participation—parties, groups, and movements. Like some analysts of voter behavior who ask whether citizens are more or less likely to participate depending on such factors as level of education, income, and age, Putnam assumes civic activity depends largely on traits and dispositions outside the polity. In keeping with this view, Putnam "holds constant" the political organizational context of civic engagement for the period 1920 to 1996. But does that make sense in light of the enormous changes in parties and groups since 1920?

Analyses of voter behavior can shed some light on this issue. The best work on voter turnout, Steven Rosenstone and John Mark Hansen's *Mobilization, Participation, and American Democracy,* shows that people don't just come to politics; politics also comes to people. The institutional setting affects who participates and how; voter traits matter much less than commonly thought. Between 1960 and 1988 voter turnout declined about 11 percentage points in presidential elections. Rosenstone and Hansen demonstrate that the weakened social involvement that Putnam describes, along with the declining age of the electorate, accounted for about 35 percent of the turnout decline. But they found that 54 percent of the drop was due to what they call "decline in mobilization." Personal contact with voters gave way to television advertising, states moved their gubernatorial campaigns to "off" years, primaries proliferated, leaving fewer resources for mobilization during general campaigns, and the civil rights and student movements weakened.

So we can't talk about the drop in voting without talking about how galvanizing parties and movements are. The 65 percent decline in unionization since 1954, for example, has critically reduced resources for mobilizing voters. Many analysts of union decline point to the rise of consulting firms than specialize in "union avoidance," sharp increases in unfair labor practices among management, the limitations of labor laws and their enforcement, and labor's strategic errors in the face of economic change. Civic disengagement has not caused trade union decline; trade union decline has caused civic disengagement.

Putnam's indictment of television is deeply and appropriately Tocquevillian. Tocqueville warned that individualism could pull Americans into private concerns and leave us vulnerable to the degradation of public life. If Putnam is right, then Tocqueville's prophecy is now urgent. Alternatively, though, the polity may have abandoned the people. Imagine if unions still organized torchlight parades on Labor Day during a presidential election year; if presidential candidates came to town in motorcades and waved at supporters, stopping to shake their hands and kiss their children; and if local party politicians, church leaders, and others contacted voters personally asking for support for one candidate or another. Amidst all this activity wouldn't you be more likely to run into someone who asked you to bowl with his league? Or invited you to come to a meeting of an investment club? Mightn't you be more trusting of the world at large? The television might be on at the bowling alley, and on election night you might watch the returns on TV at the American Legion hall or gathered with friends. But you wouldn't be a couch-potato citizen.

So maybe it's not that the people have lost interest in the polity, seduced by *Friends* one night and *Frasier* another. Maybe the polity, as it were, has lost interest in the people. It's not that Americans are tuning out. They're being left out.

Response

Robert D. Putnam

Any social change as broad gauged as that sketched in "The Strange Disappearance of Civic America" is surely complex—with multiple causes, conflicting countertrends, and uncertain consequences—so I welcome a lively discussion of these issues, especially with interlocutors as sophisticated as those in this symposium. In my view, four central questions must be considered:

1. *Is it true that civic engagement has declined in the last few decades—that is, have Americans' connections with their communities become attenuated?* My 1995 article on "Bowling Alone" surveyed this issue, and "Strange Disappearance" briefly reviewed the evidence. This is the central question addressed by Schudson.

2. *If so, why has it happened?* "Strange Disappearance" was a first attempt to sort through some possible answers to this question. Schudson, Skocpol, and Valelly all respond in part to this question.

3. *Does it matter?* That is, does civic engagement (or its absence) actually have significant consequences for the health of our communities? This question has not been debated thus far, and I shall here assume—like my critics here—that, for the most part, the answer is "yes." However, "civic engagement" comes in many forms, some healthful and others not, so exploring the diverse consequences of those different forms will be a central concern of my larger project.

4. *What can we do about it?* This is, in many respects, the question that most concerns me. It is the focus of a gathering debate in conservative circles, but until now it has been ignored by progressives. I am thus delighted that it is at the core of Skocpol's contribution.

First, has anything changed? Americans engage with our communities and with one another in many different forms—in families, around the water cooler, at church, on the street corner, over the barbecue, in voluntary associations, in political gatherings, and myriad other settings. No single archive records all these encounters, but I have tried to pull together as diverse an array of evidence as possible—multiple surveys, membership records, time budgets and so on—in order to detect and decipher underlying trends, without limiting my attention to a single sphere, such as politics. The title "Bowling Alone" was chosen precisely to suggest that civic disengagement in contemporary America is not primarily a political phenomenon, although of course it has powerful political consequences. (By way of analogy, neither universal education nor television is primarily a political phenomenon, although both have had powerful political consequences.)

Politics, however, is the focus of the critiques by Schudson and Valelly, and I am happy to address it. I am not the first scholar to notice a decades-long slump in many forms of political engagement. Valelly correctly cites, for example, Rosenstone and Hansen, whose pathbreaking work (as modestly extended in my own) shows substantial declines in such activities as attending meetings on community affairs or working for political parties. Equally ominously, interest in political and social issues among students entering college reached a 30-year low last fall.

The forms of engagement that have resisted this trend—political contributions, civil litigation, talk radio, membership in "mailing-list" and "single-issue" lobbies, such as the AARP or the NRA, and so on—are without doubt politically significant, and they betoken a widespread recognition of the power of politics, for good or ill. Americans have not stopped trying to influence government, even though most of us are increasingly skeptical about our chances of success.

For the most part, however, these rising forms of political engagement rest on a constricted notion of citizenship—citizen as disgruntled claimant, not citizen as participant in collective endeavor to define the public interest. Just as much of our community service today is "drop-by," much of our politics is "surf-by" and "call-in." We are no less free with our opinions, but we are listening to each other less. We are shouting and pressuring and suing, but we are not reasoning together, not even in the attenuated sense that we once did, with people we know well and will meet again tomorrow. Financial capital grows in political importance, while social capital declines. To those Americans who have more money than time, this may seem a mere change in coinage, but the transformation is fundamentally debasing our democracy.

Schudson is surely right that there was something special about "the long civic generation"—that is, after all, why I labeled it such—and he and Skocpol are both right that levels of civic engagement have risen and fallen in the tides of American history. In fact, the unusual civic engagement among Americans raised in the first half of this century was probably the fruit of a period of civic revitalization around the turn of the century. (I am currently engaged in research on precisely this question, in the hopes of uncovering lessons relevant to our current predicament.) If Schudson believes, however, that contemporary progressives should rest content with today's post-civic, Reaganite "normalcy," then I dissent.

Assuming for the moment that social connectedness has in fact atrophied in recent years, what could explain that trend? My greatest regret about "Strange Disappearance," I confess, is that its formulation seems to have invited hasty readers to conclude that I propose a simple-minded, mono-causal explanation—the boob tube as the root of all evil. I do believe that television has had a profoundly negative affect on community bonds in America, but I do not believe (and I did not write) that it is the sole culprit. (In the longer published version of my essay from which TAP excerpted "Strange Disappearance," I wrote that "like Agatha Christie's *Murder on the Orient Express,* this crime may have had more than one perpetrator, so that we shall need to sort out ringleaders from accomplices.") My references in "Strange Disappearance" to the Zeitgeist of World War II, to the changing role of women in America, to altered family structures, and so on, should perhaps have been less fleeting. More important, I agree with all three critics that those of us investigating this puzzle should look more systematically for evidence of what Skocpol calls "structural" effects, what Valelly terms "organizational context," and what Schudson felicitously calls "spark plugs"—in short, the supply side of civic life, as well as the demand side.

On the other hand, I would not automatically upgrade this hypothesis from "plausible" to "proven," for I have met too many conscientious leaders of community organizations around the country who are despondent about their inability, despite heroic efforts, to reverse the slow ebbing of their members' involvement—spark plugs in an engine running out of fuel. Moreover, the organizational supply or "spark plug" theory is more plausible for some forms of disengagement (political parties and women's clubs, for example) and much less so for other (fraternal groups and bowling leagues, for example). Finally, even if civic disengagement did begin among erstwhile "spark plugs," rather than among organizational back-benchers, the leaders' withdrawal still needs explanation and (if disengagement matters) remediation. "Shifting elite allegiances" is a label (or an epithet), not an explanation or prescription.

So what is to be done? So far the recent debate on how to restore social connectedness has been, as Skocpol says, largely a monopoly of the right. One important merit of Skocpol's important essay is precisely that it opens up this issue on the left. Another is that she brings historical evidence to bear on contemporary debates. For good historical reasons, progressives should resist the view, now being articulated by some simple-minded reactionaries, that government can be replaced by "civil society." As I wrote in this journal three years ago (rather plainly, I thought, and in italics, no less): "Social capital is not a substitute for effective public policy but rather a prerequisite for it and, in part, a consequence of it."

That said, progressives cannot allow ourselves to be pushed into the position that government energy can replace civic vitality or that grassroots connectedness does not matter. Surely we do not need to rehearse sterile academic debates about "the state" versus "civil society," for both are plainly important. What we need instead is a thorough, empirically grounded debate about how to revitalize civic engagement.

Public policy will be part of the answer, as I wrote three years ago. Take a single contemporary example: Neighborhood crime watch groups seem to be a notable exception to the general decline in social connectedness over the last quarter century, and most such groups emerged from community crime prevention programs sponsored by various federal, state, and local agencies, beginning in the 1970s, working often in partnership with community groups. So Skocpol is right to criticize "Tocqueville romanticists" who would claim that politics and government are irrelevant (or worse yet, intrinsically inimical) to civic vitality and who idealize "bottom-up" solutions. (Whether she is right to put me into that category is a less important question that I shall leave to others.)

On the other hand, "top-down" or government-driven solutions are hardly a panacea, and I cannot believe that Skocpol holds that extreme view, either, despite language in her commentary here that occasionally suggests that an active civic life can exist only as the product of an active government. The Washington elites whose creativity she celebrates may have played an important role in creating the American Legion, the Farm Bureau Federation, and the PTA, but so also did millions of ordinary Americans in thousands of local communities. Finding practical ways to encourage and enable their descendants (us) to reconnect with our communities, especially across lines of race and class, is a matter of high urgency, and we should not be distracted by false "either/or" debates.

Gingrich's Time Bomb

Philip Harvey, Theodore R. Marmor, and Jerry L. Mashaw

The Republicans' Contract With America is a deceptive document. While its sponsors denounce the welfare state, the Contract itself calls for cuts in only two specific areas: Aid to Families with Dependent Children (AFDC) and the crime prevention initiatives of the 1994 anti-crime bill. At the same time, the Contract promises a variety of new social benefits in the form of tax breaks. These include tax incentives for adoption and for the purchase of long-term care insurance, an elderly dependent care tax credit, a $500-per-child general tax credit, an increase in the amount of earned income retirees may receive without any reduction in their Social Security payments, and a cut in taxes on Social Security payments for the elderly with incomes over $34,000 (singles) and $44,000 (couples). These new benefits would be equivalent to entitlements—that is, no further action by government is necessary to make such benefits available to all eligible individuals.

Attacking the welfare state while creating new middle-class entitlements is a nifty political move. Conservatives can take credit for the new benefits for their more prosperous constituents while cutting benefits for the stigmatized poor. Deficit reduction may provide a cover for the cuts, but the immediate effect is a regressive redistribution of income.

The Contract's long-term consequences are likely to be more insidious. Over time the new proposals would gut the nation's safety net while creating a budgetary time bomb. The devil was never more in the details. In addition to the new tax breaks for social benefits, the Contract also promises a new tax-exempt savings account, a major new tax break for businesses, and that long-sought Republican goal, the capital gains tax cut. After seven years, when the Republicans' proposed balanced budget amendment would become effective, escalating revenue losses from the tax cuts would almost surely force major reductions in all social programs, including Medicare and Social Security. The Republicans do not admit to these consequences because they would be unpopular. But the Contract's budgetary arithmetic makes it hard to avoid the conclusion that this is what Gingrich's Republican followers seek to accomplish.

THE GREAT ROLLBACK

While various elements of the Contract contribute to the overall strategy, the Republican attack on the safety net comes primarily from the welfare reform bill, dubbed the Personal Responsibility Act of 1995 (PRA). The bill would effectively return the United States to nineteenth-century policies toward the poor and public assistance—complete with orphanages and even "indoor relief." Although provisions phasing in the new rules would soften their immediate impact, the legislation calls for radical changes, including:

- new eligibility requirements that would deny benefits to more than half of current AFDC recipients (if the requirements were fully effective immediately);
- an end to the legal right of the eligible poor, including the elderly and disabled poor, to cash and food assistance;
- a cap on total federal spending on cash, food, and housing assistance under a formula that would reduce real funds below current levels, impose larger cuts in the future, and force different groups of needy persons to compete for this diminishing pie;
- a shift of responsibility to the states for designing, administering, and paying for cash and food assistance programs, thus subjecting all of these programs to the political and fiscal pressures that have led states to cut the real value of welfare benefits in half since 1970; and
- a bar against legally admitted aliens, including children and many political refugees, from receiving virtually all forms of public assistance except for emergency medical care.

Such were the main provisions of the legislation as it stood when introduced in Congress in January. The Republicans estimate it would save about $40 billion during the first four years of operation (1996-1999). The Center on Budget and Policy Priorities (CBPP) estimates the cuts at $57 billion.

Not all these provisions, to be sure, are likely to survive in final legislation this year. However, the proposals are an index of

Republican intentions and a window on their underlying views. What they do not achieve in 1995 they may well return to do after 1996, especially if they have an all-Republican government extending from the Congress to the White House to the statehouses.

The biggest losers under the Republican plan would be children born out of wedlock, many of whom would no longer qualify for public assistance. The bill's sponsors say these changes would reduce out-of-wedlock births, which they blame for both poverty and crime in a "sense of the Congress" statement in the legislation. However, studies comparing states with different welfare benefit levels show decisively that benefits have little or no effect on out-of-wedlock birth rates. So other motives are clearly at work in these proposals: a search for scapegoats to blame for the nation's social problems, an expression of moral disapproval of unmarried teen parents, a need to target the least sympathetic groups even when cutting an unpopular program.

Under the legislation, any child without a legally established father would be ineligible for public assistance. The mother's full cooperation in efforts to establish her child's paternity would not be sufficient. Children would have to wait until the state identified their fathers even if it required lengthy legal proceedings. A state could make an exception only if it determined that efforts to establish paternity would result in physical danger to the mother or that the child was conceived as a result of rape or incest. The CBPP estimates that if this rule were effective immediately (rather than applying only to new applicants), approximately 2.8 million children would be stricken from AFDC rolls.

The bill would also permanently bar from AFDC any child born out of wedlock to a mother not yet 18, unless the mother either married the child's father or married someone else who legally adopted the child. Individual states could establish higher cutoff ages up to 21. This exclusionary rule would apply even to children conceived as a result of rape or incest. It would apply even if the mother later married, but her husband was unable to adopt the child because the natural father refused to relinquish his parental rights. Approximately 28 percent of all families on welfare were started by an unmarried mother under the age of 20. The CBPP estimates that approximately 12 percent were started by an unmarried mother under the age of 18.

Under these rules, a 30-year-old woman with a 13-year-old child born out of wedlock could never receive any welfare assistance for the child if she lost her job, even though she had never received welfare and had worked full-time ever since the child was born. States also would have the option of denying federal housing assistance to all families headed by a person who "has borne a child out of wedlock after attaining 18 years of age but before attaining 21." The exclusion would be permanent and would prohibit such a woman from ever living in housing that was subsidized under one of 14 federal programs. For example, subsidized housing for the elderly would be unavailable to a 72-year-old woman who had borne a child out of wedlock 52 years earlier.

The legislation would return some of the savings attributable to these changes to the states to promote adoption, establish orphanages, and pay for programs designed to reduce out-of-wedlock births. If the states wanted to provide income assistance to unwed mothers, they could do so only in "closely supervised residential group homes for unwed mothers," or what Gingrich's nineteenth-century forerunners used to call "indoor relief."

FROM WELFARE TO WORK?

Work requirements for welfare have been a common theme of all recent welfare reform efforts. Usually, these take the form of "workfare" programs that require welfare recipients to earn their benefits. The Republicans' plan has elements of workfare, but it also incorporates a "work test" approach that requires recipients to work under a pay scale so meager and punitive that it is likely to deter anyone who is not truly desperate from seeking benefits.

The PRA would repeal all statutory exemptions from AFDC work requirements and require the states to put target percentages of recipients to work full-time in exchange for their benefits. The states would have flexibility only in deciding how to achieve these targets. By 2003 the minimum participation rate would be one person working full-time for every two families receiving assistance. Job training and education would not qualify as work. And beneficiaries excused from full-time work because they were sick or incapacitated or took care of infants or toddlers would count also toward a state's allowed total of nonworkers on welfare.

The bill would actually prohibit states from subsidizing education and training for more than two years during a recipient's lifetime. The

JOBS program, established under the Family Support Act of 1988 to provide welfare recipients with job training and other services to enhance their employability, almost surely would wither under the PRA. States could use a restructured JOBS program to satisfy the PRA work requirements, but they would be under no obligation to do so. It would be cheaper for them to establish new work programs stripped of the extra services they are now required to provide to JOBS participants.

States also would no longer have to compensate welfare recipients at the minimum wage for their required work. In fact, under the Republican plan, many recipients would have to work for less than the minimum wage. If the new rules had been in effect in January 1994, a single parent with one child required to work full-time for her welfare benefits in Mississippi would have been compensated at a rate of only 63 cents an hour. If the state offered her the same level of food aid as the federal food stamp program—which it would not have to do under the Republican bill—this same mother would get paid at a rate of only $1.99 an hour for her combined cash and food benefits.

Time limits on welfare benefits have now become a central theme in the debate over welfare reform. The Republicans would limit a family's lifetime eligibility to five years and give states the option of limiting it to two years, provided the family had been required to participate in a work program for a total of at least 12 months.

The legislation recognizes no exceptions to the lifetime limits. High unemployment rates would be no excuse for failing to get a job. Nor would the onset of a debilitating illness or accident or any other difficulties beyond an individual's control. Recipients unlucky enough to exhaust their benefits in the middle of a recession or an illness would have to be dumped from the rolls.

Moreover, states would face considerable fiscal pressure not to extend benefits for the full five years. States that spent more than their federal allotment for welfare in any year would have to cut benefit levels, limit eligibility, transfer money from other programs, or raise taxes. The temptation to limit benefits to fewer than five years would be very strong. The PRA requires full-time work from single parents only after they have received benefits for two years. Requiring work is more expensive than sending checks, especially if child care is provided. So, continuing a family's benefits beyond two years could result in substantially greater costs than providing the same benefits to a family in the first two years of its eligibility.

JUST GET A JOB

Imagine a dog bone economy in which 100 dogs compete for 90 bones. Every morning the dogs fight over the available bones until an equilibrium is reached in which the 90 best fighters end up with the 90 available bones. The other ten dogs lick their wounds. A troupe of social scientists study the fighting and produce data showing that bigger, more aggressive dogs get bigger bones while dogs without bones tend to be weaker and dispirited. They conclude that bonelessness is caused by a lack of strength and spirit and propose exercise and motivational training for the weaker dogs as a means of ending bonelessness. Will their strategy work?

The PRA's work requirements are based on the assumption that welfare dependency stems primarily from the refusal of welfare recipients to take available jobs. How else can one justify a bill that would deny public assistance to the children of jobless parents except in orphanages or through state-subsidized foster care and adoption? How else can one justify requiring the jobless parents of dependent children to work at a scale lower than the minimum wage for a benefit far below the poverty line? Even ardent conservatives would find such treatment hard to stomach if they weren't convinced that joblessness among welfare recipients is voluntary.

But the facts do not support this view. Even at what many professional economists call "full employment," surveys of job availability consistently show that there are not enough jobs for everyone who is actively looking for work, let alone for everyone society thinks should work.

In the Milwaukee metropolitan area for example, unemployment rates in May 1994 were at a level most politicians would kill to achieve—4.2 percent. About 32,000 people in the area were unemployed and actively looking for work. In addition, there were about 23,000 able-bodied welfare recipients not counted as unemployed in government figures. Based on national averages, about 19,000 people were probably working part-time because they couldn't find full-time jobs, and perhaps another 1,800 people wanted jobs and had looked for work in the past year but gave up the search as fruitless.

Counting all these groups, probably about 75,000 people in Milwaukee were out of work and needed jobs.

A survey at the time showed that employers in the Milwaukee area were seeking to fill only 16,790 full-time and 13,845 part-time positions. There simply weren't enough jobs to go around, and the job shortage for unskilled workers or for residents of depressed neighborhoods was far worse than the area-wide averages suggest. Welfare reform that ignores this job gap and its devastating effects on families and communities is destined to fail. Proposals that blame welfare recipients for their own joblessness are not only cruel but shortsighted. Joblessness and its attendant social ills cannot be eliminated without creating more jobs.

THE ECLIPSE OF LEGAL RIGHTS

Recipients of food assistance and the elderly or disabled poor aren't as attractive targets for welfare bashing as unmarried mothers. Nevertheless, the Republicans go after them as well, drawing the purse strings tighter without saying who should be denied aid.

Our nation's major income assistance programs for needy persons are presently offered as legal and budgetary entitlements. Anyone who meets the eligibility requirements for the program is entitled to assistance. There are no waiting lists based on the availability of funds. This is true not only of AFDC but also of Medicaid, food assistance programs such as food stamps, and Supplemental Security Income (SSI), which provides cash assistance to the elderly and disabled poor.

Housing assistance is the most important form of support for the poor that the government does not provide as an entitlement, and the effects of this limitation are dramatic. For example, while virtually all welfare recipients receive food stamps, less than a quarter live in public housing or receive federal housing subsidies even though most of them would be legally eligible for assistance, if funds were available.

The Republican plan would eliminate legal rights to AFDC, SSI, and all food assistance programs. Only Medicaid would continue to be an entitlement. Henceforth, individuals could qualify for these programs but still not receive assistance because the year's budget had run out.

At the same time, the bill would put federal contributions to AFDC, SSI, and virtually all housing assistance under a single budget cap or limit. The limit would include spending on the new work programs mandated for welfare recipients, so their cost would have to be absorbed by other cuts. Federal spending on all of these programs would be permitted to grow beyond prior year levels only to account for inflation and changes in the poverty population.

The formula mandated for calculating these changes, however, would in practice force further reductions. Under the formula used to calculate changes in the poverty population, for example, adjustments would lag by almost three years. Recessions would come and go before the federal government would raise a cap to reflect increases in poverty. Spending wouldn't necessarily catch up in prosperous times either. Each year's cap would depend on the prior year's actual spending. So, if spending came in under the cap either because the economy was performing well or because of shortfalls in federal or state appropriations, subsequent caps would be permanently reduced.

The Republicans have projected that their cap will cut federal expenditures for the poor by $18 billion between 1997 and 1999. Based on more current data, the CBPP projects the cuts at $26 billion. In either case, the cuts would grow larger after 1999.

LET THEM EAT CAKE

The PRA strategy for reducing federal food assistance is even more daring. It would repeal the Food Stamp program, the National School Lunch Act, and legislation authorizing the Special Supplemental Food Program for Women, Infants and Children (WIC), along with virtually every other federal food assistance measure. A single block grant to the states would replace these programs. States would be required to spend stated percentages of their block grant on substitutes for the WIC program and for school lunches for needy children, but otherwise they would be free to fashion whatever food assistance programs they wanted. The federal government would furnish food stamps at face value to any states that wanted to use them, but states would establish their own eligibility criteria and benefit levels.

The block grant allocation for 1996 would cut federal food assistance about 9 percent compared to 1995 levels and henceforth permit increases in spending only to reflect general population growth and changes in the "food at home" component of the consumer price index. No increases would compensate for the effects of recessions or changes in poverty rates. The PRA's sponsors estimate the cuts in federal food assistance at $1 billion over four years. The CBPP estimates the cuts at $18 billion.

While generally free to establish their own criteria for food aid, states would have to impose a work test on able-bodied recipients between the ages of 18 and 62 not caring for children or for another incapacitated family member. The legislation would require these recipients to perform at least 32 hours of work in the month before receiving assistance. The current maximum food stamp benefit is $115 for a single person. Thus, beneficiaries who received this much food aid (and many would not) would effectively be paid at a rate of $3.59 per hour, substantially less than the minimum wage. They would have to complete the work the month before they received the food aid.

The intent of this rule is obvious. It is to discourage single adults, including a large proportion of the nation's homeless population, from applying for food assistance. Soup kitchens funded from the block grants would have to turn away any "nonexempt individual" who had failed to satisfy the work test. Once again, the assumption seems to be that there's no such thing as involuntary unemployment.

LET THE STATES DO IT

The Republicans have touted their strategy as turning more power over to the states to design and administer social programs. Past performance gives little cause for comfort at this prospect. The federalization of social welfare in the United States occurred in response to a collapse of the capacity of the states to handle distress during the Great Depression. With luck we will never again experience such a crisis. Recessions, however, are a fact of life—indeed, regional recessions have become common in recent decades even when the national economy is prospering. States simply do not have the resources of the federal government to increase spending when their economies go sour. Federal entitlement programs provide countercyclical benefits to the nation that boost the economy during hard times and even out the economic fortunes of different regions. To assume that states can or Congress will provide the extra aid that is needed in as timely and as well targeted a fashion is fantasy.

Whether state legislators are as warm-hearted as their federal counterparts is not the issue. States compete with each other to attract business investment. Low taxes are widely believed to be an important selling point, and the same people who argue that social welfare policy should be left to the states regularly argue on the state level that taxes and social spending should be reduced to make the state more "competitive." This conventional understanding of how best to compete for jobs acts as a brake on the more generous impulses of state legislatures and exerts a steady downward pressure on social spending.

The recent history of welfare benefits demonstrates the problem. States presently set AFDC benefit levels and completely control General Assistance, which serves destitute people not covered by federal programs. Over the past two decades states have permitted average welfare benefit levels to erode to approximately half their former value, and General Assistance programs have recently been the target of a flurry of draconian budget cuts. In Michigan, where General Assistance for "able-bodied" persons was entirely eliminated, only 20 percent of the program's former recipients found work lasting most of the year following the termination of their benefits and 25 percent reported being homeless seven months after their benefits ended.

THE RIGHT'S LONG-TERM STRATEGY

The changes proposed for poverty programs under the PRA would be devastating to the affected families. The Republicans have designed the legislation, however, to soften its immediate impact. A number of key provisions would apply only to new applicants. The net first-year cuts in spending would be small compared to subsequent cuts. In many instances (such as food aid), they have also tried to hide responsibility for federal cutbacks by making the states decide whose ox to gore.

This may reflect a recognition by the Republican leadership that the changes they propose could easily create a backlash. "Welfare" is unpopular, but most Americans do not want to reduce help provided the poor. The Republicans thus call for big changes in "welfare" without hurting too many people in the short run. Their strategy is to call for changes with only small immediate effects that will grow dramatically over time.

Strikingly, the Republican counterrevolution against the welfare state does not include any cuts in the benefits that are the core of the welfare state: the social insurance programs that together account for over 70 percent of all income transfers. In fact, the only changes in Social Security proposed in the Contract with America would increase the cost to the federal government of benefits for wealthier recipients. And far from cutting the middle-class entitlements that are richly larded into the tax code—such as the mortgage interest deduction—the Republicans are promising the new tax breaks we mentioned earlier for adoption, long-term care insurance, elderly dependent care, and the costs of child rearing, not to mention that old favorite, the capital gains tax cut.

These tax expenditures, like the new rules for Social Security, would disproportionately benefit higher-income households. Based on existing federal income tax rates, any social welfare benefit provided as a tax deduction returns 33 cents on the dollar to high-income families, 28 cents on the dollar to middle-income families, 15 cents on the dollar to working-class families, and nothing at all to families too poor to have any income tax liability. Even the $500-per-child tax credit—which looks deceptively like a European-style child allowance—would offer a bigger subsidy to the better off, since there is no suggestion the credit would be refundable (that is, payable to people with little or no tax obligation).

Moreover, just as the Republicans backload their spending cuts—concentrating them in future years—so they backload their tax breaks for the wealthy. Small at first, the new tax expenditures will produce mushrooming losses in revenue beyond the five-year official budget horizon. Viewed in Machiavellian terms, the Contract appears to be a refinement of the strategy pioneered by the Reagan administration: use tax cuts to create budget pressures in the hope that forced austerity will eventually soften popular resistance to cuts in social spending. Under the balanced budget amendment, which would require the federal government to bring its spending and revenue into balance by 2002, Republicans will bewail the necessity, but Social Security will go on the chopping block.

The Republicans describe the Contract as calling for $190 billion in tax cuts over the next five years; they estimate $40 billion in spending cuts over the same period. This imbalance alone looks like a gun pointed at social insurance spending. But three of the tax cut proposals in the Contract could more than double the government's revenue loss between the sixth and tenth year after their introduction.

The Republican's proposed new backloaded IRA—"American Dream Savings Accounts" (ADSAS)—would encourage taxpayers with existing IRAS to roll them over into new ADSAS. The rollover would generate tax revenue in the short-run, but the government would face major losses later on when the ADSAS are cashed out. The proposed capital gains tax cut would also generate new revenue in the short run by encouraging asset sales but would result in huge revenue losses later on. And proposed changes in depreciation rules would give businesses a tax break equivalent of 100 percent deductibility in the year capital equipment is purchased but extend realization of this benefit over the life of the equipment. This change is also structured to generate some immediate increases in tax revenue and major losses in the long run.

If these proposals are adopted, five years from now the pack of devils we have been describing will show up to collect the several hundred billion dollar debt left by the Contract. Where will Congress get the money? After defense spending and interest on the national debt, there is nothing left to cut in the budget that remotely approximates the requisite scale. Conservatives may then, as now, proclaim their fealty to Social Security. They will surely hope that Americans fail to see the connection between their Contract with America and the unraveling of the long-term social contract that Social Security has represented since the Depression. But if interest must be paid, defense is sacred, tax increases are unthinkable, and the budget must be balanced, Social Security programs will have to be cut—both substantially and rapidly.

HOW SHOULD LIBERALS RESPOND?

In responding to the Republican offensive, liberals would be wise to keep three things in mind. First, social spending is not unpopular as long as the public understands exactly who is being helped, how, and why. This is why conservatives prefer to attack "welfare" rather than specific entitlements (with the exception of AFDC). Liberals shouldn't let them get away with this sleight of hand. The public needs to understand that the Republicans want to deny food, shelter, and medical care to identifiable families whose needs are desperate and for whom this country does not have enough jobs.

Second, the American public has a strong sense of entitlement to social insurance benefits that goes well beyond the legal meaning of the term. Liberals should sound the alarm that the Republican's Contract with America is designed to undermine those programs by so impoverishing the Treasury with tax breaks for the wealthy that Social Security programs will have to be cut.

Third, liberals should face up to the Achilles' heel in their vision of a socially responsible government. That weak spot is their lack of an effective, politically attractive answer to joblessness. The New Deal stood for jobs when unregulated markets proved incapable of providing them. In the eyes of the public, the Great Society stood for transfer payments delivered to people who should have been working. Liberalism's New Deal image is attractive. The Great Society image is not. It is no accident that the only transfer programs that conservative politicians are willing to attack openly and vociferously are those that provide benefits to employable persons.

The best answer to the Republican welfare plan is to tell the truth about job availability. There aren't enough jobs to go around. It's not just good jobs that are in short supply. There aren't enough bad jobs either. The labor market is a giant game of musical chairs in which there aren't enough seats for everyone who is actively seeking work, let alone for others who the public thinks should work. The private sector cannot provide work for everyone. That's not a condemnation of the market. It simply recognizes its limitations. If the Republicans want to force welfare recipients to take jobs in the private sector—any jobs—they should be pressed to say who they want to go jobless instead.

Liberal support for measures designed to help welfare recipients compete more effectively for scarce jobs is insufficient. More jobs are needed. Instead of arguing with conservatives over whether welfare recipients should be expected to work, liberals should be arguing about the kind of work opportunities welfare recipients should be provided. Offering sub-minimum wage workfare is unconscionable. But so is minimum wage workfare when maximum earnings are limited to AFDC benefit levels and recipients are denied the earned income tax credit (EITC)—as they would be under the Clinton welfare reform proposal. The principle of making work pay should apply just as much to jobs created for welfare recipients as it does to other jobs.

Denying public assistance to unemployed parents will only aggravate our nation's already severe social problems. We must remember that the (imaginary) laissez-faire past that Republicans seek to recreate was not a golden age. It was an age of Dickensian social conditions and enormous suffering. The do-nothing social policies that permitted such conditions to fester constituted a failed strategy that has been rejected for nearly a century throughout the industrialized world—and for good reason. The gaps between rich and poor that an unfettered market permits are an engine of profound social and political distemper. It is this inescapable truth that welfare state programs recognize and that the Republicans' Contract with America seeks to deny.

We need a new social contract—but surely not one that combines vicious treatment of the poor with fiscally irresponsible promises to the better off. Newt Gingrich has a flair for the dramatic. But his Contract with America is much too reminiscent of the bargain made by Faust. The Republican bargain should be rejected before it has to be broken, and the devil of social discord and unrest seeks to collect its debt with interest.

EPILOGUE

This article was written in the winter of 1994-95 in response to the Republican party's initial legislation proposal for implementing the welfare reform plank of the Contract With America. The Republicans' welfare reform bill already was undergoing significant change as we wrote the article and more change followed. Throughout the legislative process, however, the same conservative views that inspired the original bill continued to dominate its revision. Moderating influences were weak. Democratic opposition to the legislation was notable mainly for its timidity until President Clinton signaled his intent to veto the bill in the form it was taking, and Democratic counterproposals, including those emanating from the White House, moved significantly toward Republican positions.

The overriding goal of the legislation remained the same: to significantly reduce both funding and eligibility for means-tested antipoverty benefits. According to an analysis by the Center on Budget and Policy Priorities (CBPP), the bill as finally enacted (and vetoed by the President) would have cut federal spending on means-tested income assistance programs by $64 billion over seven years, compared to what would have been spent if existing law remained unchanged.

The enacted bill would have required AFDC into a block grant program with work requirements and time limits similar to those described in our article. Food Stamps would have continued as a federal entitlement, but spending would have been reduced by 20 percent as a result of new eligibility restrictions and reductions in benefits. SSI also would have continued as a federal entitlement, but disabled children and the elderly poor would have suffered substantial reductions in eligibility and benefits. The number of children eligible for disability benefits would have been reduced by two thirds over time, and the minimum age at which the elderly poor could qualify for benefits would have been increased to 67 from the current 65. And although some of the original bill's most problematic provisions were eliminated or modified in the legislative process, some equally problematic ones were added—such as the elimination of the requirement that states provide Medicaid benefits to AFDC recipients.

In other words, the general character of the bill Congress sent the President is consistent with the Republicans' original proposal, even though many of the details of the legislation have changed.

Come the Devolution

Lenny Goldberg

One of the Republicans' many ideological coups has been their ability to cast important questions of federalism in wholly conservative terms. In the new Republican demonology, liberals are centralists, favoring Washington while resisting local decisionsand initiatives. Conservatives offer a decentralist new paradigm, returning, in the immortal words of born-again decentralist Senate Majority Leader Robert Dole, "power to the people."

Dole's appropriation of a 1960s new-left slogan unintentionally acknowledges the ambiguity of the decentralizing impulse. In the 1960s, community activists sought to empower local groups and individuals in the opposition to a corporatized, centralized warfare-welfare state. In the 1990s, the right uses the same power-to-the-people rhetoric to attack 60 years of liberal policies that have been anchored by federal laws, standards, and fiscal resources. The empty slogan, of course, avoids all the important questions of government: what power to what people, under what set of laws, institutions, and values?

Three things are noteworthy about this debate. First, a close look at the Dole-Gingrich brand of "devolution" reveals less a principled philosophy of federalism than a series of opportunistic forays, often contradictory. Second, the Democrats, after a few promising false starts, have fumbled a legitimate issue and allowed the Republicans to impose their own conception. And third, despite the big dose of hypocrisy in the Republican package, decentralism and community empowerment remain worthy goals for progressives. The issue is too important to simply cede to the right.

DECEPTIVE DEVOLUTION

The Gingrich revolution would roll back both the social advances associated with the New Deal-Great Society and the role of national government as guarantor. Much of what is packaged as devolution is simply opportunism. If entitlements cannot be eliminated directly, their elimination can be disguised as a block grant. The block grant for Aid to Families with Dependent Children (AFDC) over time would force state-level rationing of a program that once guaranteed income support for needy families, potentially shifting burdens to already overstrapped foster care and child welfare systems. Limited federal support for Medicaid would intensify rationing of health care. The school lunch block grant would effectively eliminate the entitlement to that program. Since the poor are not the most popular claimants for state aid, it adds up to a massive rollback of income support.

The right rails about unfunded mandates, but the Gingrich brand of devolution creates unfunded liabilities. States already in competition with each other to lower taxes to attract business will now be forced to slash programs for the poor and disadvantaged. This looming "race to the bottom" is not a function of the mean-spiritedness of states and localities. Rather, it stems from changes in federal-state relations that would create inexorable downward fiscal pressures on the safety net.

Often the right's preferred level of government is purely a matter of expediency. For example, Republicans complain about a federal requirement that San Diego build a sewage treatment plant—intrusive, micromanaging environmentalism, according to Gingrich, a means of protecting the ocean according to the EPA. California Governor Pete Wilson refuses to implement the federal motor-voter law because it is not paid for (and because it might register too many new voters). But neither Pete Wilson nor any other governor (or Republican congressman, for that matter) has complained about perhaps the most intrusive new unfunded mandate now being implemented nationwide: the requirement passed in the Bush administration for mandatory, repeated drug testing programs for all transportation and public safety employees, a program that will cost state and local governments billions of dollars on an ongoing basis, ostensibly because localities would not otherwise protect the public from drug-crazed bus drivers and police officers.

In the 1995 rewrite of the crime bill, the House Republicans demanded: Don't tell the locals how to fight crime. So they eliminated categorical crime prevention and police officer funding. But at the same time, they offered the states new prison money—but only if states strengthen their sentencing laws to keep felons in jail for 85 percent of their sentences, irrespective of local statutes, sentencing, and parole decisions. The Democrats were little better. The categorical crime prevention program was in fact a mess, only accessible by those capable of hustling grants from the Department of Justice. Clinton's defense of money earmarked for the thin blue line of police officers may have been good politics, winning support from chiefs and cops, but it is a trap for the locals, who are hard-pressed to turn down federal largess for cops on the street—and will be hard-pressed to lay those cops off when the federal money runs out, as it does very quickly in the Clinton police program.

A second closely related hypocrisy involves interest group politics. Powerful special interests seek centralized power via uniform federal standards if the locals go too far. For example, Republicans want to restrict product liability nationally because they have failed at the state level. Alternatively, the special interests seek local control when they don't like federal restrictions, such as federal lands policy in the west. Energy utilities readily move from state public utilities commissions to the Federal Energy Regulatory Commission and back again, seeking their advantage irrespective of any principle of state or federal jurisdiction. This is less new-paradigm devolution than old-fashioned venue shopping.

OPPORTUNISM IN SEARCH OF IDEOLOGY

Over the years, conservative theorists here and in Europe have articulated thoughtful versions of devolution and "subsidiarity"—the idea that government action should be carried out at the lowest possible level that can perform it competently. But in the current Republican conception, amid the myriad hypocrisies and opportunisms, it is hard to find a principled core.

Two conservative theorists of devolution, William Eggers and John O'Leary of the Reason Foundation, extol the flexibility and antibureaucracy of localism in *Revolution at the Roots*, a sort of *Reinventing Government* of the right. The principles here, however, call for limitation on all government action through tax restrictions, and "transferring responsibility from government to individuals, families, and voluntary associations." Not only should the central government be transferred downward to local government, but local government should also do less and should have less money. This is less a theory of decentralized government than pure libertarianism.

James Pinkerton, a former Bush aide, claimed a conservative "new paradigm" of decentralization and empowerment—initially a group of examples in search of a theory such as self-management, ownership of public housing projects, and school vouchers. His latest book, subtitled *The End of Big Government—and the New Paradigm Ahead*, oddly includes not only medical savings accounts and school vouchers—but also a revival of FDR's Civilian Conservation Corps.

The ostensible historical and theoretical inevitability of devolution is also touted in the "Third Wave" of futurists Alvin and Heidi Toffler. In the new information society, information is so widely dispersed and decisions have to be made so continually that centralism is impossible and government is on perpetual overload. Just as corporations have decentralized their decisionmaking, just as mass markets have fragmented, just as diversifying subgroups of the population make increasingly diverse demands, so must government decentralize decisionmaking. Thus, devolution of the central government is an inevitable trend that makes government consistent with the new decentralized economy and society. The Tofflers are neither entirely wrong nor entirely conservative: They celebrate diversity, environmentalism, feminism, and civil rights. But on close examination, they would wish away all bureaucracy without any examination of the appropriate role of government, particularly the need to maintain a well-functioning infrastructure that keeps the society running.

In short, it is difficult to find any consistent concept of devolution either in the theorists or in the actions of the Republican Congress. Conservatives would overthrow the most local of regulatory decisions—land use law—by extending "takings" theory to many local regulatory actions. A recent Medicare reform proposal would allow doctors to form health plans that would be exempt from strict state financial accountability standards. The state responsibility to protect its citizens from defective products would be overridden by a weakened national product liability standard. The policy seems to follow the constituency: If ranchers on federal lands want local control but cable companies insist on local preemption, so be it. The Tenth

Amendment—delegating powers to the states—should be in play on, for example, abortion, until a fifth antiabortion vote on the Supreme Court outlaws it entirely.

Like President Reagan's "New Federalism" proposals of the early 1980s, the Republican proposals devolve precisely the wrong programs in the wrong ways. Then, Democrats swallowed some funding cuts but blocked the dismantling of federal responsibility. This time around, the Democrats' response to devolution has been ineffectual and sometimes incoherent.

HOW DEMOCRATS DROPPED THE BALL

As a candidate for president, Bill Clinton brought a critical governor's eye to excessive federal micromanagement. The Democratic Leadership Council, likewise, has made decentralization an essential tenet of being a "new" Democrat. Budget director Alice Rivlin's most recent book, *Reviving the American Dream: the Economy, the States and the Federal Government*, written just before she joined the administration, advocated a wholesale devolution of major federal programs. Vice President Gore's National Performance Review calls federal-state relationships "fundamentally broken." And this administration has demonstrated a far greater willingness than previous ones to grant waivers to the states to permit greater innovation, experimentation, and flexibility. So what went wrong?

First, Gingrich, Dole, and company pursued a much more aggressive and populist-sounding version of decentralization. Pre-Gingrich, all of this was policy-wonk stuff: federalism, intergovernmental relations, unfunded mandates, and the like have long been yawners in the hierarchy of hot public policy issues—which, alas, is how the Clinton administration treated them. Gingrich's great achievement has been to transform a nuts-and-bolts discussion of how government should operate into grand ideology to whip the Democrats and dismantle the New Deal.

Second, the administration had many opportunities but failed to project any unifying vision of government. For example, the National Performance Review easily could have been cast as a decentralist program that breaks down unnecessary federal bureaucratic functions and devolves power to local decisionmakers. Instead, as deficit mania intensified, it has been promoted mainly as an attempt to save money. The administration's much-maligned health care plan, labeled big government incarnate, in fact gave much power and flexibility to the states and even regions to run their own programs—although few others than state-level activists knew it. In health and human services, where the administration has given states broad waivers to innovate, only insiders—public officials, policy advocates, and inhabitants of places like the National Conference of State Legislatures or the Advisory Committee on Intergovernmental Relations—have ever cared.

Further, a lot of this stuff is intrinsically of interest only to the interest groups and government functionaries who live and die by it. The difficulty of exciting the public about a principled and non-opportunistic version of devolution is partly a function of its numbing detail. In a federal system (yawn), every single program has its own set of intergovernmental issues. Every public policy area has an involved and evolved set of federal, state, and local relationships that have far more to do with institutional histories, the predilections of long-powerful congressional chairs, and lobbying groups with particular preferences than with any coherent federalist principles. Many state bureaucrats are actually happy to have federal restrictions, which offer an all-purpose excuse for failure to innovate.

It took incredible Republican packaging to place something as boring as "unfunded mandates" onto the front-burner of national policy, even as the legislation itself fails dismally to relieve localities of some of the more onerous and stupid of these actual mandates. Thus even the most astute commentators have missed the fact that Clinton potentially offers a smarter and more serious version of decentralization. Michael Kelly, writing in the *New Yorker*, understands why Gingrich would be proposing devolution, but is shocked that the Clinton administration would even halfheartedly take up this banner. Democrats came into office this time with a sensible view of devolution—but the issue got lost in the Democratic Party's general retreat.

Let's pause to recall why much of the post-1933 liberal agenda has necessarily increased the reach of the national government. Democrats in this century have relied on the federal government to secure broad gains for the majority of people. In the sweep of New Deal social insurance programs, its (partial) extension to health care in the 1960s, the triumph of civil rights over states' rights, and the need for national environmental protection, Democrats have rightly advanced the power of the federal government to provide the basic rights and protections of citizenship. For several generations, Democrats have fought against the ravages of an inhumane, anti-ecological marketplace and the perceived lack of concern by corrupt or inept state governments for their own citizenry. If devolution and decentralization means abandoning these advances, then the *New Yorker* is right to be shocked, and the Democrats are right to fight against these efforts.

In truth, since the New Deal the dominant mode of thought—governing paradigm, if you will—has been centralism of both a progressive and conservative nature. Liberal centralism describes the New Deal postwar consensus. Conservative centralists have long believed in a powerful military and an extensive domestic and international security and intelligence state.

Though it is sometimes forgotten, progressives have often fought to maintain, not eliminate, local regulatory powers and the design of programs to fit local needs. They have built an extensive set of community-based institutions—from Head Start to community development corporations to workplace committees on occupational safety and health—which began in opposition to the established bureaucratic order; and have envisioned human scale and participatory institutions.

DECENT DEVOLUTION

Just as there are both conservative and liberal brands of centralism, there are both progressive and reactionary forms of decentralism. Since so much of the congressional program is simply ideological and is aimed at the poor, it is tempting to dismiss devolution as a smokescreen. Richard Reeves, for example, observes that the use of federal power in American history has meant progress over slavery, oppression, and economic backwardness. The *Washington Monthly* has derided "devolution chic" by collecting numerous examples of corruption and venality at the local level. The *New York Times* questions whether state legislatures, many of them part-time and burdened by term limits, can rise to the task of making intelligent decisions about programs.

But the irony remains: Much of the thrust of recent progressive movements was antibureaucratic, anticentralist, and focused on empowerment of community and individuals. The civil rights movement sought fundamental personal and community rights based on decentralized moral witness—but required the full power of the federal government to establish and enforce those rights.

One of the most significant policy and institutional contributions of the progressive movements of the 1960s has been the rise of community-based nonprofit agencies—public-private partnerships, if you will—as a key element in direct service delivery, in battered women's shelters, child care agencies, community development corporations, and community health clinics, among many diverse variations on the theme. The antiwar movement long called for shrinking the bureaucratic national security state and its dependent corporations. The women's movement is fundamentally about empowerment: The personal became political at the most individual and community level. The environmental movement developed the most visionary decentralist perspectives: think globally, act locally; small is beautiful; create "human scale" institutions and bio-regional governments.

The right does not own this issue. We need to sort through what the federal government does best while identifying where devolution can and should work. The following is only an outline of a much broader discussion and debate.

RIGHTS. The first concern of any progressive like Reeves, who gets nervous about devolution, is civil rights and civil liberties. Guaranteed constitutional rights and civil liberties, like many other federal responsibilities, are simply not devolvable. As these rights become clarified by federal action or decisions—for example Miranda rights, abortion rights—they cannot be abrogated by localities.

This principle, however obvious, helps clarify the debate on unfunded mandates. If the constitutional right to an attorney is established, the fact that localities have to pay for public defenders is simply the cost that government must bear to guarantee the people their legal rights, not a federal mandate. Access for the disabled to public buildings and public transportation costs states and localities money; but since access and mobility for the disabled are legislated as a right of citizenship, not only public but private costs (disabled access to businesses) are simply the costs of serving all citizens.

But this argument goes only so far. Establishing a right to health care, for example, does not mean that local government can be mandated to provide it without financing. For the federal government to ensure rapid implementation of disability access, it should provide the funding. In general, the most effective and important intervention of the federal government is precisely what Gingrich is trying to destroy: federal financing.

FUNDING. The most critical programmatic function of the federal government is financing. The Social Security program is at once the most centralized and the most empowering program of all: The computer system and bureaucracy guarantee income without strings for millions of individuals, delivered to their doorstep. Supplemental Security Income empowers the disabled, blind, and very poor elderly with the ability to survive. The Medicare system permits millions of elderly to seek their own health care with (until now perhaps) substantial choice. So far, no one has suggested that the states take over income maintenance or medical care for the elderly for many good reasons, such as the fact of interstate personal mobility and the states' limited fiscal resources.

As Alice Rivlin has noted in her otherwise favorable treatment of devolution, devolving entitlement programs would place an unthinkable burden on the states, a burden that only the federal government is fiscally capable of carrying. Thus, entitlement programs that assure that poor children have income support, medical care, a home without abuse, and sufficient food must be federally financed. Seen this way, a simple child allowance program like that of most Western countries becomes a far more fair and efficient means of providing family support than the AFDC system, particularly one run by the states.

Federal financial power must necessarily extend to functions that the states will not or cannot undertake. Basic research, which is distributed to many locations, benefits no state or particular industry immediately but is arguably critical to long-term economic growth. A public broadcasting system, based on local stations that raise much of their own money, would have been impossible without federal financing. One can argue the legitimacy of many federal expenditures; but one cannot argue that the states can afford these broader expenditures.

FLEXIBILITY. The devolutionary aspect of federal financing should be local program flexibility. To oversimplify, the federal government must finance efforts to remedy problems; community efforts should receive every incentive to provide the solutions. The most effective programs are often those that come from the bottom up—the community development, job training, family service, and community clinic programs that fill the voids that the legislative process or the regulatory bureaucracy could not envision.

Where the federal government wants specific behavior or change, it should use incentives: In child support, for example, federal policy currently provides incentive payments to pay for the states and localities to improve collections, with limited program specifications on how the job gets done. (The program has encountered its greatest problems with federal specifications for computerization.) Such flexible programs as the Land and Water Conservation Fund encourage localities to invest in environmental improvements with a minimum of regulatory oversight. Categorical requirements for program and service delivery, representing well-intentioned efforts to replicate solutions, so often break down in the implementation.

VARIETY. As a corollary, the federal government must get used to developing enforceable standards without dictating how to get there. It is a national standard that children have the right to be free from an abusive or seriously neglectful environment. But child abuse advocates complain that there are a range of frequently contradictory family reunification requirements combined with child protection requirements that put community agencies, child protective services, courts, and families at cross-purposes. If the states or the counties are not doing the job, there must be a federal right of action that could potentially dictate drastic and expensive solutions. But in many cases—such as misguided efforts to deny states money based on their formal child abuse statutes or technical violations of federal statute—the heavy federal hand does little good and adds nothing but cost and complexity.

EMPOWERMENT. Amid all the talk of individual empowerment, conservatives are attempting to preempt community empowerment. True devolution would set baseline standards for regulation but would permit stronger action at the local level. Many corporate lobbying efforts in environment and other regulatory issues attempt to preempt local action by setting national standards; any real concern for local democracy, which is given lip service in the current debate, would maintain the ability of localities to expand on national standards.

For example, energy utilities are currently seeking federal regulatory action to preempt the ability of municipalities to buy power on behalf of their own citizens when energy markets are restructured to be competitive; phone utilities have successfully used the Federal Communications Commission to overturn state efforts to protect privacy rights of their consumers from caller ID; the cable industry has successfully sought federal preemption from local regulation of local monopolies. The opportunities for state and community actions and innovations are many, but they are often stifled by limitations enacted at the behest of powerful interests.

Another aspect of community empowerment is one that began in the 1960s—the direct relationships between the community-based sector and federal funding. Many nonprofit community organizations were stimulated by the War on Poverty; assessments of community needs led to health clinics and many other programs that, when successful, have lasted. Devolving program funding has strengthened both the public sector and the community-based sector in responding to community needs.

What functions should be directly devolved? In her book budget director Alice Rivlin calls for the states to take charge of the "productivity agenda" such as education and skills training, child care, housing, infrastructure, and economic development. "The following programs would be devolved to the states or gradually wither away: elementary and secondary education, job training, economic and community development, housing, most highways and other transportation, social services, and some pollution control programs.... Citizens and organizations concerned about better housing, training, and education would have to lobby in their state capitals, not Washington."

Rivlin's case is strongest for devolving economic development functions, which also happen to be among the most pork-laden projects. In the absence of federal assistance and strings, competition among states will still be healthy over who has the best ports, highways, mass transit, and airports, the best job training, the lowest-cost energy, and the best quality of life.

Devolving "pork" means that many massive, costly, and environmentally destructive measures (such as California's excessive water projects) would never be built if beneficiaries had to bear full cost. At the same time, other programs, such as housing and social services, need local variety but at least partial federal funding.

Pragmatism must still reign in an arena in which no strict set of principles will work. Head Start fits into no convenient typology of appropriate federal functions but has had strong support (until now) as an effective program. When Leon Panetta was asked if he does not trust the states to run the proposed revamped school lunch program, his response was, "It works." It is easy to attack distant federal bureaucrats and cite absurd anecdotes about inappropriate regulations and bureaucratic intervention; it is all too rare to hear defenses of effective programs.

Ultimately, progressives have to reclaim democratic empowerment as a politics. For most progressives and conservatives alike, the substance is more important than the structure: Advocates for interests or ideology care more about what is done than at what level the decision is made. But for those not directly involved in the public policy process—that is, the voting public—the sense of alienation from government and lack of control is deeply felt.

Efforts to bring decisions and participation closer to local communities may be an integral part of restoring connection to the political process. Devolving huge liabilities for social problems to state and local government is a recipe for disaster. Empowering communities and funding the responsibilities they have been given might help restore a sense that democracy can function.

Populist Road to Hell

Peter Schrag

There are all sorts of ironies in the term-limits movement that has swept the country in the past six years. The most obvious is that while Congress has been the prime target, it is the state legislatures that have (so far) taken the hit—some 20 states have imposed legislative term limits in the past six years, all but one through the initiative. And while generally regarded as populist, the term-limits cause in some states has depended on a few conservative deep pockets, such as Kansas oil billionaires Charles and David Koch. In California, the deep pockets were those of a conservative Los Angeles poilitician, Pete Schabarum, who recently retired after five years as a legislator and 19 years as a county supervisor—no term limits for him. Since the law prevented Schabarum from keeping for himself the $1 million-plus he still had in his campaign treasury, he decided he would use it to buy his fellow citizens a term-limits initiative.

Term limits were not, in other words, just the result of a wild round of coincidental dissatisfaction that happened to sweep every state that had the initiative in its constitution. The legislatures of Maine and California, Ohio and Idaho, Oklahoma and Michigan, didn't all turn into swamps of iniquity at the same time. But since qualifications for Congress, as the Supreme Court recently reaffirmed, are established in the Constitution—states cannot tinker with them. So it was the state legislatures that got hit and it's in the states that term limits have stuck.

Another source of irony, perhaps the most significant, is that just as term limits begin to bite, Congress is about to turn a vast range of highly complex social policies—welfare, Medicaid, food stamps—into block grants, transferring responsibility to those same state legislatures, many of which will no longer have senior members with more than six or eight years in office. And so by some strange working of the popular will, the country will take some of government's toughest decisions out of the hands of legislators with long experience and deliver them into the hands of amateurs.

California's recent experience may signal what we can expect: gridlock, bitter partisan hostility, and greater reliance on special interests for the expertise required to write complex legislation.

BITTER FRUIT

In November 1990, California became one of the first of the 20 states to adopt term limits—three two-year terms in a lifetime for the state Assembly, two four-year terms for the state Senate. And because its limits are among the most stringent, virtually all the state's legislators will be, as the phrase goes, "termed out" at the end of 1996. Thus California once again becomes the first major test of yet another grand plebiscitary experiment. The only other state where term limits kick in this year is Maine, which has a population equal to about 3 percent of California's and a part-time legislature with little professional staff. After the November 1996 election, none of California's 80 Assembly members will have had more than four years' experience. After the 1998 election, only a few of 40 state senators—those who were first elected in 1992—will have more than six.

So far the results aren't pretty. Contrary to the rosy predictions of such term-limits advocates as George Will, California has not entered a golden age of "civic republicanism." Nor has Proposition 140, the term-limits initiative, brought the state perceptibly closer to the "government of citizens representing their fellow citizens," which Schabarum promised voters in his ballot argument six years ago.

Nor has it done much, quoting the ballot argument again, to "remove the grip that vested interests have over the legislature [and] put an end to the Sacramento web of special favors and patronage." What it has done is send a new generation of politicians to Sacramento who are long on partisanship and painfully short on both legislative experience and policy background—and, worse, often seem not to care.

That's not to say that the proponents were all wrong. Because of term limits, the California Senate, one of whose members has been in public office since 1938, will cease to be what one legislator unkindly called "the geriatric ward of California." That presumably will be true in a lot of other states as well. High turnover may cause some legislatures to become more diverse in both gender and ethnicity, though that hasn't yet happened in California. It will become much harder for Assembly speakers or Senate presidents, none of whom is likely to serve more than two years, to accumulate either the power that their predecessors had or the dispensable political campaign funds on which much of that power was based. The personal arrogance and indifference of some long-term members may become a thing of the past.

But anyone looking for a new generation of citizen-legislators will probably look in vain. By general agreement, the 1995 session of the California legislature was probably the most mean-spirited and unproductive in memory, a unique combination of instability, bad behavior, political frenzy, and legislative paralysis. In the past year, California has had three Assembly speakers, two Republican Assembly leaders, two Republican Senate leaders, and six special elections, not counting runoffs. These included three recalls and there will almost certainly be more before the 1996 general election. In effect, we've witnessed an accelerating game of musical chairs prompted by the search of the nearly termed-out for jobs of longer and more secure tenure: as lobbyists, consultants, or academics, or in other public offices. That, in turn, has produced an almost continuous battle over the speakership and with it an unprecedented round of fratricidal vendettas stemming from the attempts of a group of clumsy and inexperienced Assembly Republicans to punish those who were insufficiently loyal to their caucus.

CALIFORNIA SCHEMING

A short reprise: In November of 1994, Republican Senator Marian Bergeson, a ten-year veteran of the legislature, knowing she must leave office by 1996, runs for, and wins, a seat on the Orange County Board of Supervisors, thereby setting up a special election in March that's won, after a runoff in June, by Republican Assemblyman Ross Johnson. This leaves a vacancy in the Assembly, prompting another special election, held in September. In the meantime, Republican Assemblyman Dick Mountjoy, who would have been termed out in 1996 and is looking for a place with more potential, has won a special election for the Senate seat vacated by Senator Frank Hill, who was removed from office in the summer of 1994 after his conviction on a bribery charge. But because of a closely divided Assembly, and a quirk in state law, Mountjoy delays giving up his Assembly seat even after his Senate victory so that he can cast his vote for a Republican speaker.

In the course of that maneuvering, the Republicans become so paranoid about the ability of the longtime Democratic speaker, Willie Brown, to outfox them that one of their members, a former sheriff's deputy named Larry Bowler, cuts the wires of the internal microphones in the caucus chamber where they meet out of fear that Democrats might be listening in. Eventually, in what Republicans call a coup, the Democrats, with the help of one Republican defector, Assemblyman Paul Horcher, oust Senator/Assemblyman Mountjoy from the Assembly and return Brown to the speaker's chair. Mountjoy's Assembly seat is thereupon filled in yet another special election.

In anger and revenge, Republicans organize a successful voter recall against the defecting Horcher, who is replaced by Assemblyman Gary Miller. The Republicans also organize a recall against Assemblyman Mike Machado, a Democrat, whom they accuse of breaking a promise not to vote for the Democratic speaker. That recall fails miserably, and Machado files an $800,000 claim with the state, not yet settled, under a law allowing public reimbursement of expenses to the survivor of a recall. In the meantime, Willie Brown, who also will be termed out in 1996 and is now running for mayor of San Francisco, steps down as speaker, but since Republican Assemblywoman Doris Allen is angry at the way she's been treated by the leaders of her caucus, she, like Horcher before her, refuses to vote for the Republican leader, Jim Brulte. (Also termed out, she seems to feel no fealty to her caucus.) Instead, she allows herself to be elected speaker of the nearly evenly divided house with the unanimous votes of the Democrats, plus her own vote, over the unanimous opposition of her Republican colleagues. Allen thus becomes the target of yet another GOP recall, which takes place in November 1995. By September, having succumbed to the harassment and invective of her GOP colleagues, she resigns the speakership, but not before she manages to describe them, in one very public statement, as "power-mongering males with short penises." It was that kind of year.[1]

THE COST OF LIMITS

This chain of intrigue and conflict—and the resulting legislative gridlock and partisan hostility—would probably not have been half as severe had it not been for another development: a legislative redistricting by judicially appointed special masters after the 1990 census that so evenly divided districts that it was hard for either party to get undisputed control of the lower house. If we were living in a less ideologically unforgiving time or place, there might also have been more compromise and professional respect among the members.

But term limits themselves send the message that experience is not as important as ideological purity and faithful representation of the voters of one's district. Government, said Phil Isenberg, a pragmatic Democratic assemblyman and one of the legislature's most thoughtful members, who will himself be termed out in 1996, is not "like filling sandbags in the flood"—something that a citizen does on a temporary basis and then returns to normal life. During much of 1994, Willie Brown, who has been in the Assembly for more than 30 years and was its speaker for 15, tried to train a new generation of Democratic leaders—potential speakers, chairs of key committees, and all the rest. But the effort seems to have had only marginal success at best; no one who has been there four years or less has learned enough about California's complicated system of government. Under term limits, moreover, the payoff is so limited. Who wants to stay up all night learning brain surgery when he can only practice for two years? Therefore, Brown told *Los Angeles Times* reporter Daniel Weintraub, there is going to be no "central force, no central person, who is really responsible or accountable, everyone just doing their own little number." Next year, the fights among Democrats may become as fractious as those among Republicans.

The effects will be less severe in the Senate, with its eight-year limits and its complement of members who previously served in the Assembly—and still less true in states like Oklahoma, Nevada, and Utah, which have 12-year limits for each house of their legislatures, longer than the average term is now. "The legislative process is remarkably adaptable and resilient," writes Douglas G. Brown, the director of Colorado's Office of Legislative Legal Services, about the likely effects of reforms in that state. But he does not minimize the dangers: "Experienced members know that disagreement is the default position and agreement takes time and compromise and education to achieve. Experienced members can reason by analogy from previous experiences; new members will not know the lessons of the past." Bill Lockyer, California's Senate president, puts it another way: New members arrive "convinced that those people (already in government) have screwed it all up: I'm going to fix it, whatever it is. [But after a while] people tend to meet smart people with different values . . . and they start to say 'Maybe I'm not absolutely right about this.'" With term limits, that is far less likely to happen.

What is certain, at least in California, is that term limits have increased instability and reduced legislative experience. Under the state's rigid limits, members begin looking for the next slot from the moment they arrive. The legislature has, in effect, become a bus station where some people have just arrived and others are waiting to leave, and as a result the institution itself does not elicit much loyalty or devotion. In the two-year period between the 1992 and 1994 elections, California had 12 special elections—that's 10 percent of all seats.

More than $10 million was spent on these races—more per race than the obscene amounts, now approaching a total of $80 million every two years, spent in regular legislative elections. In addition, it costs the taxpayers of each affected district an estimated $300,000 to $500,000 to run each of these special elections. We are probably already ahead of that pace in this cycle, though exact figures are not yet available, and since there are still 24 Assembly members and 12 senators who will be termed out by the end of this year, the cycle is far from over. The successful recall of Assemblyman Horcher cost the winners $400,000 and the losers $600,000. That's a little high for such a contest, but not extraordinary—and certainly not money that comes in $5 donations raised at neighborhood teas and clambakes. This year, for the first time, as California Common Cause director Ruth Holton observed, political candidates are holding fundraisers in Sacramento—which means that they're shaking down the special interests—even before they're elected.

POLITICAL PARALYSIS

It's too soon to know conclusively how all that will affect policy and the quality of government generally. There's little question that, as the sponsors of California's term limits promised, the flow of money, particularly to members of the Assembly, will be less subject to the control of a powerful speaker like Brown. There simply isn't time for anyone to develop the long-term relationships that Brown, for better or worse, managed with trial lawyers, public employee unions, land developers, and other major lobbies. The Assembly's speaker at the end of the 1995 session was a 32-year-old freshman Republican named Brian Setencich, a former professional basketball player in Europe, who had been in the legislature less than eight months and whose prior political experience was a few years on the Fresno City Council. For the same reason, it will also be hard for anyone to develop the clout to broker deals among various interest groups—which are now increasingly trying to work their own deals directly with individual members—or to keep caucus members in line.[2]

That will make it even harder than it has recently been in California to hold votes together and enact any major legislation—indeed, to do anything that takes patient compromise and thus requires the luxury of time and a relatively stable group of bargainers. In the process, it's not only politically complex and divisive issues that have bogged down in California's fractured legislature. Even such matters as the two-thirds vote to place school construction bonds on the state ballot—a vote that was once routine for both Republicans and Democrats—have become increasingly insurmountable hurdles. This summer, for the second time in two years, no school bond measure was approved, despite the fact that California's classrooms are the most crowded and among the most dilapidated in America.

But the changing power relationships are only one element contributing to California's policy paralysis. What is at least as important is the declining level of policy experience that term limits foster and celebrate. The California legislature once had a highly professional staff, but the term-limits initiative also required a 40 percent reduction in legislative personnel and funding.

Here again is an example of unintended consequences. Most observers agree that for years there had been too many political hacks on legislative payrolls, men and women earning six-figure salaries and cushy pensions to organize fundraisers, staff campaigns, and talk to lobbyists. But the initiative did little to reduce the number of hacks who, in the constant search for money, are needed more than ever. The damage, rather, was done in the nonpartisan Legislative Analyst's office, which studies and evaluates the fiscal effects of the budget and all money bills. The office lost 60 percent of its staff. The budget reductions also decimated the ranks of policy experts attached to various legislative committees—experts on budgeting, water law, taxation, environmental law, education, transportation, and all the rest—who, for the better part of a generation beginning in the mid-1960s, had made California's legislature a model of professionalism. Until 1990, someone from the Legislative Analyst's office appeared and testified at hearings on all major revenue and appropriations bills; after the office's budget was cut, that was no longer possible.

There also appears to have been a marked decline in the quality of the work done by committee policy staff, partly because they were shorthanded and partly because the new members seemed to care less. Previously, committee bill analyses were, for the most part, objective statements that laid out the arguments on a bill, pro and con, raised unanswered questions, and tried to suggest the likely effects. Now, they tend increasingly to be taken verbatim from the lobbyists pushing or opposing the measure, or simply from fantasy. That practice seems not to reflect corruption so much as the cult-politics mindset of people who fervently believe that if they hold the correct position on an issue no further information is required. They are not in Sacramento to govern; they are there to enact the agenda that they arrived with.

For example, analysis of a bill authorizing a bond issue to buy computers and other new technology for California schools—probably a dubious way of funding such inherently perishable improvements—cited "serious concerns . . . in the technology community regarding overuse of computers by young children. Scientific reports reveal that, as with TV, there is actual physiological damage and impairment to the areas of young children's brains which involve metaphorical thinking and other avenues to higher thinking skills." So far, no one has found those scientific reports, but since this analysis was written for a legislator who once announced that the Air Force had an official witch, no one really expected to. Because term limits leave everyone insecure, said one member, "this place has become a totally risk-averse environment, which is why you have so much stridency and so little achievement."

The winners from term limits will be, first, the lobbyists, who are never termed out; second, the governor and the executive branch, which still has budgeting and policymaking expertise; and, third, the bureaucrats, who will stay long after legislators go. Art Agnos, a former legislator and former mayor of San Francisco, now western regional director for the Department of Housing and Urban Development, recently remarked that the real effect of term limits is that "no one will be in office long enough to touch the bureaucrats. ... They tell us political appointees—the politocrats—that while we're the A team, they're the B team: 'We be here when you come and we be here after you're gone.'"

CYCLES OF FRUSTRATION

California has been on a plebiscitary rampage since the passage of Proposition 13 in 1978; term limits are not likely to be the end of the process. For most of the past two decades, and even before, the state has been going through a continuous cycle of reform and political frustration, with initiative after initiative imposing state and local tax limitations, spending limits, a formula for school spending, term limits, three strikes, and prohibiting public education and other services for illegal immigrants (currently blocked by the federal courts). Each initiative has put still more restrictions on the ability of elected officials—legislators, city councils, school boards, county supervisors—to make choices and set priorities. As each has made it harder for the legislature to function and more difficult for voters to comprehend the system—let alone know whom to hold accountable—yet another remedial ballot measure has sprouted from the resulting frustration. This, in turn, has further restricted the latitude of those who used to be called the people's representatives, which in turn has further exacerbated the impotence of the legislature and has reduced the accountability of those whom the voters elected.

The key was Proposition 13, which not only limited the local property tax but gave the state the power to allocate property tax revenues among counties, cities, schools, and thousands of special districts. It thus severely weakened local government and shifted power to a state government whose legislature was itself being hamstrung by a set of uncoordinated populist reforms. Equally important, Proposition 13 and the scores of bills and ballot measures that followed in its wake so divided accountability between the state and the locals (and often among various state and local agencies) that even the simplest things—how to get a new school built, for example—became virtually incomprehensible. As recently demonstrated in Los Angeles, the county or the school board slipping into bankruptcy points to Sacramento for reducing its funding; the state points to the local supervisors and their managers for failing to control mushrooming employee salaries and benefits.

They are both correct. In 20 years, California's state and local governments have become a sort of Rube Goldberg machine whose most important product may well be voter alienation. It's said, probably correctly, that only three people understand California school finance, and two of them are lobbyists. More obviously, the post-13 era has been marked by a steep slide in the quality and availability of the state's public services and a sharp rise in the kind of political corruption—sometimes indictable, sometimes not—that thrives in an increasingly unmanageable, demoralized, and unaccountable system. Since 1988, five California legislators, several staffers, and one prominent lobbyist have been convicted on federal bribery or similar charges.

Finally, there is the huge effect of the two-thirds vote that California, almost alone among the states, requires in each house of the legislature, not only for the enactment of any tax but, more important, for approval of the annual state budget and virtually every other sort of appropriation. That gives every determined political minority—from welfare Democrats to right-to-life Republicans—the power to extract concessions from the majority, both by blocking additional spending and, in times of stress, blocking desirable spending cuts. It's no coincidence that California's legislature is so often gridlocked for weeks or even months before it can agree on a budget. With the array of new political technologies—from direct mail to television to the Internet—that have evolved since Proposition 13, it's often easier for well-organized and well-heeled groups, on the left as well as the right, to use the initiative, once intended as the people's instrument, to write policy changes into law or into the budget than to get the legislative supermajority that the constitution requires. But it makes it almost impossible to set realistic annual budget priorities.

There is no space here to describe the inequities in tax and spending policies, the economic dislocations, and the other Alice-in-Wonderland policy distortions that this process has produced in the past two decades. In any number of places, property taxes on identical parcels in the same neighborhood are vastly different because one parcel was purchased recently (and thus reassessed), while the other has been in the same hands since 1978 and thus is carried on the rolls at 1975 values. And since local communities are now effectively precluded from taxing themselves to improve schools, California's per-pupil spending has declined from fifth or sixth in the nation to 42nd—a decline that started long before the recession that began in 1989. California is the state where accountability has become so entangled that the buck never stops and can never be traced.

Given that structural morass, the governmental inexperience that term limits produce can only exacerbate the difficulties of accomplishing anything. California Republicans have some hopes of gaining control of both houses of the state legislature in 1996—they now control one, more or less—but if they succeed, the thing they will learn first and foremost is how limited their ability is to accomplish anything substantial. The cycle of reform and frustration will go on.

Of course, California is unique in some of these things. But these days it is hardly alone in its search for quick constitutional fixes—balanced budget amendments, supermajority tax-enactment provisions, term limits and other autopilot mechanisms—in an effort to guarantee what never was and never will be: that government will do the right things without constant attention from a citizenry that seems to have less and less interest in, patience for, or attachment to, its institutions. The excesses and abuses of a distant, overprofessionalized government are legendary and need no further reiteration, but the alternative, in a world as complex as this one, is not some dreamy system of short-term amateurs. California is not so much apart as ahead, a cautionary tale that others ignore at their peril.

NOTES

1. Since this piece was first published, Willie Brown was elected mayor of San Francisco; his Assembly seat was filled in a special election by Carol Migden, a San Francisco political activist. On the same day, Assembly member Byron Sher, in yet another special election, replaced state Senator Tom Campbell, who had won a special election a few months earlier to a seat in Congress. Doris Allen was successfully recalled and replaced by a young Republican conservative named Scott Baugh who finally provided the Assembly Republicans with enough votes to elect their own speaker, Curt Pringle. But three months after his election, Baugh was indicted in Orange County (by a Republican district attorney) on various charges of campaign fraud in connection with a failed attempt to run a dummy candidate to split the Democratic vote and thus assure his election. By then, an aide to Pringle and another Republican staff member had already pleaded guilty to lesser campaign fraud charges. In addition, two other Republican staff members were indicted, one of them a senior aide to Republican Congressman Dana Rohrabacher, and there were persistent rumors, as this went to press, that the investigation might reach higher up.

2. When Allen was recalled and Baugh elected, Setencich's brief tenure as speaker came to an end. Curt Pringle, who replaced him, thus became California's fourth speaker in the current legislative session and, given the ongoing investigation in Orange County, perhaps not the last. And in what *Los Angeles Times* columnist George Skelton called a manifestation of California's "Mad GOP Disease," the Republican organization, funded by a wad of Christian fundamentalist money from Southern California, ran a candidate against Setencich in the March 1996 primary and beat him by five hundred votes. Setencich hasn't yet foreclosed the possibility of running as a write-in in November, when he has a reasonable choice of winning. The March primary, incidentally, in which candidates were chosen to replace more than two dozen termed-out legislators, saw the lowest turnout of any presidential primary in California history.

Contributors

BARRY BLUESTONE is the Frank L. Boyden Professor of Political Economy at the University of Massachusetts, Boston, and senior fellow at the John W. McCormack Institute of Public Affairs. His latest book is *Negotiating the Future: A Labor Perspective on American Business* (Basic Books).

ALAN BRINKLEY is a professor of American history at Columbia University and the author of *The End of Reform: New Deal Liberalism in Recession and War.*

ROBERT DREYFUSS is a freelance writer based in Alexandria, Virginia, specializing in politics and national security issues.

JEFF FAUX is president of the Economic Policy Institute and coauthor of *Rebuilding America*. He is currently writing a book on the prospects for the American economy in the twenty-first century.

JAMES K. GALBRAITH is a professor of economics at the Lyndon B. Johnson School of Public Affairs at the University of Texas, Austin, and coauthor of the textbook *Macroeconomics* (Houghton-Mifflin).

LENNY GOLDBERG is a public interest consultant and lobbyist based in Sacramento, California, serving primarily nonprofits, consumer groups, and labor unions.

STANLEY B. GREENBERG, chairman and CEO of Greenberg Research, Inc., is pollster to the president and advisor to the Democratic National Committee. His most recent book is *Middle Class Dreams: The Politics and Power of the New American Majority.*

PHILIP HARVEY is a visiting scholar at the Russell Sage Foundation; the author of *Securing the Right to Employment*; and the coauthor, with Theodore R. Marmor and Jerry L. Mashaw, of *America's Misunderstood Welfare State.*

DAVID R. HOWELL is associate professor and chair of the urban policy analysis program at the Robert J. Milano Graduate School at the New School for Social Research.

BROOKS JACKSON is a correspondent with CNN's Special Assignment Unit. He is the author of *Honest Graft: Big Money and the American Political Process.*

JOHN B. JUDIS is a senior editor at the *New Republic* and author of *Grand Illusions: Critics and Champions of the American Century.*

ROBERT KUTTNER writes for *Business Week*, the *Boston Globe*, and other magazines, and is the author most recently of *The End of Laissez-Faire.* He is founder and coeditor of the *American Prospect.*

LOUIS LOWENSTEIN is a professor of finance and law at Columbia University. His books include *Sense and Nonsense in Corporate Finance.*

THEODORE R. MARMOR is a professor of politics and public policy at Yale University's School of Management and coauthor, with Philip Harvey and Jerry L. Mashaw, of *America's Misunderstood Welfare State.*

JERRY L. MASHAW is the Sterling Professor of Law at Yale and coauthor, with Philip Harvey and Theodore R. Marmor, of *America's Misunderstood Welfare State.*

LAWRENCE MISHEL is research director of the Economic Policy Institute and coauthor, with Jared Bernstein, of *The State of Working America, 1994-95.*

ROBERT D. PUTNAM is the Dillon Professor and the director of the Center for International Affairs at Harvard University.

JOEL ROGERS is a professor of law, political science, and sociology at the University of Wisconsin, Madison, and chair of the interim executive council of the New Party.

SAMANTHA SANCHEZ is Project Director of the the Money and Western Politics Program at the Western States Center.

PETER SCHRAG, editorial page editor of the *Sacramento Bee*, has written about education and politics for more than thirty years.

MICHAEL SCHUDSON is a professor of communication and sociology at the University of California, San Diego.

THEDA SKOCPOL is a professor of government and sociology at Harvard University, and the author, most recently, of *Boomerang: Clinton's Health Security Effort and the Turn aganist Government in U.S. Politics.*

GLENN R. SIMPSON, the senior staff writer for *Roll Call* newspaper.

RUY A. TEIXEIRA is director of the Politics and Public Opinion Program at the Economic Policy Institute.

LESTER THUROW is a professor of management and economics at MIT, and the author most recently of *The Future of Capitalism* (Morrow).

RICHARD M. VALELLY is a professor of political science at Swarthmore College.

EDWARD N. WOLFF is a professor of economics at New York University, the managing editor of the "Review of Income and Wealth", and the author of several books, including, most recently, *Top Heavy: The Increasing Inequality of Wealth in America and What Can Be Done about It* (The New Press).